Informatik-Fachberichte 252

Herausgeber: W. Brauer
im Auftrag der Gesellschaft für Informatik (GI)

Subreihe Künstliche Intelligenz

Mitherausgeber: C. Freksa
in Zusammenarbeit mit dem Fachbereich 1
„Künstliche Intelligenz" der GI

G. Dorffner (Hrsg.)

Konnektionismus in Artificial Intelligence und Kognitionsforschung

6. Österreichische
Artificial-Intelligence-Tagung (KONNAI)

Salzburg, Österreich
18.-21. September 1990

Proceedings

Springer-Verlag

Berlin Heidelberg New York London
Paris Tokyo Hong Kong Barcelona

Herausgeber

Georg Dorffner
Institut für Medizinische Kybernetik
und Artificial Intelligence der Universität Wien
Freyung 6/2, A-1010 Wien, Österreich

Programmkomitee

J. Diederich (GMD Sankt Augustin)
C. Freksa (TU München)
C. Lischka (GMD Sankt Augustin)
A. Kobsa (Univ. des Saarlandes)
M. Köhle (TU Wien)
B. Neumann (Univ. Hamburg)
H. Schnelle (Ruhr-Univ. Bochum)
Z. Schreter (Univ. Zürich)

CR Subject Classification (1987): I.2.

ISBN-13:978-3-540-53131-9   e-ISBN-13:978-3-642-76070-9
DOI: 10.1007/978-3-642-76070-9

CIP-Titelaufnahme der Deutschen Bibliothek.
Konnektionismus in Artificial Intelligence und Kognitionsforschung: proceedings /
6. Österr. Artificial-Intelligence-Tagung (KONNAI), Salzburg, Österreich, 18.–21. September 1990.
G. Dorffner (Hrsg). -Berlin; Heidelberg; New York; London; Paris; Tokyo; Hong Kong; Barcelona:
Springer, 1990.
(Informatik-Fachberichte; 252: Subreihe künstliche Intelligenz)
ISBN-13:978-3-540-53131-9

NE: Dorffner, [Hrsg]; KONNAI [1990, Salzburg]; GT

2145/3140-543210 – Gedruckt auf säurefreiem Papier

Vorwort

Konnektionismus als Methode, Modellvorstellung, aber auch als Weltbild dringt immer mehr in die Domänen der AI (KI) und Kognitionsforschung vor. Obwohl es eine Reihe von Konferenzen gibt, die künstliche neuronale Netzwerke – die Basis des Konnektionismus – zum Inhalt haben, scheint dem Bereich der Intelligenzforschung und -modellierung mit Hilfe solcher Netzwerke vergleichsweise noch wenig Raum geboten zu werden. Die Konferenz, die vom 18. bis 21. 9. 1990 in Salzburg stattgefunden hat und deren Proceedings in diesem Band vorliegen, sollte diese Lücke schließen. Sie hat in Form von Vorträgen, Workshops und Panels Arbeiten zusammengebracht, die sich mit Anwendungen neuronaler Netzwerke auf Probleme der AI, mit grundlegenden Aspekten von massivem Parallelismus und Netzwerkverarbeitung in der AI sowie mit theoretischen Implikationen der Modelle auf die AI und die Kognitionsforschung im allgemeinen beschäftigen. Die vorliegenden Beiträge geben einen guten Einblick in den Stand der Forschung – besonders im deutschsprachigen Raum, aber auch darüber hinausgehend.

Diese Proceedings sind grob in zwei Teile gegliedert. Der erste enthält die Artikel des allgemeinen Teils der Tagung, die von mindestens zwei Mitgliedern des Programmkomitees begutachtet wurden. Einer der eingeladenen Vorträge [Sharkey] konnte hier ebenfalls aufgenommen werden. Der allgemeine Teil selbst ist wiederum grob in drei Teile gegliedert, die ungefähr den drei Schwerpunkten der Tagung *Sprachverarbeitung* (Arbeiten 1 [Sharkey] bis 5 [Kwasny & Faisal]), *theoretische Grundlagen und Modellierung* (Arbeiten 6 [van Gelder] bis 11 [Standfuß et al.]) und *Anwendung* (Arbeiten 12 [Bischof & Pinz] bis 18 [Salomon]) entsprechen.

Der zweite Teil enthält kürzere Beiträge der drei Workshops *Strukturierte Netzwerkmodelle*, *Konnektionismus und Sprachverarbeitung* und *Massive Parallelität und Kognition*, die vom jeweiligen Leiter ausgewählt wurden, und die die Grundlage für die Diskussionen zum genannten Thema bildeten. Die Beiträge zum Workshop *Konnektionismus und Sprachverarbeitung* sind theoretische "Position Papers", die auf Fragen eingehen, die in einer vorangestellten Einleitung zusammengefaßt sind.

Die Tagungssprachen waren Deutsch und Englisch, wobei unter den Beiträgen im allgemeinen Teil beide Sprachen vertreten sind, alle drei Workshops hingegen ausschließlich in Englisch abgehalten wurden.

An dieser Stelle möchte ich mich recht herzlich bei den Mitgliedern des Programmkomitees, bei den Leitern der Workshops, sowie bei den tatkräftigen Helfern des Organisationskomitees bedanken, ohne die diese Tagung nicht zustande gekommen wäre.

Georg Dorffner

Inhaltsverzeichnis

CONNECTIONIST REPRESENTATIONS FOR NATURAL LANGUAGE: OLD AND NEW

Noel E. Sharkey
Department of Computer Science
University of Exeter

Connectionist natural language processing research has been in the literature for less than a decade and yet it is already claimed that it has established a whole new way of looking at representation. This article presents a survey of the main representational techniques employed in connectionist research on natural language processing and assesses claims as to their novelty value i.e. whether or not they add anything new to Classical representation schemes.

Connectionist natural language processing (CNLP) research has barely been in existence for a decade (cf. Sharkey & Reilly, in press, for a potted history) and yet it has grown enough to attract criticism from some formidable guardians of the Classical tradition. For example, Fodor and Pylyshyn (1988) claimed that connectionist representations could work for NLP if and only if they were implementations of Classical representations. One of their main arguments was that only Classical representations exhibit the properties of compositionality, and structure sensitivity and therefore only Classical representations can be used for natural language processing. While it is not the purpose of this paper to address the Fodor and Pylyshyn arguments in detail, some of their arguments will be used to examine connectionist representations for their novelty value. The main aim of the paper is to present a critical survey, and the Classical criticisms are discussed in this light of the survey. The stance taken here will be that there are novel connectionist representational types which are compositional (though not in the Classical sense) and which can be manipulated by structure sensitive operations.

Natural language research is normally concerned with two main types of representation: structural or syntactic representation and semantic or meaning representation. The latter is usually divided into the representation of lexical items and the representation of larger units such as phrases or sentences. In much connectionist work it is difficult to separate syntactic and semantic representation. Nonetheless, each of the different types will be discussed in turn and a taxonomy will be proposed.

1. The representation of meaning and structure

1.1 Semantic representations

Localist v Distributed.

One of the major debates in connectionist research of the early to mid-eighties was concerned with whether or not individual items in a net should be represented by the activity on a single unit in a net - a *localist* representation (e.g. Cottrell, 1985) - or whether their representation should be a *distributed* pattern of activation across a number of units (e.g. Hinton, McClelland, and Rumelhart, 1986). Localist connectionism became almost synonymous with Jerry Feldman's group at Rochester, USA, while the proponents of distributed representations resided in San Diego (UCSD) as Rumelhart and McClelland's Parallel Distributed Processing group (c.f. Feldman, 1989 for a fuller discussion).

Hinton (1989) points out that terms *localist* and *distributed* are relative. They refer to the relationship between the terms of a descriptive language and a connectionist implementation. We can extract two simple defining - criteria for distributed representations from the Hinton paper. First, an entity that is described by a single term in the descriptive language is represented by more than one element in the connectionist implementation. For example, if the letter 'F' is a term in the descriptive language, then the distributed elements in the descriptive language may be the three features 'I ', '—' and '–'. Second, each of the elements in the connectionist implementation must be involved in representing more than one entity described by a single term in the descriptive language. For example, the features that make up the letter 'F' may also be used as part of the representation for the letter 'E'.

Figure 1 shows a fairly typical example of a localist net from the Rochester group (Shastri & Feldman, 1986). This is rather like the old semantic network idea in which each unit in the net represents a single concept and is linked to other units by either positive or negative weights. In most of the early Rochester work the weights were set by hand rather than by a learning algorithm. But there is no reason why localist representations cannot be trained using the same algorithms as those of the distributed school.

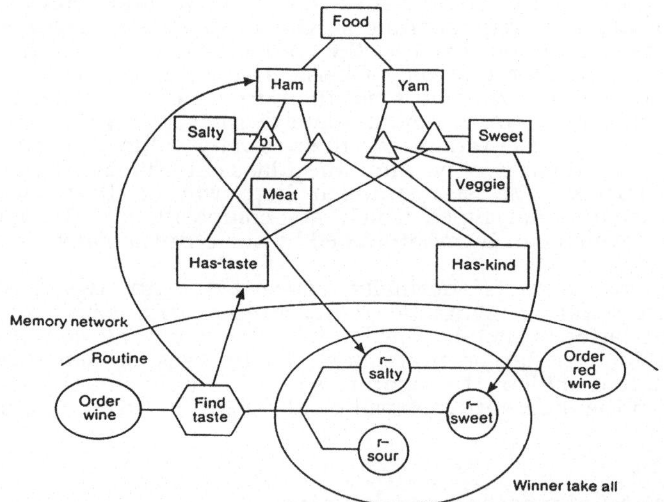

Both representational types have their advantages and disadvantages. The major advantage of localist representation is its transparency. Each unit is clearly labelled and so it is easy to see what its function is in the network. However, it is difficult to see what the novelty value of such representations amounts to. Since each unit represents a single semantically interpretable symbol, there is no new action that does not appear in the Classical tradition. Connectionists using such punctate representations must rely on the novelty value of the processing implementation as the main thrust of their research[1].

As we shall see later, despite their seeming opacity, there are advantages of distributed representation which make them more desirable. Unlike localist

---

[1]We have not discussed here the problems of building a representational theory using punctate representations for whole propositions. Such a theory would have to make the unlikely assumption that mind has a finite number of propositions which can never be unpacked and used to construct novel propositions (see Fodor & Pylyshyn, 1988).

representation, there are number of types of distributed representation. Two broad classes will be discussed here: symbolic and subsymbolic (c.f. Smolensky, 1988). All other types may be subdivided into these two groups.

Symbolic v Subsymbolic.

To understand the distinction between symbolic and subsymbolic representations, we need to look first at the notion of a *microfeature*. This is a term that has not been used entirely consistently in the literature. All would agree that microfeatures are the atomic elements in a distributed connectionist representation. However, some authors (e.g. McClelland & Kawamoto, 1986) use the term to refer to individual elements which are semantically interpretable on their own without examining their role in the representation e.g. propositional predicates such as *is human, is soft*. These sort of microfeatures are symbolic in the sense that they refer to properties in the world. That are much akin to semantic features, and are sometimes called semi-localist.

Figure 2 shows some of the microfeatures used by McClelland and Kawamoto (1986). While these are closely related to earlier semantic feature representations, they have the defining criteria for a distributed representation. That is, a single term in the descriptive language, such as the word 'ball', is represented by a number of microfeatures in the connectionist implementation i.e. non-human, soft, neuter, small, compact, rounded, unbreakable, food. In addition, the microfeatures representing the word 'ball' are shared by other words. For example, 'cheese' shares non-human, soft, neuter, small, and rounded.

Feature Dimensions & Values

NOUNS

HUMAN	human, nonhuman
SOFTNESS	soft, hard
GENDER	male, female, neuter
VOLUME	small, medium, large
FORM	compact, 1D, 2D, 3D
POINTINESS	pointed, rounded
BREAKABILITY	fragile, unbreakable
OBJ-TYPE	food, toy, tool, utensil, furniture
	animate, nat-inan

VERBS

DOER	yes, no
CAUSE	yes, no-cause, no-change
TOUCH	agent, inst, both, none, AisP
NAT-CHGE	pieces, shreds, chemical, none
	unused
AGT-MVMT	trans, part, none, NA
PT-MVMT	trans, part, none, NA
INTENSITY	low, high

Other authors (e.g. Hinton, 1981; Smolensky, 1988) use the term microfeature to refer to individual elements that are semantically uninterpretable (without participating in further processing) or subsymbolic. By this we mean that no one individual microfeature refers to a property in the world. Rather, reference to such properties emerges from a pattern of activation across several microfeatures. This style of representation is more like how many imagine information to be encoded in the nervous system. Each neuron is an unlabelled unit in a large collective from which symbolic information emerges.

There are two main ways in which subsymbolic microfeatures have been developed in the literature. In the first mention of the term, Hinton (1981) arbitrarily set a group of units to represent each word in his system (although a subvector for each word represented type information). A set of arbitrary microfeatures used in Sharkey's (1989a) Lexical Distance model (shown in Table 1) should give the general picture.

```
Doctor 111000000000000 11100000000000000000000000000000

Nurse  111000000000000 00011100000000000000000000000000

Knife  000111000000000 00000011100000000000000000000000

Fork   000111000000000 00000000011100000000000000000000

Bread  000000111000000 00000000000011100000000000000000

Butter 000000111000000 00000000000000011100000000000000

Dog    000000000111000 00000000000000000111000000000000

Bone   000000000111000 00000000000000000000111000000000

Foot   000000000000111 00000000000000000000000111000000

Shoe   000000000000111 00000000000000000000000000111000
```

Table 1. Arbitrary microfeature sets as used in Sharkey (1989a). These were used for a psychological model of word priming. Hence the vectors of microfeatures are divided into two fields. The first field represents shared microfeatures between related words, while the second field represents unique microfeatures.

Another way in which microfeatures have been developed is through the use of some learning algorithm such as the generalised delta rule (e.g. Hinton, 1986; Miikkulainen & Dyer, 1988). Figure 3 illustrates a set of microfeature activations that were learned for use in a prepositional attachment task (Sharkey, 1989b). In this instance, a net containing two weight layers was given sentences as input and was required to output a structural interpretation. The learned microfeatures are the activations on the hidden units.

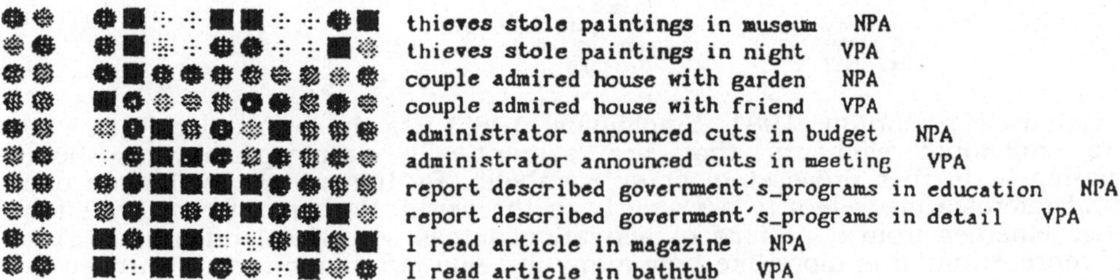

Figure 3. Learned microfeature sets as in Sharkey (1989b)

One disadvantage of using symbolic microfeatures is that the task of choosing a sufficient set of microfeatures is in the hands of the researcher. This can be problematic in that it is difficult to determine, *a priori*, what microfeatures would be required for a given task. At its worst, the use of symbolic microfeatures can lead to the sort of *ad hoc* "tuning" from which much of AI research has suffered i.e run the system and, if it doesn't work, try some different microfeatures (though it may be possible to circumvent part of this problem by conducting an empirical investigation with humans to determine a sufficient set of microfeatures).

With semantically uninterpretable microfeatures, these problems need not occur. It is possible for a net to develop a sufficient set of semantically uninterpretable microfeatures for a required task[2] (e.g. Miikkulainen & Dyer, 1987).

Some advantages of Distributed representations

Distributed representations require less memory than localist ones. More distributed items can be represented per vector element (for vectors with more than two elements). A classic example is McClelland and Rumelhart's (1981) representation of the 26 letters of the alphabet with a 16 element vector of visual features. A localist scheme would require a 26 element vector.

Localist networks can encode up to n items, where n is the dimension of the representation space; while distributed networks have the capacity to encode $2^n - (n+1)$ items. In Example 1, a comparison is given, of localist representations versus distributed representations using a four-bit vector. Note that the localist vector holds only 4 items while the distributed vector holds 11.

     Localist representations
     1000 0100 0010 0001

     Distributed representations
     1100 1010 0110 1110 1001 0101 1101 0011 1011 0111 1111

Example 1. Comparisons of a distributed versus localist representation on a four-bit vector.

The difference in storage capacity becomes more apparent as the size of the representing vector gets larger as shown in Table 2. With only 10 bits, 1013 distributed representations may be encoded, whereas a localist representation will have a storage capacity of only 10 items.

N⁰ Bits	Localist	Distributed
2	2	1
3	3	4
4	4	11
5	5	26
6	6	57
7	7	120
8	8	247
9	9	502
10	10	1013

Table 2. Comparisons of the storage capacity for localist and distributed systems.

---

[2] It is also possible that some learned microfeatures can have symbolic values as demonstrated by Hinton (1986) and Sejnowski and Rosenberg (1986).

Another important advantage of distributed representations is that they have built-in generalisation properties. In localist representations, all of the vectors representing items are, by definition, perpendicular to one another and equidistant (Hamming or Euclidean distance). Thus it is difficult to capture similarities and differences between items in localist representation space (although it can be done by explicit marking). On the other hand, distributed representations can form a denser representation space. For example, for simplicity of exposition, imagine that a set of distributed representation vectors are unit normalised (i.e. are all set to length 1). These vectors may then be described geometrically as points on a unit hypersphere as illustrated in the sphere in Figure 4.

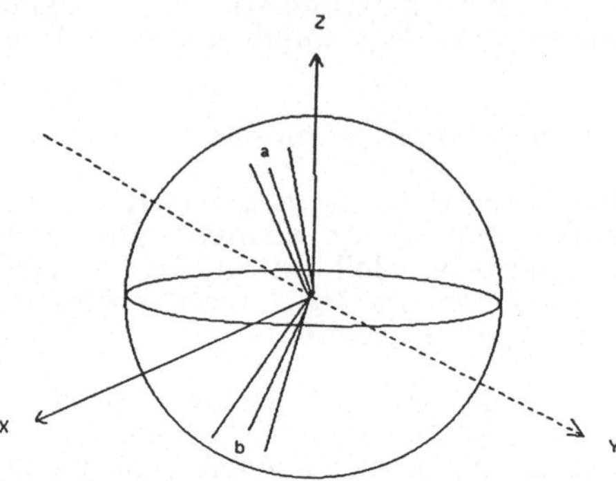

Figure 4. Two clusters of vectors, a and b, are shown on the surface of a unit sphere

The point here is that similar items will cluster on the surface of the hypersphere (two clusters are shown at a and b in Figure 4. It is then relatively easy to develop a process model in which similar items produce similar or identical results. For example, if a net was trained to take microfeatural representations of HORSE, CAT, and COW as input and map them onto ANIMAL in the output, then we would expect a microfeatural representation for DOG, which was not in the training set, to also produce the response output ANIMAL. That is, we would expect the vector representation for DOG to be sufficiently close to the vector representation for the other animals to have a similar effect.

A third advantage of distributed representations for CNLP is that they provide a natural basis for content addressable memory (e.g. Hopfield, 1982). That is, a network can be trained such that given a partial description (a subset of microfeatures), it will complete the pattern. Sharkey (1989c) has taken advantage of this property to "fill in" information not explicit in a text. This is the connectionist equivalent of default reasoning,but it comes automatically as a standard feature of distributed representations.

In summary, the various types of semantic representations for CNLP have been examined here. It was also proposed that the most powerful representation, in terms of memory efficiency, pattern completion and storage efficiency, was the distributed subsymbolic. But there is another important reason for favouring subsymbolic representations. Their examination represents a research topic that is unique to connectionism. Distributed symbolic representations have been applied in the Classical tradition in areas such as speech recognition. However, as shall be argued later, the study of subsymbolic representation is a new departure.

1.2 The Representation of Structure

A distinction can be drawn between those connectionist structures which are syntactically accessible and those which are syntactically implicit. Syntactically explicit representations are those in which structural operations rely on the actual spatial layout of theelements in the representations. Syntactically implicit representations, on the other hand, are not spatially concatenative and do not contain explicit representations ot their constituent tokens. This distinction will become clearer as the different styles of structural representation are discussed in turn.

Syntactically structured representations

A common form of structural representation in AI is the sentence *frame* (e.g. Minsky, 1975)[3]. In this notation, propositions or concepts are described as structures explicit containing a number of slots that have constraints on what items may fill them. For example, Schank (1972) developed the notion of conceptual dependency in which there were a small number of action frames (approximately 12). For example,

John drove mary to the station.

would be represented as:

```
                                      ┌──> STATION
   JOHN <==> PTRANS --> MARY ────┤
                                      └──< ?HOME?
```

where ?HOME? is a default value. This can also be represented as a frame with slots:

agent	action	object	to	from
JOHN	DROVE	MARY	STATION	?HOME?

Hinton (1981) described a distributed representation for propositions which shares a number of properties with these sentence frames. In Hinton's system, binary vectors representing distributed propositional triples are conceptually divided into three parts. The elements of the nth partition, by analogy with frames, represent all and only the permissible fillers of the nth slot. Thus the only constraint on what items may fill a slot is only that the appropriate vector partition has bits for representing the items. There are defaults for filling in missing values in the partitions/slots, but these fall out of the pattern completion process in Hinton's system.

---

[3]This notion is very similar to the linguist's case grammar (Fillmore, 1968).

These vector frames are syntactically explicit because the vector partitions act as slots in a structured frame[4]. Thus it is easy to tell at a glance what are the roles of the constituents. Probably for this reason, vector frames have been used widely (e.g. McClelland & Kawamoto, 1986; St.John & McClelland, in press; Touretzky & Hinton, 1988). Their main use is as input and output buffers to make the inputs and outputs comprehensible.

Although very useful, vector frames suffer from three particularly bad problems. First, there can be considerable redundancy in the representations. For example, most items that could appear in an Object partition could also appear in the Subject partition, and so they have to be represented twice by different elements. The second problem relates to the first in that the representation for the same item in two partitions is entirely different. Thus the system has no way of "knowing" that, for example, the *book* in the Object partition is the same as the *book* in the Subject position. A third problem with vector frames is that they have a fixed length or a fixed number of partitions. Thus all of the input sentences can be only of that length.

A number of ways have been found to get around this fixed length restriction such as having a processing window that moves along the input vector (e.g. Sejnowski & Rosenberg, 1986). Other researchers have taken the alternative approach of employing recurrent networks (e.g. Elman, in press) which accept sequential inputs. We shall return to examine these representations in more detail in the section on *Encoding temporal structure.*

The vector frame representation, it could be argued (c.f. Fodor & Pylyshyn, 1988), is simply a connectionist implementation of symbolic case frames. By being merely implementational, vector frames add nothing new to the theory of language and cognition. For a connectionist representation to add something new it must be different from classical representations. Nontheless, vector frames are useful for input and output representations. They can act as a *symbol surface* on which connectionist representations can emerge for the researcher to check out what has been happening underneath. We now turn to examine distributed representations of structure which are syntactically implicit.

Syntactically unstructured representations.

Saying that a representation is syntactically implicit means that it does not have a *concatenative* constituent structure. The most common form of syntactically implicit representations are those that result from a mapping of an input space onto a space of lower dimensionality. For example, Hinton (1981) mapped propositional triples onto a lower dimensionality PROP assembly using fixed random weights. Thus each triple, in a sense, recruits a set of PROP units to represent it in a syntactically implicit form. Through a learning process, it is possible to map the PROP activations back onto the higher dimensional Triple space, and thus recreate the structure. Coarse coding, as Hinton called it, is discussed at length in Hinton, McClelland, and Rumelhart, (1986).

Variations of this type of compact representation are common in the literature (e.g. Touretzky & Hinton, 1988; Touretzky and Geva, 1987; Willshaw & von der Malsburg, 1979; Cottrell, Munro, and Zipser, 1989) and may be set up by a simple algorithm, as in conjunctive coding (e.g. McClelland & Kawamoto, 1986), or may be learned either

---

[4]A similar technique was employed in McClelland and Rumelhart's (1981) model of word recognition. The vector partitions, in that instance, were used to represent positional information of the letters. For example, the word TART would be coded as T_1, A_2, R_3, T_4; where the subscripts indicate the appropriate vector partition.

by *supervised* (e.g. Hinton, 1986) or *unsupervised* techniques (e.g. Kohonen, 1982). Regardless of the learning technique used, the representation *encodes* statistical regularities of the input (usually) by reducing the pattern environment to a lower dimensional feature space. When required, the lower dimensional coding can be decoded onto the symbol surface again.

To make the notion of compact representations clearer, from the perspective of both semantic and structural representation, we turn now to briefly analyse one of the learning algorithms in more detail.

1.3 Representation in a back propagation net

In this section, we discuss how the generalised delta learning rule constructs representations. This is perhaps the most commonly employed learning algorithm in connectionist natural language research. We begin by discussing its application in a feedforward net architecture with two layers of weights (as shown in Figure 5).

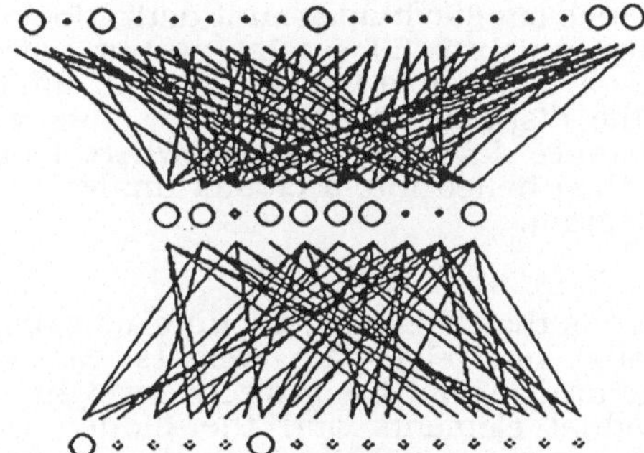

Figure 5. An illustration of a standard back propagation net with 2 layers of weights. The circles represent the units and the lines between are partial representation of the weights.

Before running the learning, all of the weights, from the input units to the hidden units and from the hidden units to the output units, are usually set to small random values in the range -1 to +1[5]. In the forward operation of the net, the input vector **v** is set to the binary states of the first input pattern. This vector is then mapped onto the hidden unit vector **h** (normally of lower dimension than **v**) by multiplying **v** by the first weight matrix W_1 and applying the squash function $S:W_1v \rightarrow h$ (where S is $1/1+e^{-x}$, $x = W_1v$). Then **h** is mapped onto the output vector **o** using the same squash function $S:W_2h \rightarrow o$

During learning **o** is compared with a target vector **t** to determine its correctness. If $0 > t - o > 0$ then an error correction procedure is set in motion which adjusts the weights matrices W_1 and W_2 such that **o** is closer to **t**. The mathematics and rationale of the weight adjustment have been given full treatment in many sources (e.g. Rumelhart, Hinton, and Williams, 1986; Hinton, 1989) and so will not be repeated here.

---

[5]A smaller range of initial values is sometimes used. Kolen and Pollack (1990) demonstrate the importance of initial conditions to learning in monte carlo simulations and show that under certain circumstances a fractal surface can appear.

What we are interested in at present is how the representations develop over time? Our first question must then be: where are the representations. Up until now the concern has only been with representations that are patterns of activation across a set of units. In this sense, the hidden unit activations are the representations (as discussed in sections 1.1 and 1.2), while the lower weights are part of the encoding function (S:W_1v -> h) and the upper weights, are part of the decoding function (S:W_2h -> o).

However, we may also describe the encoding and decoding weights as representations themselves. It is instructive to view the learning process geometrically to get an intuitive grasp of the notion of weight representation. The first step in learning is to adjust the upper (decoding) weights so that the weight vectors for output units that want to be 'on' are moved closer to the current vector of hidden unit activations; and the weight vectors for outputs that want to be 'off' are moved away from the current hidden unit vector. Secondly, the lower (encoding) weights are adjusted to push the vector of hidden unit activations even closer to the weights whose outputs should be 'on' and further away from weights whose outputs should be 'off'.

The upshot of this learning is: (i) input patterns that are required to produce similar outputs will learn to produce similar hidden unit activations and thus they will have to have similar 'projective' weights; (ii) similar output patterns will have to have similar 'receptive' weights. It is possible to examine this similarity using a Euclidean distance metric, where the distance between two vectors v_1 and v_2 in R^n is the length of v_1 - v_2 i.e. distance d = $||v_1 - v_2||$, where length $||v||$ = $v.v$. These Euclidean distances can then be fed into a cluster analysis program which plots the similarities on a 2D dendogram.

The point to be made here is that it is not just unit activations that may be studied under the representational umbrella. The weights can also be thought of as representations. It can be argued that the projective weights from the inputs are the representations of individual elements and the hidden unit activations are the compositional representation of strings of the individual elements.

2. Recent issues in natural language representation

<u>2.1 Encoding Temporal Structure</u>

One problem for researchers employing the standard feedforward back propagation nets discussed in 1.3, has been how to represent temporal sequences. In reading text and speech understanding, the input is structured in time, and thus the behaviour of a system cannot be determined solely on the basis of the current input element. What is required is some sort of memory for previous elements in a sequence (or sentence) to be combined with the current element. Up until now, the input representations we have examined involve presenting each whole sequence to the system as a single input. This is equivalent to buffering the input stream until a sequence has been completed, before acting on it. The question then reverts to how to structure the contents of the buffer.

The main approach examined here has been the vector frame (e.g. Hinton, 1981; McClelland & Rumelhart, 1981). Another approach is that of Rumelhart and McClelland (1986). They adapted Wicklegren's (1969) proposal for the representation of words as sequences of context sensitive phoneme units (Wicklephones) which represent each phone as the phone itself, its predecessor, and its successor (e.g. the vowel in the word "cat" would be represented as $_kat$). Thus a set of overlapping triples can be interpreted as a sequence. Rumelhart and McClelland represented each Wicklephone as a distributed pattern of activation over *Wicklefeatures*, where a

Wicklefeature is a single unit that conjunctively coarse codes a feature of the central phoneme, a feature of its predecessor, and a feature of its successor. A different method, employed by Sejnowski and Rosenberg (1986) for their NETtalk system, employed a window containing 7 letters that moved across an input text. The central element of the window, on each successive move was encoded using the three elements on either side of it as context.

An alternative solution to the encoding of sequential structures, without using a buffer, was proposed by Elman (1988) with the introduction of a network architecture for predicting successive elements of a sequence (sentence). This is a variant of the feedforward multi-layer perceptron which allows feedback or recurrent links from the hidden units to the input. As each element of a sequential structure, such as a sentence, is coded onto the input units, the previous hidden unit vector is copied onto memory units in the input stream[6]. In this way, the meaning of an element of a sequence will be shaded by the context of the prior elements. In a sense each input cycle contains a memory of the previous cycles in the sequence.

Elman (1989) has conducted a number of simulations using the simple recurrent net architecture (SRN). He presented short sentences to the net, one word at a time, using the next word as a target. Thus the task for the net was to predict the next word in a sentence. Elman found that the network had developed hidden unit representations for the input patterns that reflected information about the possible sequential ordering of the inputs e.g. the net knew that the lexical category VERB followed the lexical category NOUN. Cluster analyses of the hidden unit activations revealed that the verb category is broken down itno those verbs which require a direct object and those for which a direct object is optional. Furthermore, the analyses showed that the nouns were divided into animates and inanimates with a further subdivision for human and non-human. In a larger scale analysis, Elman also discovered that the tokens of particular types clustered together[7]. Thus, hidden unit representation in the simple recurrent net, after learning, can be shown to exhibit a number of properties needed for a lexical category structure and type/token hierarchies.

Elman (1989) also investigated the representation of grammatical structure in a study which used a phrase structure grammar to generate the input sentences. This grammar allowed recursion through the use of a relative clause category that expanded to NPs that permitted further relative clauses. The results suggest that the net had learned to represent abstract grammatical structure. For example, when presented with a subject noun the net correctly predicted a verb which agreed with the number of the subject noun (i.e. singular/plural), even when a relative clause intervened. In addition, given a particular noun and verb, the net was shown to correctly predict the class of the next transition allowed by the grammar, thus demonstrating the representation of verb argument structure. Finally, the results from the recursive representations showed limitations. These representation were found to degrade after about three levels of embedding.

The same type of SRN was employed by Servan-Schrieber, Cleeremans, and McClelland (1989) in a study which involved learning a finite-state grammar. There were many interesting results from this study. But the most important results, for

---

[6]Elman's recurrent net is actually a variant of Jordan's (1986) sequencing net. Jordan took his recurrent links from the output units or from the training vector to the input units whereas Elman's recurrent links are from the hidden units to the input units.

[7]The separation of the type/token from the part/whole distinction has proved to be a difficult one in connectionist research (c.f. Hinton, 1981; Robbins, 1989).

our purposes, are: (a) the net learned to be a perfect recogniser for a finite-state grammar (at least for the Reber (1967) grammar they used). (b) under some conditions, long distance sequential dependencies were exhibited, even across embedded sequences. The latter result was best when the dependencies were relevant at each step. Moreover, performance across embedded strings deteriorated as the length of the string increased.

In sum, by extending the backpropagation algorithm in a simple recurrent net, it has been possible to add a number of features to the compact representations that were discussed in Section 1. Primarily, SRNs allow the representation to encode sequential information such as the order of the input, and the path from one element to another. They also exhibit a certain ability to allow the encoding of long range sequential dependencies across embedded sequences.

2.2 Recursive distributed representations

One aspect of natural language processing that has been problematic for the connectionist community is that natural languages are recursive. We have already seen, in the last section, how this posed difficulties for SRNs. In this section, we shall discuss two recent attempts at representing recursive structures.

Tensor product representations

The tensor product system (Smolensky, in press) combines lexical items with their syntactic roles in a way which is mathematically equivalent to *outer product* learning (cf. Sharkey, 1989). That is, a vector representing an item (or role filler), i, is bound to a vector representing a role, r by the outer product ri^T. This is a tensor of rank two and results in a square matrix of activations. However the formalism goes beyond the simple outer product in that it enables the construction of recursive representation for, say, syntactic trees by using 3rd, 4th, or n^{th} order tensors. A third order tensor is a cube of unit activation and orders beyond the third are hypercubes.

There are two main problems with tensor products. First, with deep embedding the representation could grow exceedingly large. Second, when the input vectors (the fillers for the roles) are not orthogonal the tensorial representations have to be constructed by more complex incremental learning methods (e.g. the delta rule for linearly independent pattern sets, or back propagation). This makes the whole process less manageable as it is not at all obvious how such learning would take place[8]. However, processing and memory considerations aside, Smolensky presents an elegant and formally tractable theory of recursive representation. We can leave it to later research to work out how to develop it in real time and how to use it for recognition.

Recursive auto-associative memory (RAAM)

Hinton (1988) outlined an idea for handling embedded clauses by inserting a *reduced description* of them into larger representations. However, he did not detail a method by which such representations could be learned. This challenge has been taken up by Pollack (in press) who shows how such a reduced description can be learned in a Recursive Auto-Associative Memory (RAAM). The RAAM architecture is the same as the standard feedforward net with two layers of weights (for encoding and decoding the hidden unit representations) and the standard back propagation algorithm is

---

[8]Recall that the tensor operation produces vectors of unit activation and not weights.

employed for learning. Pollack has shown the power of the RAAM system for encoding a sequential stack with PUSH and POP and also for encoding and decoding syntactic trees. The whole trees are represented in a single layer of hidden units and can be decoded in cycles until the terminal symbols appear as the outputs. The difference between RAAM and the usual back propagation net rests on the method for presenting the input patterns.

We shall briefly describe the operation of a RAAM system here using the example of a simple binary tree: ((A B) (C D)). First the input space is divided into n partitions, with k units in each partition. The size of n depends directly on the maximum valency of the tree to be represented (in our simple example $n = 2$). Since this is an autoassociative net the output vector is identical to the input vector; both have nk units and there are k hidden units.

The representation of the binary tree would be formed as follows: (i) A and B are presented in the two vector partitions and autoassociated. The resulting hidden unit representation R_1 is kept to one side (on an external stack or somesuch); (ii) C and D are presented and autoassociated and the resulting hidden unit representation R_2 is put to one side; (iii) R_1 and R_2 are presented as input and autoassociated. The resulting hidden unit vector R_3 is a representation of the entire tree. R_3 can be decoded by presenting it directly to the hidden units and the outputs will be R_1 and R_2. These are then presented in turn until the terminals have been decoded.

Pollack (in press) presents a range of interesting simulation results which show RAAM to be a very effective method for encoding and decoding recursive structures. The only problem is that the method of presentation of inputs relies on an external stack and it is not altogether clear what a pure connectionist implementation of this would be. However, regardless of how the representation is constructed, Pollack has demonstrated how unstructured representations can encode recursive representation in a compact form.

2.3 Compositionality and structure sensitivity

In Section 1, connectionist representations were classified into different types. Some of these, as we have seen, are very similar to their Classical counterparts in that they contain explicit symbol tokens and/or have concatenative constituent structure (e.g. localist concept notes, symbolic microfeatures, vector frames), and some are weaker (e.g. localist proposition nodes). It is not the aim here to cast doubt on the value of the research using these representation schemes, but to consider whether or not the representations themselves (not the research) have novelty value.

From the review above, it should be quite clear that compact subsymbolic connectionist representations are different than Classical syntactic structure representation. This style of representation, Fodor and Pylyshyn (1988) argue, is not compositionally structured. However, as Van Gelder (1990) points out, Fodor and Pylyshyn are implicitly discussing only one type of compositionality: *spatially concatenative composition.* In this mode of composition, the spatial layout of the symbols (reading from left to right) is important (indeed crucial) for symbol manipulation and inference. Van Gelder states that for a mode of combination to be concatenative, "... it must preserve tokens of an expression's constituents (and the sequential relations among tokens) in the expression itself.".

In contrast, to Classical concatenative representation, the type of compact connectionist representation we have been discussing may be considered to have a different mode of combination. That is, "pure" connectionist representations are not concatenative, but are functionally compositional nonetheless. It is worth quoting van Gelder again on this point. "We have functional compositionality when there are general, effective and reliable processes for (a) producing an expression given its constituents, and (b) decomposing the expression back into those constituents." Connectionist models can certainly perform (a) and (b) as well as meet the criteria that the processes must be general, effective, and reliable. By *general*, van Gelder means that that the process can be applied, in principle, to the construction and decomposition of arbitrarily complex representations. We have seen how a simple feedforward back propogation net can learn to encode and decode representations[9]. To be *effective* the processes must be mechanistically implementible and to be *reliable* they must always generate the same answer for the same inputs. Once a connectionist net has finished learning it meets both of these criteria.

Given that connectionist representations are functionally compositional, the question is: do such seemingly unstructured representations carry structural information? And a subsiduary, though perhaps more important, question is: do these representations allow direct structure sensitive operations? The short answer to the first question is obviously "yes". Even in the early Hinton (1981) model of semantic nets, the vector frames of structured input representions were coarse coded onto a compact representation such that they could be accurately reconstructed onto an identical vector frame. To be reconstructed, the coarse coded representation must have been carrying structural information. In fact, they were carrying information about concatenative structure without themselves being concatenative.

The subsiduary question, as to whether connectionist representations allow structure sensitive operations, is partly addressed by the answer to the previous question. However, it might be argued that even the functionally compositional connectionist representation may be a variation on the Classical theme because the connectionist representations must emerge onto the symbol surface before they can be structurally manipulted. For example, Fodor & McLauglin (1990) claim that in order to support structure sensitive operations, compositional representation must contain explicit tokens of the original constituent parts. This position has been subjected to a recent empirical investigation by Chalmers (in press) which refutes it.

Chalmers constructed compact recursive distributed representations of syntactically structured sentences using Pollack's (in press) RAAM system (described in 2.2 above). After training the net to develop compact representations for both active and passive sentence structures, Chalmers set out to test the structure sensitivity of the representation. He did this by attempting to train the transformation of the compact active sentences into the compact representation of the passive sentences. This experiment was successful in that it demonstrated that connectionist representation can be structurally manipulated (passivisation) without recourse to emergence on the symbol surface.

3. Conclusions

The main classes of connectionist representation for natural language processing have been examined in this paper. For convenience these were divided into semantic representations (Section 1.1) and structural representations (Section 1.2). In Section 1.1, semantic representations were clasified into major types: localist and distributed, and a number of advantages were pointed out for distributed representations (memory efficiency, content addressibility, and built-in generalisation). In addition, two flavours of distributed representation were pinpointed: symbolic and subsymbolic. On the question of the novelty of connectionist semantic representation,

---

[9] Hornik, Stinchcombe & White (1990) have shown that a feedforward back propogation net can learn to represent any borel-measurable function.

the subsymbolic was shown to be the only contender. Distributed symbolic representation have a lot of similarities with Classical feature theory.

On the syntactic side, a distinction was drawn between representations which are syntactically explicit and syntactically implicit. It was argued that only the latter could be considered to be representationally novel. The syntactically implicit representations were discussed further in Section 2.3. It was argued that they were functionally compositional (as opposed to concatenative) and could be sensitive to structural manipulations without recourse to decoding into the original symbolic tokens of their constituent parts.

This paper displays optimism about the development and utility of unique connectionist representations i.e. subsymbolic, syntactically implicit representations. We have seen only one connectionist study in which these representations have been shown to be structure sensitive. However, this is just the beginning. We have also seen (Section 2.1) how non-concatenative distributed representations can carry information about temporal structure, long distance dependencies, lexical category structure and the type/token distinction. We have also seen how they can represent finite state grammars. In section 2.2, we saw how research on connectionist representation had begun to overcome one of the hardest problems for CNLP, the representation of recursive structures.

All in all, despite (and to some extent thanks to) Fodor and Pylyshyn's critique of connectionist representation, it looks as though the prognosis for CNLP is good. Judging by the explosion of research we have seen up until now, the next few years are expected to yield many exciting new results.

References

Chalmers, D.J. (in press) Syntactic Transformations on Distributed Representations. *Connection Science, 2.1.*

Cottrell, G.W. (1985) A Connectionist Approach to Word Sense Disambiguation. PhD Thesis, TR154, Department of Computer Science, University of Rochester, NY.

Cottrell, G.W., Munro, P. & Zipser, D. (1989) Image Compression by Back Propagation: An Example of Extensional Programming. In N.E. Sharkey (Ed) *Models of Cognition: A Review of Cognitive Science.* Norwood, N.J.: Ablex.

Dolan, C.P. & Smolensky, P. (1989) Tensor Production System: a Modular Architecture and Representation. *Connection Science* 1(1), 53-68.

Elman, J.L (1988) Finding the structure in time. TR 880, CRL, University of California, San Diego.

Elman, J.L. (1989) Representation and structure in connectionist models. TR 8903, CRL, University of California, San Diego.

Feldman, J.A. (1989) Neural Representation of Conceptual Knowledge. In N.E. Sharkey (Ed) *Models of Cognition: A Review of Cognitive Science.* Norwood, N.J.: Ablex.

Fillmore, C.J. (1968) The Case for Case. In E. Bach and R. Harris (Eds) *Universals in Linguistic Theory.* Holt, Rhinehart & Winston.

Fodor, J.A. & McLaughlin, B. (1990) Connectionism and the Problems of Systemacity l:Why Smolensky's Solution Doesn't Work. *Cognition*, 35, 183-204.

Fodor, J.A, & Pylyshyn, Z.W. (1988). Connectionism and Cognitive Architecture: A Critical Analysis. *Cognition*, 28, 2-71.

Hinton, G.E. (1981) Implementing Semantic Networks in Parallel Hardware. In G.E. Hinton & J.A. Anderson (Eds) *Parallel Models of Associative Memory*. Hillsdale, N.J.:Lawrence Erlbaum.

Hinton, G.E. (1986) Learning Distributed Representations of Concepts. *Proceedings of the Eighth Annual Conference of the Cognitive Science Society*.

Hinton, G.E. (1989) Connectionist Learning Procedures. *Artificial Intelligence*, **40**, 184-235.

Hinton, G.E., McClelland, J.L. & Rumelhart, D.E. (1986) Distributed Representations. In D.E. Rumelhart & J.L. McClelland (Eds) *Parallel Distributed Processing, Volume 1*. Cambridge, MA: MIT.

Hopfield, J.J. (1982) Neural Networks and Physical Systems with Emergent Collective Computational Abilities. *Proceedings of the National Academy of Sciences*, USA, 79, 2554-2558.

Hornik, K. Stinchcombe, M. & White, H. (1989) Multilayer Feedfoewrad Network are Univesal Approximators. *Discussion paper 88-45R.* Department of Economics, UCSD.

Jordan, M.I. (1986) Attractor Dynamics and parallelism in a Connectionist Sequential Machine. *Proceedings of the 8th Annual Conference of the Cognitive Science Society*, Amherst, MA. 531-545.

Kohonen, T. (1982) Clustering, Taxonomy, and Topological Maps of Patterns. In M. Lang (Ed) *Proceedings of the Sixth International Conference on Pattern Recognition*. Silver Spring, MD: IEEE Computer Society Press.

Kolen, J.F. & Pollack, J.B. (1990) Back Propagation is Sensitive to Initial Conditions. *Technical Report 90-JK-BPSIC.* Ohio Satat University.

McClelland, J.L. & Kawamoto A.H. (1986) Mechanisms of Sentence Processing:Assigning Roles to Constituents. In J.L. McClelland & D.E. Rumelhart (Eds) *Parallel Distributed Processing Volume 2*. Cambridge, MA: MIT.

McClelland, J.L. & Rumelhart, D.E. (1981) An Interactive Activation Model of Effects in Letter Perception: Part I. An Account of Basic Findings. *Psychological Review*, 88, 375-407.

Miikkulainen, R. & Dyer, M. G. (1987) Building Distributed Representations without Microfeatures. *Technical Report UCLA-AI-87-17*, AI Laboratory, Computer Science Department, University of California at Los Angeles, CA.

Minsky, M. (1975) A Framework for Representing Knowledge. In P.H. Winston (Ed) *The Psychology of Computer Vision*. New York:McGraw-Hill.

Pollack, J.B. (in press) Recursive Distributed Representations. *Artificial Intelligence*. Rumelhart, D.E., Hinton, G.E. & Williams, R.J. (1986) Learning Internal Representations by Error Propagation. In D.E. Rumelhart & J.L. McClelland (Eds) *Parallel Distributed Processing Volume 1*. Cambridge, MA: MIT..

Robbins, A. (1989) The Distributed Representation of Type and Category. *Connection Science* 1.4.

Schank, R.C. (1972) Conceptual dependency: a theory of natural language understanding. *Cognitive Psychology*, 3, 552-631.

Sejnowski, T.J. & Rosenberg, C.R. (1986) A Parallel Network that Learns to Read Out Loud. *Technical Report JHU/EECS-86/01*. John Hopkins University.

Servan-Schreiber, D., Cleermans, A., & McClelland, J.L.(1988) Encoding sequential structure in simple recurrent nets. TR CMU-CS-88-183. Computer Science department, Carnegie-Mellon University.

Sharkey, N.E. (1989a) The Lexical Distance Model and Word Priming. *Proceedings of the Eleventh Cognitive Science Society.*

Sharkey, N.E. (1989b) Lexical Representations for Prepositional Attachment. *Report to British Telecom CONNEX Project.*

Sharkey, N.E. (1989c) A PDP Learning Approach to Natural Language Understanding. In I. Aleksander (Ed) *Neural Computing Architectures.* London:North Oxford Academic.

Sharkey, N.E. & Reilly, R. (in press) An overview of connectionist natural language processing, *Parallel update.*

Shastri L. & Feldman J.A. (1986) Neural Nets, Routines and Semantic Networks. In N.E. Sharkey (Ed) *Advances in Cognitive Science.* Chichester: Ellis Horwood.

Smolensky, P. (1989b) Distributed Representations of Symbolic Structures Constructed with Tensor Products. *Artificial Intelligence* (in press).

Smolensky, P. (1988) On the Proper Treatment of Connectionism. *Behavioral and Brain Sciences*, **11**, 1-74.

Smolensky, P. (in press) Tensor Product Variable Binding and the Representation of Symbolic Structures in Connectionist Systems. *Artificial Intelligence.*

St John, M.F. & McClelland, J.L. (in press). In R. Reilly & N.E. Sharkey (Eds) *Connectionist Approaches to Language Processing.* Hillsdale, N.J.:LEA.

Touretzky, D.S. & Geva, S. (1987) A Distributed Connectionist Representation for Concept Structures. *Proceedings of the Ninth Annual Conference of the Cognitive Science Society*, 155-164.

Touretzky, D.S. & Hinton, G.E. (1988) A Distributed Connectionist Production System. *Cognitive Science* **12**(3), 423-466.

Van Gelder, T. (1990) Compositionality: a Connectionist Variation on a Classical Theme. *Cognitive Science, 14.*

Wickelgren,W.A.(1969) Context-sensitive coding, associative memory, and serial order in (speech) behavior. *Psychological Review*, 76,1-15.

Willshaw, D.J. & von der Malsburg, C. (1979) A Marker Induction Mechanism for the Establishment of Ordered Neural Mapping: Its Application to the Retino-tectal Connections. In *Philos, Trans, Roy, Soc, Lond. B* **287**, 203-243.

KOHÄRENZ UND MONITOR

IN KONNEKTIONISTISCHEN SPRACHPRODUKTIONSMODELLEN[*]

Ulrich Schade

Fakultät für Linguistik und Literaturwissenschaft

Universität Bielefeld

D 4800 Bielefeld / Bundesrepublik Deutschland

1. Einleitung

Eine wichtige Aufgabe der KI besteht darin, Modelle kognitiver Prozesse zu entwickeln. Diese Modelle müssen empirische Daten über den zu modellierenden kognitiven Prozeß abbilden und erklären. Da die Sprachproduktion ein sehr komplexer Prozeß ist, der nicht direkt beobachtet werden kann, empfiehlt es sich, für seine Untersuchung eine Negativmethodologie zu verwenden. Das heißt, die besten Rückschlüsse auf die Sprachproduktion gewinnt man aus den empirischen Daten über Versprecher, deren Reparaturen und ähnlichen „inkohärenten" Resultaten des Sprachproduktionsprozesses (vgl. z.B. Fromkin 1971, Butterworth 1980).

Im folgenden soll dargelegt werden, daß in einem konnektionistischen Modell inkohärente Resultate des Produktionsprozesses darauf zurückgeführt werden können, daß das Modell während des ablaufenden Prozesses in einen „inkohärenten Zustand" geraten ist. Die Beschreibung inkohärenter Prozeßzustände bietet die Möglichkeit eine Monitorkomponente für solche Modelle zu explizieren. Unter einer Monitorkomponente wird dabei derjenige Teil des Modells verstanden, der Fehler erkennt, die das Modell produziert.

---

[*] Diese Arbeit entstand im Rahmen des von der DFG geförderten Forschungsprojektes „Kohärenz", Teilprojekt „Gesprochenes Deutsch".

2. Kohärenz im konnektionistischen Modell

Als Grundlage für die vorgeschlagene Definition von Kohärenz/Inkohärenz und der darauf aufbauenden Monitorkomponente dient ein vorliegendes konnektionstisches Produktionsmodell (vgl. Schade 1988, Schade & Eikmeyer 1990). Die jeweiligen Definitionen lassen sich aber ohne größere Probleme auf andere konnektionistische Produktionsmodelle (Berg 1988; Dell 1986, 1988; MacKay 1987; Stemberger 1985, 1990) übertragen.

Im vorliegenden Modell werden linguistische Einheiten, wie Wörter, Silben und Phoneme durch jeweils einen Knoten repräsentiert (vgl. Abbildung). Exzitatorische Verbindungen zwischen diesen Knoten ergeben sich aus den syntagmatischen linguistischen Relationen zwischen diesen Einheiten. Inhibitorische Verbindungen ergeben sich aus den paradigmatischen Relationen. Letztere beschreiben Wahlmöglichkeiten für bestimmte strukturelle Positionen.

Durch die inhibitorischen Verbindungen werden also Knoten zusammengefaßt, die linguistisch gleichartige Einheiten repräsentieren und damit in ihrer Gesamtheit eine Verarbeitungsebene des Modells definieren. So existieren eine Phonemebene, eine Silbenebene, eine Wortebene usw. Die Ebenen sind hierarchisch angeordnet. Nur Knoten benachbarter Ebenen können exzitatorisch miteinander verbunden sein.

In einem solchen Modell läßt sich „Kohärenz" sehr einfach aus der Definition darüber ableiten, wann zwei benachbarte Ebenen in kohärenter Beziehung zueinander stehen. Für zwei benachbarte Ebenen definiert man, daß sie zu einem Zeitpunkt t genau dann in kohärenter Beziehung zueinander stehen, wenn die zum Zeitpunkt t jeweils höchst aktivierten Knoten dieser Ebenen auch exzitatorisch miteinander verbunden sind. Der gesamte Prozeß befindet sich genau dann in einem kohärenten Zustand, wenn für alle Paare benachbarter Ebenen gilt, daß sie in kohärenter Beziehung zueinander stehen.

Diese Definition soll anhand der Abbildung verdeutlicht werden. Betrachten wir dazu zunächst die Silbenebene und die Wortebene. Ein Knoten der Silbenebene repräsentiert eine Silbe, ein Knoten der Wortebene ein Wort. Ein Silbenknoten ist genau dann mit einem Wortknoten exzitatorisch verbunden, wenn die zugehörige Silbe eine Silbe des fraglichen Wortes ist. Nehmen wir nun an, die beiden Ebenen ständen in kohärenter Beziehung zueinander. Dann sind die am höchsten aktivierten Knoten beider Ebenen exzitatorisch miteinander verbunden, und somit ist die höchstaktivierte Silbe eine Silbe des höchst aktivierten Wortes.

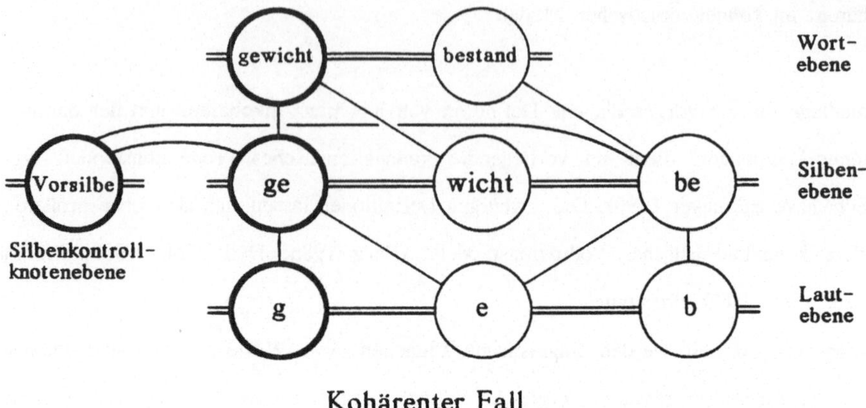

Kohärenter Fall

Inkohärenter Fall

<u>Abbildung:</u>   Ausschnitt aus dem Modell

(Der jeweils höchst aktivierte Knoten einer Ebene ist durch die dickere Umrandung hervorgehoben.)

Wie aus dem Beispiel deutlich wird, durchläuft das Modell während der Produktion genau dann eine Folge von kohärenten Zuständen, wenn das Resultat des Produktionsprozesses fehlerfrei ist. Im folgenden soll gezeigt werden, daß der so verstandene Kohärenzbegriff als Grundlage einer Monitorkomponente benutzt werden kann.

3. Die Monitorkomponente eines konnektionistischen Produktionsmodells

Die Aufgabe der Monitorkomponente besteht darin, Produktionsfehler zu entdecken, damit diese Fehler repariert werden können. Aus den empirischen Daten ergibt sich, daß der Monitor, der die menschliche Sprachproduktion überwacht, sehr effektiv arbeitet. Die hier verwendeten empirischen Daten stammen aus der umfangreichen Sammlung von Versprechern, die Berg als Grundlage für seine Untersuchungen und sein Produktionsmodell angelegt hat (vgl. Berg 1988; 1990). Die Sammlung umfaßt mehr als 6000 Einträge. Sie zeigt, daß unterschiedliche Arten von Fehlern unterschiedlich gut erkannt und entsprechend unterschiedlich häufig repariert werden. Für die meisten Fehlertypen liegt die Reparaturrate aber bei etwa 90%: so werden von den besonders häufig auftretenden syntagmatischen konsonantischen Substitutionen in Bergs Korpus 1217 von 1318, also 92.3% repariert.

Der kognitive Monitorprozeß arbeitet also sehr effektiv. Er ist aber auch sehr schnell. Wie jeder aus eigener Erfahrung weiß, werden zum Teil schon Fehler erkannt, die noch gar nicht zur Produktion gekommen sind. Monitorkomponenten in symbolverarbeitenden Modellen entsprechen dieser Anforderung nicht, da sie auf komplexen Reanalyseverfahren beruhen (vgl. Berg 1986). Im Gegensatz dazu erkennen konnektionistische Monitorkomponenten mögliche Fehler anhand von Aktivierungsmustern während des Produktionsprozesses. Konkrete Vorschläge für eine konnektionistische Monitorkomponente findet man bei MacKay (1987) und Berg (1990).

4. MacKays Monitorkonzeption

In MacKays Modell werden Knoten zu einem bestimmten Zeitpunkt des Produktionsprozesses selektiert. Danach können sie ihre Nachbarn besonders stark beeinflussen, also mit Aktivation versorgen. Sobald aber der nächste Knoten selektiert wird, erfolgt eine Dämpfung und eine anschließende Selbstinhibitionsphase für den ersten Knoten. In dem Beispiel, das durch die Abbildung vorgegeben ist, würde also der Knoten „gewicht" nach seiner Selektion seine Bestandteile „ge" und „wicht" besonders stark aktivieren. Bei einem korrekt ablaufenden Produktionsprozeß würde nach „gewicht" der Knoten „ge" selektiert. Wenn dann „ge" Aktivation verschickt, unterliegt „gewicht" im Modell von MacKay schon einer Selbstinhibition. Die die Aktivation, die „ge" an „gewicht" über das

„Feedback" schickt, verhallt ohne Wirkung.

MacKay könnte also sagen, daß sein Monitor genau dann einen Fehler anzeigt, wenn ein Knoten, der selektiert wird, nicht exzitatorisch mit einem Knoten verbunden ist, der sich in seiner Selbstinhibitionsphase befindet. Aber MacKay geht bei seiner Monitorbeschreibung (1987, Seite 169) davon aus, daß bei einem fehlerhaft ablaufenden Prozeß auf der Ebene, die der „fehlerbehafteten" Ebene übergeordnet ist, ein „falscher" Knoten aktiviert wird. An dieser Sichtweise setzt die Kritik von Berg (1990) an: Wird im gegebenen Beispiel nach der Selektion von „gewicht" etwa fälschlicherweise als nächster Knoten der Silbenknoten „be" selektiert, so befindet sich zwar „gewicht" in seiner Selbstinhibitionsphase, doch der Knoten auf der Wortebene, der nach MacKay fälschlicherweise aktiviert würde, wäre der Knoten, der „bewicht" repräsentiert. Dieser Knoten existiert jedoch nicht, da „bewicht" kein Wort ist.

Eine weitere fundamentale Schwäche von MacKays Modell, die bislang noch nicht diskutiert wurde, liegt darin, daß MacKays Monitor nicht in der Lage ist, Kontaminationsfehler zu erkennen. Gerade Kontaminationsfehler aber liefern für die Fehlererkennung und -korrektur die interessantesten empirischen Daten. Kontaminationen entstehen durch die Interaktion zweier Realisationsmöglichkeiten für das zu Produzierende. Entsprechend der Größe der involvierten Einheiten lassen sich Kontaminationsfehler in drei Gruppen einteilen; in der ersten Gruppe erfolgt der Übergang von der einen zur anderen Realisationsmöglichkeit innerhalb einer Silbe bzw. eines Morphems (vgl. Beispiel 1a). In der zweiten erfolgt sie zwischen zwei Silben/Morphemen, aber innerhalb eines Wortes (vgl. Beispiel 1b) und in der dritten Gruppe erfolgt sie zwischen zwei Wörtern (vgl. Beispiel 1c). Bei allen Beispielen sind jeweils die alternativen Realisationsmöglichkeiten zur Verdeutlichung ebenfalls genannt.

(1a)   „..., da geschah so etwas öftiger" (öfter/häufiger)

(1b)   „... Gegensprüche ..."   (Gegensätze/Widersprüche)

(1c)   „ Seh' ich irgendwo niemanden sonst?"

        (Seh' ich irgendwo noch jemanden? / Seh' ich niemanden sonst?)

In Bergs Daten werden Kontaminationen der ersten Gruppe zu 81.3%, der zweiten Gruppe zu 54.0% und die der dritten Gruppe nur zu 41.5% repariert. Die Monitorkomponente scheint also Kontaminationen grundsätzlich schlechter zu erkennen als Fehler anderer Art, was besonders für die beiden letzten Gruppen gilt.

MacKays Monitor erkennt aber überhaupt keine Kontaminationen. Nach seinem Modell entstehen diese Fehler dadurch, daß die Knoten, die die beiden Realisationsmöglichkeiten repräsentieren, *beide* gleichzeitig selektiert (MacKay 1987, Seite 123) und entsprechend beide gedämpft und mit einer Selbstinhibition versehen werden. Unabhängig davon, von welcher Realisationsmöglichkeit dann Teile selektiert werden, befindet sich der dem selektierten Knoten übergeordnete Knoten in seiner Selbstinhibitionsphase, so daß der Monitor keinerlei Anlaß hat einzugreifen.

5. Bergs Monitorkonzeption

Viele Probleme im Modell von MacKay rühren daher, daß selektierte Knoten zu früh in die Selbstinhibitionsphase geraten. In Bergs Modell werden — ebenso wie im hier vorgestellten Modell (vgl. Schade 1988) — Knoten erst dann gedämpft, wenn die Produktion aller ihrer Teile abgeschlossen ist. Bergs Monitor nimmt aber auf diesen Unterschied im Dämpfungszeitpunkt primär keinen Bezug. Er reagiert lediglich auf den Aktivierungswert der Knoten zum Zeitpunkt ihrer Selektion. Die überzeugend einfache Grundidee beruht dabei auf folgender Überlegung: Ein fehlerhaft selektierter Knoten hat den Zielknoten als Konkurrenten und wird von diesem gehemmt, wie auch er den Zielknoten hemmt. Folglich sollte ein fehlerhaft selektierter Knoten in seinem Aktivierungswert niedriger liegen, als dies im allgemeinen für selektierte Zielknoten der Fall ist, da bei einer normal ablaufenden Produktion keine hoch aktivierten Konkurrenzknoten auftreten. Entsprechend unterbricht der Monitor in Bergs Modell die Produktion, wenn der selektierte Knoten einen zu niedrigen Aktivierungswert hat.

Bergs Monitor bemerkt allerdings keine Fehler, die darauf beruhen, daß ein fehlerhaft selektierter Knoten einen *sehr* niedrigen Aktivierungswert hat. Berg erklärt dies mit der Metapher eines Fernsehzuschauers. Dieser sieht auf seinem Fernsehschirm einen Text, der sich mit unterschiedlicher Helligkeit vom Hintergrund abhebt. Der Text entspricht dann dem selektierten Knoten, während die Helligkeit seinem Aktivierungswert entspricht. Ist der Aktivierungswert sehr niedrig, so kann — nach Bergs Metapher — der „Fernsehzuschauer" (Monitor) den Text nicht mehr erkennen und folglich auch keinen Fehler feststellen.

Diese Metapher aber widerspricht Bergs Grundidee. Der Monitor hat lediglich den Aktivierungswert zu erkennen; er braucht nicht zu „wissen", was der Knoten repräsentiert. In der Sprache der Metapher betrachtet also der Monitor nur die Helligkeit, gleichgültig um welchen Text es sich handelt. Da in der Metapher der Monitor Fehler auch aufgrund des Textes erkennen soll, deutet die Wahl der Metapher an, daß der Monitor eigentlich mehr Information als nur den Aktivierungswert des selektierten Knotens benötigt.

Die Frage, ob ein Monitor mehr auswerten muß, als einen einzelnen Aktivierungswert, läßt sich an einer Ergänzung diskutieren, die Berg für sein Modell vorschlägt. Berg geht davon aus, daß dem Monitorprozeß Aufmerksamkeit zugeführt werden kann, so daß er mögliche Fehler noch besser erkennt. In einem Modell, in dem der Monitor lediglich aufgrund eines einzelnen Aktivierungswertes entscheidet, ob die Produktion abzubrechen ist, kann der Monitor nur dann mehr Fehler „erkennen", wenn der Bereich vergrößert wird, in dem ein Aktivierungswert als Ursache für einen Produktionsabbruch angesehen wird. Das bedeutet jedoch, daß in einem immer stärkeren Maße auch Produktionen abgebrochen werden, bei denen der gewünschte Zielknoten selektiert wurde.

6. Die Verschmelzung der Modelle

Die von Berg vertretene Grundidee überzeugt durch ihre einfache und klare Konzeption. Dennoch zeigt sich, daß die Auswertung eines einzelnen Aktivierungswertes nicht genügend Information beinhaltet. Dies wäre in einem vorstellbaren *distribuierten* Modell grundsätzlich anders. In einem distribuierten Modell werden Einheiten durch Aktivierungs*muster* repräsentiert. Damit spiegeln sich aber auch die syntagmatischen Relationen zwischen Einheiten in den Aktivierungsmustern wider: Aus der Ausprägung des Aktivierungsmusters einer Einheit geht hervor, welche anderen Einheiten, die mit der ersten syntagmatisch verknüpft sind, zur gleichen Zeit ebenfalls über ein ausgeprägtes Muster verfügen. Ein Monitor, der in einem solchen Modell das Aktivierungsmuster einer selektierten Einheit auswertet, erhält folglich auch Information darüber, ob die selektierte Einheit mit selektierten Einheiten höherer Modellebenen syntagmatisch verknüpft ist.

Bergs Idee ist also auf distribuierte Modelle anwendbar. Eine Übertragung dieser Monitorkonzeption auf ein lokales Modell setzt aber voraus, daß der Monitor auch eine Auswertung der Aktivierungswerte von übergeordneten Einheiten vornimmt, ähnlich wie es MacKay vorschwebt. Um MacKays Probleme zu vermeiden, sollten jedoch Knoten nach ihrer Selektion so lange aktiv bleiben, wie die Produktion ihrer Teile andauert. Erst dann sollte die Selbstinhibitionsphase einsetzen. Dies vermeidet auch Selbstinhibitionsphasen unterschiedlicher Länge je nach betroffener Modellebene (vgl. MacKay 1987, Seite 144f).

Wenn also der Monitor syntagmatische Relationen zwischen den höchst aktivierten Knoten benachbarter Ebenen auswertet, entspricht dies der Situation, für die der in Abschnitt 2 diskutierte Kohärenzbegriff einschlägig ist. Bei der Selektion eines Knotens überprüft der Monitor, ob sich die Ebene, auf der die Selektion stattfindet, mit der ihr hierarchisch übergeordneten Modellebene in einem kohärenten Zustand befindet. Das heißt nichts anderes, als daß der Monitor überprüft, ob der selektierte Knoten mit dem höchstaktivierten Knoten der übergeordneten Ebene exzitatorisch verbunden ist.

Um die Tragfähigkeit dieses Konzeptes zu prüfen, sollen noch einmal die empirischen Werte für Kontaminationsfehler herangezogen werden. Im Gegensatz zu MacKays Modell bleiben die übergeordneten Knoten aktiviert, bis die zugehörige Produktion auf den unteren Ebenen abgeschlossen ist. Demnach können Kontaminationsfehler dadurch erklärt werden, daß auf einer höheren Ebene die beiden Realisationsmöglichkeiten, die an der Kontamination beteiligt sind, während der Produktion ähnlich stark aktiviert sind. Der Fehler entsteht dadurch, daß während der Produktion die relativen Aktivierungsverhältnisse der beiden konkurrierenden Knoten wechseln. Das heißt, zunächst ist der Knoten, der die Möglichkeit 1 repräsentiert, ein wenig stärker, doch im Laufe der Produktion kommt es dazu, daß der Knoten, der die Möglichkeit 2 repräsentiert, ein Übergewicht an Aktivierung besitzt. Der postulierte Monitor aber entdeckt immer nur dann einen Fehler, wenn die jeweils höchstaktivierten Knoten der betreffenden Ebenen zum Zeitpunkt einer Selektion nicht exzitatorisch miteinander verbunden sind, also nicht zur selben Realisationsmöglichkeit gehören. Die Chance, einen inkohärenten Zustand zu erkennen, nimmt natürlich sukzessiv ab, wenn der Übergang von einer Möglichkeit zur anderen auf einer höheren Ebene, also beispielsweise zwischen Wörtern statt innerhalb eines Wortes, vollzogen wird: Im letzteren Fall kommt es nur zwischen der Wortebene und der Konzeptebene kurzzeitig zu einem inkohärenten Zustand; findet der Übergang dagegen innerhalb einer Silbe statt, so entstehen im Netz zu verschiedenen Zeiten kurzzeitig inkohärente Zustände zwischen der Lautebene und der Silbenebene, zwischen der Silbenebene und der Wortebene und· zwischen der Wortebene und der Konzeptebene. Im Gegensatz zu den inkohärenten Zuständen bei Substitutionsfehlern werden bei Kontaminationsfehlern aus den inkohärenten Zuständen wieder kohärente, sobald der Übergang von der einen Realisationsmöglichkeit zur anderen vollzogen ist. Folglich kann die Monitorkomponente, die ja nur während einer Selektion operiert, kontaminationsbedingte inkohärente

Netzzustände leicht übersehen, und dies um so leichter, je weniger Ebenen von den inkohärenten Zuständen betroffen sind, je geringer also die Gesamtzeitspanne ist, in denen inkohärente Zustände auftreten. Dies entspricht den im Abschnitt 4 vorgestellten empirischen Daten.

7. Schluß

Dieses Papier diskutiert unterschiedliche Ansätze für eine konnektionistische Monitorkomponente. Dabei wird festgestellt, daß ein Vorschlag Bergs, nach dem der Monitor während des Produktionsprozesses jeweils lediglich den Aktivierungswert eines einzelnen Knotens auswerten muß, in lokalen konnektionistischen Modellen aufgrund einer zu kleinen auswertbaren Informationsmenge nicht ausreicht. Der Vorschlag kann aber in Richtung des Ansatzes von MacKay erweitert werden, indem nicht nur ein Aktivierungswert, sondern Teile von Aktivierungsmustern ausgewertet werden. Diese Erweiterung kann als Test daraufhin verstanden werden, ob sich die betreffenden Teile des Modells in einem kohärenten Zustand befinden.

8. Literatur

Berg, T. (1986). The Problems of Language Control: Editing, Monitoring, and Feedback. *Psychological Research*, 48, 133−144.

Berg, T. (1988). *Die Abbildung des Sprachproduktionsprozesses in einem Aktivierungsflußmodell.* Tübingen: Niemeyer.

Berg, T. (1990). *Toward a Theory of Error Detection and Correction.* In Vorbereitung.

Butterworth, B. (1980). Introduction: A Brief Review of Methods of Studying Language Production. In: B. Butterworth (Hrsg.), *Language Production*, 1, 1−17. London: Academic Press.

Dell, G.S. (1986). A Spreading-Activation Theory of Retrieval in Sentence Production. *Psychological Review*, 93, 283−321.

Dell, G.S. (1988). The Retrieval of Phonological Forms in Production: Tests of Prediction from a Connectionist Model. *Journal of Memory and Language*, 27, 124−142.

Fromkin, V.A. (1971). The Non-Anomalous Nature of Anomalous Utterances. *Language*, 47, 27−52.

MacKay, D.G. (1987). *The Organisation of Peception and Action.* New York, NY: Springer.

Schade, U. (1988). Ein konnektionistisches Modell für die Satzproduktion. In: J. Kindermann & C. Lischka (Hrsg.), *Workshop Konnektionismus*, Arbeitspapiere der GMD, 329, 207−220. St. Augustin.

Schade, U. & Eikmeyer, H.-J. (1990). Modelling Attention in a Connectionist Speech Production Model. In: R. Eckmiller, G. Hartmann & G. Hauske (Hrsg.), *Parallel Processing in Neural Systems and Computers*, 495 – 498. Amsterdam: Elsevier.

Stemberger, J.P. (1985). An Interactive Activation Model of Language Production. In: A.W. Ellis (Hrsg.), *Progress in the Psychology of Language*, Vol. 1, 143 – 186. London: Erlbaum.

Stemberger, J.P. (1990). Wordshape Errors in Language Production. *Cognition*, 35, 123 – 157.

A syllable-based net-linguistic approach to lexical access

Claudia Kunze

Sprachwissenschaftliches Institut
Ruhr-Universität Bochum
Postfach 10 21 48
D-4630 Bochum 1
email: P050202@DBORUB01.BITnet

Abstract

This paper is concerned with a net-linguistic approach to the simulation of lexical access focussing on the syllable as the basic unit in speech processing. A connectionist localist architecture serves to represent a hierarchically organized multi-layered structure ranging from simple peripheral levels like the phoneme layer up to more complex conceptual levels (syllabic, morphemic and word layers) that are involved in word recognition. Besides this stratification, the parallel processing mode and an overall mechanism to shift incoming units serve to develop a network that demonstrates the growth of phonomorphological structure and its ambiguities while at the same time preserving the temporal dimension of speech.

1. Introduction: The syllable as a relevant unit in lexical access

In recent research generative phonologists have pointed out the organizational power of the syllabic unit concerning phonological rules as well as structure building and reaucing phonological processes on higher and lower levels of representation (see Wiese (1988) for a review). The epiphenomenal character of the syllable should be considered by two crucial functions: The syllable as the only prosodic unit to which stress may be assigned plays the dominant role in Metrical Phonology. Prosodic structure such as stress patterns facilitates lexical access in automatic speech recognition. On the other side the syllable is not an unordered set of segments, but requires language specific constraints on consonantal sequences in its onset and coda constituents (in German the sequence e.g. /nt/ is permitted as a coda and prohibited as an onset).

In certain psychological models of online word recognition the evidence of the syllable as a relevant unit is denied (cf. Marslen-Wilson (1978; 1984:145; 1987), Elman & McClelland (1986)). Phonemes derived from acoustic features directly influence the lexical layer without taking account of any intermediary structure. Other psychologists like Erman & Lesser (1980),Segui (1984) and Frauenfelder & Tyler (1987) argue that the syllable is the basic unit of speech segmentation that can rather easily be extracted from the speech signal. The segmentation into syllables occurs before phoneme detection and before lexical access take place. Segui gains evidence for the hypothesis of syllable-sized steps in speech recognition from shorter reaction times in detecting intrasyllabic target sequences in relation to reaction times concerning the same target sequences distributed over adjacent syllables. From an interactive point of view, Segui suggests the syllabic level to be the locus of trade-offs between bottom up (sensory) and top down (contextual) information. In spite of these insights a satisfying integration of syllabic and subsyllabic structure into an access-model is not yet realized. The model below proposes a representation in which this conceptual link between phoneme and word recognition is elaborated.

Besides neglecting the syllabic level as an intermediary hidden layer, another deficiency of current models in speech recognition concerns the representation of the temporal dimension. This issue has attracted increasing interest in recent connectionist research (cf. Elman & Zipser 1988; Waibel, Hinton et al. 1987) but has not yet been resolved in an obvious and convincing fashion for an extended number of data.

The following sections focus on the architecture of the system concerning layered concepts and time structure. On this basis the activation processes may demonstrate ambiguous syllable structure assignment resulting from variations in segmenting consonantal sequences. The correct structure is postlexically made available by matching a lexical item whereas structures without support from the lexical layer will decrease. The role of context effects is separated from the word recognition process and will be transferred to a postlexical level on which semantic, syntactic, and pragmatic information may be considered. In contrast to this it is sometimes argued that the locus of context influences interacts with the structuring process either in its beginning (Marslen-Wilson (1987)) or during the whole process (Elman & McClelland (1986)).

2. The architecture of the system

Although the model presented here is not psychologically motivated, several important properties of the system are adopted from Elman & McClelland's TRACE-model (1986):

- a layered arrangement of simple and more complex levels that comprise units standing for concepts
- a space for representing the occurrence of units in time
- a parallel processing structure among the units

There are distinctions concerning the choice of layers (TRACE comprises feature, phoneme and word level) and the quality of preserving the structure of input data (which TRACE realizes in various processing cycles on each level of representation by copying over and over again the connectivity patterns among units). Schnelle (1988) proposes a representation in which each basic concept is stored only once, whereas its temporal occurrence will be expressed in terms of simple neighbourhood relations in a shift register (see below).

The following stratification is represented in our system[1]:

1. first layer: idealized phoneme units (rows 7–45)

2. second layer: diphthongs and long vowels (rows 47–55)

3. third layer: German syllable onsets (rows 57–107)

4. fourth layer: German syllable codas (rows 109–205)

5. the inflectional morphemes /s/, /t/, /st/ that can be combined with codas (rows 207–213)

6. a frame for analyzing the segmentation of intervocalic consont sequences into onset and

   coda occurrences (rows 215–231)

7. a frame for detecting syllable margins (rows 233/234)

8. fifth layer: German syllable structures covered by CV-templates (rows 236–270)

9. a frame for recognizing extrasyllabic segments (rows 272–274)

10. sixth and seventh layer: a lexical data base that contains bounded and unbounded

    morphemes and words (rows 276–308)

The units of each layer are connected to higher levels in a feedforward processing strategy without any feedback from higher to lower levels whereas in TRACE units of neighboring levels can influence each other bidirectionally. Figure (1) may give a first impression of the connectivity structure among units of different layers.

---

[1] The frames between the conceptual layers do not contain further conceptual entities. Their function is to compile and analyze incoming units under specific aspects which will not be described in detail exceptional the essential cluster analysis frame (see below):

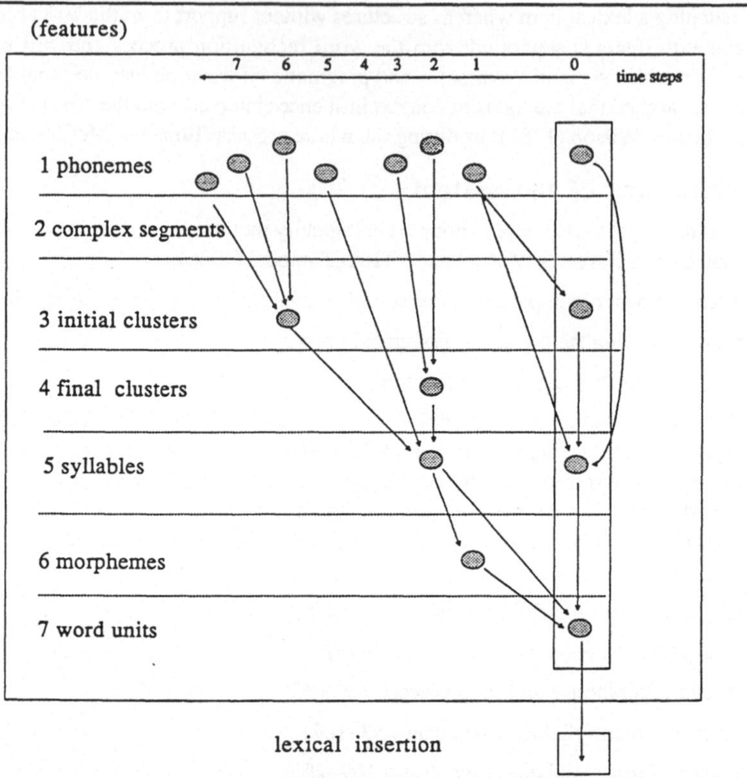

Figure 1: This Figure demonstrates the different levels of the model ranging from the phoneme layer up to the word layer. In our representation lower levels are arranged to be at the top, higher levels at the bottom of the system – just in opposite to the usual mode of description.

It can be seen how the activation of a word concept depends on the activities of various simpler concepts such as phonemes, onsets and codas, syllables and morphemes. Phoneme concepts (1) are directly connected to each further level in complex segment (2), cluster (3 + 4), syllable (5) and word (6 + 7) building processes. Units of initial and final cluster levels are not interconnected with each other; being derived from phoneme sequences, they influence both syllabic (5) and lexical layer (6 + 7). Syllable concepts are correlated to specific morpheme (6) and word (7) units; morpheme occurrences (6) may converge to word concept activations (7). By overgenerating structures on cluster levels and syllabic layer there will not be a corresponding activation of a lexical item in each case. The connections between the units are hardwired and specify a boolean state of activation (active (1) vs. inactive (0)). It is not intended to reach the flexibility that psychological models (whether connectionist or not) exhibit to compensate errors or underspecified word parts like in TRACE or an elaborated version of COHORT (cf. Marslen-Wilson 1987) that allow for partially activated units. Neither is this model is concerned with sensory input that naturally constitutes the main challenge for psychological models of speech perception. Neural networks developed by Elman & Zipser (1988) concerning the internal restructuring (by two hidden units (!)) of (320) acoustic input patterns to (320) feature types serve to provide learning labels denying the assumption of prewired structure. It is questionable whether this hidden layer is sufficient for a realistic representation of speech processing that reflects human knowledge of language. The present network is developed from a

31

linguistic point of view; it tries to provide general insights into new strategies towards processing the morphophonological structure of German up to the lexical units. In our representation about 300 linguistic features − most of them concerning concepts of units between the phoneme and word level− of growing complexity are highly interconnected in a localist architecture.

The representation of linguistic structure follows the principles of net-linguistic representation which is in our case similar to time delay neural networks (TDNN). The input units become activated in temporal sequence in the space of input units. In our case, it contains one possible unit for each phoneme; at any time exactly one of the units is active. We assume an elementary temporal interval. At the end of each elementary temporal interval the input activation pattern is shifted into a temporal delay network (or − in computer terminology − a shift register) whereas the pattern already in the delay network is shifted one position "deeper" into the network. During the elementary temporal interval the level of feature units of the first intermediate level becomes activated depending on the sequential pattern of activity in the delay network. At the end of the elementary temporal interval the features are also shifted into a delay network dedicated to the features. Thus the activation of the second level of features is determined by the sequential pattern of features of the first level as the features of the first level were determined by the input sequence. The second level features are equally shifted in a delay network for this level and thus third level features can be activated depending on its patterns and so forth for as many levels as linguistically motivated.

			#	w	a	ch	t	r	a	u	m	#
7	a	!	0	0	1	0	0	0	1	0	0	0
8	e	!	0	0	0	0	0	0	0	0	0	0
9	i	!	0	0	0	0	0	0	0	0	0	0
10	o	!	0	0	0	0	0	0	0	0	0	0
11	u	!	0	0	0	0	0	0	0	1	0	0
12	ae	!	0	0	0	0	0	0	0	0	0	0
13	oe	!	0	0	0	0	0	0	0	0	0	0
14	ue	!	0	0	0	0	0	0	0	0	0	0
15	b	!	0	0	0	0	0	0	0	0	0	0
16	c	!	0	0	0	0	0	0	0	0	0	0
17	d	!	0	0	0	0	0	0	0	0	0	0
18	f	!	0	0	0	0	0	0	0	0	0	0
19	g	!	0	0	0	0	0	0	0	0	0	0
20	h	!	0	0	0	0	0	0	0	0	0	0
21	j	!	0	0	0	0	0	0	0	0	0	0
22	k	!	0	0	0	0	0	0	0	0	0	0
23	l	!	0	0	0	0	0	0	0	0	0	0
24	m	!	0	0	0	0	0	0	0	0	1	0
25	n	!	0	0	0	0	0	0	0	0	0	0
26	p	!	0	0	0	0	0	0	0	0	0	0
27	q	!	0	0	0	0	0	0	0	0	0	0
28	r	!	0	0	0	0	0	1	0	0	0	0
29	s	!	0	0	0	0	0	0	0	0	0	0
30	t	!	0	0	0	0	1	0	0	0	0	0
31	v	!	0	0	0	0	0	0	0	0	0	0
32	w	!	0	1	0	0	0	0	0	0	0	0
33	x	!	0	0	0	0	0	0	0	0	0	0
34	z	!	0	0	0	0	0	0	0	0	0	0
35	#	!	1	0	0	0	0	0	0	0	0	1
36	ch	!	0	0	0	1	0	0	0	0	0	0
37	sch	!	0	0	0	0	0	0	0	0	0	0
38	ck	!	0	0	0	0	0	0	0	0	0	0
39	pf	!	0	0	0	0	0	0	0	0	0	0
40	ts	!	0	0	0	0	0	0	0	0	0	0
41	tz	!	0	0	0	0	0	0	0	0	0	0
42	ss	!	0	0	0	0	0	0	0	0	0	0
43	dt	!	0	0	0	0	0	0	0	0	0	0
44	Vokal	!	0	0	1	0	0	0	1	1	0	0
45	Konsonant	!	0	1	0	1	1	1	0	0	1	0

Figure 2: Activity pattern on the phoneme layer after scanning in the input string *wachtraum*. The activation of a concept is indicated by 1 whereas non-activated concepts obtain the value 0.

Figure (2) shows a pattern on the delay line corresponding to the word "Wachtraum" as well as the vowels and consonants becoming activated in dependence on the phonemes. All cluster concepts on higher levels refer to this first layer (7–45) where phonemes and their "cover symbols" are stored as explained.

51 initial clusters are represented in the rows 57–107. They are extracted from German phonotactic constraints concerning the consonantal part of the syllable preceeding the nucleus. Onsets may consist of one, two or three segments and will be activated if the individual condition is satisfied and a vowel follows, e.g. the detection of /pfl/ depends on the activation of individual /p/, /f/, /l/, /V/ in a temporally correct pattern.

No.	Sym		1	2	3	4	5	6	7	8	9	10	11	12	13	14	15	16
64	l	!	0	0	0	0	0	0	0	0	0	0	0	0	0	0	0	0
65	m	!	0	0	0	0	0	0	0	0	0	0	0	1	0	0	0	1
66	n	!	0	0	0	0	0	0	0	0	0	0	0	0	0	0	0	0
67	p	!	0	0	0	0	0	0	0	0	0	0	0	0	0	0	0	0
68	r	!	0	0	0	0	0	0	1	0	0	0	0	0	0	0	0	0
69	s	!	0	0	0	0	0	0	0	0	0	0	0	0	0	0	0	0
70	t	!	0	0	0	0	0	0	0	0	0	0	0	0	0	0	0	0
71	v	!	0	0	0	0	0	0	0	0	0	0	0	0	0	0	0	0
72	w	!	0	0	1	0	0	0	0	0	0	0	0	0	0	0	0	0
97	tr	!	0	0	0	0	0	0	1	0	0	0	0	0	0	0	0	0
98	zw	!	0	0	0	0	0	0	0	0	0	0	0	0	0	0	0	0
99	pfl	!	0	0	0	0	0	0	0	0	0	0	0	0	0	0	0	0
100	schl	!	0	0	0	0	0	0	0	0	0	0	0	0	0	0	0	0
101	schm	!	0	0	0	0	0	0	0	0	0	0	0	0	0	0	0	1
102	schn	!	0	0	0	0	0	0	0	0	0	0	0	0	0	0	0	0
					w				r tr					m				m schm

No.	Sym		1	2	3	4	5	6	7	8	9	10	11	12	13	14	15	16
114	k	!	0	0	0	0	0	0	0	0	0	0	0	0	0	0	0	0
115	l	!	0	0	0	0	0	0	0	0	0	0	0	0	0	0	0	0
116	m	!	0	0	0	0	0	0	0	0	1	0	0	0	0	0	0	0
117	n	!	0	0	0	0	0	0	0	0	0	0	0	0	0	0	0	0
118	p	!	0	0	0	0	0	0	0	0	0	0	0	0	0	0	0	0
119	r	!	0	0	0	0	0	0	0	0	0	0	0	1	0	0	0	0
120	s	!	0	0	0	0	0	0	0	0	0	0	0	0	0	0	0	0
121	t	!	0	0	0	0	0	0	0	0	0	0	0	0	0	0	0	0
122	v	!	0	0	0	0	0	0	0	0	0	0	0	0	0	0	0	0
123	z	!	0	0	0	0	0	0	0	0	0	0	0	0	0	0	0	0
124	ch	!	0	0	0	1	0	0	0	0	0	0	0	0	0	0	0	0
174	st	!	0	0	0	0	0	0	0	0	0	0	0	0	0	0	0	0
175	ts	!	0	0	0	0	0	0	0	0	0	0	0	0	0	0	0	0
176	lch	!	0	0	0	0	0	0	0	0	0	0	0	0	0	0	0	0
177	mpf	!	0	0	0	0	0	0	0	0	0	0	0	0	0	0	0	0
178	nch	!	0	0	0	0	0	0	0	0	0	0	0	0	0	0	0	0
179	chs	!	0	0	0	0	0	0	0	0	0	0	0	0	0	0	0	0
180	cht	!	0	0	0	0	1	0	0	0	0	0	0	0	0	0	0	0
181	ckt	!	0	0	0	0	0	0	0	0	0	0	0	0	0	0	0	0
182	rch	!	0	0	0	0	0	0	0	0	0	0	0	0	0	0	0	0
183	tzt	!	0	0	0	0	0	0	0	0	0	0	0	0	0	0	0	0
184	bsch	!	0	0	0	0	0	0	0	0	0	0	0	0	0	0	0	0
185	lsch	!	0	0	0	0	0	0	0	0	0	0	0	0	0	0	0	0
186	rsch	!	0	0	0	0	0	0	0	0	0	0	0	0	1	0	0	0
187	tsch	!	0	0	0	0	0	0	0	0	0	0	0	0	0	0	0	0
188	nsch2	!	0	0	0	0	0	0	0	0	0	0	0	0	0	0	0	0
189	bst	!	0	0	0	0	0	0	0	0	0	0	0	0	0	0	0	0
						ch 	cht							m	r rsch			

Figure 3: Recognized onsets and codas concerning the phoneme input *wachtraum#marschmusik* after 15 processing cycles. The last three phonemes are not yet scanned in. Initial cluster will be activated by matching its individual condition of a certain phoneme (sequence) and a following vowel. For detecting a final cluster, the specific required segment(s) must be preceeded by a vowel.

97 final clusters are available on the fourth layer (109–205). They form the postnuclear part of a syllable varying in length from 1 to 4 segments. A final cluster will be activated by fulfilling its individual conditions and the detection of a preceeding vowel. Many sequences preliminarily recognized as final clusters can underly a resyllabification process by containing parts that form initial clusters (e.g. rbst - rb.st) which are activated simultaneously.

3. Ambiguities in segmenting intervocalic consonant sequences

Phonotactic constraints on syllable onsets and codas do not provide for a single correct syllabification in many cases. Ambiguous activations must be considered and kept in mind until a solution is found. Combinations of final and initial clusters that do not occur as monomorphemic sequences are ambiguous if they overlap in at least one segment (in many cases realized by an obstruent that generally presents the last part of a coda and the first part of an onset at the same time: e.g. *rkl* to *rk.l* vs. *r.kl*). The system is able – on the basis of its parallel activation mode – to take account of such ambiguities without representing those "synthetic" medial clusters explicitly just by activating both possible segmentations in terms of recognizing coda (1) + onset (2) as well as coda (2) + onset (1).

```
215   V               !   0  0  1  0  0  0  1  1  0  0  0  1  0  0  0  1
216   C               !   0  1  0  1  2  3  0  0  1  0  1  0  1  2  3  0
217   #               !   1  0  0  0  0  0  0  0  0  1  0  0  0  0  0  0
218   CA              !   0  0  1  0  0  0  1  0  0  0  0  1  0  0  0  1
219   CCA             !   0  0  0  0  0  0  2  0  0  0  0  0  0  0  0  2
220   CCCA            !   0  0  0  0  0  0  0  0  0  0  0  0  0  0  0  0
221   V               !   0  0  1  0  0  0  1  1  0  0  0  1  0  0  0  1
222   VV              !   0  0  0  0  0  0  0  1  0  0  0  0  0  0  0  0
223   CE              !   0  0  0  1  0  0  0  0  1  0  0  0  1  0  0  0
224   CCE             !   0  0  0  0  2  0  0  0  0  0  0  0  0  2  0  0
225   CCCE            !   0  0  0  0  0  0  0  0  0  0  0  0  0  0  0  0
226   CCCCE           !   0  0  0  0  0  0  0  0  0  0  0  0  0  0  0  0
227   CE=CA           !   0  0  0  0  0  0  0  0  0  0  0  0  0  0  0  0
228   CCE=CE+CA       !   0  0  0  0  0  0  0  0  0  0  0  0  0  0  0  0
229   CCCE=CE+CCA     !   0  0  0  0  0  0  0  0  0  0  0  0  0  0  0  0
230   CCCE=CCE+CA     !   0  0  0  0  0  0  0  0  0  0  0  0  0  0  0  0
231   CCCCE=CCE+CCA       0  0  0  0  0  0  0  0  0  0  0  0  0  0  0  0

                              w                 r                 m              m
                                               tr                             schm
                                  ch                                     r
                                      cht                 m             rsch
```

Figure 4: The frame in this Figure does not provide for new concepts, but serves to summarize the activations of the lower levels at each step in time. Our string of phonemes is transferred into an abstract sequence of C- and V-units (rows 215/216) on which syllable structure assignment is based: vowels are represented by a V-slot (215), consonants by a C-slot (216). This abstract covering is adopted from the first layer (rows 44/45) and modified by indicating the number of units in consonant sequences. Thus, initial and final clusters derived from the input string are encoded corresponding to their length: CA, CCA, CCCA (in rows 218–220) refer to onsets (length 1,2,3); CE, CCE, CCCE, CCCCE (223–226) refer to codas (length 1,2,3,4). In the rows 227–231, sequences preliminarily beeing interpreted as monomorphemic final clusters but during processing resyllabified by a following segment into onset and coda occurrences are recognized; cf. the segmentation of a final cluster comprising two segments into coda + onset each consisting of one segment can be detected in row 228.

These simultaneous activities are compiled in rows 216–231 where all represented onsets and codas are encoded under their length number (CA in row 218 refers to an onset consisting of one single segment). The CV-encoding of rows 44/45 is repeated in 215/216; consonantal segments are counted until the sequence is interrupted by the detection of a vowel. In Figure (4) two medial consonantal sequences of the length 3 can be seen that are both segmented into codas and onsets in relation 1 (CE) to 2 (CCA) as well as 2 (CCE) to 1 (CA). These segmentations refer to the cluster /chtr/ (ch.tr or cht.r) in the lexical item

Wachtraum[2] (see CV-configuration between the two boundary activations in 217). Corresponding to the second consonantal sequence of three segments in the lexical item *Marschmusik* (march or military music in general) that is not yet completely scanned in, a further ambiguous segmentation is indicated by CE + CCA (r.schm) vs. CCE + CA (rsch.m). Based on the cluster analysis the assignment of syllable structure to the data is derivable.

#	Template	E	!	1	2	3	4	5	6	7	8	9	10	11	12	13	14	15	16
236	V Silben		!	0	0	0	0	0	0	0	0	0	0	0	0	0	0	0	0
237	VC		!	0	0	0	0	0	0	0	0	0	0	0	0	0	0	0	0
238	VCC		!	0	0	0	0	0	0	0	0	0	0	0	0	0	0	0	0
239	VCCC	E	!	0	0	0	0	0	0	0	0	0	0	0	0	0	0	0	0
240	VCCCC	E	!	0	0	0	0	0	0	0	0	0	0	0	0	0	0	0	0
241	VV		!	0	0	0	0	0	0	0	0	0	0	0	0	0	0	0	0
242	VVC		!	0	0	0	0	0	0	0	0	0	0	0	0	0	0	0	0
243	VVCC		!	0	0	0	0	0	0	0	0	0	0	0	0	0	0	0	0
244	VVCCC	E	!	0	0	0	0	0	0	0	0	0	0	0	0	0	0	0	0
245	CV		!	0	0	0	0	0	0	0	0	0	0	0	0	1	0	0	0
246	CVC		!	1	0	0	0	0	0	0	0	0	1	0	0	0	0	0	1
247	CVCC		!	0	1	0	0	0	0	0	0	0	0	1	0	0	0	0	0
248	CVCCC	E	!	0	0	0	0	0	0	0	0	0	0	0	0	0	0	0	0
249	CVCCCC	E	!	0	0	0	0	0	0	0	0	0	0	0	0	0	0	0	0
250	CVV		!	0	0	0	0	0	0	0	0	0	0	0	0	0	0	0	0
251	CVVC		!	0	0	0	0	0	1	0	0	0	0	0	0	0	0	0	0
252	CVVCC		!	0	0	0	0	0	0	0	0	0	0	0	0	0	0	0	0
253	CVVCCC	E	!	0	0	0	0	0	0	0	0	0	0	0	0	0	0	0	0
254	CCV		!	0	0	0	0	0	0	0	0	0	0	0	0	1	0	0	0
255	CCVC		!	0	0	0	0	0	0	0	0	0	0	0	0	0	0	0	0
256	CCVCC		!	0	0	0	0	0	0	0	0	0	0	0	0	0	0	0	0
257	CCVCCC	E	!	0	0	0	0	0	0	0	0	0	0	0	0	0	0	0	0
258	CCVV		!	0	0	0	0	0	0	0	0	0	0	0	0	0	0	0	0
259	CCVVC		!	0	0	0	0	0	1	0	0	0	0	0	0	0	0	0	0
260	CCVVCC		!	0	0	0	0	0	0	0	0	0	0	0	0	0	0	0	0
261	CCVVCCC	E	!	0	0	0	0	0	0	0	0	0	0	0	0	0	0	0	0
262	CCCV	E	!	0	0	0	0	0	0	0	0	0	0	0	0	0	0	0	0
263	CCCVC	E	!	0	0	0	0	0	0	0	0	0	0	0	0	0	0	0	0
264	CCCVCC	E	!	0	0	0	0	0	0	0	0	0	0	0	0	0	0	0	0
265	CCCVV	E	!	0	0	0	0	0	0	0	0	0	0	0	0	0	0	0	0
266	CCCVVC	E	!	0	0	0	0	0	0	0	0	0	0	0	0	0	0	0	0
267	CCCVVCC	E	!	0	0	0	0	0	0	0	0	0	0	0	0	0	0	0	0
268	CCCVVCCC	E	!	0	0	0	0	0	0	0	0	0	0	0	0	0	0	0	0
269	CCCVCCCC	E	!	0	0	0	0	0	0	0	0	0	0	0	0	0	0	0	0
270	CCCVVCCC	E	!	0	0	0	0	0	0	0	0	0	0	0	0	0	0	0	0

Figure 5: 35 templates serve as CV-encodings of possible. German syllable structures of increasing complexity. The canonical syllable template is realized by CCVCC (row 256). Syllables that overstep two segmental positions in onset or coda contain extrasyllabic segments (indicated by E). This Figure shows the activity pattern on the syllabic layer after 23 processing cycles (four cycles after the item *marschmusik* is completely recognized. Ambigious cluster analysis of the previous frame evokes ambiguous syllable structure assignment.

On the syllabic layer (236–270) 35 syllable templates (see Figure 5) are represented starting with a syllable simply consisting of a short vowel (V) up to templates comprising extrasyllabic segments at each margin and a diphthong (CCCVVCCC). The alternative syllable structure assignments CVC and CCVVC vs. CVCC and CVVC concerning *Wachtraum* and CVC + CCV + CVC vs. CVCC + CV + CVC concerning *Marschmusik* result from the ambiguous activity patterns in cluster segmentation. In contrast

---

[2] This expression is ambiguous. It can mean: 1. daydream' if with a morpheme boundary after *Wach-* or 2. `guard room' if with a morpheme boundary after *Wacht-*

to the online process of cluster analysis, the assignment of syllable structure is delayed for four processing cycles to check the right context for an onset of a following syllable. Thus, ambiguities on the syllabic level based on missing context are excluded and only the essential phonotactically motivated ambiguities are retained. The remaining ambiguous segmentations can only be resolved by integrating the lexical layer.

4. The lexical solution of ambiguous segmentation and syllabification

In TRACE and COHORT detected phonemes directly influence the lexical layer by activating a pool of candidates that is narrowed down during processing when combinations of units become more specific. In the model presented here, there will only be an activation on the lexical level after every discrete phoneme of an item has been recognized. If the generated structures correspond to a lexical activation they will exhibit a correct parse of the system. Structures that do not conform to the requirement of a lexical item will not reach the lexical level and decrease.

```
276   wach A,3          !   1  0  0  0  0  0  0  0  0  0  0  0  0  0  0  0
277   wacht N,4         !   0  1  0  0  0  0  0  0  0  0  0  0  0  0  0  0
278   raum N,4          !   0  0  0  0  0  1  0  0  0  0  0  0  0  0  0  0
279   traum N,5         !   0  0  0  0  0  1  0  0  0  0  0  0  0  0  0  0
280   musik N,5         !   0  0  0  0  0  0  0  0  0  0  0  0  0  0  0  1
281   marsch N,4        !   0  0  0  0  0  0  0  0  0  0  1  0  0  0  0  0
282   schau N,3         !   0  0  0  0  0  0  0  0  0  0  0  0  0  0  0  0
283   spiel N,5         !   0  0  0  0  0  0  0  0  0  0  0  0  0  0  0  0
284   gleich A,5        !   0  0  0  0  0  0  0  0  0  0  0  0  0  0  0  0
285   tritt N,4         !   0  0  0  0  0  0  0  0  0  0  0  0  0  0  0  0

286   faeng V,4         !   0  0  0  0  0  0  0  0  0  0  0  0  0  0  0  0
287   schreib V,5       !   0  0  0  0  0  0  0  0  0  0  0  0  0  0  0  0
288   unter P,5         !   0  0  0  0  0  0  0  0  0  0  0  0  0  0  0  0
289   zwischen P,6      !   0  0  0  0  0  0  0  0  0  0  0  0  0  0  0  0
290   problem N,7       !   0  0  0  0  0  0  0  0  0  0  0  0  0  0  0  0
291   wirk V,4          !   0  0  0  0  0  0  0  0  0  0  0  0  0  0  0  0
292   ge Prae,2         !   0  0  0  0  0  0  0  0  0  0  0  0  0  0  0  0
293   in Prae,2         !   0  0  0  0  0  0  0  0  0  0  0  0  0  0  0  0
294   un Prae,2         !   0  0  0  0  0  0  0  0  0  0  0  0  0  0  0  0
295   ver Prae,3        !   0  0  0  0  0  0  0  0  0  0  0  0  0  0  0  0
296   nis Su,3          !   0  0  0  0  0  0  0  0  0  0  0  0  0  0  0  0
297   lich Su,3         !   0  0  0  0  0  0  0  0  0  0  0  0  0  0  0  0
298   zu Prae,2         !   0  0  0  0  0  0  0  0  0  0  0  0  0  0  0  0
299   er Su,2           !   0  0  0  0  0  0  0  0  0  0  0  0  0  0  0  0
300   wach.traum N,8    0  0  0  0  0  1  0  0  0  0  0  0  0  0  0  0
301   wacht.raum N,8    0  0  0  0  0  1  0  0  0  0  0  0  0  0  0  0
302   marsch.musik N,9   0  0  0  0  0  0  0  0  0  0  0  0  0  0  0  1
303   schau.spiel N,8  0  0  0  0  0  0  0  0  0  0  0  0  0  0  0  0
304   un.ver.gleich.lichA14  0  0  0  0  0  0  0  0  0  0  0  0  0  0  0  0
305   zu.tritt N,6       0  0  0  0  0  0  0  0  0  0  0  0  0  0  0  0
306   unter.schreib.er N,12  0  0  0  0  0  0  0  0  0  0  0  0  0  0  0  0
307   in.zwischen Adv,8    0  0  0  0  0  0  0  0  0  0  0  0  0  0  0  0
308   ge.faeng.nis N,9     0  0  0  0  0  0  0  0  0  0  0  0  0  0  0  0
```

Figure 6: The lexical layer after 23 processing cycles. On the one side, the activation of morphemes and words depends on matching activations of phoneme, cluster and syllable concept-occurrences, on the other side the former determine the correct parse on cluster and syllabic level so that in the case of recognizing *Marschmusik* the developed structures CVC and CCV on the syllabic level and /r/ as final cluster activation as well as /schm/ as initial cluster activation will not be supported by correlating to the lexical layer.

The present model contains only a small lexical data base (see Figure 6) consisting of a few bounded and unbounded morpheme and word units for exemplifying the processing strategy. We are intending to extend it soon.

There are 24 morphemes varying in their respective categories (adjectives, nouns, verbs, prepositions) and length (276–299) and nine composita (nouns, adjectives, adverbs in rows 300–308) represented. A specific morpheme is recognized if the required activations on the phonemic, cluster and syllabic layers converge. Words refer to the activation of the morphemic level. In the case of the processed item "Wachtraum" the ambiguous syllable structure assignments are justified by corresponding to lexical entries because both segmentations are correct: Wacht.raum and Wach.traum (see Figure 6). Concerning the item "Marschmusik" structures like CVC.CCV.CVC without a correlation to the morphemic layer are not able to survive as a stable pattern. Hence, the ambiguity is resolved by morphemic accounts and we obtain the segmentation into CVCC.CV.CVC as the sole correct parse.

5. Conclusion

Based on an analysis of German syllable structure a net-linguistic model of lexical access has been developed that is able to detect and represent ambiguous structures and partially resolve them by integrating a lexical data base. Converging activations of simple units to complex concepts constitute a highly interconnected network in a system that includes a dynamic component and an adequate representation of time structure in word recognition. A crucial property to be pointed out is the segmentation of intervocalic sequences which is elaborated on the base of represented onset and coda concepts in a parallel processing structure. Phonemes, clusters, peaks, syllables and morphemes as parts of lexical entries are necessarily to be included in lexical access. The highly conceptualized field between phoneme and word units that is evident in modern phonology and morphology is in a first step transferred into a connectionist localist architecture of online speech processing. Hence, this may support the hypothesis of a powerful structured "hidden layer" in the human brain. The lack of physiological reality (concerning real acoustic input) and psychological reality (tested by reaction times in phoneme monitoring and word detection) is obvious, but not harmful. We believe that physiological and psychological adequacy should be added as a variation to models of implementing linguistic insights. We deliberately take the position of implementational connectionism.

References

Bouda, H. & Bouwhuis, D. (1984). *Attention and performance X. Control of language processes.* [Proceedings of the 10th International Symposium on Attention and Performance, Venlo July 4–9, 1982.] London: n.p.

Erman, L.E & Lesser, V.R. (1980). The HEARSAY-II speech understanding system: A tutorial. In: W.A. Lea (ed.) *Trends in speech recognition* Eaglewood Cliffs: New York, pp.361–381.

Elman,J. &Zipser,D. (1988). "Discovering the hidden structure of speech." *Journal of the Acoustical Society of America* 83, pp. 1615–1626.

Frauenfelder, U. & Segui, J. (1989). "Phoneme monitoring and lexical processing: Evidence for associative context effects." *Memory and Cognition* 17, pp. 134–140.

Frauenfelder, U. & Tyler, L. (1987). "The process of spoken word recognition. An introduction." *Cognition* 25, pp. 1–20.

Marslen-Wilson, W. (1984). "Function and process in spoken word recognition." In: Bouda & Bouwhuis (1984), pp. 125–150.

Marslen-Wilson, W. (1987). "Functional parallelism in spoken word recognition." *Cognition* 25, pp. 71–102.

Marslen-Wilson, W. & Welsh, A. (1978). "Processing interactions and lexical access during word recognition in continuous speech." *Cognitive Psychology* 10, pp. 29–63.

McClelland, J. & Elman, J. (1986). "Interactive processes in speech perception: The TRACE model." In: McClelland, J., Rumelhart, D. & The PDP Research Group. *Parallel Distributed Processing. Explorations in the microstructure of cognition. Vol. 2: Psychological and biological models.* Cambridge, Mass.: MIT Press, pp. 58–121.

Schnelle, H. (1988). "Ansätze zur prozessualen Linguistik." In: Schnelle, H. & Rickheit, G. *Sprache in Mensch und Computer.* Opladen: Westdeutscher Verlag.

Segui, J. (1984). "The syllable: A basic perceptual unit in speech processing?" In: Bouda & Bouwhuis (1984). pp. 165–181.

Waibel, A., Hazanawa, A., Hinton, G., Shikano, K., & Lang, K. (1987). "Phoneme recognition using time-delay neural networks." ATR Technical Report TR-1-0006. ATR Interpreting Telephony Research Laboratories.

Wiese, R. (1988). *Silbische und lexikalische Phonologie. Studien zum Chinesischen und Deutschen.* Tübingen: Niemeyer.

A connectionist parser for context-free phrase structure grammars

Rolf Wilkens   Helmut Schnelle

Sprachwissenschaftliches Institut
Ruhr-Universität Bochum
Postfach 10 21 48
D-4630 Bochum 1
email: P050202@DBORUB01.BITnet

Abstract

Most connectionist networks in present use employ built-in learning algorithms. Their major disadvantage however is their inability to handle complex knowledge structures. In this paper a connectionist network is presented which can handle highly developed cognitive structures not by making use of learning processes but by the integration of a powerful initial structure. Parsing of context-free phrase structure grammars shall exemplify the workings of the network.

1. Introduction

"Positive results in the field of parallel computation will be based on existing knowledge of computational structures, not on mystical emergent properties of unstructured networks." (Feldmann (1988)). There are no convincing arguments against this statement, at least not in the field of complicated perceptual behavior, such as language processing. As a consequence, we should study ways of translating existing knowledge of computational structures into massively parallel systems, in particular into connectionist systems.

For a start, we choose the field of computational knowledge expressed in constituent structure grammars, in particular context-free phrase structure grammars (CF-PSGs). We present a compiler which translates any given CF-PSG into a connectionist network, which has two essential features:

1. The representation used in the connectionist network is equivalent to any tree or bracket notation used in symbolic processing.
2. The connectivity structure of the resulting network corresponds directly to the logical dependencies between the terminal and nonterminal symbol occurrences in the constituent structure rules used to describe the productions of any CF-PSG. In this way, the connectivity structure mirrors the dominance and precedence relations embodied in CF-PSGs.

In other words: The connectivity structure is a quasi-neuronal representation of the computational knowledge which is usually presented in terms of rules and algorithms. Our system thus provides the proof that connectionist networks can represent cognitive knowledge of high complexity — a fact that has recently been questioned by critics of connectionism (cp. Fodor & Pylyshyn (1988)). However, our system is of the variety of an implementational connectionism implementing systems whose computational knowledge is already defined by rules — it is not a system which generates new knowledge structures through learning.

We believe that studies of implementational connectionism are presently more important for high-level language processing than attempts to define learning systems. It seems to be the case that the knowledge embodied in high-level modules is highly structured and can only be learned in systems with a powerful initial structure, but not at all by systems which are initially practically unstructured (like the systems underlying present studies of connectionist learning). Further research will gain a better understanding of the required initial structures by studying empirically the knowledge structures which are the outcome of the learning procedures.

We therefore turned to studies of massively parallel parsers in terms of connectionist architectures, i.e. systems whose units have minimal computational power (such as Boolean operators or threshold units). We developed a connectionist parser which is algorithmically based on the Earley chart parser. The parser is implemented via the definition of a set of Boolean equations assigned to the units of our network. These equations will then define the connectivity relations between the units. Furthermore our system has a compiler which translates any CF-PSG into the set of Boolean equations needed to parse this CF-PSG.

We shall now explain the essential ideas which lead to our implementation of massively parallel (connectionist) networks compiled from CF-PSGs through parallelizing Earley's algorithm.[1] The essential ideas of our parser will be outlined in the following paragraphs by using our example grammar[2]

$$G = \{\{S, A\}, \{a, b\}, \{S \to Ab, S \to aA, A \to aa, A \to a\}, S\}$$

The string to be analyzied will be 'aab'.

2. Earley's Representation

Let us first summarize the essential features of Earley's algorithm. The parser described by this algorithm works top down and online. It operates in two stages: in the first stage, a parse list is computed and in the second stage the correct parse is filtered out from the generated parse list. The parse list is represented as a set of triples of the form: <*number of input symbol, dotted rule, scope of dominance*>, in our representation abbreviated as $< X, Y, Z >$. A dotted rule is a special notation used in Earley parsers. It has the general form $N \to \alpha.\beta$. The rule $N \to \alpha.\beta$ is derived from all productions $N \to \gamma$ where γ is dividable into $\alpha\beta$ (All dotted rules for our example grammar are shown in figure (2)). The occurence of a dotted rule $N \to \alpha.\beta$ in the parse list means that there already exists a derivation $\alpha \Rightarrow t_i \ldots t_n$ with t_n as the last scanned terminal. Therefore, the production $N \to \gamma$ has been processed to $N \Rightarrow t_i \ldots t_n\beta$, and the next terminals have to be derived from β.

When the parser is running all derivations which are possible in the assigned grammar will be processed parallely. Figure (1) shows all these possibilities in a tree notation and in the triple notation used by Earley.

After the scanning-in of the first two terminals two derivations are possible: $S \Rightarrow aA$ and $S \Rightarrow Ab$. Only by scanning the third terminal the ambiguity can be dissolved and we get the correct derivation: $S \Rightarrow Ab \Rightarrow aab$.

To give an idea of how the Earley parser works we look a little closer at the actions carried out before the second terminal is read. At first all possible start-terminals will be predicted. This is done by adding the triples $< 0, S \to .Ab, 0 >$, $< 0, S \to .aA, 0 >$, $< 0, A \to .a, 0 >$ and $< 0, A \to .aa, 0 >$ to the empty parse list. When the parser scans the first terminal 'a' the predictions can all be confirmed, i.e. the parse list must be expanded by the triples $< 1, A \to a., 1 >$, $< 1, A \to a.a, 1 >$ and $< 1, S \to a.A, 1 >$. This is the general idea of the Earley parser: Before the parser scans a terminal all terminals which can follow all previous derivations will be predicted by adding a triple to the parse list where the dot in the dotted rule is situated immediately in

---

[1] The formal definition of the compilation algorithm and the definition of the resulting connectionist network can be found in Schnelle & Doust (1989) and Wilkens (1990).

[2] We write all nonterminals as capitals, all terminals as noncapitals. With lowercase greek letters we denote strings of any length (even the zero string) of terminals or nonterminals. With N we denote any nonterminal and with t any terminal. Both N and t are always nonempty.

front of this predicted terminal. When scanning the next terminal all triples which predict this terminal will be confirmed by adding a triple to the parse list with a dotted rule where the dot is immediately situated after the terminal. Obviously the number of input symbols is increased by one and so is the scope of the dominance.

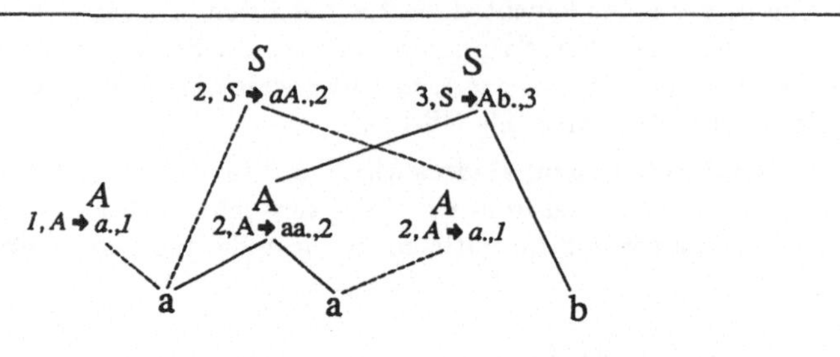

Figure 1 : All possible parse trees and some triples generated during the analysis of 'aab'

After the number of triples is increased by the triple $< 1, S \rightarrow a.A, 1 >$ the parser must predict all terminals t if there is a possible derivation $A \Rightarrow t\alpha$ in the grammar. This can be done by simply adding all triples $< X, A \rightarrow .t\alpha, 0 >$ to the parse list. (X is the number of the scanned terminals.) If there exists a triple $< X, A \rightarrow \gamma., Z >$ in the parse list, all triples $< X', N \rightarrow \alpha.A\beta, Z' >$ have to be confirmed. In this case the latter triple will be completed by adding the triple $< X, N \rightarrow \alpha A.\beta, Z + Z' >$ to the parse list.

$$S \rightarrow aA. \quad S \rightarrow a.A \quad S \rightarrow .aA \quad S \rightarrow Ab. \quad S \rightarrow A.b \quad S \rightarrow .Ab$$
$$A \rightarrow aa. \quad A \rightarrow a.a \quad A \rightarrow .aa \quad A \rightarrow a. \quad A \rightarrow .a$$

Figure 2 : The set of dotted rule symbols derived from the example grammar

3. The architecture of our system

How are we going to implement Earley's algorithm in a connectionist net? We follow the localist principle of connectionist implementation — One concept - one unit — but we apply it to the triples in Earley's representation: One triple - one unit. All possible triples in this example parse list with 11 dotted rules (as enumerated in figure (2)) and with 3 as the longest possible dominance are $< 0 \ldots 3, \text{dotted rule}, 0 \ldots 3 >$. In general we have the triples $< 0 \ldots n, \text{dotted rule}, 0 \ldots n >$ with n as the longest possible dominance. To this set of triples we add the triple $< 0, .S., 0 >$ and the triples $< 1 \ldots n, .t., 1 >$ to indicate a scanned terminal. The connections between the units must be defined in such a way that they generate activity patterns over a three-dimensional system of units (each member of a triple indicating a dimension), such that a unit becomes active (the logical value *true*) exactly when the corresponding triple is specified in the Earley algorithm. All other units not specified in the algorithm must remain inactive (logical *false*).

The representation just outlined has an essential disadvantage: The space built by the units which represent the parse list has to be unlimited, since it depends on the length of the input string. To solve this problem we will divide our system into three spaces: One space for computing the parse list, one space for representing the parse list, and another one for representing the correct parse and to be use as an internal storage space during the parsing process. Since the length of the word to be analyzed is not limited — even in a known grammar (cp. a grammar with some recursive productions like $A \rightarrow \alpha A \beta$) — it is not possible to limit these three spaces in general.

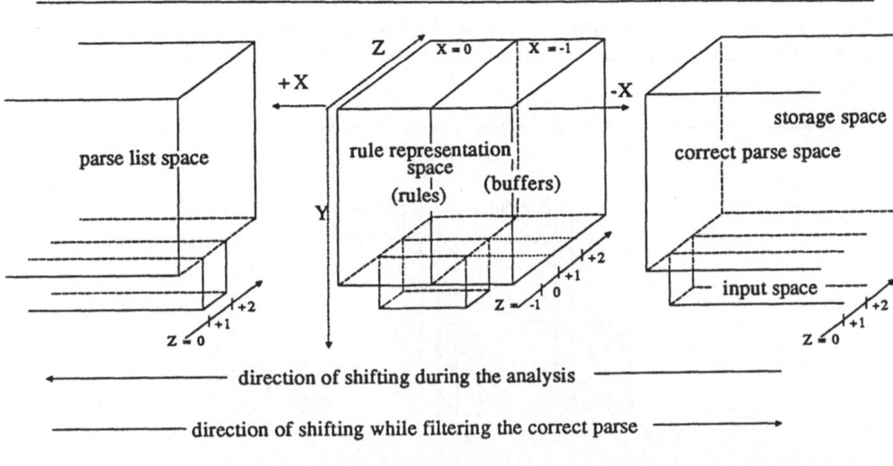

Figure 3 : The architecture of the connectionist parser. From left to right there are the parse list representation space, the rule representation space, and a space which is used as memory during the parse process and as correct parse representation space, when the parse list is completely generated.

Figure (3) shows these three spaces in our system. It must be pointed out that the X-dimensions of the parse list representation space and of the correct parse space are unlimited. Only the rule representation space has a fixed localization on $X = 0$ and $X = -1$ (for another used buffer). All Z-dimensions can not be limited since the length of dominance is not limited. But because there is a fixed number of dotted rules for every grammar all Y-dimensions are limited.

Our challenge is now to connect infinite units in a way that every unit has only a finite number of neighbors. In terms of connectionism: The fan-in (and also the fan-out) of every unit must be fixed. To explain this task we need a more detailled explanation of the representation in our system. At the beginning the word is represented in the input space. The units in this space are the input units of the system. They can be regarded as output units of a morpho-phonological parser. All other units execpt the ones located in the correct parse space are hidden units in the system. Only the units in the correct parse space are the output units. Therefore the first terminal to be scanned is located at $X = -2$, the second at $X = -3$ and so on. To scan the first terminal the whole input string has to be shifted one step to the left so that a terminal is present in the rule representation space. This shifting process can be described as follows: Each unit will receive a signal to take on the activity of its right neighbor. Because every unit has a right neighbor the complete pattern of activation is shifted one step to the left.

This is the main action of our parser. In short words the complete process can be described as follows:

1. Shift the complete input string through the rule representation space into the parse list space. At the end of this shifting process the last terminal of the word to be scanned is located at $X = 1$ and the parsing process is finished.
2. Activate some units in dependency of the pattern of activity (i.e. the structure already recognized) and of the scanned input symbol (i.e. activation of the unit representing this symbol)

in the rule representation space. This process corresponds directly to the parse process determined by the productions of the grammar.

3. Every time a new input symbol is shifted in the rule representation space shift the pattern of activity in the rule representation space into the parse list space.

4. When the process is finished repeat the steps 1 to 3 with the only modification that the activation pattern in the parse list space is shifted from right to left through the rule representation space into the correct parse space. This time the correct parse is computed by filtering out all activations which are not necessary to represent the assigned structure.

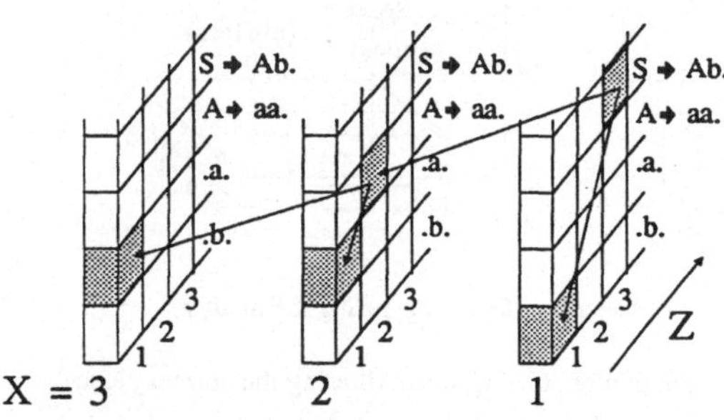

Figure 4 : A schematic diagram of some triples in our system after the complete word has been scanned. Note that the arrows do not represent the connections in this system.

The outlined process demonstrates another very important feature of our system: Most of the process can be achieved by a simple shifting operation. The consequence of this fact is that we have no problems handling infinite units, i.e. an infinite parse list. We associate the following formula with all units:

$$\forall_X X \geq 0 \lor X \leq -2, \ \forall_Y Y = \textit{dotted rules}, \ \forall_Z Z \geq 0$$
$$\text{Activation of } (X, Y, Z) = \text{Activation of } (X+1, Y, Z)$$

Figure 5 : The formula for shifting all units one step to the left. Every unit has only a fixed fan-in: the unit located at $X+1, Y, Z$.

Formulas like the above containing a quantifyer $\forall$ allow us to modify the limits of the spaces in a current implementation without any modification of the computational structure of the system in general. This is a direct analogy to the memory of a Turing machine: To increase the memory of a Turing machine means nothing more than to make more tape available. This adds up to nothing more than to add more units associated with the shifting formula to our system.

This does not mean that a learning process will take place. The units will not "learn" the shifting formula. In general it is not possible that a network will increase the number of the units during runtime since the connectivity is build up by the network compiler. This compiler will assign the associating formulas to all units. On the other hand, adding more units will not affect the computational structure of the system (in opposition to Fodor & Pylyshyn (1988:34f)) since all added units will have a homogenous connectivity structure, as expressed by the shifting formula.

The reason for this is that the computational structure of our system is only represented in the rule representation space. Only the units in this space have a complex connectivity which mirrors directly the dominance and precedence relations embodied in the rules of the grammar.

4. An outline of the connectionist parsing process

As we have shown, the connectivities of all units in the parse list representation space can be described with formulas like the one in figure (5). In this paragraph we want to demonstrate how the other units have to be connected to compute the parse list. This implies a more technical discussion. We want to define some abbreviations and will have a closer look at some connectionist features of our system. We define a function S which maps the *State* of activity of every unit into the logical values *true* or *false*. Since we associate every unit with a Boolean formula we do not distinguish between the *rule of activation* and the *rule of propagation*. So the whole network can be defined by formulas of the form:

$$S'(X_i, Y_i, Z_i) = S(X_i, Y_i, Z_i) \odot S(X_j, Y_j, Z_j) \odot S(X_k, Y_k, Z_k) \odot \ldots$$

Figure 6 : Typical form of all formulas in the system. The sign $\odot$ stands for any logical operator.

The formula in figure (6) has to be read as follows: The activity of the unit u_i at time $t + 1$ (notated as $S'(u_i)$) is computed from the activity of units $u_i, u_j, u_k \ldots$ at time t. This means that the formula in figure (6) is evaluated and the computed logical value is assigned as the new activation value for unit u_i. This can be done simply because the output function of every unit is nothing but the identity function. The next step we have to do is to define the meaning of neighborhood in our system. We have to show that the neighbors of every unit are always limited in number and that there is no formula like the one in figure (7)

$$S'(0, Y, Z) = \forall_X S(X, Y, Z) \ldots$$

Figure 7 : Prohibited formula. One unit is connected with infinitly many others.

To verify this restriction we take a closer look at the parsing process in detail. Assume that the unit $(0, A \rightarrow .aa, 0)$ has been activated by the predictor. This is for example the case after the predictor has run for the first time. The next terminal to be scanned is at this moment located at $X = -2$, i.e. the unit $(-2, .a., 1)$ is active. To scan this terminal the complete pattern needs to be shifted one step to the left. After this shifting action has been completed the two units $(1, A \rightarrow .aa, 0)$ and $(0, .a., 1)$ are active. But also unit $(0, A \rightarrow a.a, 1)$ must be activated. This action can be described as follows:

If unit $(0, A \rightarrow .aa, 0)$ and unit $(-2, .a., 1)$ are active (the predicted terminal 'a' *will* be read next) and the complete pattern is shifted (the terminal *is* read) then activate the unit $(0, A \rightarrow a.a, 1)$.

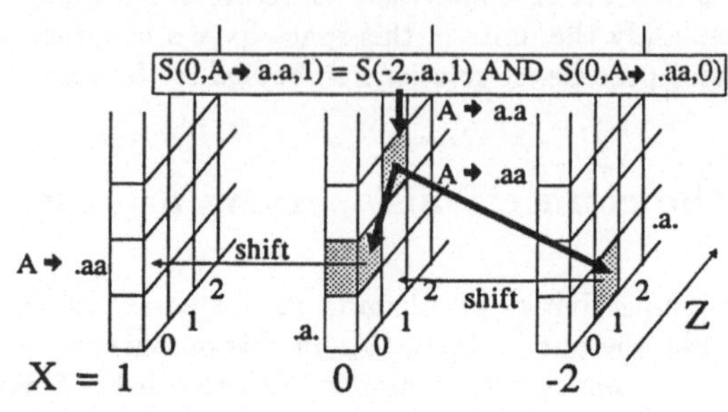

Figure 8 : The action of the scanner in our system

The figure (8) shows this action schematically. This idea can easily be formalized. For every dotted rule $N \rightarrow \alpha\gamma.\beta$ the length of dominance is exactly computed by:

$$(9) \qquad Z_{N \rightarrow \alpha\gamma.\beta} = Z_{N \rightarrow \alpha.\gamma\beta} + Z_\gamma$$

Since for every terminal the scope of dominance is 1 the formula in figure (8) can be generalized as follows:

$$(10) \qquad S(0, N \rightarrow \alpha t.\beta, Z+1) = S(0, N \rightarrow \alpha.t\beta, Z) \; AND \; S(-2, .t., 1) \; \Big\{ AND \; shift \Big\}$$

With this formula we have all we need to define the neighborhood relation:

> Neighbors are units which are either *spatial* neighbors (i.e. the X and/or Z coordinates differ by 1 as could be seen in the description of the shifting process) or *functional* neighbors which means that their dotted rules are derived from one and the same production of the grammar.[3]

It is obvious that this definition limits the units which can be neighbors of any other unit.

We have seen that formula (10) is only the generalization of formula (8). Of course formula (9) holds if the dot is moved over a nonterminal. But the dominance of a nonterminal could be of variable length. This is the reason why it is not possible to use a formula like (10) in a case like this. A formula like (10) assigned to a unit $(0, N \rightarrow \alpha M.\beta, Z)$ must lead to an impossible formula like the one in (7) because the unit $(0, N \rightarrow \alpha M.\beta, Z)$ has to be connected with all units $(1 \ldots n, N \rightarrow \alpha.M\beta, 0 \ldots Z)$. All we know is that if a unit $(0, M \rightarrow \gamma., Z')$ is active there must also an active unit $(Z', N \rightarrow \alpha.M\beta, Z)$. Beforehand the dotted rule $M \rightarrow .\gamma$ was predicted by the latter unit. After scanning Z' terminals the unit $(0, M \rightarrow \gamma., Z')$ is active (we assume of course that the correct terminals have been scanned). We now apply the technique of shifting to the above case. Since an analyzed structure has to be checked we have to shift back this structure to the right. Then the activity of unit $(Z', N \rightarrow \alpha.M\beta, Z)$ can be transferred to $X = 0$. But how do we know for how many steps the activation pattern has to be shifted? Now the consideration above shows that the X coordinate of the required unit $(X = Z', N \rightarrow \alpha.M\beta, Z)$ is the same as the Z coordinate of unit $(0, M \rightarrow \gamma., Z')$. The only thing we have to do now is to shift back the activation of unit $(X = Z', N \rightarrow \alpha.M\beta, Z)$ and simultaneously shift the activation of unit $(0, M \rightarrow \gamma., Z')$ down the Z-axis to $Z = 0$.

Now consider the following: After this shifting process both units $(Z' - Z' = 0, N \rightarrow \alpha.M\beta, Z)$ and $(0, M \rightarrow \gamma., 0)$ must be active at the same time. This leads us directly to the following formula:

$$(11) \qquad S(0, N \rightarrow \alpha M.\beta, Z + Z') = S(0, N \rightarrow \alpha.M\beta, Z) \; AND \; S(0, M \rightarrow \gamma., Z' - Z' = 0)$$

---

[3] We also take the symbol $.t.$ as a dotted rule and derive it from all productions $N \rightarrow \alpha t \beta$.

The crux in this formula is that we have to perform an addition: $Z + Z'$. But this is no problem if we modify our shifting process. As formula (11) shows we have to add to the Z-coordinate of unit $S(Z', N \to \alpha.M\beta, Z)$ the Z-coordinate of unit $S(0, M \to \gamma., Z')$ (denoted as Z'). But also we have to shift both activations for Z' steps. We now modify the shifting process in such a way that at every shifting step we increase the Z-coordinate by one. In other words we shift back diagonally. This means that unit $(0, N \to \alpha.M\beta, Z + Z')$ will be active when the shifting process is finished and that we have performed an addition by shifting. So the following formula holds:

$$(12) \qquad S(0, N \to \alpha M.\beta, Z) = S(0, N \to \alpha.M\beta, Z) \; AND \; S(0, M \to \gamma., 0)$$

One can easily see that all mentioned units are in the (functional) neighborhood relation defined above. Figure (13) demonstrates both shifting operations schematically.

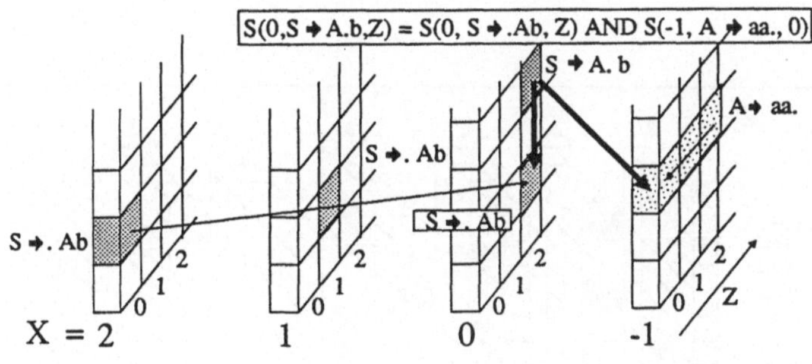

Figure 13 : The complex shifting operations to move the dot over a nonterminal. The dotted rule $S \to .Ab$ is shifted diagonally back and the dotted rule $A \to aa.$ is shifted down the Z-axis.

These shifting processes are controlled by special units. The units which control this process are situated in the control space. This is a subspace of the rule representation space located at $Z = -1$. The units at $X = 0$ control both shifting processes. The units at $X = -1$ are used of another process not explained in this outline. For the shifting process down the Z-axis we have to use the buffer in the rule representation space as shown in figure (13). For the shifting-back diagonally we use the buffer space by first copying the units from the parse list space into the buffer space and then shifting them in this space. This is to do to avoid mismatches of shifted and computed activity.

The next two figures show this process. Figure (14) shows the state after the copying has been performed and figure (15) shows the state after the complete shifting has been done. These two figures are screen copies of our system.

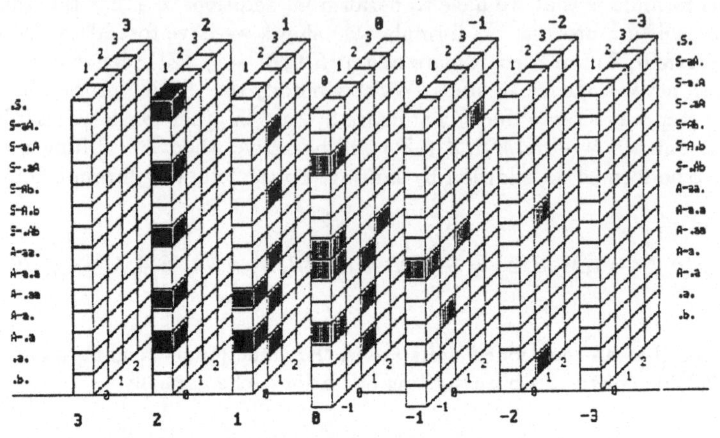

Figure 14 : A screen copy of the system after performing the copy process. The state of activity of the units in the control space is controlling the shifting process. Now the parser is ready to perform the required addition by shifting.

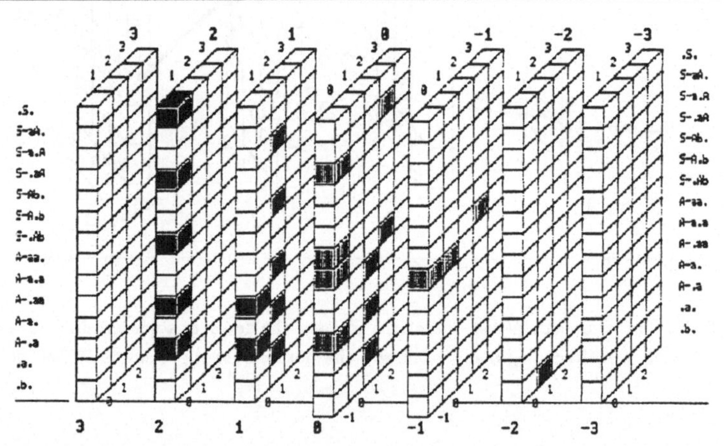

Figure 15 : Final stage of shifting. The activation of unit $(-1, A \to aa\bullet, 0)$ and unit $(-1, S \to \bullet Ab, 2)$ will cause activation of unit $(0, S \to A\bullet b, 2)$ in the next step. Unit $(0, S \to aA\bullet, 2)$ has already been activated by the step before.

Let us now consider a less formal example. We try to parse the simple sentence "*the boy hit the ball*". We assume that we have a grammar with the productions $\{S \to NP\ VP, NP \to det\ n, VP \to v\ NP\}$. It should be clear by now how the initialization will work and that scanning the first two terminals yields the activity of the dotted rule units $(0, NP \to det\ n\bullet, 2)$. In other words, the parser has detected an NP which dominates two terminals, the words "*the*" and "*boy*". Since the dot is at the end of this dotted production, the parser has to search for all productions having the dot immediately before an NP. This action will be carried out by our shifting process. The activity of the dotted rule $S \to \bullet NP\ VP$ (the one which predicted the just completed dotted rule) will be copied from $X = 2, Z = 0$ to $X = -2, Z = 1$ into the buffer space by increasing the scope of dominance by 1. Simultaneously the activity of the dotted rule unit $(0, NP \rightarrow det\ n., 2)$ will be copied into the parse buffer located at $X = -1$ by decreasing the scope of dominance: unit $(-1, NP \rightarrow det\ n., 1)$ will be activated. This modification of the dominance means that one shifting step has already been performed. At the next shifting step the activity of unit $(-2, S \rightarrow .NP\ VP, 1)$ is transferred to $(-1, S \rightarrow .NP\ VP, 2)$ (diagonal shift) and the activity of unit $(-1, NP \rightarrow det\ n., 1)$ is transferred to $(-1, NP \rightarrow det\ n., 0)$ (shifting down the Z-line). Now the formula (12) yields the correct activation of unit $(0, S \rightarrow NP.\ VP, 2)$, and the parser has to predict a verbal phrase. After the scanning-in of the verb "*hit*" another nominal phrase is predicted. Let us now have a closer look at the situation when the next two terminals ("*the ball*") are read. In the bracket notation of linguists the parser has activated the unit representing the concept "a nominalphrase [NP *the ball*] $(Z = 2)$ has just $(X = 0)$been read". Since unit $(2, VP \rightarrow v.NP, 1)$ is also active the parser can merge (by shifting) these two concepts to the concept "[VP *hit*[NP *the ball*]] has just been detected". Obviously this VP dominates exactly 3 terminals. So after another shifting process the parser has performed the correct derivation [S[NP *the man*][VP *hit*[NP *the ball*]]].

5. Conclusion

This paper aims at showing that it should be possible to implement a highly structured system (such as the one expressed in CF-PSGs) in a connectionist network. The question arises how this technique can be carried over to a system which is not based on CF-PSGs but on unification based grammars or on the principles-and-parameters approach such as recently developed by Chomsky. Some of the necessary modifications of the spaces for such systems are shown in Hoelter (1990). We are optimistic that we can also translate these grammars into a connectionist network like the one developed in this article.

References

Feldman, J.A. (1988) "Structured neural networks in nature and in computer science." In: Eckmiller, R. & v.d.Malsburg, Chr. *Neural Computers*, Berlin etc.: Springer.

Fodor, J.A. & Pylyshyn, Z.W. (1988) "Connectionism and cognitive architecture, A critical analysis", *Cognition* 28: 3-71.

Hoelter, M. (1990) "Net-linguistic representation of complex feature structures". unpublished Ms. Ruhr-Universität Bochum

Schnelle, H. & Doust, R. (1989) "A net-linguistic "Earley" chart-parser." To appear in: Reilly, R. & Sharkey, N. *Connectionist approaches to language. Vol. 1.* Amsterdam: North Holland.

Wilkens, R. (1990) "Ein netzlinguistischer Parser für kontextfreie Phrasenstrukturgrammatiken" M.A. thesis. Ruhr-Universität Bochum, Sprachwissenschaftliches Institut.

OVERCOMING LIMITATIONS OF RULE-BASED SYSTEMS: AN EXAMPLE OF A HYBRID DETERMINISTIC PARSER

Stan C. Kwasny

Center for Intelligent Computer Systems[†], Washington University
St. Louis, Missouri 63130, U.S.A.

Kanaan A. Faisal

Information and Computer Science Department
King Fahd University of Petroleum and Minerals[‡]
Dhahran 31261, Kingdom of Saudi Arabia

1. Introduction

The rule-based approach to building intelligent systems is prevalent throughout the enterprise of Artificial Intelligence. Many famous systems have succeeded because they rely on rules at least to some extent. Through good knowledge engineering, the representation and encodement of the elements required to find adequate problem solutions can be facilitated. But despite enormous efforts, rule-based systems are far from perfect in their performance. What are the limitations and how can they be overcome?

Our work focuses on combining a symbolic rule-based system with a (connectionist) neural network. This marriage works exceptionally well in our domain. Some limitations of symbolic systems can be overcome through connectionism while some limitations of connectionism can be overcome through symbolic means. We offer one example which shows progress that would be difficult to make using either single approach. Specifically, rule-based deterministic parsing, as first articulated in a complete and convincing manner by Marcus [1], lends itself to experimentation as a hybrid system. We show how the rules of a deterministic parser can be re-tooled to serve as training data for a neural network. We demonstrate that the resultant hybrid system outperforms all other published attempts at robust deterministic parsing and syntax-based lexical disambiguation.

2. Limitations of Rule-Based Systems

Rule-based (expert) systems have become classical in the approach they offer for solving difficult problems. Many intelligent systems rely on rules as a vehicle for representing procedural solutions to individual pieces of large and complex problems. The rules often arise

---

[†] The sponsors of the Center are McDonnell Douglas Corporation and Southwestern Bell Telephone Company.

[‡] The second author gratefully acknowledge the support of King Fahd University of Petroleum and Minerals.

from the efforts of knowledge engineering in which the knowledge that an expert brings to bear on a problem is codified in an "if .. then .." form. The left-hand (if) side of the rule represents the preconditions under which that rule can activate and eventually fire. The right-hand (then) side specifies actions specific to the situation which, upon firing the rule, move the system closer to a solution. Often the relationship between left-hand and right-hand sides is specified approximately through numeric certainty factors. These factors can often be solicited from the expert and used to determine what credence should be placed on the conclusions reached from firing a rule. Rule-based systems assume a knowledge base which holds a representation of the state of the system's knowledge as it develops solutions to problems. Generally, this knowledge is stored and manipulated symbolically. Initially, the knowledge base will usually contain all factual knowledge and is updated and revised dynamically as the system runs.

At any given point in the process, several rules may be active. Under a process of conflict resolution, one rule is selected to be fired. The particular strategy for resolving conflicts may vary from system to system. Often the system-builder is given the choice of what strategy should be employed for his purposes. Several strategies are well known, but none is considered universally optimal for all situations. Upon firing, one rule may cause another rule to become activated and thus be chosen to fire. The chaining of rules in this manner is a distinctive feature of the rule-based approach.

2.1. State of the Art

According to Davis [2] expert systems can be characterized by the features in Figure 1. Each of these features reflect a limitation of rule-based expert systems. All of them, however, touch on properties that connectionism possesses to some extent. It is very natural, therefore, to examine the potential for combining a rule-based approach with one based on connectionism. The success of constructing such a hybrid system depends on whether the combination retains the benefits of the two approaches and introduces no new problems. We shall return to this later after examining a system which takes such an approach.

As Davis stated, expert systems possess expertise in a narrow task domain. They exhibit very uneven behavior as they are asked to consider problems at the boundaries of their domain. The task domain must be anticipated totally by the rules in order to be successful. Since rules are at the heart of these systems, we now closely examine some properties which rules bring to these systems.

- Narrow domain of expertise
- Fragile behavior at the boundaries
- Limited knowledge representation language
- Limited input/output
- Limited explanation
- One expert as knowledge base "czar"

Figure 1: State of the Art of Expert Systems (after Davis [2])

2.2. Rules

The language of "if..then.." is the de facto programming language of rule-based systems. Rules tie together the symptoms (facts, premises, observables, situations, states) with their treatments (actions, conclusions, goals). But rules are often determined in ad hoc ways either from some poorly articulated fragment of expertise or from some requirement of the system to track its own state during a computation. Furthermore, the relation between rule premise and conclusion is often captured with an ad hoc mechanism such as certainty factors.

A single rule incorporates procedural knowledge about a very tiny "rule domain" that is a small part of the task domain. It is specific to particular values and events that exist within the knowledge base. Rule domains are necessarily small and specialized since a large rule domain is only possible if an algorithmic solution exists for some large part of the task domain. Most task domains do not have that property. Combining many rules combines many rule domains and thus widens the task domain of the system.

If rule domains do not overlap, then each rule is independent of the other. However, there are bound to be gaps in the task domain of the system since only in the simplest cases would rule domains fit together snuggly like the pieces of a jig-saw puzzle.

If rule domains do overlap, on the other hand, then conflict resolution strategies are necessary to decide which rule is most appropriate. This greatly complicates the task of the rule builder (programmer) since it is difficult to cleanly abstract the behavior of a rule from its environment and the mechanism of its implementation. Rule specificity, as a conflict resolution strategy, makes it possible to layer rules so that a more specific exception to a rule is considered in preference to a general rule. Rule interactions create many difficulties for the programmer. Much of the effort to build, debug, maintain, or extend a system is taken up with the concern of how to manage rule interaction.

In a rule-based expert system, knowledge is acquired from an expert and encoded in both the knowledge base and the rules. This can be an extremely difficult undertaking. Part of the problem comes from trying to understand the task domain in ways that the expert understands it. More of the difficulty comes in properly formulating a set of rules that work up to the level of the expert.

Often there are not one but many experts available who may provide contradictory advice about the task domain. How to reconcile these differing opinions becomes a real question. In domains in which the expertise has been recorded, as in a textbook, situations may arise in practice that the textbook does not consider nor cover. It is always useful to consider actual cases and to observe as the expert examines the evidence at hand in reaching his solution in the task domain. However, relying on a textbook as an expert source for building rules can often accelerate knowledge acquisition. Rules from textbooks are generally accepted wisdom and can serve to guide a system even when cases presented are quite far afield.

TEIRESIAS [3] is one system that permits the expert himself to examine the behavior of the system and suggest changes to rules. This works well if the expert can formulate his critique in terms of rules or rule changes. However, the expert may not think about his task domain in terms of rules. In that sense TEIRESIAS provides a very artificial environment for system development.

State of the Art (after Davis [2])	Features of Connectionism
• Narrow domain of expertise	• Generalization
• Fragile behavior at the boundaries	• Graceful degradation
• Limited knowledge representation language	• Localist/distributed encoding
• Limited input/output	• Training/learning
• Limited explanation	• "Probes"
• One expert as knowledge base "czar"	• Multiple experts

Figure 2: Potential of Connectionism

3. Connectionism

Every limitation of rule-based systems mentioned above can be examined in light of connectionism. While connectionism has its own weaknesses, it offers a better approach than rules to most of the weaknesses mentioned by Davis as shown in Figure 2.

Connectionist networks generalize to novel inputs. This serves to broaden the domain covered by the system. Training need not include every possible situation to which the network will be applied. If a representative set of patterns are utilized in training and the network generalizes, then novel patterns will be treated in line with similar training cases. A rule-based system in combination with a connectionist neural network can potentially generalize better within the task domain.

Connectionist systems degrade gracefully. There is a shared responsibility among the units of the network for decision making. Thus, any single unit can become disabled or non-functional and the system degrades little. This feature, coupled with generalization, smooths out the boundaries of the system and reduces the fragility of its behavior.

Representation of knowledge is difficult symbolically since it requires a detailed analysis of the elements of the domain and how they interact. Connectionism permits encodings that are distributed as well as localist. Furthermore, network training is an important part of constructing most connectionist models for a task. It is through training that the network learns to adapt to its training situations. Preferred responses are rewarded while others are not. Furthermore, expertise need not be articulated in the form of esoteric, convoluted rules. Connectionism relies upon extensional specification of input/output associations, which are more natural than rules for most tasks.

Explanation in rule-based systems comes from the rules. In particular, "how" and "why" questions are often answered by merely articulating a rule. Connectionist networks do not have rules and cannot respond in this way. Since representations are often distributed, there is no easy interpretation of the activated units and no easy explanation for decisions made by the system. The use of "probes" [4] is one promising approach to this problem. These are special input units which are trained to evoke a particular descriptive pattern when turned on. These patterns can serve to elucidate the nature of the decision being made.

If expertise happens to lie with multiple experts, conflicting rules may result during knowledge acquisition. Conflict resolution strategies offer no real solution to this problem.

In a connectionist network, training can permit conflicting rules to compete. The winning rule is the one which resonates best with other training patterns. It has been shown in other systems [5] that a neural network can often be configured to perform as well or better than any individual expert from which training data has been constructed.

Training from rules can lead to a network whose behavior emulates the rules, but does so in a robust manner. This can be tested by presenting both expected and unexpected cases to the system. Rule-based training is a good way to provide very general coverage in a task domain. In the early stages of knowledge acquisition, it is an excellent way to prototype an initial set of general rules from the expert. We call this form of training "deductive" training in the sense that very general situations are presented during training, but the resultant network is expected to perform on specific, real situations.

Rule-based training is analogous to textbook learning. For example, a new medical intern possesses all the knowledge that textbooks can convey. He is ready to treat actual patients, but lacks the depth of skill that experience brings. He must, therefore, spend a number of years as an intern looking at real data in actual situations to become equipped to perform as an expert doctor would.

For this reason, a second type of training, called "inductive" training, is necessary. While rule-based training takes its training patterns from idealized situations (as in a textbook), inductive training uses actual cases with real data. It is inductive in the sense that training from very specific situations is expected to generalize to other cases of a similar nature.

Deductive and inductive training can be utilized individually, but we have found that combining the two in a mixed form of training yields the best overall results. Returning to the case of the young doctor, we would expect this to be the case since the doctor is not ready to take on a full load of patients just after emerging from the classroom. Additional "on the job" training is necessary to completely master the field. In our experiments, we construct training data from both rules and real situations and present them together in the same training pass. See [6] for additional discussion of the two types of training.

4. Example: Deterministic Parsing

Rule-based deterministic parsing is chosen as a setting in which to illustrate the benefits of a hybrid architecture. Here, only a very brief description of the system is presented. In [7] some of the linguistic properties of our system are examined while [8] contains more details of the system and further results.

Our hybrid deterministic parser combines the notions of deterministic parsing as implemented in the PARSIFAL system with that of connectionism. The result is a parser which is decidedly more robust than PARSIFAL and which compares favorably with various of its extensions. Our hybrid deterministic parser represents a departure from traditional deterministic parsers in its combination of both symbolic and connectionist components. The symbolic component manages the stack as well as the flow of sentence elements into the buffer while the connectionist component decides how these structures should be managed. Training of the connectionist component is based on patterns derived from the rules of a symbolic deterministic grammar.

Three generations of experiments have been conducted. In each set of experiments the size of the grammar increases as does the complexity of the task. Nevertheless, the results actually get better as the system is scaled up to successively larger grammars. Our training techniques are shown to be applicable to successively larger subsets of English. The approach also permits some simplification over traditional deterministic parsers, including the elimination of both rule packets and priorities. Furthermore, parsing is performed more robustly by the connectionist component and with more tolerance for error in the parsing process. Experimentation has shown that a network trained with rules from a deterministic grammar can generalize to parse grammatical, ungrammatical, and lexically ambiguous sentence forms.

4.1. Architecture

Deterministic parsing is based on the determinism hypothesis posed by Marcus. If we accept the determinism hypothesis it must follow that sentence processing need not depend in any fundamental way on backtracking. As a further consequence, no partial structures need be produced during parsing which fail to become part of the final structure. Several extensions to PARSIFAL have been researched independently. In PARAGRAM [9] methods for parsing ungrammatical sentences are presented. In ROBIE [10] the resolution of lexical ambiguities is performed by extending the rules and slightly modifying the interpreter. In LPARSIFAL [11] it is shown how syntactic rules can be acquired from sentence examples. The three extensions to PARSIFAL are all derivatives of deterministic parsing, but represent independent solutions in specific problem areas. One goal of our work is the integration of their processing capabilities. The ultimate goal is to produce a parser that is capable of learning some reasonable facility with language, but does not fail on inputs that are only slightly different from expected inputs.

For contrast, the approach of PARSIFAL is now reviewed. Determinism is accomplished by permitting lookahead of up to three constituents within a buffer designated for that purpose. A stack is present to permit the recursive processing of embedded structures and to facilitate processing generally. Rules are partitioned into packets which become active or inactive during parsing, but are usually associated with the current (top-level) node of the structure being built. A single processing step consists of selecting a rule from an active rule packet and firing the rule. Conflicts are resolved from the static ordering (priority) of rules within the packet. The action effects changes to the stack and buffer and, after a series of processing steps, a termination rule fires which terminates processing and leaves the final structure on top of the stack.

The hybrid parser is organized into a symbolic component and a connectionist component. The latter component is implemented as a three-layer neural network and is trained using backward propagation [12] from rule ''templates'' which are derived from a PARSIFAL-like deterministic grammar. Rule templates are intermediate between symbolic rules and the training patterns required by the network. Each rule template typically represents a large number of patterns each of which characterizes a situation that can occur during parsing. Output from the network indicates an action to be performed. Actions are performed symbolically on traditional data structures which are also maintained symbolically.

The symbolic component manages the input sentence and the flow of constituents into the buffer, coding them as required for use by the network in the connectionist component. It is the responsibility of the connectionist component to show a preference for a specific action. These preferences are a result of many iterations of back-propagation learning with instances of the rule templates. Once trained, the system makes decisions very efficiently. The feed-forward multiplication of weights and computation of activation levels for individual units produce the pattern of activation on the output level. Activation of output units is interpreted in a winner-take-all manner, with the highest activated unit determining the action to be taken. Actions are then performed by the symbolic component.

During sentence processing, the network is presented with encodings of the buffer and the top of the stack. The model does not actual see the words of the sentence but a canonical representation of each word in a form that could be produced by a simple lexicon, although such a lexicon is not part of the model in its present form. The encoding scheme is developed according to what features are required by the grammar rules and are, therefore, primarily syntactic. The network produces the action to be taken which is then performed. If the action creates a vacancy in the buffer and if more of the sentence is left to be processed then the next sentence component is moved into the buffer. The process then repeats until a stop action is performed, usually when the buffer becomes empty. Iteration over the input stream is achieved in this fashion, allowing sentences of unlimited length to be processed.

4.2. Training

Training of the parser proceeds by presenting patterns to the network and teaching it to respond with an appropriate action. The input patterns represent encodings of the buffer positions and the top of the stack from the deterministic parser. The output of the network contains a series of units representing actions to be performed during processing and judged in a winner-take-all fashion. Network convergence is observed once the network can achieve a perfect score on the training patterns themselves and the error measure has decreased to an acceptable level (set as a parameter).

For deductive training, each grammar rule is coded as a training template which is a list of feature values. In general, each constituent of the buffer is represented by an ordered feature vector in which one or more values is ON(+1) when a feature is present in the form and OFF(−1) when not. Additionally, in a rule template, the feature vector can show a DO NOT CARE (?) value for features not relevant to the situation represented by the rule. A rule template is then instantiated by randomly changing ? to either +1 or −1 in order to yield a training pattern. In this way, each template can be instantiated to give many training patterns and each training epoch is slightly different. Since it is obviously impossible to test the performance of all possible instantiations of templates, for the purpose of judging convergence a zero is substituted for each ? in the rule template to provide testing patterns.

Inductive training is performed from actual sentences. The deterministic grammar rules are applied to several sentences yielding many sentence traces. Each rule application gives a single sentence trace which includes both the pattern of features in the buffer and stack and the action that is performed. The collection of traces are merged to eliminate duplicates and the resultant set of patterns are utilized in training the network inductively.

	Target Grammars		
	Small	Medium	Large
Number of Rules	13	22	73
Number of Actions	5	20	40
Network Size (Units)	44-15-5	35-20-20	66-40-40
Network Size (Weights)	735	1100	4240
Presentations ($\times$ 1000)	200	500	1000
Based On	Example (Winston, 1984)	Appendix C (Marcus, 1980)	Appendix D (Marcus, 1980)

Figure 3: Summary of Target Grammars Used in the Hybrid Parser

Besides experimenting with deductive and inductive training strategies individually, we have also examined a mixed strategy in which rule templates and sentence traces are combined to give the patterns for training. There is evidence that the mixed strategy may exceed either of the other two strategies in performance.

4.3. Summary of Results

Our experimentation has examined three very different target grammars, which we shall call small, medium, and large. Figure 3 shows some of the characteristics of these grammars for comparison. The small grammar is based on an example from the Winston [13] AI textbook. The network requires 44 input units to encode the stack and three-place buffer. Our choice of 15 hidden units is determined empirically. The medium and large grammars, based loosely on appendices C and D in [1] contain 22 and 73 rules respectively. The network configurations reflect an increase from 5 to 20 to 40 actions. A variety of training runs have been made with each grammar. Shown is the number of presentations of training patterns sufficient to get good convergence and generalization results, although fewer presentations may suffice.

In our initial attempt to demonstrate the feasibility of our approach, a small, simple grammar is used. It features S, NP, VP, and PP structures with an assumed preprocessing for noun phrases. Coding of three rule packets (S, VP, and PP) as rule templates provides training data for the 44-15-5 unit network. Perfect performance, as determined by presentation of a limited number of test sentences, is achieved for the 13 grammar rules coded. No generalization experiments were performed due to the limited nature of the grammar.

A second set of experiments shows how a variety of more complicated mechanisms essential to PARSIFAL are realized in our architecture. The medium grammar is much more sophisticated than the small one and permits reasonable generalization experiments to be conducted. It is capable of processing a variety of simple sentence forms such as simple declaratives, simple passives, imperative sentences, and yes-no questions. Appendix C of [1] serves as the model for the rules of this grammar. All of the basic mechanisms of deterministic parsing are represented.

In a third set of experiments, a much larger and more general grammar is used. In this case, the grammar consists of 73 rules and represents rules for parsing many sentence forms such as simple declarative sentences, passives, imperatives, yes-no questions, wh-questions, wh-clauses, and other embedded sentences.

With the medium and large grammars, several sentences are coded for testing and comparison purposes. Some would parse correctly by the rules of the deterministic parser, while others are mildly ungrammatical and lexically ambiguous. Most of these examples are drawn from work cited earlier by Charniak and Milne. In parsing the sentences, the performance of the network is measured in two ways: first, by the validity of the structure produced; and second, by the average strength of the response of the neural network. Strength is measured as the reciprocal of the average error for each step. In this way, it is determined if the network is generalizing in any useful way and whether its responses are being challenged by other ones. Several dozen sentences have been examined and tested and desirable generalization properties have been shown.

In examining grammars of varying sizes, our objective is to determine whether the same generalization properties seen in the medium grammar would scale up to a much larger and more realistic set of grammar rules. Our data supports this conclusion.

5. Conclusions

Our hybrid system for deterministic parsing has demonstrated some of the advantages of introducing connectionism in a rule-based setting. While we have not addressed explanation capabilities in our system, many of the limitations of rule-based expert systems pointed out by Davis have been reduced. The result, in this case, has been a parser that broadens the domain of expertise and is much less fragile at the boundaries. Utilizing one of the three types of training, (deductive, inductive, or mixed), the system is guided by either idealized rules, concrete cases, or both. If multiple sources of knowledge exist, the system can be trained even if some of that knowledge overlaps or contradicts. Knowledge competes for appropriateness in a given situation. Furthermore, the form of the knowledge need not be rules, but merely an extensional specification of input/output pairs.

Our example of hybrid deterministic parsing illustrates one method of combining a rule-based, symbolic approach with connectionism to provide some of the best features of both.

References

1. Mitchell P. Marcus, *A Theory of Syntactic Recognition for Natural Language,* MIT Press, Cambridge, MA, 1980.

2. Randall Davis, "Amplifying Expertise with Expert Systems," in *The AI Business: Commercial Uses of Artificial Intelligence*, ed. P.H. Winston and K.A. Prendergast, MIT Press, Cambridge, MA, 1984.

3. Randall Davis, "Teiresias: Applications of Meta-Level Knowledge," in *Knowledge-Based Systems in Artificial Intelligence*, ed. R. Davis and D.B. Lenat, McGraw-Hill, New York, NY, 1982.

4. M.F. St. John and J.L. McClelland, "Learning and Applying Contextual Constraints in Sentence Comprehension," Technical Report AIP-39, Department of Psychology, Carnegie-Mellon University, Pittsburgh, PA, June 8, 1988.

5. E. Collins, S. Ghosh, and C.L. Scofield, "An Application of a Multiple Neural Network Learning System to Emulation of Mortgage Underwriting Judgements," in *Proceedings of IEEE International Confernce on Neural Networks II*, pp. 459-466, 1988.

6. Kanaan A. Faisal and Stan C. Kwasny, "Deductive and Inductive Learning in a Connectionist Deterministic Parser," in *Proceedings of the International Joint Conference on Neural Networks*, vol. 2, pp. 471-474, Lawrence Erlbaum Associates, Hillsdale, NJ, January 15-19, 1990.

7. Kanaan A. Faisal and Stan C. Kwasny, "Design of a Hybrid Deterministic Parser," in *Proceedings of the 13th International Conference on Computational Linguistics*, Helsinki, Finland, August, 1990. (FORTHCOMING)

8. Stan C. Kwasny and Kanaan A. Faisal, "Connectionism and Determinism in a Syntactic Parser," *Connection Science: Journal of Neural Computing, Artificial Intelligence, and Cognitive Research — Special Issue on Connectionist Research on Natural Language*, Carfax Publishing Company, Abingdon, Oxfordshire, England, 1990. (in press)

9. Eugene Charniak, "A Parser with Something for Everyone," in *Parsing Natural Language*, ed. M. King, pp. 117-150, Academic Press, New York, NY, 1983.

10. Robert Milne, "Resolving Lexical Ambiguity in a Deterministic Parser," *Computational Linguistics*, vol. 12, no. 1, pp. 1-12, January-March, 1986.

11. Robert C. Berwick, *The Acquisition of Syntactic Knowledge,* MIT Press, Cambridge, MA, 1985.

12. David E. Rumelhart, Geoffrey Hinton, and Ronald J. Williams, "Learning Internal Representations by Error Propagation," in *Parallel Distributed Processing*, ed. D.E. Rumelhart and J.L. McClelland, pp. 318-364, MIT Press, Cambridge, MA, 1986.

13. Patrick H. Winston, *Artificial Intelligence,* Addison-Wesley, Reading, Ma, 1984.

WHY DISTRIBUTED REPRESENTATION IS INHERENTLY NON-SYMBOLIC

Tim van Gelder
Department of Philosophy, Indiana University
Bloomington Indiana 47405 USA

There are many conflicting views concerning the nature of distributed representation, its compatibility or otherwise with symbolic representation, and its importance in characterizing the nature of connectionist models and their relationship to more traditional symbolic approaches to understanding cognition. Many have simply assumed that distribution is merely an implementation issue, and that symbolic mechanisms can be designed to take advantage of the virtues of distribution if so desired. Others, meanwhile, see the use of distributed representation as marking a fundamental difference between the two approaches. One reason for this diversity of opinion is the fact that the relevant notions — especially that of *distribution* — are rarely adequately characterized before addressing the issues. At this level of generality, an adequate characterization is one that is sufficiently abstract to subsume most paradigm cases of representation of a given type, yet also sufficiently precise to give real theoretical bite when addressing questions such as those raised above. This paper advances a definition of distributed representation and shows that, understood this way, distribution is in fact incompatible with the core notion of symbolic representation found in the cognitive science literature. For this reason, genuinely distributed connectionist models cannot be, or implement, physical symbol systems (Newell & Simon 1976) or "classical" symbolic models (Fodor and Pylyshyn 1988). Thus, I am endorsing the view that distributed connectionist models do indeed present a radical new approach to modeling cognitive processes.

1. The Nature of Distribution

Despite the fact that distribution is a central feature of a very large proportion of connectionist models, almost no attention has been given to the problem of providing a comprehensive, systematic definition of the concept. Numerous brief characterizations have been offered — see van Gelder (1990b) for a survey of scores of attempts — but when examined closely they turn out to draw on a wide range of themes, ranging from relatively trivial notions of spatial or neural "spread-out-ness" at one extreme to complete functional equipotentiality at the other. As a consequence, *distribution* is currently one of the murkiest concepts in the whole of cognitive science.

Fortunately, one concept in particular both figures in a relatively large proportion of characterizations and turns out to describe a very high proportion of the paradigm cases of distribution: namely, the non-discreteness or non-localizability of representations. From this perspective a representation is distributed when multiple items are encoded over the same extent of the available resources, without any more fine-grained correspondence of items to particular locations. For an obvious example, consider the connection weights in a standard feed-forward connectionist network, encoding many different associations over the very same connections.

If the representings of a number of different items are in fact fully superimposed, every part of the representation R must be implicated in representing each item. If this is achieved in a non-trivial way there must be some encoding process that generates R given the various items to be stored, and which makes R vary, at every point, as a function of each item. This process will be implementing a certain kind of *transformation* from items to representations. This suggests thinking of distribution more generally in terms of mathematical transformations exhibiting as certain abstract structure of dependency of the output on the input. More precisely, define any transformation from a function F to another function G as *strongly distributing* just in case the value of G at any point varies with the value of F at any point; the Fourier transform is a classic example. Similarly, a transformation from F to G is *weakly distributing*, relative to a division of the domain of F into a number of sub-domains, just in case the value of G at every point varies as a function of the value of F at at least one point in each sub-domain. The classic example here is the linear associator, in which a series of vector pairs are stored in a weight matrix by first forming, and then adding together, their respective outer products. Each element of the matrix varies with every stored vector, but only with one element of each of those vectors.

Clearly, a given distributing transformation yields a whole space of functions resulting from applying that transformation to different inputs. If we think of these output functions as descriptions of representations, and the input functions as descriptions of items to be represented, the distributing transformation is defining a whole space or scheme of *distributed representations*. To be a distributed representation, then, is to be a member of such a scheme; it is to be a representation R of a series of items C such that the encoding process which generates R on the basis of C implements a given distributing transformation.

Distributing transformations (and hence distributed representations) are ubiquitous in connectionist models. Consider for example the transition from input to hidden-layer representation in a fully connected feed-forward network. If we think of the represented items as the elements of the input vector, then the transition is implementing a simple case of a strongly distributing transformation since the activation of any given hidden unit varies as a function of the activation of every input unit. The precise form of this distributing transformation can easily be written down in an equation in terms of the connection weights and the activation function of the units. Because the transformation which generates the hidden unit pattern is strongly distributing, the hidden unit pattern itself is appropriately classified as a (strongly) distributed representation.

An excellent example of *weakly* distributed representation is the working memory (WM) in Touretzky and Hinton's (1988) Distributed Connectionist Production System model (DCPS). This model processes triples of basic elements, where each triple is encoded as a unique pattern of activity over 2000 binary units. Patterns are generated by means of a coarse-coding scheme which activates approximately 28 units for each triple. At any time a number of these triple patterns can be stored in a central 2000-unit WM by activating the relevant units for each pattern. The process of storing patterns in WM — essentially just vector addition — is one that superimposes the basic patterns. It implements a weakly distributing transformation because the activation level of any given unit in WM varies with every pattern to be stored, but at one and only point in that pattern (i.e., whether a given unit is activated depends on whether there is a 1 or a 0 at one specific point in each of the patterns to be stored).

Note that, although this characterization of distribution in terms of a core notion of superposition captures most of the standard cases of distributed representation found in connectionist work, some familiar examples are excluded. An example is the "Wickelfeature"-based representation of verb forms in Rumelhart & McClelland's (1986) well-known model of past tense acquisition . (Care is needed here, for the connections which represent the associations of present with past tense forms *do* in fact constitute a genuinely distributed representation). For this reason the present characterization is sometimes accused of being too *narrow*. Now, it is true that my analysis disagrees with previous usage to some extent, as in this case. However, given the extraordinary state of disarray of the concept, any decent analysis will *inevitably* have to reject some previous usage as mistaken or misleading. The most important thing is that the analysis itself carve up the relevant phenomena at their true conceptual joints. Any taxonomy of forms of representation which casually lumps together genuinely superposed representations *and* merely feature-based representations is failing to recognize deep differences and is therefore too *wide* to be really useful. (Further argument that superposition is in fact the really central feature of genuinely distributed representations — and that this category does indeed deserve the label "distributed" — is given in van Gelder 1990b.)

2. Symbolic Representation

There is already considerable consensus in the cognitive science literature on the nature of symbolic representation. The following definition is merely a synthesis of proposals advanced by Newell and Simon, Haugeland, Fodor, and Pylyshyn among others. A scheme of symbolic representation consists of:

(a) a primitive vocabulary consisting of a finite set of disjoint and digital symbol classes (or *types*); each class is made up of a potentially unbounded number of physical tokens known as *symbols*;

(b) a set of grammatical rules governing the combining of symbols;

(c) a concatenative mode of combination;

(d) an unbounded set of expression classes (or *types*), where expression tokens are constructed by concatenation of symbols in conformity with the grammatical rules;

(e) primitive semantic assignments to symbols; and

(f) principles for making semantic assignments to expressions on the basis of the primitive assignments and the syntactic structure of the expression.

For a particular representation to count as symbolic it must belong to such a scheme, and consequently must itself satisfy the above conditions.

Some details are worth noting. First, basic symbol classes are completely *disjoint* — i.e., no primitive symbol token belongs to more than one class. A consequence of this condition is that expression classes themselves are disjoint. Second, these disjoint classes are *digital*, which is to say that it is always possible to determine, positively and reliably whether a given token falls into a particular symbol class (see Haugeland 1981). In practice, symbol tokens usually instantiate some characteristic physical shape or configuration, and it is this fact which underlies the digital separability of symbol classes. (Thus, it is because tokens of the word "cat" have a characteristic shape that we can reliably distinguish them from tokens of the word "bat".) Third, condition (3) makes explicit the requirement that when primitive symbols are grammatically combined to generate compound expressions, actual tokens of the primitive symbol classes can be found physically instantiated in the expression itself. A concatenative mode of combination just is a way of combining symbols to obtain expressions such that each of the expression's primitive constituents are "tokened" every time the expression itself is tokened. As Newell & Simon (1976) put it, "...a symbol structure is composed of a number of instances (or tokens) of symbols related in some physical way (such as one token being next to another)." It is satisfying this requirement, more than any other, which justifies the description *symbolic*.

This last point is worth stressing. Only when defined in the above reasonably strong and precise terms does symbolic representation form the basis of the computational theory of mind as that theory has been articulated by Fodor, Pylyshyn and others. Though it is not difficult to find weaker formulations in the literature, on any such weaker account symbolic representation is not appropriately connected with the notion of computation construed as symbol manipulation. In particular, if we surrendered the concatenation requirement, we would thereby be surrendering the kind of rule-governed structure-sensitive algorithmic operations that lie at the heart of the computational approach, since those operations rely directly on the causal role of the constituents of the expressions being transformed. (For elaboration and defense of this point see van Gelder 1990a, Fodor & McLaughlin (forthcoming), Fodor & Pylyshyn 1988, Pylyshyn 1984 Ch. 3.)

3. Incompatibility

It should be obvious that distribution and symbolic representation have significantly different flavor. It is moreover hardly controversial that some cases of distributed representation are patently non-symbolic, and vice versa. But can there be, nevertheless, an overlap between the two categories? Can symbolic representation ever be genuinely distributed? The surprising answer is *no*. This can be demonstrated relatively easily with the above clarifications of the relevant concepts in hand. In a nutshell, the argument is this: as indicated above, there are quite precise formal and semantic conditions that representations have to satisfy in order to count as symbolic, and it is impossible to satisfy these while remaining genuinely distributed.

3.1 Formal Incompatibility

To count as symbolic a representation must satisfy at least three purely formal conditions: it must belong to a space of expression tokens that is digitally structured; the expression itself must be grammatically well-formed; and it must be concatenatively structured. Distribution is incompatible with symbolic representation because distribution, by its very nature, typically violates the first two conditions and always violates the third.

(a) Analog nature of distributed schemes

While symbolic representation is essentially digital, distributed schemes are typically analog in that they allow a smooth continuum of acceptable representation instances, and so fail to guarantee the possibility of unambiguous determination of a given representation's type identity. Interestingly, this particular difference is often touted as one of the *virtues* of distribution, giving rise to computational advantages such as the ability to handle very fine shades of meaning. An explanation of the analog nature of most distributed schemes is to be found in the fact that nothing in the definition of distributing transformations, around which distributed schemes are constructed, requires that the output be digitally structured; indeed, the most natural mathematical form for distributing transformations to take is continuous.

(b) Distributed representations are standardly non-grammatical

To count as symbolic, a representation must be grammatically well-formed; it must be constructed in accordance with the rules of the scheme in question. Distributing transformations, however, are typically not grammatically constrained; they will happily output a single representation of *any* series of items they are presented with. Whenever generation of the distributed representation is not governed by grammatical rules, the representation cannot be properly regarded as symbolic; yet nothing in the nature of distribution provides for such grammatical constraints.

(c) Distributed representations are invariably non-concatenative

Although these first two considerations are generally sufficient in practice to differentiate distributed and symbolic representations, they cannot *conclusively* establish incompatibility since there are ways in which the transformations generating distributed representations can be externally constrained to produce digital output in accordance with grammatical formation rules (for an example see below). However it is not possible to design distributing transformations producing representations meeting the third requirement on symbolic representations, that of *concatenative* structure. It is in the very nature of distributing transformations that, when a number of items are superimposed to form one representation, the items themselves are lost, in the sense that there are no longer distinct *tokens* of the stored items to be found. In short, it is impossible to combine symbol tokens to form grammatically well-formed structures in a way that both *superimposes* them and *concatenates* them.

3.2 Incompatibility of Semantic Structure

An important advantage of symbolic representation is that it is generally *possible* to determine the meaning of the whole on the basis of basic semantic assignments to its primitive constituents. This is because such representations are constructed out of tokens of their parts, and there is a localist correspondence between parts of the representation and basic features of the represented domain. Thus, when we have a symbolic representation of the situation where the cat is on the mat, there is a localist correspondence between the cat itself and the term "cat". A consequence is that a local change in the situation being represented only requires local, "modular" variation in the representation; for example, if the cat is now replaced by a dog, we need only change "cat" to "dog" to get an accurate representation of the new situation.

Contrast this with distributed representation, where (by definition) the representation at any point varies as a function of the content at every point. There is no localist correspondence of features of the representation to features of the world at all; rather, *all* the representation corresponds to the whole (i.e., each part) of the represented situation. Consequently, any change in the represented situation requires changes across the whole representation. This fundamental difference is often conveyed by describing distributed representations as "holistic," or by pointing out that storage is context dependent: i.e., any given item is only stored *in the context of* other items or content parts.

4. Case Study: BoltzCONS

One of the main sources of resistance to incompatibility arguments of the above kind is the existence of connectionist models utilizing representations that at least *appear* to be both distributed and symbolic. Strategically at least is essential for me to show clearly why such models do not in fact constitute counterexamples. Basically, in such models, where the representations are genuinely distributed they turn out to be non-symbolic; and where symbolic, they are not genuinely distributed (though they may have some features on the basis of which current confused usage often classifies them as distributed).

Thus, consider Touretzky's BoltzCONS extension of the DCPS model. This "distributed symbol processing" model contains a WM of essentially the same type as DCPS, except that in this case the basic triple-patterns stored in WM are treated like LISP "cons" cells. By carefully storing the right combination of triples, the overall state of WM is able to function as a representation of a complex data structure. Now, there is no doubt that this memory is genuinely distributed, since the basic patterns were stored there by a weak distributing transformation (see Sec. 1). A number of considerations seem to suggest that it is also symbolic. Symbols are stored in WM and can be retrieved; these basic symbols are sufficiently distinct that, under normal working conditions, WM states fall into a digitally structured space; and just which symbols are stored at any time is governed by what can be regarded as grammatical constraints.

The crucial difference, however, is that *the BoltzCONS WM is not concatenatively structured*. Recall that a concatenatively structured representation contains actual tokens of its basic constituents. But when triple A and triple B are stored in WM as part of the representation of a complex expression, it is impossible to find that particular, distinctive pattern of approximately 28 out of 2000 units which the coarse-coding scheme assigned to triple A. *That* pattern was lost when it was stored in memory with the pattern for triple B. So where is the required token of triple A? We cannot say that the current overall pattern is itself a token of triple A (i.e., including the current pattern which is the state of WM among the class of A-tokens), since — by the very same reasoning — that pattern would also have to count as an instance of triple B. This would be an egregious violation of the requirement that the basic symbol classes be *disjoint*.

5. Discussion

The upshot of these arguments is no representation can be both distributed (i.e., belonging to a *scheme* fixed by a given distributing transformation) and symbolic at the same time. It is important to see that this is not just terminological bickering; rather, it follows from the very nature of the forms of representation themselves. It has been shown that representations with certain properties do not have certain other properties. These properties are those which are central the categories of distributed representation and symbolic representation respectively. The only matter of terminology is whether it is wisest to use the *labels* "distributed" for the first category and "symbolic" for the second; this latter relatively trivial matter has not been discussed here.

What consequences does this have for our understanding of connectionism and its relation to classical models of cognition? First, a crucial clarification. While no representation can be both distributed and symbolic, it is quite possible to *represent* a symbolic structure in distributed form - i.e., to have a distributed representation *of* a symbolic structure. (The WM of BoltzCONS is a pertinent example; alternatively, think of a hologram of a page of text.) In such a case the representation itself is distributed while its *content* is a symbolic entity. It is essential to distinguish between the form of a representation and the form of its content, whatever that content may happen to be.

Now, in a recent authoritative restatement of the classical, symbol-processing conception of cognitive processes, Fodor and Pylyshyn have argued that the use of symbolic representations and structure-sensitive processes lies the very heart of that approach. From this and the general incompatibility thesis it follows that *connectionist models based on distributed representations cannot be, or implement, any classical symbolic model.* (The flip side, of course, is this: if the brain turns out in fact to be a genuinely distributed connectionist-style machine, the Language of Thought hypothesis will have been proven false.)

Where does this leave connectionist modeling of cognitive processes? There are, broadly speaking, three basic strategies, each of which currently has its adherents:
(a) Reject distribution in favor of symbolic representations. This strategy directly implements classical symbol-processing models of cognition in purely localist connectionist networks. Note that such an approach may still have computational advantages over standard implementations even if distributed representations and processes are nowhere employed.

(b) Construct hybrid models which utilize various possible combinations of symbolic and distributed representations. DCPS/BoltzCONS is a good example: the WM is a distributed central store, while the real processing takes place on symbols in auxiliary networks.

(c) Reject symbolic representations in favor of a wholesale move to genuinely distributed representations and processes (e.g., Pollack 1988; Chalmers 1990). In cases where symbol structures are themselves the target of processing - e.g., when modeling language processing capacities - this kind of connectionist model operates on the basis of distributed representations *of* the symbol structures in question. Insofar as connectionist modeling takes this third option, it presents a truly radical and interesting new alternative to the classical approach.

In my view the main practical benefit of the analysis sketched in this paper is that it clearly delineates this third approach. It is now apparent that models of cognition can be constructed on the basis of representations and processes that are very different from standard symbolic paradigms, and that this is true even when the domain being modeled itself includes linguistic or symbolic structures. Constructing such models means focusing attention on the distinctive properties of distributed representations themselves, developing optimal distributed schemes, and developing processes suited to dealing with information represented in that form. This shift to the wholly distributed arena has a liberating effect in that cognitive modeling need not be dominated by the kind of algorithmic, rule-governed processes which are only natural as long as information is represented in strictly symbolic form. If this is correct, we should expect the continued emergence of connectionist models in which cognitive functions which previously seemed to require complex symbol-processing are achieved on the basis of direct transformations of distributed representations.

References

Chalmers D.J. (1990) Syntactic transformations on distributed representations. forthcoming in *Connection Science*.

Fodor J. & McLaughlin B. (forthcoming) What is wrong with tensor product connectionism? in Horgan T. & Tienson J. (eds) *Connectionism and the Philosophy of Mind*.

Fodor J.A. & Pylyshyn Z.W. (1988) Connectionism and cognitive architecture: A critical analysis. *Cognition* ; 28: 3-71.

Elman J. L. (1989) Representation and structure in connectionist models. CRL Technical Report 8903, Center for Research in Language, University of California San Diego La Jolla CA 92093.

Haugeland J. (1981) Analog and analog. *Philosophical Topics*; 12: 213-225.

Newell A. and Simon H. (1976) Computer science as an empirical inquiry. *Communications of the Association for Computing Machinery*; 19: 113-126.

Pollack J. (1988) Recursive auto-associative memory: Devising compositional distributed representations. *Proceedings of the Tenth Annual Conference of the Cognitive Science Society. Montreal, Quebec, Canada.*

Pylyshyn Z. (1984) *Computation and Cognition: Toward a Foundation for Cognitive Science.* Cambridge: MIT/Bradford.

Rumelhart and McClelland (1986): On learning the past tenses of English verbs. in McClelland

J.L., Rumelhart D.E. and the PDP Research Group *Parallel Distributed Processing: Explorations in the Microstructure of Cognition*. Cambridge MA: Bradford/MIT Press; 216-271.

Touretzky D.S. & Hinton G.E. (1988) A distributed connectionist production system. *Cognitive Science*; 12: 423-466.

Touretzky D. S. (1989) BoltzCONS: Dynamic Symbol Structures in a Connectionist Network. Technical Report CMU-CS-89-182, Department of Computer Science, Carnegie Mellon. (To appear in a special issue of *Artificial Intelligence* on connectionist symbol processing.)

van Gelder T.J. (1990a) Compositionality: A Connectionist Variation on a Classical Theme. *Cognitive Science* (forthcoming).

— (1990b) What is the 'D' in 'PDP'? An Overview of the Concept of Distribution. forthcoming in Stich S., Rumelhart D. & Ramsey W. (eds) *Philosophy and Connectionist Theory* Hillsdale N.J.: Lawrence Erlbaum Associates 1990.

CONNECTIONIST COGNITION

MARTIN KURTHEN DETLEF B. LINKE PATRICK HAMILTON
Department of Neurosurgery
University Hospital of Bonn
Sigmund-Freud-Str. 25
D - 5300 Bonn 1
FRG

I.

In an influential and provocative paper, Fodor and Pylyshyn (1988) have argued that the architecture of mind cannot be connectionist "at the cognitive level". Very briefly, they maintain that explanation of cognitive capacities requires a domain of complex mental representations with combinatorial syntactic and semantic structure to account for features of cognition like systematicity, compositionality and inferential coherence. Since connectionist models lack these complex representations (while still being committed, as Fodor and Pylyshyn claim, to the concept of representation as such), these models are inadequate for the explanation of cognitive skills. But (so they generously concede) connectionist models might still turn out to be - or be *interpreted as - implementations* of "classical" symbol-processing accounts.

Smolensky (1988) has tried (successfully, in our view) to reject this "implementationalism" by arguing that due to different principles of computation at the sub-conceptual and the conceptual level, there can only be an *approximate* description of "soft" subconceptual processing in "hard" terms (see also Smolensky 1987 for further elaboration of this thesis). In what follows, we will take this rejection of implementationalism for granted, although the development of our argument does not *depend* on the assumption that connectionism provides a genuine alternative to the "classical" symbol-processing paradigm. As for "complex representations", Smolensky (1987) has argued that contrary to Fodor´s and Pylyshyn´s interpretation connectionist models *do* provide the composite structures required for cognitive processing *without* literally implementing a symbolic language of thought (see also Helm 1989 and Goschke and Koppelberg 1990a for arguments in a similar spirit). Leaving this question open, we will now (section II) shortly pursue an argument advanced by Clark (1988 and 1989) to the effect that from the (presumably correct) demand for *structured* representations it does not follow that these representations make up a language of thought in Fodor´s sense. In the final section (III) it is argued that classical and connectionist AI are alike in *not* providing an adequate account of *intentionality* (and hence *cognition)* and that such an account might be given by a teleologically oriented theory of content, the principles of which will be embodied in a connectionist rather than a "classical" system.

II.

In his critique of Fodor (1987) and Fodor and Pylyshyn (1988), Clark (1988 and 1989) focuses on the systematicity argument which can be briefly summarized as follows: "Just as the fact that linguistic capacities are systematic (in that the ´ability to produce/understand some sentences is *intrinsically* connected to the ability to produce/understand certain others´ (Fodor and Pylyshyn 1988: 37)) can only be accounted for if the sentences of the given language have some *constituent structure,* so the systematicity of *thought* can only be explained if *mental representations* have that syntactic and semantic structure, too". Now Clark (1989) holds that this argument fails because it mistakes the *conceptual* fact that belief *ascription* is generally *holistic* in nature (in that the ascription of *one* thought only *makes sense* if a background of a whole network of thoughts is assumed) for an *empirical* fact concerning the "mental lives" of intelligent beings. But the *actual* empirical fact to be explained is just the complexity of the intelligent beings´ *behavior,* a complexity *we* make sense of by ascribing "a systematic network of abstract thoughts" (Clark 1989: 147). And from the fact that these complex behavioral patterns will indeed have to be explained by some underlying "in-the-head--processing", it does not follow that this processing must be systematic in exactly the same sense as the thoughts thus ascribed, although the complexity of our behavior *does* suggest that the underlying processing has *some* sort of recombinatorial structure (see Clark 1988: 615). But if *this* is all the argument from systematicity amounts to, there is no reason to rule out *from the start* the possibility that a connectionist network could do the job (furthermore, there is some *empirical* evidence against Fodor´s and Pylyshyn´s claims as well; see Goschke and Koppelberg 1990b for review).

What makes Fodor (1987) adhere so strongly to "intentional realism", the thesis that beliefs and desires must somehow reappear as *real* structures "in the head" (that is, in the *mind* and, ultimately, in the *brain)?* Is it because he believes that this is the only way to let intentional states function as *causes,* as "parts of the physical story behind intelligent behavior", as Clark (1989: 160) assumes? Well, if the above argument is valid, it is not necessary that beliefs and desires literally act as causes of behavior: "All we need is that there should be *some* physical, causal story, and that talk of beliefs and desires should make sense of behavior" (Clark 1989: 160).

In the following section, we take this statement as a starting point for some critical remarks on Clark. But his counter-argument to the "argument from systematicity" fully survives, so that - contrary to Fodor´s and Pylyshyn´s claims - the question for "connectionist cognition" is left open for further evaluation.

III.

According to Clark, we should neatly seperate two "stories": the causal one, which tells how some in-the-head-processing brings about complex behavior, and the belief/desire story, which is primarily a folk psychological tale aiming at a holistic *interpretation* of such behavior. Although we agree with Clark on the inappropriateness of an amalgamation of the two stories in Fodor´s and Pylyshyn´s way, we still find that one of the goals of a "mature cognitive science" should be to tell *one* coherent story to which the causal and the folk psychological one are finally worked in. In fact, Clark himself tries to make one story out of two later in his book (1989: 196-201) by arguing that beliefs and desires might turn up in a proper causal explanation in scientific psychology *without* being causally efficacious themselves (in his argument, he employs Jackson´s and Pettit´s (1988) distinction between causal *process* and causal *program* explanations; see Rowlands (1989) for a criticism of such a strategy). But this Clarkian story is told in a more or less *instrumentalistic* mood (in that the belief/desire story is found to be a heuristically valuable "vocabulary"; see Clark 1989: 197) - and since *instrumentalism* concerning intentional states is not under consideration in our present argument, we leave this for another occasion.
But *should* we try to make "one story out of two" after all? Well, it depends on what we want to get a theory of: if we are only interested in a neurobiologically grounded theory of complex behavior, we can well focus on the causal story alone. But if our goal is a scientific theory of what we prescientifically *take* to be the core of human (and perhaps animal) intelligence, we have to *relate* the concepts of *that* "cognitive science" to our well-established folk psychological concepts. This is not to be understood as an a priori realistic interpretation of beliefs and desires, since the *final status* of intentional states is entirely left open. It´s just the project of a more ambitious and complete theory. The causal story could only constitute a theory of human cognition if it were able to not only reconstruct the causal chains leading from in-the-head-processing to overt behavior, but also tell us "what happened to" beliefs and desires: did they survive till the end? If not, who killed them and how? - Less metaphorically, it goes like this: even if we recognize *behavior* as the primary explanandum, we cannot simply exclude beliefs and desires from our theory of cognition, for - at least in the case of humans - behavior will be found "intelligent" *only under some folk psychological interpretation*. In Sellars´ (1956) interpretation, inner intentional states can be reconstructed as *theo-*

retical entities introduced in order to account for complex and somehow "intelligence-driven" behavior. According to this view, "thoughts" or beliefs belong to a *second stratum* of concepts pertaining to conceptual activity, a stratum which is superimposed on a *basic stratum* where "thinking" is just a propensity to *utter* the respective sentence (see Sellars 1979: 115-117 for an elaboration of this thesis). The most interesting point in this is that if we take talk about inner intentional states as *theoretical* talk about (primarily) overt verbal behavior, we find that these intentional states are not at all construed as *causal antecedents* of intelligent behavior. It is just that the positing of intentional states renders an "enriched and more subtle account" (Sellars 1979: 117) of intelligent behavior possible, so that thoughts and beliefs simply *are* the behavior "more adequately conceived". They *are* the behavior, now *relocalized* in a stronger theory. So if we hold that the (scientific) story about intelligent behavior will finally turn out to be a story about some in-the-head-processing, concepts pertaining to *neurological* (or *computational,* or whatever) processes and states - as belonging to the third and final stratum of explanation - must prove to be adequate "successor concepts" (to borrow another term from Sellars) of the concepts of the second stratum, viz. the intentional states of folk psychological discourse.

This excursion into Sellarsian thought may help to illustrate our view that a "mature cognitive science" should try to merge Clark´s two stories in the end. The neurological (or computational) story will have to tell us a lot about the lot of intentional states. That is, to count as a complete theory of cognition, both classical symbol-processing and connectionist accounts would have to provide an explanation of *intentionality* in general, that is, the specific *aboutness* of beliefs and desires as semantically characterized states. And it is exactly Fodor´s (1987) claim that *his* version of the classical account (known as the "Representational Theory of Mind") *does* provide such an explanation, while connectionism, dispensing with the idea of a "language of thought", does not. As things now stand, we claim that they both don´t. Our paradigmatic connectionist seems to admit the present incapacity of connectionism in *this* respect and - with an eye on classical accounts - at the same time points to an important *advancement* when he says that "if we succeed in building symbols and symbol manipulation out of ´connectoplasm´ then we will have an explanation of *where symbols and symbol manipulation come from...*" (Smolensky 1987: 141). Indeed, an explanation of where symbols "come from" might help to understand where *intentionality* comes from (see below). But what about Fodor´s account of intentionality? In its most recent guises, the Representational Theory of Mind still traces the intentionality of beliefs and desires back to the semantic content of mental representations: ´to believe that p´ *is* to be in a certain computational relation to a representation the semantic content of which is ´p´. But here the question arises: "Where does that semantic content come from in the first place?" By analogizing the whole set of representations with a *language* in the full sense and by further reducing intentionality to semanticity, Fodor in fact saddles himself with a theory of *meaning.* But the Representational

Theory of Mind does not yield a theory of meaning. For all it says is that (1) "the *syntactic* structure of mental states *mirrors* the *semantic* relations among their intentional objects" (Fodor 1987: 138; our emphasis) and (2) for a token in the language of thought to "be about" (that is, to represent) some thing in the world, a relation of "causally reliable covariation" (Fodor 1987: 119) is sufficient. Now these two claims are problematic in themselves. As for (1), it is quite unclear how a language with the semantic richness of, say, English or German, could be so constituted that its syntax would systematically "mirror" its semantics. Fodor and Pylyshyn (1988: 28f) are optimistic about the possibility to "construct" such a language, but they give us no further reason to share their optimism. And regarding (2), Cummins (1989) has shown that any covariance theory *that is also committed to computationalism* (as in Fodor´s case) fails because it already *presupposes* the notion of representation (and hence content) in that according to computationalism, distal objects and their correlating tokens of Mentalese covary *in virtue of* preexisting representational ressources (stored knowledge etc.; see Cummins 1989: 63 - 66). For in order to *"be about"* a distal object in any cognitively relevant sense, a token of Mentalese must be processed *as a representation of that object;* it´s just being "activated" by some "causal contact" with the represented does not suffice. And this "being processed *as"* a representation surely requires a sort of *embeddedness* into a preexisting network of representational states. Thus the Representational Theory of Mind does not *explain* the semanticity of mental representations, but presupposes it. As Bogdan (1989: 697f) puts it: "...Fodor is talking about the (sufficient) naturalized conditions for *semantic success* (such as concept application), NOT about the antecedent conditions of ... having a concept in the first place. ... I would have thought that the question a naturalizer of psychosemantics must ask is, What makes *brain states* be *about* protons or horses or anything at all?, and not, GIVEN that brain states are about protons or whatever, when do they *succeed to be about* protons or whatever?"
The Representational Theory of Mind *evades* what it had better *faced* in order to contribute to a theory of cognition: an account of *meaning* in the "language of thought". And remember that the very move that made this account of meaning *necessary* in the first place - the assumption of a language-like set of representations - was meant to guarantee the superiority of the classical approach to connectionism. Neither the classical nor the connectionist approach has yet yielded an explanation of *intentionality* (qua semanticity) - but only the connectionists are ready to concede that fact.
So what might a theory of intentionality look like? We are not prepared (indeed, not *able)* to answer *that* question. But at least it seems to us that there is one promising candidate: the teleological theory of content which has been developed mainly by Millikan (1984 and 1989) and eloquently championed by McGinn (1989). We cannot review this theory here, but we can at least point to some of its most interesting facets with regard to the classical/connectionist debate (and add some reflections inspired by this "teleosemantics" and by recent "hermeneutical AI" as

prepared by the work of Winograd and Flores 1986 and brought to our knowledge by Lischka 1987). Very briefly and offhand: if you just *cannot* provide intentionality by stuffing your desired intelligent artifact with rich and subtle symbol manipulations and *then* asking yourself how these symbols might come to "be about" something (that is, be related to "the world"), why don´t you just drop some (implicit or explicit) classical premises and try the other way round? That is,

(1) try to find the basis of intentionality in a system´s being "in the world" and being *related* to it *ab initio* instead of "placing" that system "into" the world and thus artificially seperating it from environmental contexts;

(2) try to explain an intelligent system´s intentionality primarily in terms of its *desires* and *needs* instead of *beliefs* and abstract reasoning (see McGinn 1989: 155). That is, assume that internal states can only "point to" the world "if there is a point *for* the organism in their so pointing" (McGinn 1989: 199). This *"for* the organism" is not the mentalistic "intentional *for"*: it is not assumed that the organism itself must be consciously *aware* of the representational relation between internal states and worldly states of affairs (see also Kurthen 1990: 48 - 64). It is just assumed that the "pointing" or "not pointing" of the internal states *makes a difference* for the success - according to biological standards - of the organism´s actual and future actions;

(3) in AI, try not to *project* your (the programmer´s) rationalistic concepts of cognitive activity into the artifact by providing it with a complete and fixed set of learning (and other) algorithms (see Winograd and Flores 1986, Lischka 1987). Instead, supply your artifact with some basic goals (some objects of *ersatz*-desires) and leave enough room for an *autonomous* development of strategies to achieve those goals;

(4) try to trace back a cognitive system´s intentionality to the ontogenetic (and maybe phylogenetic) *history* of that system instead of just pondering about the final product, ahistorically construed (see also Dennett 1987 and Millikan 1984). Let your artifact have an "infancy", a learning period in which it comes to *(adequately)* react to - and act upon - the world it finds itself placed into and *by that* develops "cognitive skills". Don´t try to create an *"adult* android"...

These four advices are grounded in a general dissatisfaction with the classical approach as exemplified by the RTM. If cognitive theorizing *solipsistically* confines itself to the syntactic characteristics of a system´s "in-the-head-processing", it irreversibly excludes the internal symbols world-relatedness and hence the intentionality of the whole system´s behavior (first advice above). For if the mind is "syntax-driven", *semantics* goes epiphenomenal (see Stich 1983 and McGinn 1989). And the attempt to reintegrate the world-relatedness of the symbols of the language of thought is either *circular* (due to the presupposition of representation; see Cummins´ critique above) or does not arrive at the concept of a representation of something *as something* (if the approach is restricted to the mere *covariance* between a representation and its represented). In order to *achieve* a certain content, an internal state - qua indicating *one* and not *the other* worldly state of affairs -

must have some sort of *relevance to* the organism; it must make a difference for the success of the organism´s behavior (second advice; see also Dretske 1988). And such an acquisition of content will only take place if the cognitive system itself can pass through a period of development (ontogenetically and maybe phylogenetically; fourth advice) and if it can *itself* form and "recruit" (Dretske´s term) the internal structures adequate for the production of successful behavioral output (where "successful" behavior is behavior that leads to the fulfillment of the system´s desires; third advice).

Thus the "teleosemanticist" assumes that a system cannot develop internal states that "are about" things in the world unless their indicating (or not indicating) those worldly things makes a difference *for* that system *as being in the world* and *as being adapted to it.* Now if something like that were true (and we cannot discuss the further pros and cons here), one would indeed expect a *connectionist* system to meet the requirements rather than a classical one. For the classical systems *are* fixed on the symbolic level in so far as they are already supplied with a complete set of "representations" *before* they had a chance to develop genuine world--relatedness and to form and recruit internal structures that are relevant to the achievement of their goals (see also Lischka 1987). By way of contrast, connectionist systems could develop adequate processing patterns primarily on a *subsymbolic* level in a domain of concrete interaction with their environment, thus being free (at least partially) from the rationalistic constraints of the programmer´s pre-understanding of the "standards of cognition" (see Lischka 1987 and, in greater detail, Winograd and Flores 1986 for a criticism of rationalism in cognitive science). Further, these processing patterns could be selected according to their capacity to bring about actions adequate to environmental demands. Thus, the adequateness of the recruited patterns would "make a difference" *for* the system - on the condition that it is equipped with some (probably built-in) basic (equivalents of) "needs" and world-related "goals". - If these differences between classical and connectionist systems *do* hold, we can end with the provisional result that while *both* sorts of systems have hitherto failed to instantiate intentionality (and hence *cognition),* the principles of the theoretical account of intentionality which to us looks most promising will be embodied in a connectionist rather than a classical system.

Acknowledgements
We are indebted to Christoph Lischka and Barbara Becker for having drawn our attention to the problems in the first place and for helpful discussions on the subject afterwards. We are further indebted to our ever-helpful librarian, Mrs. Karin Mutlaq.

REFERENCES

Bogdan, R.J. (1989): Does semantics run the psyche? *Philosophy and Phenomenological Research* 49: 687-700.

Clark, A. (1988): Critical notice: Psychosemantics: the problem of meaning in the philosophy of mind (J.A. Fodor). *Mind* 97: 605-617.

Clark, A. (1989): *Microcognition: philosophy, cognitive science, and parallel distributed processing.* Cambridge, Mass.: MIT Press.

Cummins, R. (1989): *Meaning and mental representation.* Cambridge, Mass.: MIT Press.

Dennett, D. (1987): Evolution, error, and intentionality. In: Dennett, D.: *The intentional stance.* Cambridge, Mass.: MIT Press: 287-321.

Dretske, F. (1988): *Explaining behavior. Reasons in a world of causes.* Cambridge, Mass.: MIT Press.

Fodor, J.A. (1987): *Psychosemantics: the problem of meaning in the philosophy of mind.* Cambridge, Mass.: MIT Press.

Fodor, J.A., Pylyshyn, Z.W. (1988): Connectionism and cognitive architecture: a critical analysis. *Cognition* 28: 3-71.

Goschke, Th., Koppelberg, D. (1990a): Connectionism and the semantic content of internal representation. *Revue Internationale de Philosophie* 172: 87-103.

Goschke, Th., Koppelberg, D. (1990b): The concept of representation and the representation of concepts in connectionist models. *Psychological Research* (in press).

Helm, G. (1989): Klassische vs. konnektionistische Modelle in der Kognitiven Psychologie. In: Becker, B. (Hrsg.): *Zur Terminologie in der Kognitionsforschung.* St. Augustin: GMD: 103-111.

Jackson, F., Pettit, P. (1988): Functionalism and broad content. *Mind* 97: 381-400.

Kurthen, M. (1990): *Das Problem des Bewußtseins in der Kognitionswissenschaft.* Stuttgart: Enke.

Lischka, C. (1987): Über die Blindheit des Wissensingenieurs, die Geworfenheit kognitiver Systeme und anderes... . *KI* 4: 15-19.

McGinn, C. (1989): *Mental content.* Oxford: Basil Blackwell.

Millikan, R.G. (1984): *Language, thought, and other biological categories.* Cambridge, Mass.: MIT Press.

Millikan, R.G. (1989): Biosemantics. *Journal of Philosophy* 86: 281-297.

Rowlands, M. (1989): Discussion of Jackson and Pettit, ´Functionalism and broad content´. *Mind* 98: 269-275.

Sellars, W. (1956): Empiricism and the philosophy of mind. In: Feigl, H., Scriven, M. (eds.): *Minnesota studies in the philosophy of science, Vol. 1.* Minneapolis: University of Minnesota Press: 253-329.

Sellars, W. (1979): *Naturalism and ontology.* Reseda, Cal.: Ridgeview.

Smolensky, P. (1987): The constituent structure of connectionist mental states: a reply to Fodor and Pylyshyn. *The Southern Journal of Philosophy* 26 (Suppl.): 137-160.

Stich, S. (1983): *From folk psychology to cognitive science.* Cambridge, Mass.: MIT Press.

Winograd, T., Flores, F.: *Understanding computers and cognition.* Norwood: Ablex.

On the importance of pictorial representations for the symbolic/subsymbolic distinction

Michael Mohnhaupt
University of Hamburg, Department of Computer Science
Bodenstedtstr. 16, D-2000 Hamburg 50

1 Introduction

This paper is concerned with representational aspects of cognition. It is based on the two assumptions: 1) that cognition is information processing and 2) that mental representations and their manipulation are essential for cognitive processes. Both assumptions are the basis of the cognitive science research program. Given these assumptions there are mainly two different representational positions.

First, the *symbolic* position (e.g. [Fodor + Pylyshyn 88]) that favors the symbol system hypothesis. Symbolic and structured expressions composed of atomic representing entities are favored as representations within this theory, and structure sensitive operations are essential to process these representations. Second, the *subsymbolic*[1] position (e.g. [Smolensky 88]) that proposes the use of simple neuron-like elements as atomic representing entities and local activation and inhibition operations as mode of processing to model cognition. The dominant advocates of the symbolic camp claim that the mind/brain architecture is not connectionist at the cognitive level. On the other hand, the radical advocates of the subsymbolic camp completely reject symbolic accounts for cognition.

There is a third position besides the purely symbolic and the purely subsymbolic position: modeling cognitive processes by exploiting *pictorial* representations (see e.g. [Paivio 71], [Kosslyn 80], [Pinker + Kosslyn 83], [Sterelny 86], [Rehkämper 87], [Lindsay 88]). In general, the model of pictorial representations is supported by: 1) empirical evidence from experiments in psychology and physiology, 2) computational experiments in artificial intelligence, and theoretical insights, e.g., into complexity constraints and the usefulness of different representations and different styles of processing. Pictorial representations are only proposed for modeling a subclass of cognitive phenomena. Additional and more abstract propositional representations are necessarily assumed within these approaches. Typically, propositional representations complement pictorial representation to deal with high-level cognitive functions, e.g., for several aspects of language processing and for recognition. In addition, propositional representations are exploited as long-term memory.

Pictorial representations are mainly favored to model cognitive processes which are based on spatial or spatiotemporal relations between objects and object parts. Typical examples include the computation of spatiotemporal distances between visual objects, e.g., to avoid collisions, the mental rotation of objects, comparing the size of different objects, learning of typical object motion, the prediction of spatiotemporal behavior of objects, or top-down control of visual processes (see e.g. [Kosslyn 80], [Pinker 88], [Gardin + Meltzer 89], [Steels 90], [Mohnhaupt + Neumann 90a], [Mohnhaupt + Neumann 90b]).

In this paper, we focus on the importance of pictorial representations for the symbolic/subsymbolic distinction. Because we see significant evidence for pictorial representations, we want to elaborate what these models contribute to the symbolic/subsymbolic debate. We derive two main conclusions:

1. For two reasons, we view pictorial representations as specialized subsymbolic representations. First, local activation and local inhibition operations are essential for these representations. Second, pictorial representations do not have composed representing entities and structure sensitive operations. The representing entities are typically cells, which mainly represent location information and which are connected to its neighbors. These cells are in the same sense subsymbolic as in classical subsymbolic representations, because they slice represented entities into small atomic pieces (see [Rehkämper 88]).

---

[1] The term subsymbolic might be misleading because of the commitment to mental representations and therefore to symbols (see also [Fodor + Pylyshyn 88]), although these symbols might differ from symbols in 'classical' approaches. But in this paper we use it following Smolensky's definition.

2. Following conclusion one, we reject both the purely subsymbolic and the purely symbolic position. The reason is that using pictorial representations leads automatically to a hybrid representational system including pictorial subsymbolic and propositional symbolic parts. A hybrid model is necessarily assumed within the different approaches on pictorial representations, in psychological studies as well as in computational experiments. Pictorial subsymbolic and propositional symbolic representations are used at different levels of abstraction for different cognitive tasks.

Therefore, the symbolic/subsymbolic debate changes from an 'all or none' question into a 'what is best for which tasks' question. Instead of finding out about one single 'language of thought', we view it as more important to identify subclasses of cognitive tasks, which are based on the same underlying computational architectures and the same style of processing. In addition, it has to be investigated how the different subsystems interact.

In Section 2 we review briefly the current discussion on symbol systems and connectionism. In Section 3 we consider the main empirical and computational arguments for favoring pictorial representations to model several cognitive tasks. In addition, we elaborate why pictorial representations should be viewed as specialized subsymbolic representations, which are complemented by propositional symbolic representations.

2 Symbol Systems and Connectionism

Recent discussions between the subsymbolic position (see [*Smolensky 88*]) and the symbolic position (see [*Fodor + Pylyshyn 88*]) offer very different models for cognition at the representational level. The authors have opposite views about the adequate description language for cognitive phenomena and about the appropriate level of description for many relevant phenomena. Below, we briefly review the two different positions. In addition, we add two general comments to the discussion, one concerning the importance of the debate for cognitive science, and the other concerning an assumption on which the debate is based.

2.1 Symbol Systems

Fodor and Pylyshyn define symbol systems as having representational states with combinatorial syntactic and semantic structure. They postulate one 'language of thought' based on structurally atomic and structurally molecular representations. The semantic content of molecular expressions depends on the semantic content of its syntactic parts. In addition, there are processes operating on the representations which are sensitive to the structure of the representation.

In Fodor and Pylyshyn's view several important aspects of cognition can be appropriately described by symbol systems: First, the unbounded expressive power of language (productivity of thoughts) can be explained only by non-atomic expressions. Second, the systematicity and the compositionality of thoughts should be viewed as a result of applying syntactic rules. Denying syntactic aspects of language would lead to an unnecessarily complex explanation. Third, the inferential coherence of thoughts can also be explained by a syntactic analysis. By inferential coherence the authors refer to several empirical facts, e.g. to the observation that humans know that P can be logically deduced from $P \wedge Q$ if they know that P can be logically deduced from $P \wedge Q \wedge R$. Composed syntactic structures lead to a natural explanation of these empirical observations, because they would result from intrinsic properties of the representation and its processes. Explaining the same effects within a connectionist framework would require additional assumptions in terms of extra explicit connections between different substructures of a connectionist network.

Because composed syntactic expressions and structure sensitive operations cannot be found in the current connectionist framework, following Fodor and Pylyshyn, they draw the conclusion that connectionist theories are insufficient to explain cognition. They view connectionism as an implementation theory at the neural level.

2.2 Connectionism

On the contrary, Smolensky argues that connectionist[2] models can account for many, possibly all cognitive phenomena. He admits that structured expressions and structure sensitive operations are currently not completely understood or missing within connectionist framework, but he views these constructs as less important; in addition he is convinced that they could be developed in future connectionist work.

In his view the adequate description of cognition should be at a subsymbolic level, which is an intermediate level above the neural level but below a symbolic level. It is well suited to describe the 'intuitive processor', which Smolensky views to be the most important cognitive level. The subsymbolic level is composed of representations distributed over a large number of simple atomic neuron-like elements and their dynamic behavior. It is characterized by differential equations: the 'activation evolution equation' describing the temporal evolution of activations within the network, and the 'connection evolution equation' describing the evolution of the connection strength between elements. 'Hard' rules are replaced by 'soft' constraints and logical inference is replaced by statistical inference. The neuron-like style of processing includes local activation and inhibition operations between neighboring elements. It is called subsymbolic or numeric.

Smolensky's view does not eliminate high-level entities like goals, intentions and plans from cognitive theories, but by using the connectionist framework, he tries to explain these phenomena as emerging from the subsymbolic level.

2.3 Two comments

The symbolic/subsymbolic discussion received significant attention within the cognitive science literature. Unfortunately, the debate often leads to the impression that the symbolic/subsymbolic distinction is fundamental to any aspect of cognitive science. The reason for this misinterpretation is that two important questions often remain unanswered: 1) What is the domain of the debate, which aspects of cognitive science are completely unaffected by the debate?, and 2) What are the assumptions on which the discussion is based? Below, we comment on these two questions.

1. According to [Marr 82] information processing tasks like cognition must be understood at three different levels: at the level of the computational theory, at the level of representation and algorithms, and at the implementation level.

   It is important to note that symbolic and subsymbolic theories as described above are mainly concerned with the representational and algorithmic level of cognition.[3] Therefore, the computational theory is largely unaffected, although the choice of an adequate representation can lead to additional insight into the computational theory. But we cannot think of a situation where we discuss a representational system without a computational theory in mind, which is the core of any cognitive theory. Hence, discussing representational theories in isolation is important (and the main focus of this paper), but it does not address other significant questions concerning cognition.

2. The basic assumption underlying the symbolic/subsymbolic discussion in the version described above is the following: All aspects of cognition are based on one single computational architecture including one basic style of processing[4] (see [Newell 80], [Fodor 81], [Pylyshyn 84], [Pylyshyn 87], [Fodor + Pylyshyn 88], [Smolensky 88]). Following this view, the main research goal is to investigate this basic 'language of thought'.

   There are other approaches which reject this strong hypothesis. Basically, proponents of the alternative models postulate that different cognitive task demands require differently adapted computational architectures including different styles of processing.. This is analogous to the concept of different 'virtual machines' in computer science. The number of proposed cognitive

---

[2]By connectionism we refer like Smolensky to PDP models (see [Rumelhart + McClelland 87]); localist models are viewed to be symbolic representations using a connectionist style of processing.

[3]This was also pointed out in a recent article by [Chandrasekaran + Goel + Allemang 88]

[4]In [Clark 89] this assumption is called the uniformity assumption

virtual machines ranges from a small number (see e.g. [Boden 88], [Lindsay 88], [Clark 89], [Zimmer + Engelkamp 88]) to a possibly very large number (see [Minsky 85]).

As an example, consider the two tasks of predicting the path of a baseball in order to catch it, and of predicting the stock market development. The path of the ball is determined by universal physical laws (e.g. about gravity and air friction), and the knowledge necessary to solve the problem is well defined. The task can only be learnt through observation based on visual data and ongoing motor reaction. One very important constraint is the time available for an analysis (less than a second). Also, it seems advantageous to feed back the results of the ongoing analysis to the visual system to constrain the visual processes, which are generally very expensive.

On the other hand the behavior of the stock market is largely nondeterministic and a prediction must be based on a large portion of world knowledge. The knowledge can be acquired through different conscious processes, e.g., tutorial instruction. Universal laws are unknown. There is no obvious low dimensional and fixed parameter space by which the behavior can be modeled. A prediction is not constrained by very fast interaction between sensors and effectors.

Although we cannot rule out that these two tasks (modeled by two very different computational theories) are solved by the same kind of representation and the same style of processing, it does seem unlikely. In general, it seems more likely that the cognitive system consists of several (somewhat) specialized subsystems that are dedicated to certain classes of tasks. For example, subsystems might be specialized to deal specifically with 1) a collection of tasks all related to similar objects, or 2) a collection of tasks, the solutions to which are all well suited to a certain mode of computation. It is this latter type of specialization for which a pictorial subsystem seems to be designed. It is natural to view cognitive tasks in terms of the domain knowledge involved and the appropriate form of computation so that efficient use of modular design can be made.

3 Pictorial representations

Investigating the nature and the causal role of pictorial representations for cognition is a well known research topic since Paivio's work in the early seventies (see [Paivio 71]). The most prominent opponents of the so called 'imagery' debate are Kosslyn ([Kosslyn 80]) and Pylyshyn ([Pylyshyn 84]). Support for pictorial representation can be mainly based on two different kinds of arguments. First, they can be based on empirical results in psychology (e.g., reaction-time experiments and error analysis) and neurophysiology (e.g., experiments on brain damaged patients). Second, support for pictorial representations can be derived from computational experiments in artificial intelligence, and from theoretical considerations, e.g. about complexity constraints and the usefullness of different representations and different styles of processing.

3.1 Experimental and computational evidence

From research in Psychology, there is significant evidence for a distinct pictorial subsystem. Many empirical results can be explained by assuming an 2-dimensional image-like representation in which spatiotemporal relations (e.g. spatiotemporal neighborhood) of objects are explicitly available (see e.g. [Shepard 78], [Kosslyn 80], [Pinker + Kosslyn 83], [Pinker 85], and [Pinker 88]). There is also evidence that this representation is shared by perceptual and cognitive processes ([Finke 85]). Here, we do not review the experiments in detail, an excellent overview can be found in [Finke + Shepard 86] and [Finke 89]. The main empirical phenomena for which a pictorial subsystem leads to a natural explanation are the following: 1) identification and comparison tasks for viewed and imagined objects, 2) constraints on the resolution of non-visible objects, 3) judgement tasks for distances and angles between objects, 4) spatial transformation tasks of objects, e.g. mental rotation, 5) results on the interference of perceptual and cognitive tasks, and 6) conditions under which perception can be enhanced by cognition.

Recent findings in neurology also support the cognitive plausibility of a pictorial subsystem. These results suggest that: 1) mental images interact with perceptions (see [Farah 85], [Farah + Peronnet + Gonon + Giard 88]), and 2) the pictorial system itself is composed of distinguishable subsystems

(see [Farah 85], [Kosslyn 87], [Farah + Hammond + Levine + Calvanio 88], [Farah + Hammond 88]).
In particular, experiments on impaired patients show that a visual[5] pictorial representation can be
distinguished from a spatial[6] pictorial representation.

Additional evidence for the usefullness of pictorial representations results from computational experiments and theoretical considerations. The main goals of these investigations are: 1) to answer
the question why a pictorial representation would make sense for several information processing tasks
from a computational point of view, and 2) to develop criteria to evaluate and to compare different
representational schemes. Computational experiments are also important to test different representational frameworks, e.g. for consistency and temporal behavior. The different computational models
have different degrees of psychological plausibility. The main tasks for which computational aspects of
pictorial representations have been investigated are:

- *Understanding the behavior of physical objects and physical systems:* There are several approaches
  that model the behavior of physical objects using a quantitative spatial or quantitative spatiotemporal representation. In Funt's ([Funt 80]) approach, the interference of falling objects can be
  predicted using a spatial array and local operations to simulate object motion. [Gardin + Meltzer
  89] also use a pictorial representation. They express the behavior of non-rigid objects and liquids
  by local interaction rules within a 2-dimensional representation. Inferences can be derived through
  simulation. In [Larkin + Simon 87] diagrammatic representations are exploited to understand
  the behavior of physical systems, e.g. pulley problems.

- *Path planning:* Steels ([Steels 88]) proposes a model to compute a path through obstacles based
  on a 2-dimensional array and a reaction-diffusion model of local interaction rules. [Mohnhaupt
  + Neumann 90a] use an explicit 4-dimensional representation (two spatial and two velocity dimensions) and local rules to model the behavior of observed objects. The model allows to predict
  object motion in the presence of obstacles and to predict the interference of moving objects.

- *Understanding verbal descriptions:* Other approaches are concerned with the use of pictorial
  representations to understand spatiotemporal relations such as the proposition 'in front of', to
  understand abstract descriptions (e.g. propositional descriptions of geometric figures) and to understand language in general. By visualizing the content of the description, that is filling relevant
  information into a pictorial representation, inferences can be simplified, previously implicit information is available, and consistency can be checked. (see e.g. [Gelernter 63], [Waltz + Boggess
  79], [Kosslyn 80], [Adorni and Di Manzo 83], [Pribbenow 90]). There are also indications that
  a pictorial representation is advantageous for an adequate hearer model in some domains (see
  [Neumann + Novak 86]).

- *High-level control of perceptual processes:* This topic has mainly been investigated in computational vision, e.g. in the areas of expectation-based identification of objects or object motion (see
  [Binford 82], [Tsotsos 87] for overviews). Typically, object models can be used to compute the
  spatiotemporal appearence of objects from a certain viewpoint, which is then used for matching against bottom-up data provided by perceptual processes. The representation of a certain
  viewpoint is represented pictorially[7] to facilitate the matching process. In the area of motion
  prediction, [Mohnhaupt + Neumann 90b] use pictorial event models to predict the behavior
  of moving objects. The predictions allow to focus the visual processes and thereby lead to a
  significant speed up.

  The use of pictorial representations for top-down control of visual processes is psychologically
  plausible: It is known (see [Rosch + Mervis + Gray + Johnson + Boyes-Bream 76], [Rosch
  78]) that information about basic level categories can facilitate perception, but priming with
  a superordinate category does not lead to a significant speed up. Basic level categories are

---

[5]for representing the appearence of objects
[6]for representing spatial relations between objects
[7]There are also logic-based representations for high-level vision (see [Reiter + Mackworth 90], and see [Provan 90]
for counterarguments)

the highest level of abstraction for which there is a clearly definable visual shape. Rosch and coauthors conclude that top-down control is performed by forming mental images, which cannot be generated from superordinate categories. The results are consistent with a complexity level analysis of visual processes (see [*Tsotsos 90*] and [*Mohnhaupt + Neumann 90c*]).

Learning: In [*Mohnhaupt + Neumann 89*] and [*Mohnhaupt + Neumann 90a*] several learning tasks with respect to object motion are considered using a pictorial representation. Starting with basic physical observables (location and speed) for describing event instances, typical object motion can be learned using local operations. There is a natural transition from single instances to prototypes. To make experience applicable to new situations, perceptual primitives like distances and relative orientations are computed. They can be extracted within the pictorial representation by simple spreading activation operations. This kind of representation as a starting point for further learning is plausible, because it is closely related to and can therefore be directly filled from perceptual processes. By building the model from observations within the pictorial representation, physical plausibility can be maintained without extra computation.

3.2 Central features

In this subsection we summarize important *computational* and *representational* features of pictorial representations. The representational features are then exploited to relate theories on pictorial representations to the symbolic/subsymbolic distinction.

The computational experiments on pictorial representations show that even if two representations are equivalent in terms of information content, they can differ drastically with respect to their temporal characteristics, e.g. the time needed to access relevant information. There are theoretical results showing the limitations with respect to tractability and efficiency of a general purely logic-based framework (see e.g. [*Levesque 86*]). Choosing representations which are specialized as a consequence of incorporated constraints of a particular domain is one way to overcome the limitations. Another strategy is to make relevant information explicit (see [*Palmer 78*]), that is, accessible at low costs. Of course, there is a trade-off between explicitness of information and storage requirements. In addition, several important physical constraints can be made intrinsic within pictorial representations. For example, the representation in [*Steels 90*] automatically allows only one object per position. Dynamic behavior; e.g. the behavior of moving objects, can be coded by explicit representation of the temporal dimension or by local interaction rules. Inferences can be derived through simulation. The inference process is non-proof-procedural ([*Lindsay 88*]). Physical plausibility can also be maintained by building up the models from concrete observations and subsequent local processing.

Pictorial representation allow for a natural integration of bottom-up perceptual data and top-down information computed from cognitive processes. This is advantageous because many cognitive processes are either based on visual data, or relate to visual data.

The symbolic/subsymbolic distinction is based on representational features (see Section 2), that is characteristics of the representing entities and the mode of processing. From this perspective two features are central to pictorial representations: 1) they are **subsymbolic**, and 2) they are **short-term** representations, which are complemented by propositional symbolic long-term representations. In the following, we focuss on these two aspects in more detail.

The representing entities of pictorial representations are typically cells connected to its local neighbors. They divide the spatial content and possibly other dimensions of a represented entity into small pieces. For example, a house can be represented by a rectangular set of connected cells, each representing a certain location on the xy-plane, or a non-rigid moving bar can be represented by set of connected cells each representing a certain piece of the bar. The cells as representing entities are in Smolensky's sense subsymbolic. They slice the represented entity into small entities (symbols) which are similar to entities in a distributed representation within the connectionist framework. The entities do not have any syntactic substructure.

The mode of processing includes the use of simple, local and parallel operations. The operations are either activation and inhibition operations or local search operations. They are used for different tasks, e.g. to compute spatial relations, or to compute a path through obstacles. There is no dependence on structural properties of the cell or its connected neighbors, the local search operations only depend on scalar values of the neighbors. Hence, the operations share important properties with operations in connectionist networks.

Pictorial representations are short-term representations complemented by symbolic long-term representations. The different approaches agree on the need for additional, more abstract, symbolic representations, e.g. to support long-term memory, for recognition, and for natural language communication. There is psychological evidence that pictorial representations do not serve as long-term memory (e.g. [Phillips 83], [Marschark 88]), but that they are instantiated on demand from long-term memory (see [Kosslyn 80], [Pinker 88], [Kosslyn + Cave + Provost + Gierke 88]).

From a computational point of view, efficiency supplies strong reasons to assume representations in long-term memory, which are more abstract and more compact than pictorial representations. Several computational models exploit propositional symbolic long-term representations for high-level tasks. For example, object recognition and event recognition is mainly treated within propositional frameworks (see e.g. [Tsotsos 87] [Neumann + Novak 83], [Andre + Bosch + Herzog + Rist 86]). It is interesting to note that a more fine-grained recognition might require an interplay between a propositional representation and a pictorial representation (see [Mohnhaupt + Neumann 90a]).

The work on event recognition also shows that propositional descriptions are well suited as a starting point for natural language communication. In [Neumann + Novak 86] propositional event models are used to fill a case-frame deep structure for natural language generation. The arguments for using 'classical' symbolic models in this domain are similar to the arguments by Fodor and Pylyshyn (see Section 2).

4 Summary

Within cognitive science several different representational theories are under investigation. Two extreme positions include those that favor a symbol system hypothesis and those that favor a subsymbolic account for cognition. We argue in favor of a theory which consists of both, symbolic and subsymbolic parts. Our argumentation is based on the importance of theories on pictorial representations for the symbolic/subsymbolic distinction. It consists of three steps:

First, there is empirical and computational evidence supporting Fodor's and Pylyshyn's arguments, that there are some tasks which can only be modeled by a symbolic representation, mainly in the area of language understanding. But this does not exclude different representations for other tasks. In fact, there is empirical and computational evidence that pictorial representations are used for several important tasks, e.g. for the computation of spatiotemporal relations between objects, mental rotation, path planning, and several prediction tasks with respect to object motion. For efficiency reasons and empirical evidence, pictorial representations are short-term representations instantiated under certain definable condition as a 'cognitive virtual machine'.

Second, we view pictorial representations as subsymbolic representations because local activation and local inhibition operations are essential for these representations. In addition, there are no composed representing entities and no structure sensitive operations within these approaches. The representing entities are in the same sense subsymbolic as in classical subsymbolic representations, because they slice a represented entity into small atomic pieces.

Third, modeling some cognitive processes with pictorial short-term representations necessarily results in rejecting the purely subsymbolic and the purely symbolic model. The reason is that additional symbolic long-term representations which complement pictorial subsymbolic short-term representation are viewed to be necessary. This leads to a hybrid model which includes subsymbolic and symbolic parts at different levels of abstraction for different tasks.

Following our view, the symbolic/subsymbolic debate changes from an 'all or none' question into a 'what is best for which tasks' question. Therefore, instead of finding out about the 'language of thought', it is more important to identify subclasses of cognitive tasks, which are based on the same

underlying computational architectures and the same style of processing, and to investigate how dif
ferent subsystems interact.

Acknowledgements: I thank Bernd Neumann and Klaus Rehkämper for many interesting discussions, and
I thank David Fleet and Siegfried Stiehl for comments on an earlier version of this paper.

References

[Adorni and Di Manzo 83] *Top-down Approaches to Scene Interpretation.* G. Adorni, M. Di Manzo. Proc.
CIL 83, Barcelona, Spain, June 1983.

[Andre + Bosch + Herzog + Rist 86] *Characterizing Trajectories of Moving Objects Using Natural Language
Path Descriptions.* E. Andre, G. Bosch, G. Herzog, T. Rist. in Proc. 7th ECAI, 1986.

[Binford 82] *Survey of Model-Based Image Analysis Systems.* Thomas O. Binford. *International Journal of
Robotics* **1** (1982) 18-64.

[Boden 88] *Computer Models of Mind.* Margret A. Boden. Cambridge University Press, 1988.

[Boff + Kaufman + Thomas 86] *Handbook of Perception and Human Performance, Volume I + II.* Kenneth
R. Boff, Lloyd Kaufman, James P. Thomas. John Wiley and Sons, 1986.

[Chandrasekaran + Goel + Allemang 88] *Connectionism and Information-Processing Abstractions.* B. Chan-
drasekaran, Ashok Goel, Dean Allemang. *AI Magazine* **Winter** (1988) 24-34.

[Clark 89] *Connectionism and the multiplicity of mind.* A. Clark. *Artificial Intelligence Review* **3** (1989)
49-65.

[Denis + Engelkamp + Richardson 88] *Cognitive and Neuropsychological Approaches to Mental Imagery.* M.
Denis, J. Engelkamp, J. T. E. Richardson (Ed.). Martinus Nijhoff Publisher 1988.

[Farah 85] *A neurological basis of mental imagery: A componential analysis.* Martha J. Farah. in 'Visual
Cognition', Steven Pinker (Ed.), MIT Press 1985.

[Farah 85] *Psychophysical Evidence for a Shared Representational Medium for Mental Images and Percepts.*
Martha J. Farah. *Journal on Experimental Psychology: General* **114** (1985) 91-103.

[Farah + Hammond 88] *Mental rotation and orientation-invariant object recognition: Dissociable processes.*
Martha J. Farah, Katherine M. Hammond. *Cognition* **29** (1988) 29-46.

[Farah + Hammond + Levine + Calvanio 88] *Visual and Spatial Mental Imagery: Disassociable Systems of
Representations.* Martha J. Farah, Katherine M. Hammond, David N. Levine, Ronald Calvanio. *Cognitive Psychology* **20** (1988) 439-462.

[Farah + Peronnet + Gonon + Giard 88] *Electrophysiological Evidence for a Shared Representational Medium
for Visual Images and Visual Percepts.* Martha J. Farah, Franck Peronnet, Marie A. Gonon, Marie H.
Giard. *Journal of Experimental Psychology: General* **117** (1988) 248-257.

[Finke 85] *Theories Relating Mental Imagery to Perception.* Ronald A. Finke. *Psychological Bulletin* **98** (1985)
236-259.

[Finke 89] *Principles of mental imagery.* Ronald A. Finke. A Bradford Book, MIT Press 1989.

[Finke + Shepard 86] *Visual Functions of Mental Imagery.* Ronald A. Finke, Roger N. Shepard. in *Boff +
Kaufman + Thomas 86.*

[Fodor 81] *Representations.* Jerry A. Fodor. MIT Press, Cambridge, Mass. 1981.

[Fodor + Pylyshyn 88] *Connectionism and Cognitive Architecture: A Critical Analysis.* Jerry A. Fodor, Zenon
W. Pylyshyn. *Cognition* **28** (1988) 3-71.

[Funt 80] *Problem solving with diagrammatic representations.* B. V. Funt. *Artificial Intelligence* **13** (1980)
201-230.

[Gardin + Meltzer 89] *Analogical Representation of Naive Physics*. Francesco Gardin, Bernhard Meltzer. *Artificial Intelligence* **38** (1989) 139-159.

[Gelernter 63] *Realization of a geometry theorem-proving machine*. H. Gelernter. in 'Computer and thought', E. Feigenbaum and J. Feldman (Ed.), McGraw Hill 1963.

[Kosslyn 80] *Image and Mind*. Stephen M. Kosslyn. Harvard University Press, 1980.

[Kosslyn 87] *Seeing and Imagining in the Cerebal Hemispheres: A Computational Approach*. Stephen M. Kosslyn. Psychological Review, 94, 1987, pp. 148-175.

[Kosslyn + Cave + Provost + Gierke 88] *Sequential Processes in Image Generation*. Stephen M. Kosslyn, Carolyn Backer Cave, David A. Provost, Susanne M. von Gierke. *Cognitive Psychology* **20** (1988) 319-343.

[Larkin + Simon 87] *Why a Diagramm is (Sometimes) Worth Ten Thousand Words*. Jill H. Larkin, Herbert A. Simon. *Cognitive Science* **11** (1987) 65-99.

[Levesque 86] *Making Believers out of Computers*. Hector J. Levesque. *Artificial Intelligence* **30** (1986) 81-108.

[Lindsay 88] *Images and inference*. Robert K. Lindsay. *Cognition* **29** (1988) 229-250.

[Marr 82] *Vision*. David Marr. W. H. Freeman, San Francisco 1982.

[Marschark 88] *The Functional Role of Imagery in Cognition*. Marc Marschark. in *Denis + Engelkamp + Richardson 88*, pp. 405-417.

[Minsky 85] *The Society of Mind*. Marvin Minsky. Touchstone Book, Simon and Schuster, 1985.

[Mohnhaupt + Neumann 89] *Some aspects of learning and reorganisation in an analogical representation*. Michael Mohnhaupt, Bernd Neumann. in 'Knowledge representation and organisation in machine learning', K. Morik (Ed.), Lecture Notes in Artificial Intelligence, Springer Verlag 1989, pp. 50-64.

[Mohnhaupt + Neumann 90a] *Understanding Object Motion: Recognition, Learning and Spatio-Temporal Reasoning*. Michael Mohnhaupt, Bernd Neumann. to appear in 'Journal of Robotics and Autonomous Systems', North Holland 1990.

[Mohnhaupt + Neumann 90b] *On the Use of Motion Concepts for Top-Down Control in Traffic Scenes*. Michael Mohnhaupt, Bernd Neumann. Proc. European Conf. on Computer Vision ECCV-1, 1990, 598-601, Antibes (France), O. Faugeras (Ed.), Springer Verlag.

[Mohnhaupt + Neumann 90c] *Support for an intermediate pictorial representation*. Michael Mohnhaupt, Bernd Neumann. Commentary, to appear in *The Behavioral and Brain Science* **13** (1990) .

[Neumann + Novak 83] *Event models for recognition and natural-language description of events in real-world image sequences*. Bernd Neumann, Hans-Joachim Novak. Proc. Int. Joint Conf. on Art. Intell. IJCAI-8, 1983, 724-726.

[Neumann + Novak 86] *NAOS: Ein System zur natürlichsprachlichen Beschreibung zeitveränderlicher Szenen*. Bernd Neumann, Hans-Joachim Novak. *Informatik Forsch. Entw.* 1 (1986) 83-92.

[Newell 80] *Physical Symbol Systems*. Allan Newell. *Cognitive Science* 4 (1980) 135-83.

[Palmer 78] *Fundamental Aspects of Cognitive Representation*. S. P. Palmer. in: E. Rosch, B.B. Lloyd (Ed.): Cognition and Categorisation, Hillsdale, N.Y.: Erlbaum Press 1978.

[Paivio 71] *Imagery and verbal processes*. Allan Paivio. Holt, Rinehart and Winston, New York 1971.

[Phillips 83] *Short-term visual memory*. W. A. Phillips. Phil. Trans. R. Soc. Lond., B 302, pp. 295-309, 1983.

[Pinker 85] *Visual Cognition: An Introduction*. Steven Pinker. in 'Visual Cognition', Steven Pinker (Ed.), MIT Press 1985.

[Pinker 88] *A computational theory of the mental imagery medium.* Steven Pinker. in *Denis + Engelkamp + Richardson 88*, pp. 17-32.

[Pinker + Kosslyn 83] *Theories of Mental Imagery.* Steven Pinker, Stephen M. Kosslyn. in A. A. Sheikh (Ed.) 'Imagery: Current Theory, Research and Application', New York, Wiley 1983.

[Pribbenow 90] *Interaktion von propositionalen und bildhaften Repräsentationen.* Simone Pribbenow. in 'Repräsentation und Verarbeitung räumlichen Wissens', C. Freksa und C. Habel (Hrsg.), Springer Verlag 1990.

[Provan 90] *An analysis of knowledge representation schemes for high-level vision.* Gregory M. Provan. Proc. European Conf. on Computer Vision ECCV-1, 1990, 537-41, Antibes (France), O. Faugeras (Ed.), Springer Verlag.

[Pylyshyn 84] *Computation and Cognition.* Zenon W. Pylyshyn. MIT Press, Cambridge, Mass. 1984.

[Pylyshyn 87] *What's in a Mind?.* Zenon W. Pylyshyn. *Synthese* 70 (1987) 97-122.

[Rehkämper 87] *Mentale Bilder und Wegbedeutungen.* Klaus Rehkämper. Proc. German Workshop on Artificial Intelligence GWAI-11, 1987, 296-305.

[Rehkämper 88] *Mentale Bilder - Analoge Repräsentationen.* Klaus Rehkämper. LILOG-Report 65, IBM Deutschland, Oktober 1988.

[Reiter + Mackworth 90] *A Logical Framework for Depiction and Image Interpretation.* Raymond Reiter, Alan K. Mackworth. *Artificial Intelligence* 41 (1990) 125-155.

[Rosch 78] *Principles of Categorization.* Eleanor Rosch. in: E. Rosch, B.B. Lloyd (Ed.): Cognition and Categorisation, Hillsdale, N.Y.: Erlbaum Press 1978.

[Rosch + Mervis + Gray + Johnson + Boyes-Bream 76] *Basic Objects in Natural Categories.* Eleanor Rosch, Corolyn B. Mervis, Wayne D. Gray, David M. Johnson, Penny Boyes-Bream. *Cognitive Psychology* 8 (1976) 382-439.

[Rumelhart + McClelland 87] *Parallel Distributed Processing I + II.* David E. Rumelhart, James L. McClelland and the PDP research group. MIT Press, Cambridge, Mass. 1987.

[Shepard 78] *The Mental Image.* Roger N. Shepard. *American Psychologist* 33 (125-137) .

[Smolensky 88] *On the Proper Treatment of Connectionism.* P. Smolensky. *The Behavioral and Brain Science* 11 (1988) 1-74.

[Steels 88] *Steps Towards Common Sense.* Luc Steels. Proc. 8th ECAI, 1988, pp. 49-54.

[Steels 90] *Exploiting Analogical Representations.* Luc Steels. to appear in 'Journal of Robotics and Autonomous Systems', North Holland 1990.

[Sterelny 86] *The Imagery Debate.* Kim Sterelny. *Philosophy of Science* 53 (1986) 560-85.

[Tsotsos 87] *Image Understanding.* John K. Tsotsos. in: S. Shapiro (Ed.), The encyclopedia of artificial intelligence, 389-409, John Wiley and Sons, New York.

[Tsotsos 90] *Analyzing Vision at the Complexity Level.* John K. Tsotsos. to appear in *The Behavioral and Brain Science* (1990) , Cambridge University Press.

[Waltz + Boggess 79] *Visual Analog Representations for Natural Language Understanding.* David L. Waltz, Lois Boggess. Proc. Int. Joint Conf. on Art. Intell. IJCAI-6, 1979, 926-934.

[Zimmer + Engelkamp 88] *Informationsverarbeitung zwischen Modalitätsspezifität und propositionalem Einheitssystem.* Hubert D. Zimmer, Johannes Engelkamp. in 'Wissensarten und ihre Darstellung', G. Heyer u.a. (Hrsg.), Springer Verlag 1988.

Struktur und Konzeptrelationen in verteilten Netzwerken[1]

Martin Rotter   Georg Dorffner

Institut für Med. Kybernetik und Artificial Intelligence, Universität Wien
und Österreichisches Forschungsinstitut für Artificial Intelligence

Zusammenfassung

Es wird an verteilten konnektionistischen Modellen gerne kritisiert, daß sie nicht in der Lage wären, komplexe Beziehungen zwischen Konzepten in Form von Strukturen eindeutig darzustellen (Fodor & Pylyshyn 1988). In diesem Artikel soll argumentiert werden, daß dies auf einem inkorrekten Verständnis solcher Modelle beruht, und daß Konzeptbeziehungen sehr wohl in verteilten Aktivierungsmustern einen Niederschlag finden können. Dazu wird zunächst beschrieben, was Struktur in einem subsymbolischen Modell bedeuten sollte; danach wird ein Lösungsansatz – die Bindingvektor-Repräsentation – vorgeschlagen und anhand eines Beispiels beleuchtet. Dieser Ansatz geht von der strengen Auffassung klassischer Symbolstrukturen ab und unterscheidet sich daher von anderen Lösungsvorschlägen, wie zum Beispiel denen von Smolensky (1987) oder Schnelle & Doust (in press).

Einleitung

Zwischen einem informationsverarbeitenden System und dessen Außenwelt besteht eine wechselseitige Beziehung: Einflüsse von außen werden vom System aufgenommen und verarbeitet, wonach gegebenenfalls eine Reaktion des Systems auf die Außenwelt zurückwirkt. Umgekehrt kann auch das informationsverarbeitende System selbst auf die Außenwelt einwirken und so eine Reaktion dieser hervorrufen.

Beide Seiten halten sich dabei an ganz bestimmte „Spielregeln": Den Ereignissen der Außenwelt liegt eine Ordnung (Struktur) zugrunde, die ein Lernen über diese Ereignisse ermöglicht; die verarbeitenden Systeme versuchen, die Ordnung zu entdecken, zu lernen und so immer mehr über die Außenbedingungen in Erfahrung zu bringen. Die „Gesetzmäßigkeiten" der Außenwelt sind dabei nicht völlig begründbar, klar ist hingegen, daß informationsverarbeitende Systeme Gesetze kennen *müssen*, um bestehen zu können.

Um aber den äußeren Gesetzmäßigkeiten folgen zu können, muß das informationsverarbeitende System für diese eine innere Entsprechung finden.

In diesem Artikel soll die Möglichkeit betrachtet werden, *Struktur* in Netzwerken darzustellen, also eine solche innere Entsprechung zu implementieren. Dazu wäre zunächst eine Definition von „Struktur" angebracht. Dies führt aber zu der Schwierigkeit, daß Struktur meist klassisch – d.h. prädikatenlogisch – definiert ist, verteilte konnektionistische Modelle aber ein grundsätzlich anderer Ansatz sind. Daher brauchen Netzwerke eine eigene – konnektionistische – Definition von Struktur. Ziel soll es somit sein, den Unterschied zwischen beiden Auffassungen von Struktur zu beschreiben, und so den konnektionistischen Standpunkt zu verdeutlichen.

---

1 Diese Arbeit wurde vom Öst. Bundesministerium f. Wissenschaft und Forschung unterstützt.

Konzeptstrukturen und das Bindingproblem

Die Bausteine klassischer Informationsbeschreibungen sind *Symbole*. Diese sind unteilbar und können zu Symbolstrukturen zusammengesetzt werden. Der grundlegende Mechanismus zur Erzeugung von Symbolstrukturen besteht darin, Argumente und einen Relationsbegriff zusammenzubinden, und zwar *in richtiger Reihenfolge*. Diese Reihenfolge wird meist implizit durch die Reihenfolge des „Hinschreibens" bestimmt (z.B. $p(a_1,...,a_n)$), kann aber auch explizit angegeben werden, z.B. durch Durchnumerieren: $\{\{0,p\},\{1,a_1\},\{2,a_2\},...,\{n,a_n\}\}$. Wir nennen im folgenden die Argumente einer Struktur *„Konstituenten"*, ihre Reihenfolge *„Konstellation"*.

Diesem klassischen Symbolbegriff wird in der Beschreibung verteilter konnektionistischer Modelle jener des *Konzeptes* entgegengesetzt. Ein Konzept bildet ebenfalls eine Entität ab, aber auf eine andere Weise: Konnektionistische Konzepte sind nie atomar, sondern immer zusammengesetzt. Die Teilung in immer mehr Untereinheiten (Teile, Features) findet zwar auch bei kleinsten Einheiten – den Units eines Netzwerkes – ein Ende. Diese stellen aber selbst keine Konzepte dar.

Für eine „subsymbolische" Repräsentation wird nämlich vorausgesetzt, daß die Units noch keine direkte Interpretation – so wie Symbole – besitzen. Units stellen damit keine klar definierten Eigenschaften sondern „Mikrofeatures" dar. Mikrofeatures entsprechen winzigen Teileigenschaften, welche mit der (symbolischen) menschlichen Sprache nicht mehr beschreibbar sind. Eine kleine Menge von Mikrofeatures zusammengenommen stellt auch noch kein Konzept dar. Vielmehr aktiviert ein Konzept eine sehr große Anzahl von Units, also ein charakteristisches über viele Units verteiltes Muster von Mikrofeatures. Darstellungen dieser Art werden daher auch als „verteilte" bezeichnet.

Ein wichtiger formaler Unterschied im Aufbau von Symbolen und Konzepten ist dabei zu beachten: Während Symbole – wie oben beschrieben – sich mit Hilfe des Kompositionalitätsprinzips Struktur aneignen können, sind Konzeptdarstellungen nur aus Mengen aktivierter Units zusammengesetzt. Und an eben dieser Stelle melden sich Kritiker mit folgenden Überlegungen:

Wenn nämlich ein zusammengesetztes Konzept, z.B. der Satz *„Hans liebt Maria"* aus seinen Teilkonzepten *Hans, Maria* und *lieben* dargestellt werde, so geschehe dies nur durch Aktivieren der Teilkonzepte. Das heißt, daß eine Mengenvereinigung der Unitmengen, die die drei Konzepte darstellen, gebildet wird: *{Maria,Hans,lieben}*. Aus einer Vereinigungsmenge sei aber nur ersichtlich, aus welchen Konstituenten das Gesamtkonzept bestehe, nicht aber in welcher Konstellation diese zueinander stehen. Daher sei es unmöglich, die Darstellungen von *„Hans liebt Maria"* und *„Maria liebt Hans"* zu unterscheiden, da beide aus der Vereinigung der selben Teilkonzepte bestehen.

Es müßte also z.B. dem Konzept *Hans* (bzw. *Maria*) das Konzept *Subjekt* (bzw. *Objekt*) zugeordnet sein, damit eine explizite Beschreibung der Konstellation die Reihenfolge definiert. Für eine derartige „Zuordnung" genüge es aber nicht, die Vereinigungsmenge aller Konzeptdarstellungen zu bilden, da aus der Menge *{Maria,Hans,lieben,Subjekt,Objekt}* wieder nicht ersichtlich ist, ob nun *Hans* oder *Maria* das Objekt oder das Subjekt sei.

Vielmehr müßte das Gesamtkonzept durch verschachtelte Mengen beschrieben werden: *{{Maria,Objekt},{Hans,Subjekt},lieben}*. Dies sei aber mittels Aktivierung der Teilkonzepte allein nicht verwirklichbar, weil dadurch nur beschrieben werde, welche Konzepte beteiligt sind

(Konstituenteninformation), nicht aber welche *zusammengebunden* sind (Konstellationsinforma-
tion). Diese Schwierigkeit hat folglich die Bezeichnung „Bindingproblem" erhalten.

Konnektionistische Struktur

In diesem Artikel soll gezeigt werden, daß konnektionistische Modelle sehr wohl Struktur darstellen können. Es wird aber eine andere Art von Struktur sein, die dennoch in ihren Möglichkeiten
mit den üblichen Strukturdarstellungen vergleichbar ist.

Dazu muß zunächst beachtet werden, daß das menschliche Denken sowohl auf einer bewußten
als auch auf einer nicht-bewußten Ebene abläuft: Die symbolische Strukturauffassung deckt sich
am ehesten mit der bewußten. In subsymbolischen Repräsentationen wird aber versucht, zunächst
die nicht-bewußte und auch nicht-symbolische „Datenverrechnung" zu modellieren, weshalb der
symbolische Strukturbegriff nicht unreflektiert übernommen werden darf. Wo eine derartige
Struktur anzusiedeln ist, kann folgendes Verhältnis verdeutlichen:

$$\frac{\text{klassisches Symbol}}{\text{verteiltes Konzept}} \; :: \; \frac{\text{klassische Struktur}}{\text{„verteilte" Struktur}}$$

Es soll also eine „verteilte" Strukturdarstellung gefunden werden, die sich von der klassischen so
unterscheidet, wie ein verteiltes Konzept von einem klassischen Symbol. Dadurch sollten die
Vorteile, die Konzepte gegenüber Symbolen haben, auch auf das Prinzip einer „verteilten" Struktur übertragbar sein.

Folgende zusätzliche Eigenschaften müßte diese verteilte Struktur haben:

◇ Zunächst wird nur gefordert, daß verschiedene Relationen zwischen Konzepten unterschiedliche interne Zustände hervorrufen können, sodaß das System unterschiedlich darauf reagieren
kann. Die Struktur der Beschreibung (Beziehungen disjunkter Elemente) muß nicht in der Struktur des Aktivierungsmusters reflektiert sein.

◇ Eine verteilte Strukturdarstellung muß nur diejenigen Aspekte beinhalten, die im assoziativen
und intuitiven Handeln eine Rolle spielen. So ist etwa die Relation „Objekt *A* ist oberhalb von
Objekt *B*" beim assoziativen Erkennen relevant, während „Hans liebt Maria" sehr oft sequen-
tielles Schließen voraussetzt.

◇ Sie muß hauptsächlich lokale Beziehungen ausdrücken können. So ist es etwa kaum notwendig,
ein Objekt auf allen Ebenen einer Begriffshierarchie (z.B. *Pudel, Hund, Haustier, Tier, Ding*) mit
allen seinen Eigenschaften (z.B: *schwarz, Kraushaar, weiblich*, etc.) gleichzeitig darstellen zu
können. Das Erkennen dieser multiplen Beschreibungsebenen setzt ebenfalls sequentielle und
sogar bewußte oder bewußtmachende Prozesse voraus.

◇ Sie muß keineswegs immer vollständig und fehlerfrei sein. Experimente mit Versuchspersonen
zeigen, daß wir Menschen assoziativ nicht immer alle Relationen korrekt weiterverarbeiten (Stenning & Levy 1988), sondern durchaus auch „falsche Bindings" machen.

Ein Vorschlag: Die Bindingvektor-Repräsentation

Eine mögliche Lösung zur Darstellung von beliebigen Relationen zwischen Konzepten wurde von
Smolensky (1987) vorgeschlagen. In seiner *Tensorprodukt-Repräsentation* teilt er die Konzepte in

Rollen (z.B. *0,...,n*) und Füller (z.B. *p,a$_1$,...,a$_n$*) ein und repräsentiert sie in zwei verschiedenen Unitvektoren. Nun existiert für jede mögliche Kombination einer Rollenunit mit einer Füllerunit eine Bindingunit, die immer dann aktiviert wird, wenn die Rolle und der Füller zusammengebunden werden sollen. Es wird somit die Struktur $\{\{0,p\},\{1,a_1\},...,\{n,a_n\}\}$ repräsentiert. Diese Darstellungsweise erinnert noch extrem an symbolische Kompositionen: Rollen und Füller werden exakt getrennt, man kann nicht von verteilter Struktur sprechen.

Daher soll ein einfacher alternativer Ansatz vorgeschlagen werden, der Struktur mit den obigen Eigenschaften in verteilter Form realisieren kann: die *Bindingvektor-Repräsentation*.

Binding:

Gegeben sei ein Netzwerk mit einem Input- und einem Outputvektor (siehe Bild 1). Jede Unit des Inputs sei mit jeder Outputunit verbunden, wobei die Gewichte der Verbindungen zufällig (oBdA größer 0) gewählt sind.

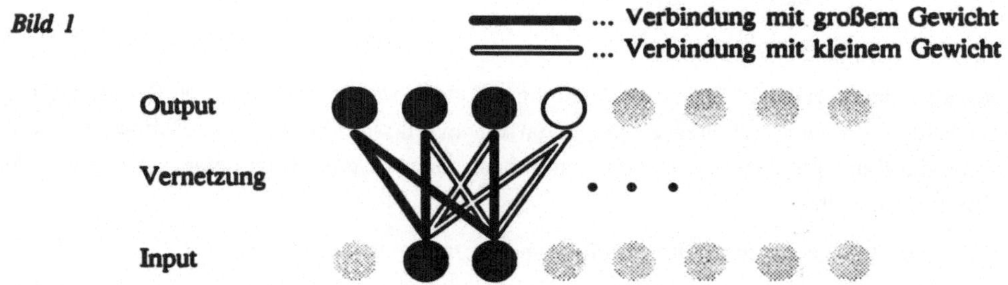

Nehmen wir an, im Input seien genau zwei Units aktiv. Werden nun die Aktivierungen zum Output propagiert, so erscheint dort ein Aktivierungsmuster folgender Art:
Besitzt eine Outputunit stark gewichtete Verbindungen von beiden aktiven Inputunits, so ist diese selbst stark aktiviert. Besitzt eine Outputunit nur mit einer der beiden Inputunits eine Verbindung mit großem Gewicht, so wird sie schwächer aktiviert. Alle anderen Outputunits werden nur schwach oder gar nicht aktiviert.
Es erscheint also ein charakteristisches Outputmuster, das die gemeinsame Aktivierung dieser beiden Inputunits signalisiert. Dieses Muster wird in den meisten Fällen von allen anderen Kombinationen zweier Inputunits unterschiedlich sein.
Nun kann eine der Inputunits als Rolle, die andere als Füller interpretiert werden. Die besonders aktiven Outputunits können dann als jene Bindingunits angesehen werden, die das Binding der Rolle mit dem Füller darstellen.

Die Outputunits übernehmen somit die Funktion von Bindingunits. Ihre Anzahl ist nicht von der Zahl der Rollen- und Füllerunits abhängig (so wie es beim Tensorprodukt der Fall ist), sondern frei wählbar, und somit an die Anforderungen anpaßbar.
Bei einer ausreichenden Anzahl von Outputunits – und wenn man kein ausgesprochenes Pech bei der Zufallsverteilung der Gewichte hat – ist nun jeder möglichen Kombination zweier Inputunits ein charakteristisches, von allen anderen unterschiedliches Outputmuster (bzw. Bindingmuster) zugeordnet. Dabei entziehen sich die einzelnen Outputaktivierungen einer genauen Interpretation, da die Bindinginformation im gesamten Muster steckt.

Überlagerung:

Für eine komplexe Struktur genügt es nicht, nur einzelne Rolle/Füller-Bindings darzustellen, sondern es sollten mehrere davon gleichzeitig im Output repräsentierbar sein. Wenn z.B. die Struktur $\{\{A,a\},\{B,b\}\}$ darzustellen ist, so müssen beide Bindings – $\{A,a\}$ und $\{B,b\}$ – im Output aktiviert sein, wodurch aber die Bindinginformation nicht verloren gehen darf. Dies kann durch eine *nichtkommutative* Überlagerung der beiden Bindingmuster geschehen:

Zuerst werden A und a gemeinsam an den Output propagiert, wonach dieser das Binding $A+a$ darstellt[1]. Dieses Muster wird „zwischengespeichert" und dann mit dem zweiten Bindingmuster $B+b$ überlagert. Die Nicht-Kommutativität läßt sich dadurch erreichen, daß die Bindingmuster vor der Überlagerung einem (beliebigen) Thresholding unterzogen werden. Die Überlagerung der Bindings, also *threshold(A+a)+threshold(B+b)* ist dann ungleich *threshold(A+b)+threshold(B+a)*. Es kann dann zwar Ähnlichkeiten zwischen den Ergebnisvektoren geben, eine Übereinstimmung ist aber sehr unwahrscheinlich.

In den folgenden Bildern sind derartige – vom Computer errechnete – Bindingvektoren zu sehen. Im Input gibt es zwei Rollenunits A, B und zwei Füllerunits a, b. Im Output wird immer das Bindingmuster nach Anwendung der Thresholdfunktion gezeigt (Bild 2).

Bild 2   threshold(A+a):

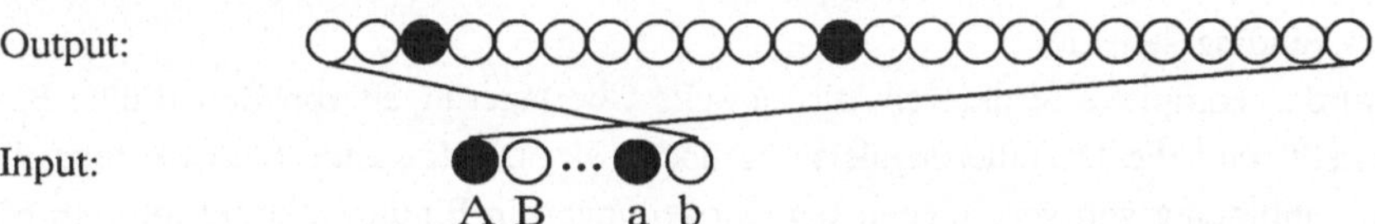

Die Outputmuster für die vier Bindings $A+a$, $A+b$, $B+a$ und $B+b$ sind – wie aus Bild 3 ersichtlich – alle verschieden:

Bild 3   Outputmuster für threshold(X+X):

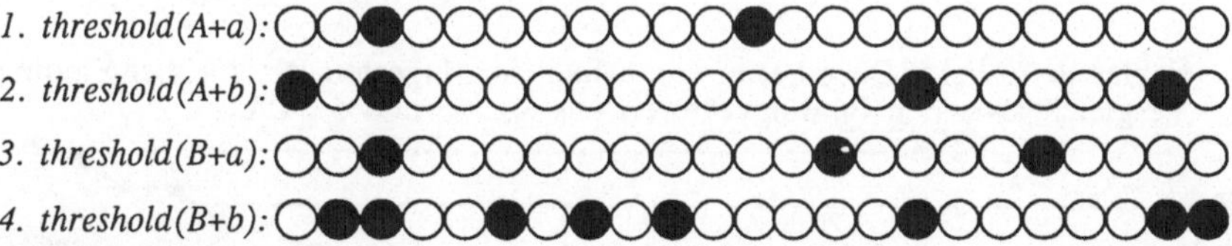

Nun können die Bindings additiv überlagert werden (Bild 4). Zuerst ist der Bindingvektor nach der Überlagerung von $A+a$ und $B+b$ angegeben, darunter jener von $A+b$ und $B+a$. Beide Muster sind eindeutig verschieden.

Bild 4   Überlagerungen[2] von je zwei Bindings:

---

1 Im folgenden sei das Binding zweier Inputdarstellungen durch das **Zeichen** ,+' symbolisiert.
2 Die Überlagerung mit Threshold sei durch das Zeichen ,&' symbolisiert.

Auf diese einfache Art kann also durch einen Outputvektor die Akkumulation von mehreren Rolle/Füller-Bindings dargestellt werden. Der Outputvektor soll in der Folge „Bindingvektor" (BV), die Methode „Bindingvektor-Repräsentation" (BVR) genannt werden. Die Outputunits können damit auch als Bindingunits bezeichnet werden, wenn auf deren spezielle Funktion hinsichtlich der Strukturrepräsentation hingewiesen werden soll.

Decodierung:

Da es sich bei einem Aktivierungsmuster des BV um eine verteilte Darstellung handelt, ist eine direkte Interpretation der dargestellten Information unmöglich. Für assoziative Vorgänge ist dies aber auch gar nicht notwendig. Wesentlich ist, daß verschiedene Bindings distinkte Aktivierungsmuster erzeugen, auf die das Netzwerk dann gesondert reagieren kann. Will man die Muster auf ihre Vollständigkeit überprüfen, so müssen sie in eine lesbare Darstellung decodiert werden. Zu diesem Zweck wurde ein Assoziationsnetzwerk verwendet, das die Bindingmuster in eine Tensorprodukt-Repräsentation umwandelt, die dann leicht analysiert werden kann. Man kann sich vorstellen, daß ähnliche Prozesse bei der Generierung einer sprachlichen Beschreibung der verteilten Konzeptstruktur ablaufen.

In mehreren Versuchen wurden alle 100 möglichen einfachen Bindings von je 10 Rollen und 10 Füllern in Bindingvektoren verschiedener Größe lokal dargestellt, und die Assoziationen auf eine 10×10 Matrix von Tensorprodukt-Bindigunits gelernt. Jede Unit im Output war dann für ein bestimmtes Binding sensitiv.

Danach wurden komplexe Strukturen, also jeweils Überlagerungen von Rolle/Füller-Bindings im BV dargestellt, und die Decodierungsleistung überprüft. Die folgende Statistik zeigt die Fehlerraten beim Unbinding von verschiedensten Darstellungen in Bindingvektoren mit 80, 65 bzw. 55 Units. Auf der horizontalen Achse sind die Fehler nach der „Überlagerungsdichte" n aufgeschlüsselt. Diese Dichte gibt die Anzahl der im BV gleichzeitig dargestellten – also überlagerten – Bindings an. Für jedes n wurden 200 zufällige Darstellungen getestet und die durchschnittliche Fehlerrate[3] beim Unbinding berechnet. Diese ist auf der Vertikalachse in Prozenten aufgetragen (Bild 5).

Bild 5 Fehler in % beim Decodieren von n-fach überlagerten Rolle/Füller-Bindings: Vergleich zwischen Bindingvektoren aus 80, 65 und 55 Units.

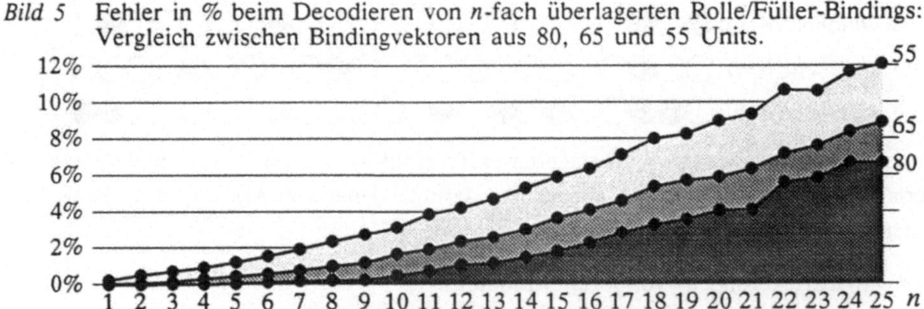

Wie zu erwarten ist, steigt mit zunehmender Überlagerungsdichte die Anzahl der Fehler. Wenn wir für die Darstellung von Strukturen annehmen, daß an jede Rolle genau ein Füller gebunden ist (wie es z.B. bei prädikatenlogischen Strukturen der Form $p(a_1,...,a_n)$ zutrifft), so entspricht dies bei 10 Rollen einer Dichte von 10 Bindings. Für diesen Fall existieren 10^{10} verschiedene

---

3 Die Fehlerrate ist die Anzahl der beim Unbinding einer Struktur falsch aktivierten Units der Outputmatrix.

Bindingmuster. Die Fehlerrate des Decodierens des Bindingvektors mit 80 Bindingunits liegt hier lediglich bei 0,5%.

Eigenschaften „verteilter" Struktur

Die BVR ist demnach eine Methode, Strukturen in einer an sich strukturlosen Menge einfacher Units darzustellen. Kommen wir nun zu den Eigenschaften zurück und betrachten sie im Licht der vorgestellten Ergebnisse:

◇ Vollständigkeit: Für viele Anwendungen müssen nicht alle möglichen Kombinationen von Bindings darstellbar sein. Eine vollständige Kapazität ist also nicht notwendig. Es genügt nämlich oft (wie z.B. in Konstituentenstrukturen) wenige bestimmte Kombinationen darzustellen. In solchen Fällen kann die Anzahl der Bindingunits stark reduziert werden, je nachdem, wieviele verschiedenartige Bindings zu erwarten sind.

◇ Auch bei einer beliebig großen Zahl von Units kann eine (zufällige) Gleichheit von Bindingmustern verschiedener Rollen und Füller nicht vollständig ausgeschlossen werden. Die Wahrscheinlichkeit hierfür ist aber sehr gering – sie fällt exponentiell mit der Bindingunitanzahl.
Dies läßt sich gut anhand der Decodierungsergebnisse verdeutlichen: Die Strukturen mit Überlagerungsdichte 1 (also alle Lernbeispiele) wurden in den Bindingvektoren zwar so dargestellt, daß eine saubere Decodierung möglich war. Bei zunehmender Dichte treten aber vermehrt Fälle auf, in denen das Überlagerungsmuster einer Struktur dem Muster einer anderen an bestimmten „Stellen" zu ähnlich (bzw. gleich) wird. Das Decodierungsnetzwerk kann dann einzelne Bindings nicht mehr erkennen, und aktiviert so einige der Outputunits falsch. Experimente bestätigen, daß auch Menschen Grenzen der Zuordnungsfähigkeit erreichen können und bevorzugt Fehlern durch falsches Binding erliegen (siehe Stenning & Levy 1988).

◇ Ausgangspunkt der Komposition sind nicht unbedingt Rollen- oder Füllerdarstellungen. Da beide Formen gleichberechtigt sind, muß nämlich nicht zwischen diesen unterschieden werden. Ihre Funktion ergibt sich erst durch ihre Verwendung, und somit implizit von selbst. So sind auch „Zwischenformen" denkbar. Damit verschwindet die Grenze zwischen Konstellations- und Konstituenteninformation.
Auch ist das Binding nicht auf zwei Entitäten (Rolle+Füller) beschränkt, sondern kann – ohne Veränderung der BVR-Architektur – auf beliebig viele Features erweitert werden. Daraus ergibt sich für das Binding eine allgemeinere Interpretation:

◇ Die Bindingunits signalisieren die gemeinsame Aktivität bestimmter Features. Die Beziehung zwischen diesen Features kann daher als eine Art „Zusammengehörigkeit" interpretitert werden. Da Units bzw. Unitmuster verschiedene Aktivierungsstärken einnehmen können, kann auch die Bestimmtheit der Zusammengehörigkeit variabel sein.
Das Binding ist somit ein „Grundtypus" der Beziehung zwischen Features, aus der sich Relationen aller Art generieren lassen. (siehe folgendes Beispiel)

◇ Die wichtigste Eigenschaft konnektionistischer Strukturen ist, daß deren „Elemente" – die Konzepte selbst – subsymbolisch dargestellt sind. So sind alle, Rollen, Füller und die darauf aufbauenden Bindingmuster subsymbolische Darstellungen. Da die Mikrofeatures subsymbolischer Darstellungen aber keine Interpretation besitzen, das Bindingprinzip sich aber schon in dieser Ebene ansiedeln läßt, haben auch die dort dargestellten „Mikrostrukturen" keine Interpretation. Diese Vorstellung geht soweit, alle Units als Bindingunits anzusehen, da es ja die Funktion jeder Unit ist, das Aktivierungsmuster vorgeschalteter Units zu analysieren. Dadurch sind Mikrostrukturen und Mikrofeatures gleichzusetzen.

Es ist somit klar, daß in Netzwerken Struktur darstellbar ist, ohne die Nachteile symbolischer Darstellungen zu übernehmen und ohne auf die Vorteile subsymbolischer Darstellungen verzichten zu müssen.

Ein Beispiel

Ein typischer Fall für Konzeptrelationen, die in der assoziativen Verarbeitung vorkommen, sind geometrische Zusammenhänge in der visuellen Mustererkennung. Das folgende Beispiel zeigt, wie eine BVR damit fertig werden kann.

Dazu betrachte man zwei einfache Bilder mit je zwei Objektdarstellungen (die man etwa als „Tisch" und „Sessel" interpretieren könnte, siehe Bild 6 oben). Beide Bilder enthalten die Rela-

Bild 6

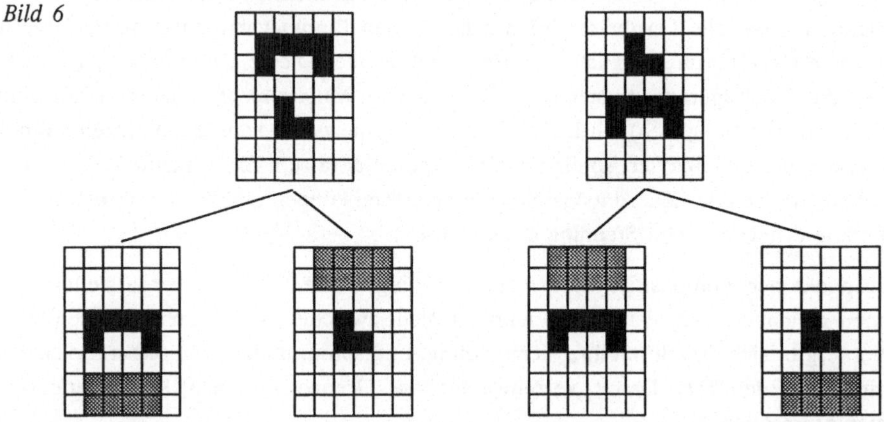

tion „*A auf B*" mit verschiedenen Belegungen: links „Tisch *auf* Sessel", rechts „Sessel *auf* Tisch". Setzt man zunächst voraus, daß die Erkennung der beiden Gegenstände ein sequentieller Vorgang mit sich verschiebendem Fokus der Aufmerksamkeit ist, so könnten sich die Muster in Bild 6 unten ergeben. Hier ist die Aufmerksamkeit auf jeweils eines der beiden Teilmuster gerichtet, während das Umfeld als „verschwommene" Aktivierung erscheint.

Man könnte nun jeweils das stark aktivierte Muster als einen „Füller", bzw. das Umfeld als die zugehörige „Rolle" interpretieren (wie wir aber schon gesehen haben, ist diese Interpretation nicht notwendig). Die Muster stellen demnach die Bindings „Sessel + oben" und „Tisch + unten", bzw. umgekehrt dar.

Wendet man nun die oben beschriebene Bindingvektor-Technik auf jeweils eines der beiden Musterpaare an, so ergeben sich eindeutig unterschiedliche Aktivierungsmuster, die aber dennoch Ähnlichkeiten miteinander aufweisen, also Informationen **über** die Gemeinsamkeiten enthalten (Bild 7). Das Netzwerk kann also unterschiedlich auf die beiden Bilder reagieren, obwohl – wie man leicht erkennt – in beiden Fällen in Summe gesehen die vier gleichen Teilmuster präsentiert werden.

Bild 7

Dieser Ansatz wurde in ein einfaches Modell zur Konzeptbildung (Dorffner 1989) eingebettet und getestet. Interessant dabei ist zu beobachten, daß die Gewichte zwischen Input und BV nicht notwendigerweise zufällig sein müssen, sondern auch durch Lernen verschieden ausgeprägt sein können. Hat das Netzwerk zum Beispiel gelernt, auf die beiden als „Tisch" und „Sessel" bezeichneten Muster mit einer stark aktivierten Unit (während die anderen Units sehr schwach aktiviert bleiben) zu reagieren, so kann die BVR-Technik dennoch distinkte Muster für die beiden Beziehungen erzeugen.

Selbstorganisation des Bindingvektors

Wie dieses Beispiel zeigt, kann Struktur ohne Verwendung ihrerselbst in Netzwerken repräsentiert werden. Die Vorgänge des Binding und des Überlagerns der Bindingmuster sind dabei sehr plausibel, weil sie bereits von der Struktur der Umwelt vorgegeben werden:

◇ Binding: Features, die zugleich aktiv sind (zeitliche Koinzidenz), aktivieren die Bindingunits gleichzeitig, und werden so als zusammengehörend in den Bindingunits dargestellt.

◇ Überlagerung: Bindings, die hintereinander aktiv sind (größerer Abstand, etwa aufgrund des sequentiellen Verschiebens der Aufmerksamkeit), werden in den Bindingunits überlagert. Die Thresholdbildung in den Units ist dabei ebenso plausibel, wie die Tatsache, daß die Aktivität einer Unit durch ihren vorhergehenden Zustand stark beeinflußt ist, was einer Überlagerungsfunktion entspricht.

Ein zeitliches Verhalten scheint also für den Aufbau von Strukturen unabdingbar zu sein. Das zeigt, wie sehr die Beschreibung der Repräsentation in einem Netzwerk von dynamischen Vorgängen – also der *Verarbeitung* der Darstellungen – abhängig ist.

Die Möglichkeit, auf eine Einteilung in Rollen und Füller verzichten zu können, ist ein wichtiger Schritt in Richtung Selbstorganisation. Die Funktion eines Features muß dann durch Lernen aus der Umwelt bestimmt werden. Im Falle einer Relation (z.B. „oben und unten") kann dies so geschehen: Aus den Lernbeispielen sind sowohl Konstituenten (Objekte) als auch deren Konstellation (räumliche Anordnung) ersichtlich. „Erkannt" werden beide erst nach einer komplexen Verarbeitung: So wie ein Objekt aus verschiedenen Blickwinkeln als dasselbe erkannt wird (Konstanzleistung[4]), kann auch eine Konstellation – die sich auf der Netzhaut völlig verschieden abbilden mag – als dieselbe erkannt werden. Aufgrund von Konstanzleistungen könnten sich also Konzepte sowohl über Objekte als auch über Konstellationen herausbilden.

Wird beim Lernen zwischen verschiedenen Objekten variiert, so ist die Konstellation – als Konzept aus Rollen – ein immer wiederkehrendes Muster, das später auch mit nicht gelernten Objekten (Füllern) wiedererkannt werden kann. Dieses Muster gilt dann als die Repräsentation der Relation.

---

4 Über die Funktionsweise von Prozessen mit Konstanzleistung ist nur wenig bekannt.

Konklusion ...

Die BVR hat also gezeigt, daß verteilte konnektionistische Netzwerke sehr wohl in der Lage sind, Konzeptbeziehungen darzustellen und geeignet zu verarbeiten. Dies geschieht, ohne daß die symbolische Beschreibung mittels Rollen und Füllern direkt eine Entsprechung in den Aktivierungsmustern finden muß. Allerdings muß dabei von der starren klassischen Auffassung einer vollständigen und umfassenden (Symbol-) Struktur abgegangen werden, was – wie gezeigt – jedoch sehr plausibel erscheint.

In weiterer Folge sind auch einige Möglichkeiten zur Optimierung der BVR denkbar:

◇ So könnte zum Beispiel die Zahl der Bindingunits dynamisch verändert werden. Ergeben sich aufgrund schlechter Zufallsverteilungen oder einer Übersättigung zu große Gemeinsamkeiten zwischen verschiedenen Bindings, so könnte der BV um einige Units erweitert werden. Zu diesen sollten dann ebenfalls zufällig gewichtete Verbindungen vom Input her verlaufen. Die neuen Bindingunits verbesserten dann die Bindingaktivierungen, indem sie das Bindingmuster erweitern und so die Unterschiede zwischen diesen vergrößern.

◇ Auf der anderen Seite wäre es möglich, von einer eher großen Anzahl von Bindingunits auszugehen – wodurch gleiche Muster sehr unwahrscheinlich sind – und diese dann systematisch zu reduzieren: Jene Units, die immer bzw. nie aktiv sind[5], können entfernt werden, da sie die Differenzierung zwischen den Mustern nicht erhöhen. Ebenso kann, wenn sich zwei Units identisch verhalten[6], eine davon entfernt werden.

◇ Darüber hinaus wären auch Optimierungen der Zufallsgewichte von Interesse, um die Kapazität weiter zu erhöhen.

Versuche zu diesen Vorschlägen sind im Gange.

Literatur

Fodor J.A. & Pylyshyn Z.W.: *Connectionism and cognitive architecture: A critical analysis*, in: Cognition 28 (88) p.3-71 1988

Dorffner G.: *A Sub-Symbolic Connectionist Model of Basic Language Functions*, Indiana University Computer Science Dept., Dissertation 1989

Rotter M.: *Über die Darstellung und Verarbeitung von Struktur in konnektionistischen Modellen*, TU-Wien, Diplomarbeit 1990

Smolensky P.: *On variable binding and the representation of symbolic structures in connectionist systems*, University of Colorado, tech. report CU-CS-355-87 1987

Schnelle H. & Doust R.: *A net-linguistic 'Earley' Chart Parser*, to appear in: Sharkey N., Reilly R. (eds.): Connectionist Approaches of Language, Erlbaum (in press)

Stenning K. & Levy L.: *Knowledge-rich solutions to the binding problem: a simulation of some human computational mechanisms*, in: Knowledge-Based Systems 3(1)143-152 1988

---

5 z.B. in Bild 3, jeweils die 3., 4. oder 5. Unit von links
6 z.B. in Bild 3, die 5. und die 10. Unit von rechts

Learning Sensory-Motor Coordination by Experimentation and Reinforcement Learning

CHRISTIAN MANNES

Austrian Research Institute

for Artificial Intelligence

ABSTRACT

This work shows how a neural network can learn a motor control task by trial and error using a reinforcement learning scheme, exemplified by a system that learns to focus an "eye" on moving objects or salient parts of pictures. No explicit knowledge about the details of the "oculomotor system" is used during training. The system described is embedded in an environment in which it acts. It can perceive the changes it causes in its environment and evaluates them with respect to some goal implicit in its architecture. The solutions the network arrives at are achieved by correlation of visual input with random gestures (experimentation) by a reinforcement learning scheme that makes use of "heterosynaptic modulation," as proposed by Reeke & Edelman (1989). Through learning, the performance of the system gradually improves so that random move generation becomes obsolete. Simulations have shown that the system is able to learn to track moving objects, as well as to trace the contours of stationary pictures.

1 Introduction

This work deals with the problem of having a neural network learn a motor control task in a situation where perception of the environment leads to actions that affect the environment, and the change in the perceived part of the environment is taken to be the only means of assessing the performance of the network. Solutions of this problem could have many applications to problems where the characteristics of perceiving or acting devices are not known, e.g. a camera that distorts visual input in an unknown way, a robot or speech synthesizer whose parameters are unknown, and so forth.

Connectionist approaches to motor control usually rely on some knowledge of desired input-output pairs. Kuperstein & Rubinstein (1989) describe a system that learns to grasp objects with a robot hand. It learns to do so by correlating input from two video cameras and random postural codes of the robot. During the training phase, the robot arm is holding the object it should learn to grasp. The arm is then driven by a random generator, and the weights between the camera input reflecting the position of the object and the motor command layer are adapted by back propagation. Thus during the training phase whatever the robot arm does is right by definition. In contrast to this method—a very similar system is described by Pabon & Gossard (1988)—, this paper describes a model that makes use of a built-in evaluation scheme that assesses actions ("experiments") in terms of reward or punishment.

Reeke, Sporns, and Edelman (1989), whose "synthetic modelling approach" provided the incentive to this work, propose a model called "Darwin III" that models a sessile creature with an eye and a multi-jointed arm. The arm is equipped with tactile and kinesthetic sensors. The system incorporates models of focussing, grasping, contour tracing, and classification of objects by integration of different sensory modalities. Their model, which uses neurophysiological data as well as model neurons in abundance (it is implemented using some 50 000 neurons and well over 620 000 connections), is meant to provide evidence for the *theory of neuronal group selection* (Edelman 1978). They use a learning rule that selects from preexisting diversity to strengthen successful responses.

This paper describes a solution to the problem outlined above in the framework of a simple connectionist system (as opposed to the large-scale biologically motivated simulations of Reeke et al.) that consists of an "environment" containing pictures, an "eye," and "muscles" that move the eye. The task of the network is to learn to center its eye over bright spots or areas of high contrast and to explore the environment by "jumping" to a new place after focussing. No knowledge about the way the "eye" reflects external input or about how the motor units affect the position of the eye is available or used for training, in contrast to learning strategies that employ some target output to compute a unit-by-unit error signal.

Since the correct transformations of visual input into appropriate motor action are not known in advance, the network explores possible solutions by experimentation. Random motor gestures are associated with patterns of activations in the "retina," and a learning rule strengthens or weakens connections depending on a global evaluation of success (focussing) or failure (objects drifting out of the visible area) of recent motor action. Preexisting associations are "tested" by the same mechanism. As the system improves, random move generation becomes more and more obsolete.

This paper discusses aspects of this method and describes a learning rule that implements a primitive form of reinforcement learning that selects from diversity generated by a random generator.

It is important to note that, although the components of the system are given names that correspond to biological entities (retina, fovea, eye, muscles etc.), no attempt is made to actually model biological phenomena.

2 Model Architecture

The neural network model described consists of the components shown in fig. 1: The "environment" providing visual input is modelled as an array of points of varying brightness. The system was tested with moving points operated by the mouse of the computer system, and with stationary scanned pictures. Parts of the pictures of the environment are projected onto the "retina" (R, a 9 by 9 array of units in my experiments), where they are preprocessed and subjected to habituation (i.e. decay of activity in the absence of change). Which part of the environment is visible depends on the position of the eye. Scanned pictures are preprocessed by a contrast enhancement algorithm that reduces a gray-scaled picture to areas of highest contrast, i.e. contours. For computational reasons, preprocessing is carried out before patterns reach the retina. The retina is connected to a layer of processing units named "motor layer" (M), whose activity moves the eye. The four units in M are assigned arbitrary directions, in which the eye is moved when the respective unit is highly activated. Units that correspond to opposing directions are interconnected by inhibitory links to form agonist-antagonist pairs, so the synchronous activation of "left" and "right"-units becomes unlikely.

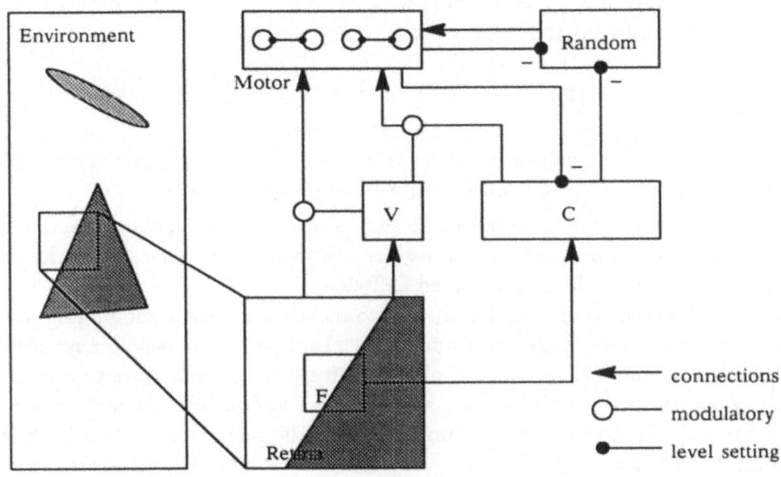

Fig. 1: The architecture of the model

The central part of the retina (the innermost 3 by 3 square), called the "fovea," is connected to a "classification layer" (C). The updating of units and the modification of connection strengths from R to C is guided by a competitive scheme, like v. d. Malsburg's model of the development of orientation sensitive cells (v. d. Malsburg 1973), Grossberg's ART (Carpenter & Grossberg 1987), Kohonen's topographical maps (Kohonen 1982), Rumelhart & Zipser's competitive learning (Rumelhart & Zipser, 1986), or the like. When the system is run with a picture that contains lines, the units in C gradually learn to respond to lines of different orientation. C is also connected to the motor layer via feed-forward links.

Another component, labeled "Random" in fig. 1, provides random input to M. It is active whenever either activity in R drops below a certain threshold, or no motor activity occurs in spite of sufficient activity in the central region of the retina. The retina, the classification layer, and the random input generator thus compete for access to the motor layer.

Finally, a component labeled "Value" (V) assesses the success or failure of recent actions (this is what Reeke, Sporns & Edelman (1989) call a "value scheme"). It assigns each pattern in the retina a value that is higher when objects are closer to the "fovea." It does so by scaling the activation value of each processing unit in R by a factor that reflects its proximity to the center of R. The output of V is used by the learning rule that strengthens weights that led to an increased value.

3 Operation and learning

An object (i.e. a bright spot) in the visible area activates corresponding units in R. Each unit in R is connected to each unit in M by modifiable weights that are initially assigned random values. All units update according to the following rule:

$$x_j(t+1) = f\left(\alpha \sum_i x_i(t)w_{ij} + \lambda x_j(t)\right)$$

where x_i, x_j denote units whose values range from 0 to 1, w_{ij} the weight from unit i to j, $f(\cdot)$ is the sigmoid function $f(x) = \frac{1}{1+e^{Gx-\frac{G}{2}}}$, and α and λ (decay) are constants.

Through learning, the weights are adapted in such a way that, for instance, active units in the left part of R activate the motor units that move the eye to the left. This moves the projection of the object close to the center, which is achieved as follows:

When a unit in R activates a unit in M, the connection enters a modifiable state, i.e. the connection is marked by a value (modelling some chemical substance allowing for synaptic plasticity, see Reeke, Sporns & Edelman (1989)) that can be positive or negative. More precisely, if both the pre- and the postsynaptic units (units i and j respectively) are on, the connection is marked with a positive value $m_{ij} = \mu$. If the presynaptic unit is on and the postsynaptic unit is off (i.e. below a certain threshold), then the connection is marked with a lower negative value ($m_{ij} = -\frac{\mu}{2}$). In any other case, m_{ij} decays. More formally, this can be expressed as follows:

$$m_{ij} = \begin{cases} \mu & x_i \geq \theta, x_j \geq \theta \\ -\frac{\mu}{2} & x_i \geq \theta, x_j < \theta \\ \lambda m_{ij} & \text{otherwise } (0 \leq \lambda < 1) \end{cases}$$

After the pattern of activation in M has changed the position of the eye and consequently the pattern in R, the difference in value (V) between the two successive situations is measured. Then all marked connections are updated according to the following rule:

$$\Delta w_{ij} = \epsilon \cdot m_{ij} \cdot \frac{dV}{dt}$$

where w_{ij} denotes the weight from unit i to unit j, ϵ is the learning rate, and V is the value of the situation in R.

This has the effect that all weights that were "used" in a situation leading to improved focussing are strengthened, whereas weights that were used in an action that led to a worse situation are weakened. The same mechanism applies to the connections from C to M.

Once an object is correctly focussed, its projection onto the fovea habituates (i.e. without change, all activity decays). With the decrease of activity in the fovea, the random module comes into play, and so soon after focussing a random movement occurs that moves the eye to a new region, where the process begins anew. Doing that, the system generates training examples for itself.

The classification layer C learns to respond selectively to lines of different orientation, or, in the case of blob-like objects, to blobs in different regions of the fovea. The classification is based on surface similarities only. If the classification codes that emerge in C correspond to cues that indicate in which direction a move could be successful (success in terms of sustained or repeated focussing), those patterns will eventually be associated with successful motor patterns. The weights from C to M are treated like those from R to M, but their effect is taken to be stronger, so that movements induced by R cause "jumps" that bring the eye to a new region. As learning proceeds, C can take the role of the random module, only in a more goal-oriented fashion. In the case of pictures that contain lines, this leads to limited tracing of contours (limited in the sense that the system cannot memorize the locations it has seen, and so tends to repeatedly visit certain areas of a picture).

Objects presented to the network are allowed to move. Although m_{ij} decays, there are situations where no muscular actions take place but the movement of an object leads to a different value that could change weights that are still modifiable. Therefore, a feedback mechanism has to be included that ensures a muscle has actually contributed to a changed situation before it is "made responsible for it." This is done by preventing modification of weights to muscles that did not move.

4 Generation of diversity

If the scheme described above would be applied only to preexisting connections from R to M, either a vast amount of connections would have to be used (as it is done by Reeke, Sporns, and Edelman), or the system could never learn anything new. Therefore, new patterns in M need to be generated and associated with patterns in R. This is accomplished in two ways: firstly, by randomly generated patterns in M, and secondly by the effect of the learning rule on the weights from R to M. When the activity in R drops below a threshold, a random pattern in M is generated, which is then treated as if it had been the result of firing in R.

The learning rule strengthens or weakens the weights from an active unit to another active unit, depending on the change of value in V. According to the learning rule, connection strengths from active to inactive units are changed in the opposite direction. For instance, if a pattern in R activates the unit that moves the eye to the left and the gesture leads to improved focussing, the weights from the active units in R to that unit are strengthened, but the weights to all other motor units are weakened. Conversly, when motor action leads to a lower value, the weights to inactive units in M are increased.

Both this mechanism and random moves generate diversity in connections from which the learning rule selects working solutions. Still, it is important that the entire range of possible action be covered by the random generator.

5   Results

The system has been tested with scanned pictures that remained stationary, and with small moving objects. In the first case, preprocessing was carried out that transformed a scanned picture first into an array of gray values, then by contrast enhancement into a line drawing that contained mainly contours, as shown in fig. 2. The first step was carried out by assigning each pixel a gray value according to the number of active pixels in its neighbourhood. The second step, the contrast enhancement, was carried out by local interaction of units connected as shown in fig. 2 (compare Yamaguchi, Fukushima, Yasuda, & Nagata 1971).

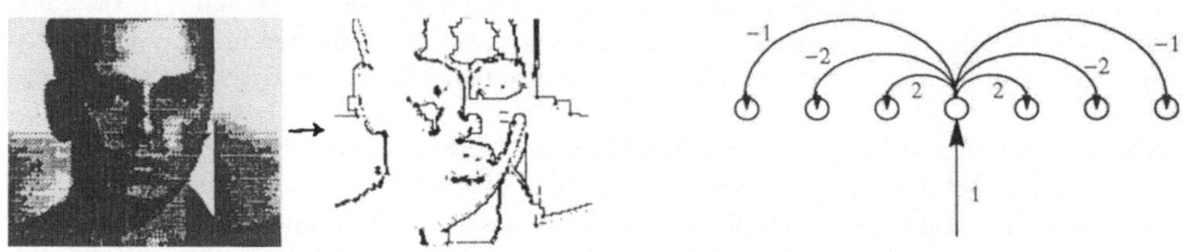

Fig. 2: Preprocessing (left); Connection scheme: relative connection strengths depend on the distance between units (right)

All units and weights were updated about 250 times. By then, the system acquired the ability to quickly focus over bright areas of the picture, staying there for a while, then changing its position to "explore" a new area, and so forth.

In the case of training with small moving objects the eye was stimulated with a small (2 by 2) rectangular blob that was moved by a human operator. In the first phase, the system was given enough time to focus on the blob, but as the performance of the network improved, the blob was moved continuously so the eye had to track it. It could be observed that even under such conditions, the system learned very well. On average, 150 cycles were needed to achieve weight constellations as shown in fig. 3.

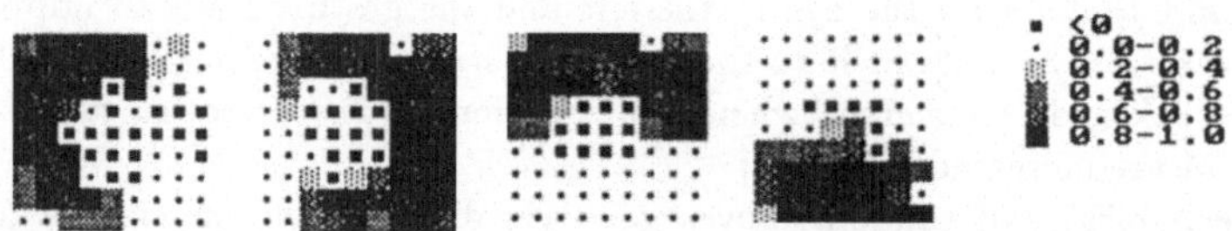

Fig. 3: Weights from R to units in M after 150 cycles

In another experiment, the projection from the environment to the eye was mirrored. The system learned without any distraction, compensating for the changed projection from the environment onto the retina.

6 Discussion

This paper describes a method for learning motor control tasks that uses feedback via the environment instead of detailed knowledge of desired input-output pairs. The system employs a mechanism of assigning a value to situations that is higher when the system proceeds towards a desirable solution. That value is used in modifying the weights in use during recent action. Learning a task is achieved by "experimentation," i.e. by using a random generator to provide responses to input patterns, and assessing the value of that combination. Provided the random generator is able to cover the whole range of useful output patterns, the network will eventually learn to associate sensory perception with appropriate motor actions. Therefore, the success of any such system depends on the quality of the random generator.

The limits of the algorithm are met when the network is to learn complicated motor gestures whose success depends on delicate temporal coordination of actions. Learning such motor actions is hard because all weights used in some time interval are treated the same way. This is also the reason why the system must fail in situations where the "blame" is to be assigned to situations that occured too far in the past.

The method described in this paper could be particularily useful with problems where neither the way the desired output is to be generated is known, nor how the input should be mapped to the output, but the goal of the system can be expressed by some "value scheme." Applications could include the learning of speech production by examples, in a setup where recordings of speech activate speech production "organs" and the match between input and output is taken to be the value function.

References

Carpenter G.A. & Grossberg S. (1987): *A Massively Parallel Architecture for a Self-Organizing Neural Pattern Recognition Machine.* in: Computer Vision, Graphics, and Image Processing 1987, 37, 54–115. In: *Neural Networks and Natural Intelligence.* A Bradford Book, MIT Press, Cambridge, Mass. 1988.

Edelman G. M. (1978): *Group Selection and Phasic Reentrant Signalling: A Theory of Higher Brain Function.* in: Edelman G. M., Mountcastle V. B. (Eds.): The Mindful Brain., MIT Press, Cambridge, Massachusetts.

Kohonen T. (1982): *Self-organized formation of topologically correct feature maps.* Biological Cybernetics 43:59-69.

Kuperstein M. & Rubinstein J. (1989): *Implementation of an Adaptive Neural Controller for Sensory-Motor Coordination.* in: Connectionism in Perspective, R. Pfeifer, Z. Schreter, F. Fogelman-Soulie, L. Steels, eds., pp. 49-61, Elsevier, Amsterdam.

v. d. Malsburg C., 1973: *Self-organization of orientation sensitive cells in the striata cortex.* Kybernetik 14:85–100.

Pabon J., Gossard D. (1988): *Connectionist Networks for Learning Coordinated Motion in Autonomous Systems.* in: Proc. AAAI 1988.

Reeke G.N., Sporns O., and Edelman G.M., (1989): *Synthetic Neural Modelling: Comparisons of Population and Connectionist Approaches.* in: Connectionism in Perspective, R. Pfeifer, Z. Schreter, F. Fogelman-Soulie, L. Steels, eds., pp. 113-139, Elsevier, Amsterdam.

Rumelhart D. E., Zipser D. (1986): *Feature Discovery by Competitive Learning,* in: Rumelhart D. E., McClelland J. L. (Eds.): Parallel Distributed Processing. Vol. 1, MIT Press, Cambridge, Massachusetts.

Yamaguchi Y., Fukushima K., Yasuda M., Nagata S. (1971): *Electronic Retina* NHK Laboratories Note 141.

WISSENSERWERB ÜBER DYNAMISCHE SYSTEME: BEFUNDE KONNEKTIONISTISCHER MODELLIERUNG

Anette Standfuss[†], Knut Möller[†] & Joachim Funke[‡]

[†]Institut für Informatik & [‡]Psychologisches Institut
Universität Bonn[1]

ZUSAMMENFASSUNG

Die vorliegende Arbeit untersucht Möglichkeiten und Grenzen der Verwendung von einfachen konnektionistischen Systemen als Modelle für den Erwerb und die Repräsentation von Wissen über zeitdiskrete lineare dynamische Systeme in der Kognitionspsychologie. Ein ausgewähltes dynamisches System namens SINUS wird in Form eines "pattern associators" repräsentiert und dessen Lernverhalten untersucht. Es wird versucht, daraus Annahmen über den Wissenserwerb von Probanden im Umgang mit solchen dynamischen Systemen abzuleiten, um insbesondere Hinweise darauf zu erhalten, was "gute" von "schlechten" Probanden unterscheidet. Ein weiterer hier betrachteter Aspekt ist die Steuerung eines dynamischen Systems in einen vorgegebenen Zielzustand, der unter Beibehaltung des konnektionistischen Modells durch einen variierten Lernalgorithmus modelliert wird. Die abschließende Diskussion geht auf die Bedeutung der Modellierung für die kognitionspsychologische Theorienbildung ein.

1   EINFÜHRUNG

In aktuellen kognitionspsychologischen Arbeiten spielen Überlegungen zum Einfluß von Wissen, dessen Erwerb und dessen Anwendung eine wichtige Rolle (vgl. Mandl & Spada, 1988). Auch innerhalb der neueren KI-Forschung wird diesem Konzept verstärkt Aufmerksamkeit zugewendet, was etwa in der Beschäftigung mit wissensbasierten Systemen zum Ausdruck kommt. Für Psychologie und Informatik hat sich mit dem Aufkommen neokonnektionistischer Modellvorstellungen eine mögliche Alternative zum herkömmlichen Standpunkt der Symbolverarbeitungstradition ergeben (vgl. zur Übersicht: Kemke, 1988; McClelland & Rumelhart, 1986; Rumelhart & McClelland, 1986).

Die vorliegende Arbeit demonstriert an einem konkreten Beispiel, dem Wissenserwerb über zeitdiskrete lineare dynamische Systeme, einige Möglichkeiten und Grenzen eines konnektionistischen Lernverfahrens.

---

[1] Anschrift der Verfasser: Römerstr. 164, D-5300 Bonn 1. Die Arbeit im DYNAMIS-Projekt wurde durch eine Sachbeihilfe der DFG unterstützt (Az. Fu 173/1).

1.1 Darstellung der Wissenserwerbssituation

Innerhalb des Forschungsprojekts DYNAMIS (vgl. Funke, 1986a) werden Probanden (Pbn) mit folgender, aus zwei Teilanforderungen bestehenden Aufgabe konfrontiert: (1) in direkter Interaktion mit einem Computer die Parameter eines ihnen zunächst unbekannten dynamischen Systems zu identifizieren und (2) anschließend auf der Basis des angenommenen Wirkungsmodells das System zu kontrollieren. Die verwendeten Systeme lassen sich als zeitdiskrete lineare Strukturgleichungsmodelle bzw. als autoregressive Prozesse erster Ordnung darstellen. Es wird unterstellt, daß Pbn im Laufe längerer Interaktionen mit dem zunächst unbekannten System ein zunehmend besseres Modell dieses Systems erwerben (vgl. Funke, 1985).

Das im folgenden verwendete System SINUS ist auf einem fremden Planeten angesiedelt. Der Pb soll die Wirkungen der drei exogenen Variablen (X) auf die drei endogenen Variablen (Y) sowie die Wirkungen der endogenen Variablen untereinander erkunden. SINUS kann durch die folgenden drei Gleichungen beschrieben werden, wobei t den Zeittakt beschreibt:

$$y1(t+1)=1.0^*y1(t)+10.0^*x1(t),$$

$$y2(t+1)=1.0^*y2(t)+ 0.2^*y3(t)+ 3.0^*x3(t),$$

$$y3(t+1)=0.9^*y3(t)+ 2.0^*x2(t)+ 0.5^*x3(t).$$

Hat der Pb das System vollständig durchschaut, so müßte sich sein internes Modell durch die folgende Parametermatrix repräsentieren lassen:

	x1(t)	x2(t)	x3(t)	y1(t)	y2(t)	y3(t)
y1(t+1)	10	0	0	1	0	0
y2(t+1)	0	0	3	0	1	0.2
y3(t+1)	0	2	0.5	0	0	0.9

Da es sich bei dem System SINUS um ein fiktives Szenario handelt, kann davon ausgegangen werden, daß der Pb so gut wie kein Vorwissen darüber besitzt, seine subjektive Parametermatrix also als Nullmatrix beschrieben werden darf.

1.2 Darstellung der konnektionistischen Modellierung

Im folgenden soll das konnektionistische Modell eines Pb konstruiert werden, der sich mit dem System SINUS befaßt. Es soll nd über folgende Eigenschaften verfügen: (a) es soll lernfähig sein in dem Sinn, daß es die Verbindungsstärken zwischen den SINUS-Variablen identifiziert, und (b) es soll Wissen in Form von Matrizen repräsentieren, deren Elemente Verbindungsstärken darstellen.

Abstrakt kann die Aufgabenstellung als Musterassoziation (=prediction problem) beschrieben werden: Gelernt werden soll die Verbindung zwischen den Variablenwerten (=exogene und endogene Werte) zum Zeitpunkt t und den Zustandswerten (=endogene Werte) des Systems zum Zeitpunkt t+1. Für die Modellierung von SINUS werden somit sechs Input-Einheiten mit drei Output-Einheiten verknüpft:

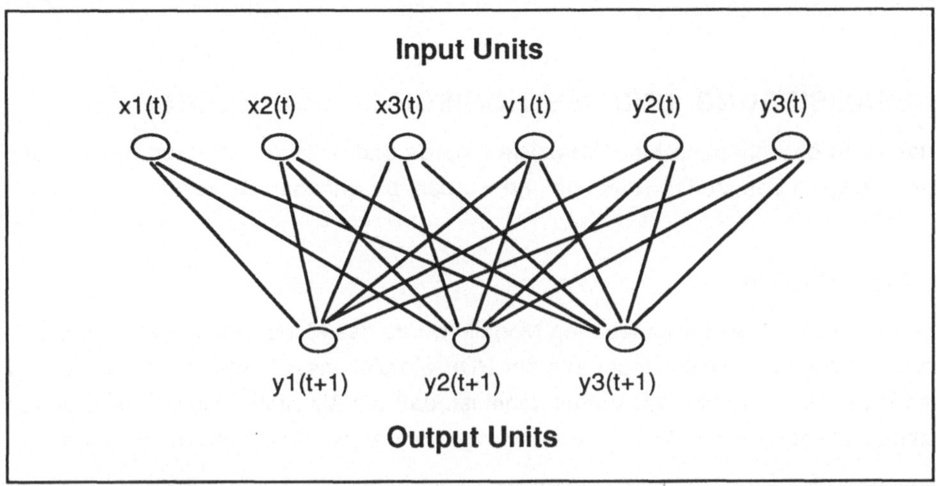

<u>Abbildung 1</u>. Vernetzung der sechs Inputs mit den drei Outputs

Dabei realisiert die Struktur des Netzwerks die zeitliche Komponente und die Gewichte der Kanten die Parameter der zu lernenden Matrix. Eine Zwischenschicht von Einheiten ("hidden units") wird nicht benötigt, da die dem System SINUS zugrundeliegenden Gleichungen linear sind.

Als <u>Einheiten</u> eignen sich hier lineare Einheiten, also solche, die ihre Aktivität als Summe der gewichteten Eingaben bestimmen. Entsprechen die Kantengewichte der optimalen Matrix, sind dadurch die Aktivitäten der Output-Einheiten den endogenen Werten des Systems SI-NUS äquivalent, die bei Eingabe der Daten zum Takt t als Werte im Takt t+1 resultieren würden.

Bei der Bestimmung der <u>Lernregel</u> wurde wie folgt vorgegangen. Das eben beschriebene Netz soll das Modell eines Pb darstellen, der über die exogenen Variablen in das System eingreifen kann und auf diese Art Information gewinnt. Plant dieses Netz einen Eingriff in einen bestimmten Systemzustand, so stellt die Netzausgabe die Prognose über den folgen-den Systemzustand dar auf der Grundlage der bisherigen Repräsentation des Simulations-systems. Wird der Eingriff in die Tat umgesetzt, gibt das Simulationssystem eine Rückmel-dung über die tatsächlich resultierenden Werte der endogenen Variablen. Dieses Feedback stellt somit den "Lehrer" des Systems dar. Aufgrund dieser Tatsache wie auch aufgrund der Tatsache, daß keine verborgenen Einheiten benötigt werden, bietet sich die einfache Delta-Regel als Lernregel an. Bei dieser wird als Fehlersignal ei die Differenz der Zielaktivität für die Output-Einheit i (=der "Prognose") und der aktuellen Aktivität der Output-Einheit i (=der tatsächlich resultierende Wert) gewählt, d.h. $e_i = t_i - a_i$ (e für "error", t für "target" und a für "activity"; die Indizes bezeichnen Einheiten). Die Delta-Regel lautet dann:

$$\delta\, w_{ij} = \varepsilon * e_i * a_j,$$

wobei ε die Lernrate (=Schrittweite des Gradientenverfahrens) und w_{ij} das Gewicht der Kante von Einheit j (der Input-Einheit) zur Einheit i (der Output-Einheit) darstellen.

2 REALISIERUNG UND METHODISCHES VORGEHEN

Wie das eben beschriebene Modell realisiert wurde und welche Tests zur Überprüfung der Leistungsfähigkeit des Modells durchgeführt wurden, beschreiben die folgenden Abschnitte.

2.1 Algorithmen

Für die Realisierung des beschriebenen Modells wurde das Modul PA (pattern associator) mit linearen Einheiten und Delta-Regel aus der PDP-Simulationssoftware von McClelland & Rumelhart (1988) ausgewählt. Von Vorteil dabei ist, daß die Aktivitäten nicht zwischen Null und Eins liegen müssen, so daß keine Veränderungen am Algorithmus notwendig waren.

Die benötigte Pattern-Datei mit den Trainingsmustern wurde mit dem DYNAMIS-Programm (Funke, Fahnenbruck & Müller, 1986) erzeugt. Um Fehlermeldungen wegen Überschreitung des Bereichs zwischen MaxInt und MinInt zu vermeiden, wurden Start-, Ziel-, Maximal- und Minimalwerte der SINUS-Steuerdatei durch 10000 dividiert.

2.2 Vorgehen

Zwei verschiedene Validierungsstrategien sollen Verwendung finden. Zum einen wird eine selbstkonstruierte Trainingsmenge als Pattern-Datei verwendet, von der anzunehmen ist, daß sie hinsichtlich der Lernmöglichkeiten maximal viel Information enthält. Zum anderen sollte aber auch geprüft werden, inwiefern empirisch realisierte Trainingsmengen, d.h. von Pbn erzeugte Systemzustände, zu akzeptablen Ergebnissen des Simulationsmodells führen können. Hierfür wurden exemplarisch Daten von zwei Pbn aus dem DYNAMIS-Projekt ausgewählt, die nach den dort entwickelten Gütekriterien ("Güte der Kausaldiagramme", GdK; vgl. Funke & Kleinemas, 1989) als gute bzw. schlechte Identifizierer bezeichnet werden können.

Für die selbst konstruierte Lernmenge wurde eine Pattern-Datei erzeugt, wobei die gewählten Werte für die exogenen Variablen möglichst zufällig aus dem positiven wie negativen Bereich gewählt und auf dreistellige Zahlen beschränkt wurden.

3 ERGEBNISSE

Entsprechend dem eben dargelegten Vorgehen bei der Überprüfung der Leistungsfähigkeit des konnektionistischen Lernmodells werden zunächst die Ergebnisse für die optimalen

Lernbedingungen berichtet. Daran schließt sich die Darstellung der Lernergebnisse auf der Basis empirisch beobachteter Lernmengen an. Schließlich geht es um die Modellierung zielgerichteten Lernens.

3.1 Lernen bei Verwendung selbst konstruierter Lernmengen

Nach 280 Lerndurchgängen (wobei ein Durchgang aus der Präsentation aller Muster besteht) und einer Lernrate $\varepsilon=1.0$ ergab sich, ausgehend von einer Nullmatrix zu Beginn des ersten Durchgangs, die folgende Gewichtsmatrix:

	x1(t)	x2(t)	x3(t)	y1(t)	y2(t)	y3(t)
y1(t+1)	9.99	0.00	0.00	0.99	0.00	0.00
y2(t+1)	0.00	0.00	2.99	0.00	0.99	0.19
y3(t+1)	0.00	1.99	0.50	0.00	0.00	0.89

Ein Vergleich mit der zugrundeliegenden Gewichtsmatrix (siehe weiter oben) ergibt eine fast optimale Reproduktion der Gewichte; Abweichungen liegen nur noch auf der zweiten Nachkommastelle vor. Damit ist die Lernbarkeit der Parameter des Systems SINUS durch ein konnektionistisches Modell demonstriert.

3.2 Lernen bei Verwendung von empirisch vorkommenden Lernmengen

In einem zweiten Schritt wurde überprüft, zu welchen Lernleistungen dieses Netzwerk fähig ist, wenn anstelle einer weitgehend optimalen Lernmenge die empirisch beobachteten, von den Pbn selbst erzeugten Lernmengen verwendet werden. Hierzu konnten die Systemdaten von zwei Pbn (DI24M und XX23M mit GdK-Werten von 2.00 resp. 0.46) herangezogen werden, die zu guter bzw. schlechter Identifikation fähig waren. Das Maß GdK skaliert die Qualität der von einem Pbn korrekt erkannten Kausalstruktur des Systems SINUS auf einem Bereich von 0 (Min) bis 2 (Max) unter Verwendung von Diagrammen, in denen der Pb die von ihm vermuteten Wirkungen auf unterschiedlichen Präzisionsgraden eintragen kann.

DI24M und XX23M haben sich jeweils fünf Durchgänge lang mit dem System SINUS beschäftigt. Während DI24M das System nach fünf Durchgängen vollständig durchschaut hatte (er gibt im Kausaldiagramm - dem Diagnostikum für die subjektive Kausalstruktur - die korrekten Parameter an), gelingt dies XX23M nicht.

<u>Lernvorgang mit den Daten von DI24M</u>: Die Lernrate wurde $\varepsilon=1.0$ gewählt. Aufgrund der geringeren Anzahl von Trainings-Patterns im Vergleich zu den selbstgenerierten Trainings-Patterns war hier eine größere Zahl von benötigten Lernepochen zu erwarten. Nach 3500 Epochen ergab sich die folgende Matrix:

	x1(t)	x2(t)	x3(t)	y1(t)	y2(t)	y3(t)
y1(t+1)	9.99	0.00	0.01	1.00	0.00	-0.01
y2(t+1)	0.00	0.02	2.95	0.00	0.98	0.23
y3(t+1)	0.00	1.98	0.52	0.00	0.01	0.88

<u>Lernvorgang mit den Daten von XX23M</u>: Hier wurde die Lernrate ebenfalls ε=1.0 gewählt. Nach 14500 (!) Epochen ergab sich die folgende Matrix

	x1(t)	x2(t)	x3(t)	y1(t)	y2(t)	y3(t)
y1(t+1)	9.98	0.00	0.00	0.99	0.00	0.00
y2(t+1)	0.00	0.00	3.00	0.00	0.99	0.20
y3(t+1)	0.00	1.99	0.49	0.00	0.00	0.90

Es zeigt sich also, daß die Korrektheit der resultierenden Matrix unabhängig von der Güte der Systemidentifikation durch die Versuchsperson ist. Demnach ist DI24M im Gegensatz zu XX23M in der Lage, die durch seine Eingriffe gewonnenen Informationen richtig auszuwerten. Daß allerdings die von XX23M erzeugten Daten "schwerer" auswertbare Informationen enthalten, macht die wesentlich erhöhte Zahl von Lernepochen deutlich.

3.3 Zielgerichtet Lernen

Ein weiterer Aspekt, der bisher nicht betrachtet wurde, betrifft die Erreichung eines Ziels, d.h. die Steuerung des Systems SINUS in einen vorgegebenen Systemzustand. Für die Pbn stellt sich diese Anforderung zusätzlich zu derjenigen der Identifikation; während der Identifikationstätigkeit kann der Pb spielerisch "ausprobieren", wie gut ihm die Erreichung eines vorgegebenen Zielzustands gelingt (vgl. 1.1). Diese Teilaufgabe der Steuerung kann mit demselben Modell wie bisher, jedoch unter Verwendung eines erweiterten Lernalgorithmus, realisiert werden (vgl. Linden, 1989).

<u>Beschreibung des Algorithmus</u>: Die Einheiten sind wie bisher lineare Einheiten und die Gewichte werden mit der Delta-Regel modifiziert. Folgende sechs Schritte sind zu leisten: (1) Anlegen eines Input-Patterns; (2) Berechnung der Ausgabe der Output-Einhe ten; (3) Berechnung des Target-Patterns, d.h. der sich aufgrund der Eingabe ergebenden tatsächlichen Systemzustands; (4) Berechnung des Fehlers für jede Output-Einheit (=Target-Output); (5) Veränderung der Gewichte mit der Delta-Regel; (6) Ermittlung des Eingriffs, der basierend auf

dem aktuellen Modell des Systems, gegeben durch die aktuellen Gewichte, das Target-Pattern als Ausgabe der Output-Patterns erzeugt.

(a) Der unter (4) berechnete Fehler wird über die Kanten an die Input-Einheiten geschickt, die den exogenen Variablen entsprechen, d.h. mit dem Kantengewicht multipliziert, und dort aufsummiert (entspricht der Netzeingabe bei einem inversen Durchgang.)

(b) Diese Eingabe für die Input-Einheiten, die den exogenen Variablen entsprechen, wird dazu benutzt, deren Aktivität zu verändern. Die Aktivität der Input-Einheiten, die den endogenen Variablen entsprechen, bleibt erhalten. Das so bestimmte modifizierte Input-Pattern wird als neue Eingabe verwendet.

(c) Die Ausgabe der Output-Einheiten wird berechnet.

(d) Der Fehler für die Output-Einheiten wird mit dem alten Target-Pattern berechnet.

(e) Goto (a), falls der Fehler größer ist als ein Schwellenwert, sonst goto (1).

Bei Verwendung dieses Lernalgorithmus konnte ein vorgegebener Zielzustand erreicht und über mehrere Schritte gehalten werden. Inwiefern dieser Algorithmus menschlichen Lernprozessen zugrundegelegt werden kann, behandelt die folgende Diskussion.

4 DISKUSSION DER ERGEBNISSE

Welche psychologische Bedeutung hat der Nachweis, daß ein bestimmtes konnektionistisches Modell die Parameter eines zu identifizierenden dynamischen Systems korrekt lernt? Damit ist zunächst einmal gezeigt, daß es hinsichtlich der internen Repräsentation des dynamischen Systems ausreicht, die Parametermatrix verfügbar zu haben: ein Netzwerk aus neun Knoten sowie den zwischen den sechs Alt- und drei Neu-Werten bestehenden gewichteten Kanten genügt hierfür ("Repräsentationsannahme").

Ein interessanter Aspekt besteht in der Frage, ob das konnektionistische Modell möglicherweise nicht nur vom Ergebnis her, sondern auch vom Lernverlauf her plausible Eigenschaften besitzt. Hierzu kann auf eine "Ökonomieannahme" zurückgegriffen werden (vgl. Funke, 1986b, p. 113), wonach Pbn zu Beginn der Identifikation mit möglichst einfachen Modellen anfangen. Dabei werden direkte Wirkungen (solche, bei denen exogene Variablen auf endogene Variablen einwirken) eher erkannt als indirekte Wirkungen (Nebenwirkungen, Eigendynamik). Im folgenden sind die direkten (=D) und indirekten (=I) Wirkungen des Systems SINUS dargestellt:

	x1(t)	x2(t)	x3(t)	y1(t)	y2(t)	y3(t)
y1(t+1)	D	-	-	I	I	-
y2(t+1)	-	-	D	-	I	I
y3(t+1)	-	D	D	-	-	I

Untersucht man den mit dem Pattern-Associator durchgeführten Lernvorgang hinsichtlich der Reihenfolge korrekt erkannter Kanten, so zeigt sich bei mehrfacher Wiederholung, daß als erstes zwischen 'Einfluß' und 'kein Einfluß' unterschieden wird, d.h. tendenziell werden die

Parameter der Matrix als erstes korrekt gelernt, deren Wert 0 ist. Erst danach wird der Einfluß genau differefziert. Dabei läßt sich keine genaue Reihenfolge angeben, vielmehr kann man diesen Vorgang als ein gleichmäßiges Ausdifferenzieren beschreiben, bei dem Rundungsfehler und ausgewählte Trainings-Patterns eine gewisse Rolle spielen.

Dieses Nichtunterscheiden-Können zwischen direktem und indirektem Einfluß ergibt sich aus der Architektur des Netzes, bei der die Werte endogener und exogener Variablen gleichbedeutende Eingaben sind. Die Begriffe direkter und indirekter Einfluß ergeben sich jedoch erst aus der Unterscheidung direkt und indirekt beeinflußbarer Variablen. Bei dieser Architektur steckt die Unterscheidung zwischen direkten und indirekten Variablen lediglich in der Erzeugung der Input-Patterns. Desweiteren ist das Lernverfahren im Pattern-Associator ein Gradientenverfahren, d.h. es beruht gerade auf der gleichzeitigen Veränderung aller Gewichte entlang des Gradienten. - Es muß also gesagt werden, daß sich die Ökonomieannahme mit diesem Modell nicht untersuchen läßt, da der Lernvorgang nicht adäquat ist.

Eine für dieses Modell sinnvolle Anwendung wäre die folgende Untersuchung: Es wird die Anzahl der Lernepochen untersucht, die für verschiedene Trainingsmengen benötigt werden. Dabei sollen die Input-Patterns und die Output-Patterns alle in demselben Winkel zueinander stehen. Zwischen den einzelnen Trainingsmengen wird dann der Winkel variiert, wobei die beiden Extrema 'linearabhängige Vektoren' und 'orthogonale Vektoren' sind.

Die zu testende Hypothese ist nun die folgende: Die Anzahl der benötigten Lernepochen ist umgekehrt proportional zur Größe des Winkels, wobei im Extremfall eines Winkels von 0 Grad kein korrektes Lernen mehr möglich ist. Da solche Trainingsmengen nur dann erzeugt werden können, wenn diese nicht in einem Simulationsdurchgang mit dem DYNAMIS-Programm erzeugt werden, muß anschließend untersucht werden, welche Eingaben die optimalsten Bedingungen in dem Sinne schaffen, daß die so erzeugten Vektoren $(X1(t), X2(t), X3(t), Y1(t), Y2(t), Y3(t))$ bzw. $(Y1(t+1), Y2(t+1), Y3(t+1))$ in einem möglichst großen Winkel zueinanderstehen.

Als nächstes kann dann die folgende Hypothese an realen Versuchspersonendaten untersucht werden: Die Güte der Systemerkennung durch eine Versuchsperson ist umso größer, je optimaler, in dem eben beschriebene Sinne, die von ihr durch Systemeingriffe erzeugten Vektoren sind. Diese Hypothese wird demnächst überprüft.

Abschließend möchten wir festhalten, daß gerade bei dem zur Diskussion stehenden Aufgabentyp kritisiert werden könnte, menschliche Pbn würden stärker hypothesengeleitet (symbolisch) vorgehen. Dem sind experimentelle Befunde mit diesem Paradigma (z.B. Berry & Broadbent, 1988) entgegenzusetzen, die für die Existenz assoziativer Mechanismen sprechen könnten. Mit unserer Arbeit haben wir einen Beitrag zur Beschreibung eines von möglicherweise mehreren Mechanismen geleistet.

Literatur

Berry, D.C. & Broadbent, D.E. (1988). Interactive tasks and the implicit-explicit distinction. *British Journal of Psychology*, *79*, 251-272.

Funke, J. (1985). Steuerung dynamischer System durch Aufbau und Anwendung subjektiver Kausalmodelle. *Zeitschrift für Psychologie*, *193*, 435-457.

Funke, J. (1986a). Ein Forschungsprogramm zur subjektiven Repräsentation dynamischer Kleinsysteme: Aufbau und Anwendung von Wissen in Abhängigkeit von Person- und Systemmerkmalen. *Berichte aus dem Psychologischen Institut der Universität Bonn, 12*, Heft 1.

Funke, J. (1986b). *Komplexes Problemlösen - Bestandsaufnahme und Perspektiven*. Heidelberg: Springer.

Funke, J., & Kleinemas, U. (1989). Theoretische und empirische Beiträge zur Diagnostik strukturellen Wissens im Kontext dynamischer Systeme. *Berichte aus dem Psychologischen Institut der Universität Bonn, 15*, Heft 1.

Funke, J., Fahnenbruck, G., & Müller, H. (1986). DYNAMIS - Ein Computerprogramm zur Simulation dynamischer Systeme. *Berichte aus dem Psychologischen Institut der Universität Bonn, 12*, Heft 3.

Kemke, C. (1988). Der neuere Konnektionismus. Ein Überblick. *Informatik-Spektrum, 11*, 143-162.

Linden, A. (1989). *Untersuchungen von Backpropagation in konnektionistischen Systemen*. Bonn: Institut für Informatik der Universität (Diplomarbeit).

Mandl, H., & Spada, H. (Eds.) (1988). *Wissenspsychologie*. München: Psychologie Verlags Union.

McClelland, J.L., & Rumelhart, D.E. (Eds.) (1986). *Parallel distributed processing. Explorations in the microstructure of cognition. Volume 2: Psychological and biological models*. Cambridge, Mass.: MIT Press.

McClelland, J.L., & Rumelhart, D.E. (1988). *Explorations in parallel distributed processing. A handbook of models, programs, and exercises*. Cambridge, Mass.: MIT Press.

Rumelhart, D.E., & McClelland, J.L. (Eds.) (1986). *Parallel distributed processing. Explorations in the microstructure of cognition. Volume 1: Foundations*. Cambridge, Mass.: MIT Press.

Verwendung von neuralen Netzwerken zur Klassifikation natürlicher Objekte am Beispiel der Baumerkennung aus Farb-Infrarot-Luftbildern

H. Bischof A. Pinz
Inst. f. Vermessungswesen u. Fernerkundung Univ. f. Bodenkultur
Peter Jordan Str. 82   A-1190 Wien

Abstract Es wird die Verwendung von neuralen Netzwerken zur Klassifikation von natürlichen Objekten erörtert, als Beispiel dient die Baumartenbestimmung von Bäumen auf Farb-Infrarot-Luftbildern. Es wird gezeigt, wie die Vorhersagegenauigkeit durch das Zusammenbauen von Netzwerken, die mit verschiedenen Parametern trainiert wurden, gesteigert werden kann, wobei WV-Diagramme (weight visualization diagrams) ein wertvolles Hilfsmittel darstellen. Weiters wird die Einbindung von neuralen Netzwerken in konventionelle bildverstehende Systeme diskutiert.

1. Einleitung

Konnektionistische Modelle scheinen speziell für den Bereich der Mustererkennung und des Bildverstehens besonders gut geeignet zu sein. In diesem Artikel wird versucht, die besonderen Vorteile aber auch die Nachteile dieser Methoden beim Erkennen und Klassifizieren von natürlichen Objekten aufzuzeigen. Natürliche Objekte wie Pflanzen, Tiere, Landschaftsformen usw. im Gegensatz zu künstlichen Objekten wie Gebäude, Straßen, Fahrzeuge usw. zeichnen sich dadurch aus, daß eine Beschreibung (dh. ein Objektmodell) wesentlich schwieriger zu erstellen ist, als bei künstlichen Objekten. Dadurch wird es auch wesentlich schwieriger, konventionelle Programme wie Expertensysteme zu entwickeln, die solche Objekte erkennen können. Man findet in der Literatur auch wesentlich mehr Beispiele zum Erkennen von künstlichen Objekten z.B. [2,9] und nur sehr wenige zum Erkennen natürlicher Objekte [5,10,11]. Natürliche Objekte können oft viel schwerer in Kategorien eingeteilt werden, d.h. die Grenzen zwischen den einzelnen Klassen sind viel fließender, und weniger leicht zu beschreiben.

All dies läßt konnektionistische Modelle mit ihrer Lernfähigkeit besonders gut geeignet erscheinen, natürliche Objekte zu erkennen. Es muß keine Objektbeschreibung mehr vorhanden sein, diese sowie die Grenze zwischen einzelnen Kategorien ergibt sich in natürlicher Weise aus den Beispielen der Trainingsmenge.

Als konkretes Beispiel für eine Klassifikation von natürlichen Objekten soll die Bestimmung der Baumart von Bäumen auf Farb-Infrarot-Luftbildern dienen. In Abb. 1 ist der grüne Farbauszug eines Farb-Infrarot-Luftbildes dargestellt, wie er auch bei den Untersuchungen verwendet wurde. In diesem Ausschnitt sind zwei Baumarten (Fichte = F, Kiefer = K) vorhanden. Die Verwendung von Luftbildmaterial ist in zweierlei Hinsicht interessant: Einerseits bildet ein System, das die Baumart von Bäumen bestimmen kann, die Grundlage für ein System zur Erfassung des Waldzustandes, und andererseits sind diese Daten für konnektionistische Modelle interessant, da mit einem relativ kleinen Bildausschnitt gearbeitet werden kann (Kronen-durchmesser), aber sich in diesem kleinen Ausschnitt eine ungeheure Vielfalt an Formen, Farben und Textur findet. Außerdem handelt es sich hierbei um natürliche Daten die etwas "verrauscht" sind, sodaß konnektionistische Modelle ihre volle Stärke entfalten können.

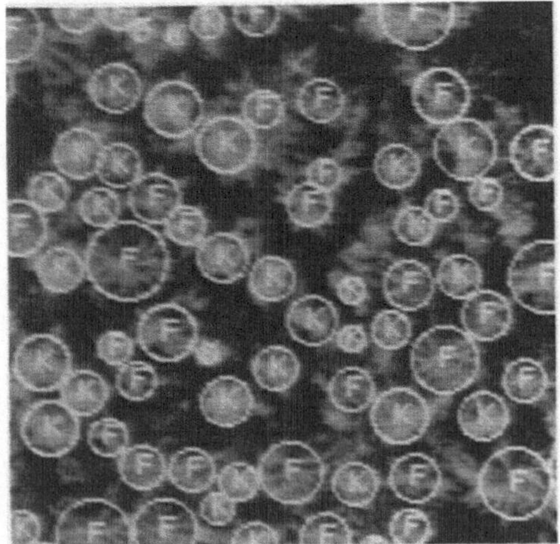

Abb. 1　　　　　　　　　　　Luftbild

Die Aufgabe die das neurale Netzwerk erlernen sollte, war es, die Baumart der einzelnen Bäume zu bestimmen. Dabei sollten ohne wesentliche Vorverarbeitung direkt die Pixel des digitalisierten Luftbildes als Input für das Netz verwendet werden. Menschliche Interpreten, die für diese Aufgabe eigens geschult werden, betrachten die Luftbilder mit einem Stereoskop (drei-dimensionales Bild), und interpretieren annähernd 100% der Bäume richtig. Das läßt darauf schließen, daß die visuelle Information zum Bestimmen der Baumart ausreichend ist.

Die Baumart eines Baumes läßt sich durch folgende Eigenschaften charakterisieren: Form (dies ist vor allem im Zusammenhang mit Stereosehen interessant), Farbe (die jedoch von Bildqualität und Kronenzustand des Baumes abhängt), Textur und Hintergrundinformation (wie z.B., daß ab einer gewissen Seehöhe eine Baumart nicht mehr auftritt).

In weiterer Folge wird zuerst das neurale Netzwerk und einige wesentliche Versuche besprochen, dann wird auf die Zusammenarbeit zwischen dem Vision Expert System (VES), das die Information liefert, wo ein Baum im Bild steht, und Netzwerk eingegangen. Es wird versucht aufzuzeigen, wie Systeme der klassischen AI mit jenen der Sub-symbolischen AI in geeigneter Weise zu einem hybriden Gesamtsystem verbunden werden können.

2. Netzwerk, Daten und Codierung

Das Netzwerk wie es in Abb. 2 dargstellt ist, ist ein 3 Layer Feed-Forward Netzwerk, das mit Backpropa-gation [13,14] trainiert wurde (Versuche mit einem 4. Layer brachten wesentlich schlechtere Ergebnisse. Außerdem wurde in [7] bewiesen, daß ein 3 Layer Netzwerk jede Borel-Meßbare Funktion beliebig genau approximieren kann, sofern die Anzahl der Hidden Units ausreichend ist.). Der Input Layer besteht aus 480 Units. Als Input dienen die Pixel von zwei Farbkanälen (grün und rot) und noch zusätzlich 30 Units für eine lokale Codierung des Baumkronenradius. Der Bildausschnitt, der mit einem solchen Netz bearbeitet wird, ist ein Quadrat mit einer Seitenlänge von 15 Pixel. Es wurden nur zwei der insgesamt drei verfügbaren Farbkanäle verwendet, weil der blaue und grüne Kanal (in der Natur entspricht dies dem grünen und roten Spektralbereich) bei Farb-Infrarot-Luftbildern stark korreliert sind, sodaß es nur zu einem minimalen Infor-mationsgewinn kommen würde, der in keiner Relation zur Zunahme an Rechenzeit stünde.

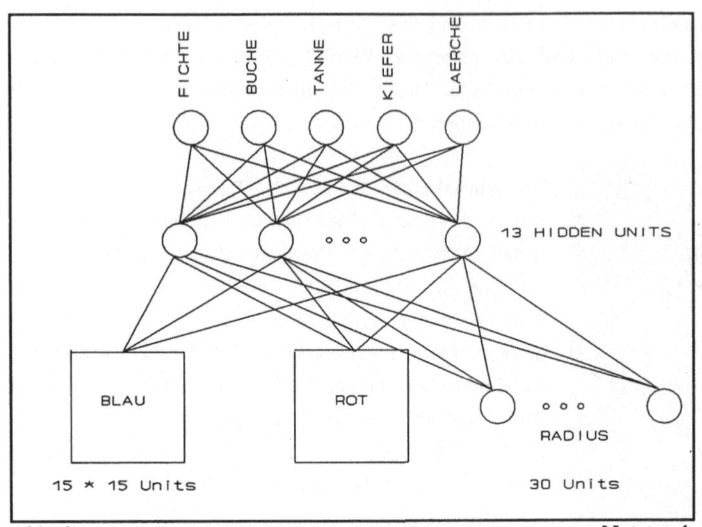

Abb. 2   Netzwerk

Das Bild wird zuerst mit einer kontrasterhöhenden Funktion, die den gesamten Grauwertebereich von [0 .. 255] ausnützt, vorverarbeitet. Die Pixelwerte werden nun mit Hilfe einer nichtlinearen sigmoiden Funktion, die eine weitere Kontrasterhöhung für Pixelwerte des mittleren Grauwertebereichs bewirkt, auf das Intervall [-0.5 .. 0.5] abgebildet. Diese Werte dienen dann als Input für das Netzwerk.

Der Output Layer besteht aus 5 Units. Der Output, der angeben soll, welche Baumart der Baum besitzt, der am Input angelegt wurde, wird lokal codiert. Bei diesen Untersuchungen wurde mit fünf verschiedenen Baumarten (Fichte, Buche, Tanne, Kiefer und Lärche) gearbeitet.

Bei anfänglichen Versuchen [3,4] hat sich 13 als ideale Anzahl von Hidden Units herausgestellt. Bei weniger Hidden Units konnte das Problem nicht mehr vollständig gelernt werden, und bei mehr als 13 Hidden Units nahm die Generalisieriungsfähigkeit ab. Dies geht völlig konform mit der Theorie, denn in [1] wurde gezeigt, daß mit einer möglichst geringen Anzahl von Hidden Units die beste Generalisierungsfähigkeit erzielt wird.

Die Daten, welche zum Trainieren und Testen der Vorhersagegenauigkeit verwendet wurden, stammten aus zwei unterschiedlichen Bildern. Dabei hatte das erste Bild den kleinstmöglichen Maßstab, der eine Erkennung der Baumart noch zuläßt (ca. 1:15000), und das zweite Bild hatte den größten Maßstab, der bei der Befliegung zur Waldschadenserfassung zu Testzwecken angefertigt wurde (1:4000). Vom ersten Bild wurden 258 Bäume in die Trainingsmenge aufgenommen, dabei wurden die Kiefern und Lärchen doppelt aufgenommen, da sie sonst in der Trainingsmenge unterrepräsentiert gewesen wären. Von diesem Bild wurden 110 Bäume die nicht in der Trainingsmenge enthalten waren, zum Testen der Vorhersagegenauigkeit verwendet. Vom zweiten Bild, das nur Fichten und Kiefern enthielt, wurden 52 Bäume in die Trainingsmenge und 190 Bäume in die Testmenge aufgenommen. Außerdem wurden noch zwanzig zufällig generierte Muster der Trainingsmenge hinzugefügt, diese Muster sollten für alle Output Units den Wert 0 liefern (nicht klassifiziert bzw. kein Baum), dies diente dazu, das Lernen zu stabilisieren.

Die Trainingsmenge von 330 Bäumen ist sicher noch zu klein um optimale Vorhersageresultate zu erzielen, jedoch standen für diese Untersuchungen keine weiteren Daten zur Verfügung. Dennoch lassen die Ergebnisse diese Methode vielversprechend erscheinen.

Da die hier vorgestellte Methode auch auf Bilder unterschiedlichen Maßstabs angewendet werden soll (für die Erkennung der Baumart scheinen Maßstäbe zwischen 1:4000 bis 1:15000 sinnvoll), und in Abhängigkeit von Bildmaßstab und Baumart recht unterschiedliche Kronenradien auftreten, ist es nötig, die Baumkronen an das Inputfenster anzupassen. Die Form der Maßstabskalibrierung, die sich bei den Versuchen als ideal herausgestellt hat, wird als Mittelcoding bezeichnet. In Abb. 3 ist sie schematisch dargestellt. Dabei wird in Abhängigkeit von Eingabe-und Ausgabemaßstab eine Schrittweite errechnet. Nun wird beim linken oberen Pixel des zu bearbeitenden Bildausschnittes begonnen. Trifft man genau auf ein Pixel, ist dies auch der Wert des Ausgabepixels. Trifft man hingegen nicht genau auf ein Pixel im Eingabebild, dann ergibt sich das Ausgabepixel

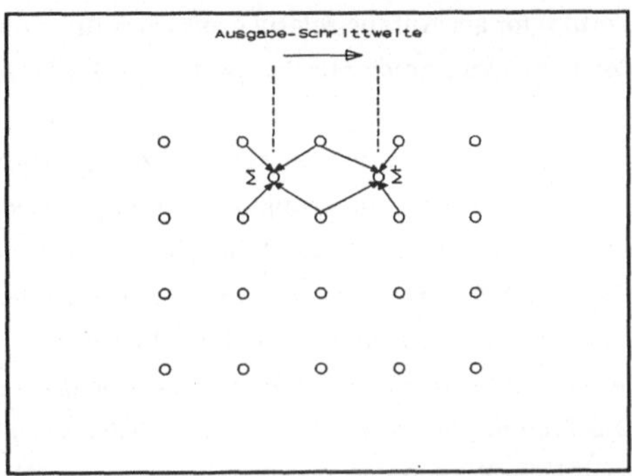

Abb. 3 Mittelcoding

aus der gewichteten Summe der vier am nächsten liegenden Pixel. Anschließend wird wieder um den Wert der Schrittweite weitergegangen.

Diese Form der Maßstabskalibrierung wird immer für ein ganzes Bild mit dem selben Ausgabemaßstab angewandt. Dadurch werden alle Bilder auf einen einheitlichen Normmaßstab bezogen. In den hier dargestellten Versuchen wurde mit einem Normmaßstab von ca. 1:15000 gearbeitet, was bei einem Inputfenster von 15 * 15 Pixel einen optimalen Kronenradius von 7 Pixel = 5,2m ergibt. Kleinere Kronen werden außen mit der Farbe schwarz aufgefüllt, von größeren Kronen wird nur ein Ausschnitt des zentralen Wipfelbereichs genommen.

Ein solches Vorgehen zeigt für das Netzwerk ein wesentlich besseres Ergebnis als die Anpassung jedes Baumes an das Input Fenster, denn dadurch bleiben artspezifische Merkmale der einzelnen Baumarten besser erhalten. Dieses Verfahren zeigt auch geringfügig bessere Resultate als ein Coarse Coding Schema [6]. Da immer nur die vier Nachbarpixel den Wert eines Ausgabepixels bestimmen, geht zwar bei einer Verkleinerung um mehr als den Faktor zwei Information verloren, aber der Kontrast im Bild bleibt viel besser erhalten. Wie sich bei den Versuchen gezeigt hat, ist das Netzwerk relativ sensitiv gegenüber Veränderungen des Kontrastes, wodurch auch erklärt wird warum Coarse Coding etwas schlechter als Mittelcoding ist.

3. Training und Ergebnisse

Es wurde mit einer großen Zahl verschiedener Parameterkonfigurationen experimentiert, die Ergebnisse sind in [3] genau beschrieben. Als ideale Parameter haben sich dabei folgende erwiesen: Die Gewichte wurden zu Beginn des Lernens mit gleichverteilen Zufallszahlen aus dem Intervall [-0.3 .. 0.3] und die Schwellwerte mit -1.8 initialisiert. Es wurde nicht mit einem fixen Lernfaktor gearbeitet sondern der Lernfaktor wurde zu Beginn relativ groß gewählt (um 0.7) und im Laufe des Lernprozesses automatisch gesenkt. Dazu wird der Summed Squared Error (SSE) beobachtet. Immer wenn der SSE inherhalb von 20 Durchläufen mindestens zweimal steigt, wird der Lernfaktor um einen fixen Wert vermindert (typischerweise 0.05), außer er ist bereits kleiner oder gleich diesem fixen Wert. Durch diese Form der Wahl des Lernfaktors kann der

Lernfaktor am Anfang relativ groß gewählt werden, und wenn es im Netzwerk zu Oszillationen kommt, wird der Lernfaktor automatisch gesenkt, wodurch das Netzwerk den Fehler dann weiter reduzieren kann.

Ein weiterer Parameter der sich als sehr nützlich erwiesen hat war "Gaussian Weight Update". Dabei wird nicht die Gewichtsänderung verwendet, wie sie von der Backpropagation geliefert wird, sondern eine Zufallszahl, die normalverteilt ist, generiert. Der Erwartungswert dieser Zufallszahl entspricht der Gewichtsänderung wie sie von der Backpropagation geliefert wird. Die so erhaltene Zahl wird als Gewichtsänderung zum alten Gewicht addiert. Durch diese Form des Updates können lokale Minima, die bei Gradientenverfahren wie der Backpropagation immer eine Gefahr darstellen, leichter vermieden werden. Die Trainingsdaten werden dem Netzwerk während des Lernens in zufälliger Reihenfolge präsentiert, und nach jeder Präsentation um 90 Grad gedreht. Dies wurde vor allem deshalb gemacht, weil meist ein Teil der Baumkrone aufgrund von Sonnenstand und Blickwinkel im Schatten liegen, und in diesem Bereich das Netzwerk sehr wenig lernen kann (Die Inputwerte sind sehr klein). Da aber Bäume in jeder Orientierung erkannt werden sollten und in der vorhandenen Trainingsmenge ein bestimmter Sonnenstand vorgegeben war, wurde es nötig, diese Operation einzuführen.

Die so trainierten Netzwerke erzielten Vorhersagegenauigkeiten von ca. 80% (für den Datensatz mit Fichte und Kiefer) bzw. 84% (für den Datensatz mit fünf Baumarten). Diese Vorhersagegenauigkeiten konnten durch das Zusammenbauen von Netzen, das nachfolgend erörtert wird, noch gesteigert werden.

4. WV-Diagramme und Zusammenbau von Netzwerken

Zum Betrachten der Gewichte eines Netzwerkes wurde eine Darstellung entwickelt, die Hinton Diagrammen ähnlich, jedoch für Bilddaten wesentlich übersichtlicher ist, und sich als sehr nützlich herausgestellt hat. Diese "Weight-Visualization Diagrams" (WV-Diagramme) wurden bereits in [3,4,12] genauer erörtert. Sie entstehen dadurch, daß man die Gewichte der Hidden Units, die ja die Eingabe Pixel gewichten, wieder in der gleichen Form wie die Pixel des ursprünglichen Bildes darstellt. Je nach Betrag und Größe des Gewichtes erhält jetzt ein Pixel des WV-Diagrammes eine Farbe zugeordnet. Positive Gewichte werden in Rot und negative Gewichte in Cyan (blau und grün) dargestellt. Je größer der Absolutbetrag eines Gewichtes, desto heller wird es dargestellt (d.h. das Größte positive Gewicht ist ganz rot). Außerdem werden die Gewichte für die beiden Farbauszüge in zwei verschiedenen WV-Diagrammen dargestellt. Oberhalb eines WV-Diagrammes werden die Gewichte die eine Hidden Unit zu den Output Units besitzt gezeigt, und links neben dem Diagramm wird der Schwellwert und der zusätzliche Input (lokal codierter Kronenradius) dargestellt. In Abb. 4 ist ein typisches WV-Diagramm gezeigt. Abb. 5 zeigt die WV-Diagramme für alle 13 Hidden Units eines Netzes (insgesamt 26 WV-Diagramme, da für jeden Farbauszug ein Diagramm entsteht). Hier mußte jedoch aus reproduktionstechnischen Gründen auf die Farbe verzichtet werden, und negative Gewichte dunkel und positive Gewichte hell dargestellt werden. Wie man sieht, bildet sich in den Gewichten der Hidden Units eine "baumkronenartige Struktur" heran. Aber man sieht auch, daß es Hidden Units gibt, deren Gewichte des rezeptiven wie auch des projektiven Feldes [8] alle annähernd gleich sind. Dieses Fehlen von Struktur läßt sich durch die Berechnung der empirischen Varianz der Gewichte quantifizieren. Da diese Hidden Units offensichtlich nichts zu einer Unterscheidung der einzelnen Baumarten beitragen, können sie weggelassen werden, ohne die Performanz des Netzwerkes zu beeinträchtigen. Außerdem läßt sich beobachten, daß Netze, die mit unterschiedlichen Parameterkonfigurationen trainiert wurden, unterschiedliche Schwächen aufweisen. Daher liegt der Gedanke nahe, daß Hidden Units verschiedener Netze ausgetauscht werden können, um so die Vorhersagegenauigkeit zu steigern.

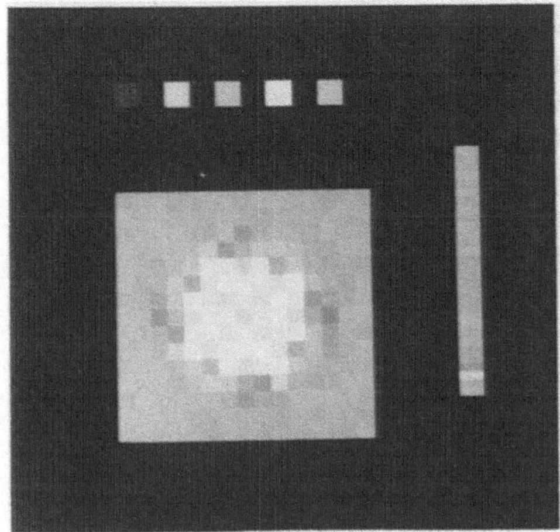

Abb. 4   WV-Diagramm

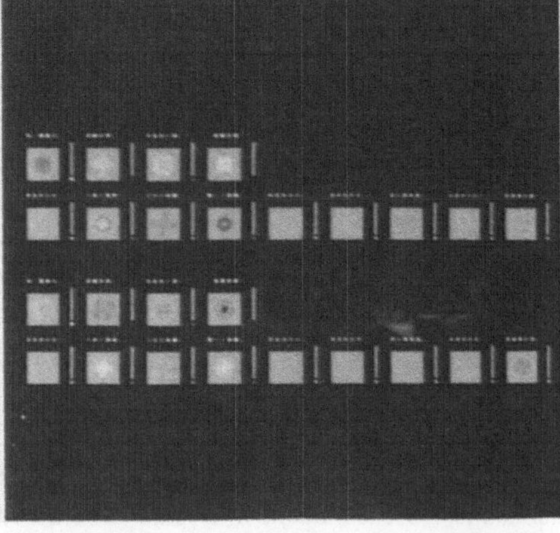

Abb. 5   WV-Diagramme

Beim Zusammenbau verschiedener Netze wurden zuerst die Hidden Units ohne Struktur ersetzt. Die Gewichte der Output Units wurden wieder zufällig gewählt. Dann wurde das Netzwerk mit einem sehr kleinen Lernfaktor (um 0.05) ca. 100 Schritte trainiert. Danach wurden wieder die WV-Diagramme betrachtet und eventuell weitere Ersetzungen vorgenommen. Wie in [3,12] beschrieben, ist das Finden einer geeigneten Ersetzung keineswegs ein triviales Unterfangen, vor allem deshalb weil die Repräsentation, die das Netzwerk entwickelt, hochgradig verteilt ist, und es sehr schwierig ist die geeigneten Hidden Units zu finden. Eine Heuristik die vielfach Verwendung fand war, solche Hidden Units auszuwählen die ein stark positives Gewicht zu einer Baumart hatten, die im ursprünglichen Netz schwer erkannt wurde.

Durch das Zusammenbauen von Netzwerken konnte die Vorhersagegenauigkeit auf ca. 84% (Datensatzatz mit Fichte und Kiefer) bis 88% (Datensatz mit fünf Baumarten) verbessert werden, was eine deutliche Steigerung darstellt. Eine Möglichkeit, diesen Ansatz zu systematisieren, wäre die Verwendung von genetischen Algorithmen. Dabei würde die Anfangspopulation bereits trainierte Netze darstellen. Danach werden die besten Individuen (beste Vorhersagegenauigkeit) zur Rekombination (Austausch von Hidden Units) ausgewählt. Die daraus neu entstehende Population wird wieder bewertet, die schlechtesten Individuen sterben, und der Prozeß beginnt von neuem.

Die Netzwerke sind auch fehlertolerant. Es können bis zu 10% der Pixel gestört werden, ohne daß sich dies auf die Performanz negativ auswirken würde. Beim Lernen wirken sich Störungen allerdings wesentlich nachteiliger aus, das Netzwerk kann nur ca. 75% des Trainingssets erlernen, gegenüber 92% bei nicht gestörtem Input. Daher sollte darauf geachtet werden, daß die Bilder die zum Trainieren verwendet werden, eine möglichst gute Qualität aufweisen (kleine Störungen sind fast immer in den Luftbildern enthalten und können nie ganz beseitigt werden).

5.Integration in VES

Da das hier vorgestellte System zum Erkennen der Baumart bereits wissen muß, wo ein Baum ungefähr steht (Verschiebungen bis zu zwei Pixeln kann das System noch ohne nennenswerte Verschlechterung der Ergebnisse bewältigen), ist unbedingt ein System notwendig, das angeben kann, wo ein Baum im Bild zu finden ist. Dies leistet das Vision Expert System VES das in [10,11] ausführlich beschrieben ist. VES liefert aufgrund des verwendeten Algorithmus im Zentrum des besonnten Wipfelteiles Mittelpunkt und Radius an das neurale Netzwerk. Verschiebungen um einige Pixel sind durchaus möglich. Die Zusammenarbeit zwischen VES und dem neuralen Netzwerk ist zur Zeit noch nicht voll ausgebaut, und beschränkt sich darauf, daß das Netzwerk von VES aus mit allen relevanten Parametern initialisiert wird. Das Wissen über diese Parameter ist in VES in Procedure-Frames gespeichert. Nach der Initialisierung schickt VES an das Netzwerk den Baumkronenmittelpunkt und Radius, das Netzwerkmodul sucht den Baum im Bild, nimmt die notwendigen Codierungen vor, und schickt an VES die Aktivierungen der Output Units zurück. VES entscheidet aufgrund dieser Information und eventuell anderen Informationen, welche Baumart vorhanden ist.

VES dient in diesem Fall dazu, die Aufmerksamkeit des Netzwerkes auf einen kleinen Bildausschnitt zu fokussieren, der dann vom Netz näher untersucht wird. Diese Vorgangsweise scheint generell für konnektionistische Modelle interessant, da ein Netzwerk, das mit einem ganzen Bild (von typischerweise 512 * 512 Pixel) arbeitet, zur Zeit noch nicht realisierbar scheint. Wenn nun aber ein konventionelles bildverstehendes System dazu in der Lage ist, die Aufmerksamkeit eines Netzes auf einen kleinen Bildbereich zu fokussieren, kann in diesem kleinen Bereich ein Netzwerk effizient eingesetzt werden. Diese Vorgangsweise bietet noch weitere Vorteile. Im übergeordneten System kann das Wissen, das symbolisch beschreibbar ist, gespeichert und effizient genutzt werden. In diesem Beispiel wäre dies z.B. das Wissen, daß ab einer gewissen Seehöhe eine bestimmte Baumart nicht mehr vorkommt. Dieses Wissen kann von VES verwaltet und zur Entscheidungsfindung herangezogen werden.

Eine andere Perspektive ergibt sich, wenn man Expertensysteme dazu einsetzt, Netze zu trainieren. Im Falle von VES könnte dies wie folgt aussehen: VES ist in der Lage, Bäume auf Farb-Infrarot-Luftbildern zu finden. Bei diesem Prozeß erzeugt es eine Reihe von Hypothesen, wo ein Baum stehen könnte. Im Laufe der Abarbeitung werden diese Hypothesen in einem relativ zeitaufwendigen Verfahren dann sukzessive angenommen oder verworfen. Wenn nun aber VES zusätzlich ein Netzwerk trainiert, dann würde das Netzwerk im Laufe der Zeit lernen, welches Objekt ein Baum und welches Objekt kein Baum ist. Da das Netzwerk wesentlich schneller arbeitet als VES, könnte, wenn das Netzwerk die nötige Performanz erreicht hat, der Prozeß des Testens von Hypothesen vollständig vom Netzwerk übernommen werden, und VES würde nur mehr dazu dienen, die Hypothesen zu generieren. Diese Vorgangsweise erscheint sinnvoller als ein Netzwerk mit einer fixen Trainingsmenge zu trainieren, da das Netzwerk, wenn es von VES trainiert wird, nur mehr jene Fälle lernen muß, die VES tatsächlich generiert. Dies ergibt sich daraus, daß das Netzwerk keinen "unnötigen Balast" lernen muß der im praktischen Einsatz nie auftreten würde, dadurch müßte auch das Generalisierungsverhalten des Netzwerkes gesteigert werden.

6. Diskussion

In dieser Arbeit wurde gezeigt, wie neurale Netzwerke sinnvoll zum Erkennen von natürlichen Objekten eingesetzt werden können. Es wurden Vorhersagegenauigkeiten von 88% erreicht, die aber durch eine größere Trainingsmenge noch gesteigert werden sollten. Es wurde auch gezeigt, daß die Methode mit Bildern unterschiedlichen Maßstabs arbeiten kann und relativ unempfindlich gegenüber Störungen beim Klassifizieren ist. Der Zusammenbau von Netzwerken stellt eine Möglichkeit dar, wie das Wissen das in einem Netzwerk herangebildet wird beeinflußt werden kann. Es wäre aber wünschenswert diesen Ansatz zu verallgemeinern und zu automatisieren. Dazu wurde die Verwendung von genetischen Algorithmen kurz diskutiert, die Gegenstand künftiger Forschungen sein wird.

Der Aufbau eines kompletten bildverstehenden Systems ausschließlich aus konnektionistischen Modellen erscheint zwar interessant, stößt aber auf eine Vielzahl von Problemen. Die Verbindung von klassischen Systemen mit neuralen Netzwerken zu einem hybriden Gesamtsystem scheint ein Weg zu sein, die Vorteile beider Methoden voll zu nutzen und zu vereinigen.

Literatur

[1] Anshelerich, V.V., Amirikian, A.V., Lukashin, A.V., Frank-Komenetskii, M.D.,
On the Ability of Neural Networks to Perform Generalisation by Induction,
Biol. Cybernetics, 61,125-128, 1989.

[2] Behrens, K., Gabler, H., Gabler, R., Nicolin, B., Sties, M.,
Ein wissensbasiertes System zur Analyse von Luftbildern in:
Hartmann G. (Hrsg.): Mustererkennung 1986, 8. DAGM-Symposion
Paderborn IFB 125, Springer 1986.

[3] Bischof H.,
Interpretation von Fernerkundungsdaten mit Hilfe von Backpropagation
Netzwerken am Beispiel der Baumerkennung aus Farb-Infrarot Luftbildern,
Diplomarbeit der TU-Wien, 1989.

[4] Bischof, H., Pinz, A.,
Verwendung von neuralen Netzwerken zur Bestimmung der Baumart
aus digitalen Rasterbildern, in:
Pinz (ed.): Wissensbasierte Mustererkennung, OCG Schriftenreihe 49, Oldenbourg 1989.

[5] Haenel S., Tränker H., Eckstein W.,
Automatic Detection of Tree Crowns in Aerial Photographs: The Path trough
the Bottelneck, in: 2. DFVLR-Statusseminar, Oberpfaffenhofen, 1987.

[6] Hinton, G.E., McCelland, J.L., Rumelhart, D.E.,
Distributed Representations, in: Rumelhart,McCelland (Hrsg),
Parallel Distributed Processing, Vol I, MIT Press, 1986.

[7] Hornik, K.,
Multilayer Feedforward Networks are Universal Approximators,
Neural Networks, Vol 2, 359-366, 1989.

[8] Lehky, S.R., Sejnowski, T.J.,
Network model of shape-from-shading:
neural function arises from both receptive and projective fields,
Nature, 333, 452-454, 1988.

[9] Matsuyama T., Hwang V.,
SIGMA: a framework for image understanding, integration of bottom-up and top-down processes
9. IJCAI 1985 Proc. Vol.2

[10] Pinz, A.,
Final Results of the Vision Expert System VES: Finding Trees
in Aerial Photographs, in:
Pinz (ed.): Wissensbasierte Mustererkennung, OCG Schriftenreihe 49, Oldenbourg 1989.

[11] Pinz, A.,
Ein bildverstehendes Experten System zur Erkennung von Bäumen auf
Farb-Infrarot-Luftbildern,
Dissertation TU Wien, Okt. 1988.

[12] Pinz, A., Bischof, H.,
Constructing a Neural Network for the Interpretation of the Species of Trees
in Aerial Photographs, Proc. 10. ICPR, IEEE Atlantic City, 1990.

[13] Rumelhart, D.E., Hinton, G.E., Williams, R.J.,
Learning Internal Representations by Error Propagation,
in Rumelhart,McClelland (Hrsg.),
Parallel Distributed Processing, Vol I, MIT Press, 1986.

[14] Rumelhart, D.E., Hinton, G.E., Williams, R.J.,
Learning representations by back-propagating errors,
Nature, 323, 533-536, 1986.

Diese Arbeiten wurden im Rahmen des Forschungsschwerpunktes "Schwerpunkt Fernerkundung", Projekt S38/2 des Fonds zur Förderung der wissenschaftlichen Forschung finanziert.

A Connectionist Realization Applying Knowledge-Compilation and Auto-Segmentation in a Symbolic Assignment Problem

Holger G. Ziegeler   *Karl W. Kratky*

Universität Wien
Institut für Experimentalphysik, Boltzmanngasse 5, A–1090 Wien
email: hgz@awirap.bitnet

Abstract

A symbolic assignment problem has been solved by making use of the fact that it can be represented as a decomposable production system. We explain how the structure of the given constraint satisfaction problem (CSP) can be exploited to design a two component architecture of a neural net interacting with a scheduler. We describe the relation of problem parameters to the net design, using a feedforward net with error backpropagation. Different versions of the net design are contrasted. We discuss the advantages of our architecture and relate the results of the connectionist approach to a solving of the problem with backtrack search. The CSP was part of a case study, a knowledge-based system for the automatic configuration of telephone exchanges. An enlargement of the architecture and its application is foreseen.

1 Introduction and Summary

This article intends to contribute to the discussion on the applicability of neural nets in the area of *symbolic* computation. The connectionist approach has widely proven to yield valuable solutions in *subsymbolic* processing tasks (often viewed as pre-processing) like those that are presented by vision and speech. Problems above this level can certainly be treated by neural nets, but despite of their parallel processing capability their performance often seems to be estimated less favourable than that of conventional computation due to excessive size or time complexity [1]. Refined architectures have been designed to manipulate complex symbolic data structures [2]. For problems of limited complexity a direct translation of problem structure to the net's connectivity can be tried (as for the problem of non-attacking queens treated by [11]). We want to show that a certain constellation of a given task can enable a net solution, although the problem is regarded to be too complex to allow an *a priori* specification of the knowledge representation in the net. The given task is of potentially unlimited size, and although there appear some global invariances in the problem solutions, they are yet unknown when the problem is posed.

We addressed this question in the course of a case study, an automatic configuration system for telephone exchanges (TELEPRO). This *knowledge-based system* was meant to represent more than just a task-specific solution. Its realization shows distinct innovative features in the overall design as well as in certain problem solving aspects. A general strategy in this study was to clarify the notion of reasoning and to relate it to different AI programming paradigms. This lead to the integration of different mechanisms in the sense of hybrid (or *eclectic*) programming, using for each subproblem the method fitting "best" to it [5].

Here we present a description of the solving of a formal *constraint satisfaction problem* (CSP), which was achieved with a two-component architecture of a neural net interacting with a scheduler. An aim was to generalize conditions how to proceed from a formal description to the design of an implementation. In this article, we describe the use of the connectionist component to learn the knowledge on partial solutions in the sense of knowledge-compilation. In another architecture, solutions are found performing a constraint satisfaction search in an informed backtracking algorithm [12], where the knowledge has to be cast into the implementation of static look-ahead and look-back.

After general remarks on the case study and a formal definition of the problem, we explain the two-component architecture of the system. The reasons which made this problem accessible for this solution are mentioned. The most important issue here is the emergence of a cyclic pattern due the decomposable character of the CSP. The consequences for the net design follow, concluded by a discussion of the performance of different versions. The basic correspondences and differences to the conventional (backtrack) solution and an enlargement of the architecture are outlined.

2 Definition of the Problem

The case study has been conducted in the domain of the configuration of telephone exchanges. In this context *configuration* means determining the *dimensions* of the exchange including calculations based on traffic theory, combined with subsequent *material assignment* and *placement*. Since the telephone system in question has a world-wide distribution and comes in numerous variants with frequent updates, a solution in this domain requires a high degree of flexibility.

As part of the configuration task, basically two different constraint satisfaction problems can be found. One is the assignment and placement of various modules to module frames, the other deals with the connections between different logical units (realized by certain physical components). Only the latter problem, which poses the more interesting aspects, has been realized comparing a conventional symbolic and a connectionist approach.

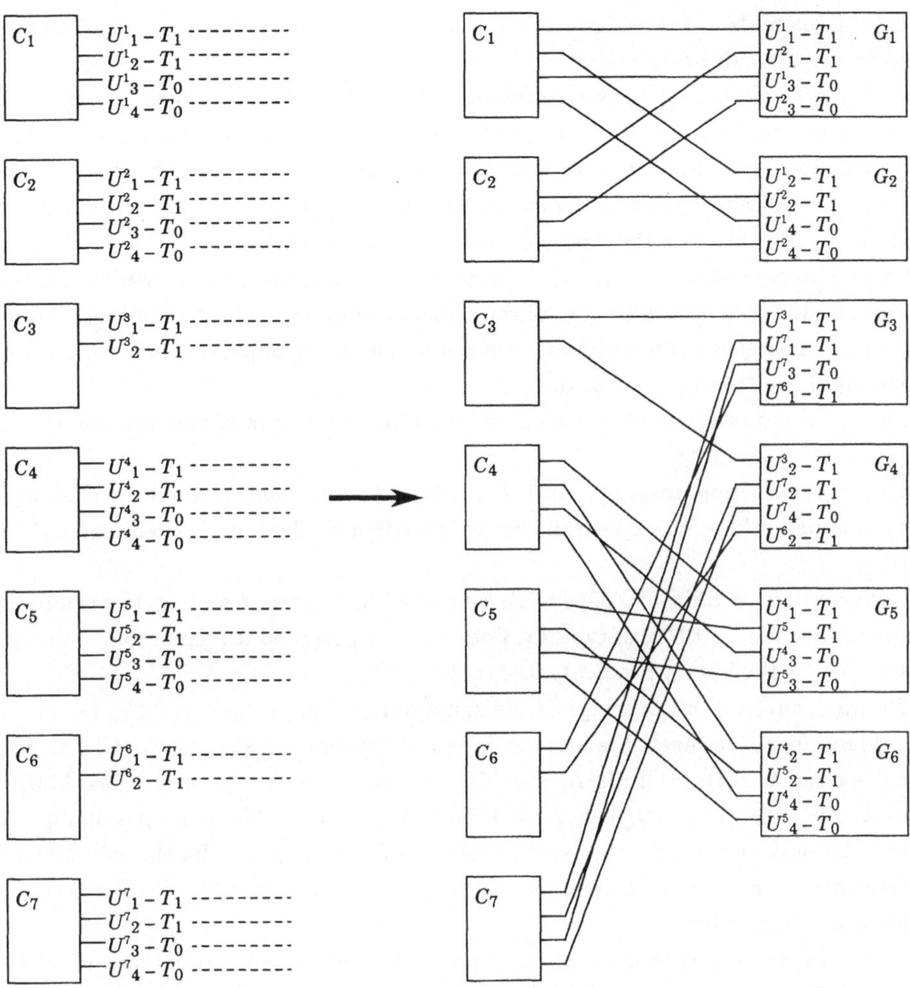

Fig. 1. An example of the assignment of connections generated by the system
(left part: given problem, right part: solution)

In the domain, the term "connection" means a link between different objects, physically being realized by cables. This notion must be distinguished from the meaning in the design of a neural net, where a "connection" describes the mechanism in which the output of a certain neuron serves as input for some other neuron. Similarly, the "units" of the domain must not be identified with the neurons in the net, although a certain correspondence was established via the input and output coding of the net (see Section 4.2).

Consider the following formal (and symbolic) representation of the CSP, stated in the usual formalism [7] (for the domain related reasons of the conditions see [12]). Fig. 1, which shows a small example of the assignment of connections generated by the system, may serve as a help to visualize the description.

Given is a known number n_C of concentrators $C_1 \ldots C_{n_C}$. The concentrators are connected to n_U connection units $U_1 \ldots U_{n_U}$ of a given type T_1 or T_0 according to the following rule. Each concentrator C_k is connected either to 2 connection units $U^k{}_{i_1}$ and $U^k{}_{i_2}$ (both of type T_1) or to 4 connection units $U^k{}_{i_1} \ldots U^k{}_{i_4}$ (two pairs each consisting of one unit of type T_1 and one of type T_0). (This is one of a variety of possible cases in the domain).

The goal is to assemble all connection units in a minimal number n_G (which is unknown and therefore subject to minimization) of connection groups $G_1 \ldots G_{n_G}$ satisfying certain conditions. This is modelled as an assignment of the connection group G_j to each connection unit $U^k{}_i$ satisfying the following constraints:

(C1)   Each connection group G_j must be assigned to a minimum of one and a maximum of four connection units.

(C2)   The two connection units $U^k{}_{i_1}$ and $U^k{}_{i_2}$ of type T_1 connected to a concentrator C_k must be assigned different connection groups, specified by the binary predicate $DIFF(U^k{}_{i_1}, U^k{}_{i_2})$.

(C3)   Each connection unit $U^k{}_{i_1}$ of type T_0 connected to a concentrator C_k forms a pair with one connection unit $U^k{}_{i_2}$ of type T_1. Both must be assigned the same connection group, specified by the binary predicate $SAME(U^k{}_{i_1}, U^k{}_{i_2})$.

(C4)   For all connection units assigned the same connection group $U_{i_1} \ldots U_{i_K}$ ($K=1\ldots4$) the total number of connected telephone lines (via the concentrators) $l(U_{i_k})$ ($k=1\ldots K$) must not exceed a certain limit L, specified by unary to 4-ary predicates $LIMIT(U_{i_k}, k=1\ldots K) \equiv \Sigma_{k=1\ldots K} \, l(U_{i_k}) \leqq L$. (C4) does not apply in the example of Fig. 1, and actually only very rarely applies. For this reason, we neglect it for the solving methods described in this article. It must be mentioned, however, that (C4) destroys the regular patterns if it applies.

In addition to the requested minimization of n_G, the problem also contains certain other optimizations. Unfortunately, the criteria for these are only somewhat informally specified in the domain, so that no explicit cost function could be given. Instead, we modelled these as heuristics and defined a solution to be *optimal* if it found an assignment to a minimal number of connection groups using these heuristics:

(H1)   The requested minimality of the number of connection groups n_G urges to assign as many connection units to one connection group as possible (maximum 4), as long as this does not violate the constraints.

(H2)   The first two connection units assigned to a connection group shall preferably be of type T_1, the last two preferably of type T_0, as long as this does not violate the constraints or contradict (H1).

(H3)   Connection units connected to concentrators serving telephone lines with a certain attribute shall be grouped together, as long as this does not violate the constraints or contradict (H1) or (H2).

(H4)   Apart from consequences of the previous constraints and heuristics, the connection
units shall not be reordered.

The search tries to find appropriate connections satisfying the constraints and using the heuristics. Their consequences can be exemplified using the example of Fig. 1. Given there is a problem consisting of seven concentrators (and the related predicates, which are not shown in the figure) for which connection units and groups must be created and assigned. (C1) determines the size of connection groups and prevents the senseless creation of unconnected connection groups, and (H1) obviously leads to fully assigned connection groups. (H4) is reflected in the fact that the concentrators appear in the order of their numbering. Due to the $DIFF$-predicate (C2) e.g. $U^1{}_1$ and $U^1{}_2$ are assigned the different connection groups G_1 and G_2, whereas due to the $SAME$-predicate (C3) e.g. $U^1{}_1$ and $U^1{}_3$ are assigned the same connection group G_1. With the exception of G_3 and G_4 (H2) is generally fulfilled. (H3) results in the visible crossing of connections due to the assumption that C_1, C_2, C_3, and C_7 contain the prerequisite attribute.

3   Embedding of Net Application in the Problem Analysis

In general, an analysis of given constraints and heuristics leads to results about the topology of the search space and may allow an automatic deduction of the algorithmic realization. In our case, several insights can be gained, which are described in detail in [12], where also a generalization of the underlying translation mechanisms from problem statement to solving algorithm is attempted. Here, we mention only those results which allow an implementation using a neural net.

The most important issue here is the emergence of a cyclic pattern in the solution due to the decomposable character of the CSP [8], since it can be split accordingly into component sub-problems. The size of the sub-problems is derived from structural parameters and a composition of the predicates formulating the problem constraints. This composition can be interpreted as the task to decouple the predicates, since it produces a decomposition of disjoint sets of variables with a composed predicate applying to each set. Yet another interpretation may view this as orthogonalization of search sub-spaces. More specifically, the assignment problem divides into these cyclic sub-problems, which have "ideal pairs" as their solution, and a certain limited size rest-problem.

This should be put in concrete terms. According to (H1) an optimal solution contains as many as possible fully connected groups. On the other hand, a kind of "multiplication" of the solution sets of the constraints (C2) and (C3) reveals that each concentrator is connected to exactly two connection groups. It can be shown that – depending on the number of actual connection units – between two and four concentrators can be combined together to fully satisfy two connection groups, which we then call an "ideal pair" (e.g. in Fig. 1 G_1G_2 with the connected concentrators C_1C_2). This defines the decomposable components of the CSP. A dedication to a partial solution is justified without risking the optimality of the global solution, if there are a minimum of four concentrators left in the rest problem. Then, rest problems contain up to seven (2·4−1) concentrators, and can be solved optimally.

Finally, it must be mentioned that heuristics (H2) and (H3) can be dealt with by sorting the order of concentrators from the start and satisfying a certain order internal to "ideal pairs". (H4) mainly states that the problem is not trivial.

Summarizing, there appear two different types of sub-problems, those which have "ideal pairs" as their solution, and a rest-problem which is different, because its solution may contain not fully assigned connection groups. This division is a consequence of the heuristics which must be followed in order to guarantee optimality. A special property of the decomposability is that we cannot specify a method to recognize the components (nor that there are components, let alone their type) before the actual partial solutions are known. This is a border case of decomposability which is usually exploited for the solving of a problem by segmentation into components, which can be solved individually. Such a beforehand segmentation cannot be done for this problem. Therefore, a special two-component architecture has been devised in which a *scheduler* presents possible concentrator candidates for a maximum size "ideal pair" or a rest-problem to a sub-problem recognizer-and-solver which iteratively picks out a partial solution and hands the yet unassigned concentrators back for the next step. The important point is that the sub-problem recognizer-and-solver is not an implementation of a (here unknown) solving method, but learns the necessary knowledge from examples (or by doing, see Section 4.3). The sub-problem solver must be able to deal with a sub-problem of both kinds in one step. This domain inherent splitting into limited size sub-problems that present a pattern recognition task (both concerning segmentation and solving) allows a realization by a connectionist approach. Below, we describe the choice of a neural net as such a sub-problem solver. On the other hand, it is hard to directly implement an algorithm for this task (see Section 5).

4 Net architecture and Performance

4.1 General

These previous considerations, in a first step, design a processing net which is capable to deal with a number of concentrators that always permits to find a sub-problem and its solution among them. From the problem analysis [12] we know that this must be larger than the maximum size of a rest-problem (so that this can be recognized) and comprises therefore the concentrators of two maximum size component sub-problems of the "ideal pair" type. This is how the problem structure determines the size of the net. It must therefore encode eight (2·4) concentrators (or 32 connection units) as input and a maximum of 32^2 possibilities of connections (from each concentrator to the place of the connection unit in the connection group) as output. Iteratively, the net will be presented this number of concentrators out of all yet unassigned concentrators by the scheduler. It must process these by recognizing and assigning an "ideal pair" and handing back unassigned concentrators for the next presentation, or recognizing a rest-problem and solving it completely. This results in a total number of required processing steps between only $n_C/4$ to $n_C/2$, provided that the net can learn the segmentation task and the partial solutions. The problem solving behaviour of the net is therefore linear in time.

The net was constructed following the standard architecture of Rumelhart et al. [10] as a feedforward network with error backpropagation and synchronous update of neurons. This could be directly mapped on the problem structure, therefore the more general case of recurrent nets [6] was not considered. Due to the large number of patterns, learning was chosen to take place after each presentation. This theoretically violates the premises of guaranteed learning success for gradient descent, but for sufficiently small update factors empirically (as usual) the learning task was managed. We provided the patterns for the learning phase by backtrack searches. The following paragraphs describe the net architecture in detail.

4.2 Neurons

The *neurons* of the input layer can assume the values 0 and 1. Thereby the coding of the input denoted the presence or absence of a connection unit for all places of the concentrators. An experiment series which used the values 0.1 and 0.9 instead to represent this fact resulted in worse performance. Although such a coding is often used to restrain the growth of weights and biases, we interpret its failure here as an unwanted un-learning effect when the outputs exceed these values.

Intentionally, the type and the constraints of the units are not encoded, since they represent features which create the geometrical symmetries of the solutions, and therefore are meant to be learnt by the net as a property of the solutions. Also, no preprocessing was done in order to specifically test the structure detection of the net.

Neurons in the hidden layer(s) could take continuous values between 0 and 1.

The output representation presented a larger problem due to the sparse population of given assignments in the domain of possible assignments. It is impossible to give every possible connection ($32^2 = 2^{10}$) a detecting neuron. Again a geometrically oriented picture (focussing on the places of the connection units) was adopted, each assignment being binary coded by five neurons (to code the number of one out of $32 = 2^5$ connections units). Again, the neurons can assume continuous values between 0 and 1, where all values below (above) 0.5 denote the bit value 0 (1).

4.3 Error function

As candidates for the *error function* we considered two different choices. The first is the sum of the squares of the deviations between calculated and desired output (given by the solutions). This method of "learning-from-examples" was applied throughout the simulations.

Although we cannot formulate an exact cost function, still a function which assigns arbitrary values to the violation of constraints and heuristics is possible. This method results in very slow learning, since it only estimates actual deviations, but is necessary in a scenario in which the desired patterns can not be explicitly specified. This is e.g. the case, when (C4) applies which in general destroys the regular pattern structure. To generalize, this method to provide an error function in order to "learn-by-doing" is applicable if the violation of optimality can be quantitatively specified by a well-behaving monotonous function (well-behaving in the sense that is does not show local minima).

4.4 Layers

Although two *layers* in general would allow to store a larger number of patterns than required, this has been shown to be impossible. The input patterns have a very large overlap, and slightly different input patterns can lead to serious alterations in the output grouping. The structure of the solution mirrors interactions not only among connection units for each concentrator, but also pairs, triples and quadruples of concentrators [3]. This forced us to adopt a semi-linear activation (sigmoid) function and to introduce hidden units.

The actual number of layers was determined in a step by step experimental process (see Section 4.5), relating intermediate results to the problem analysis. A three layer design (e.g. with 32–32–160 neurons) with full connectivity turned out to be inefficient, but the activations of the neurons in the middle layer allowed the conclusion that the net had tried to code the *DIFF* and *SAME* predicates in the weights and biases between input and hidden layer. In order to ease this task, we introduced the restriction that between first and second layer, connections are possible only within groups of four neurons ($fan\text{-}out_1 = fan\text{-}in_2 = 4$), which was meant as, and actually was learnt as, recoding of the input to calculate the *DIFF* and *SAME* predicates for each concentrator.

Unfortunately, this design turned out to be too restrictive for the three layer net, so eventually four layers (with e.g. 32–32–32–160 neurons) were adopted, which were supposed to make use of their first two layers as such a preprocessor. Namely, a fully connected four layer design was again unable to learn the patterns, due its dynamical instability resulting from the immense size of theoretically possible storage.

The remaining structure information must certainly be stored in the connection strengths and biases of the remaining layers. Here, yet another improvement could be achieved by exploiting the facts that groups of five output neurons code a single connection and that the predicates formulate restrictions mainly internal to connection groups. Therefore we introduced a distance dependent weight update for the connections to (and biases of) the last layer. There, the update factor for weights and biases was designed to come in three (decreasing) sizes:

- internal to an assigned connection of a connection group,
- leading to other units of one connection group, or
- leading to other connection groups.

The latter measure is again a restriction against dynamical instabilities. It reduced the learning time significantly.

4.5 Results

Fig. 1 shows the solution for the assignment of 7 concentrators with 24 connection units to 6 connection groups, which is derived in a one-step calculation (since it poses a rest-problem). The figure displays especially the emanent feature of the formation of "ideal pairs" of connection groups.

Fig. 2 shows a comparison of the learning curves for four typical experiments with three fully connected layers ('nn3'), three partially connected layers ('nn3l'), four fully connected layers ('nn4') and four partially connected layers with weighted update ('nn4lw'). Fig. 3 shows a comparison of the development of the mean square error per pattern for the same experiments. Experiment 'nn3' displays an initially very steep learning curve, but reaches saturation and exhibits unstable dynamics. This unstability has been eliminated in experiment 'nn3l', but the restrictions are obviously too strong and limit the storage capacity. Four fully connected layers ('nn4') do not succeed in learning, either, which we explain as dynamical instability due to the excessive number of parameters. The relatively steep and over a wide range nearly linear slope of the curve for four partially connected layers with weighted update ('nn4lw') indicates that the learning capacity of the net still is much larger than the number of presented patterns. This is also supported by the distribution histogram of weights and biases in Fig. 4. The weights typically are very small and centered around zero. We have not yet analyzed which connections can be removed without impairing the learning performance. The bias distribution, however, is very broad which we interpret as a clue not to decrease the number of neurons. The curve of the mean square error displays also the stable dynamics of the chosen architecture.

Also, there are indications that the presentation order of the patterns influences the learning performance. Efficient training means to present patterns with more participating units before the presentation of patterns that are part of them. The momentum term for the weight and bias updates is very important to avoid cancellation of the effects of successive similar patterns with distinctly different desired outputs. A small decay term for weights and

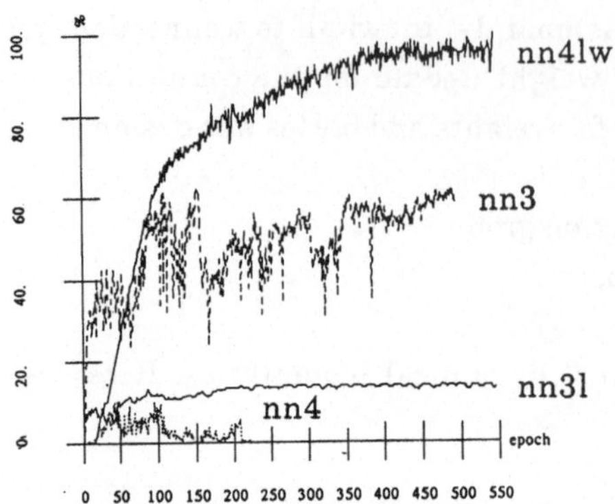

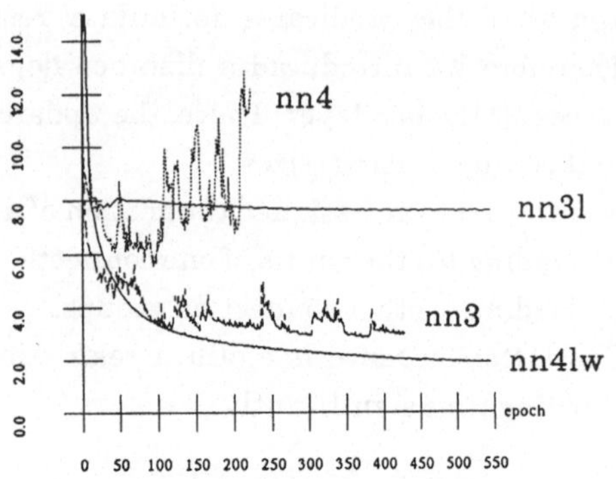

Fig. 2. Learning curves (learnt patterns vs. teaching epochs) for different experiments.
nn3: three layers fully connected.
nn3l: three layers partially connected.
nn4: four layers fully connected.
nn4lw: four layers partially connected with weighted updates.

Fig. 3. Mean square error per pattern. Same experiments as in Fig. 2.

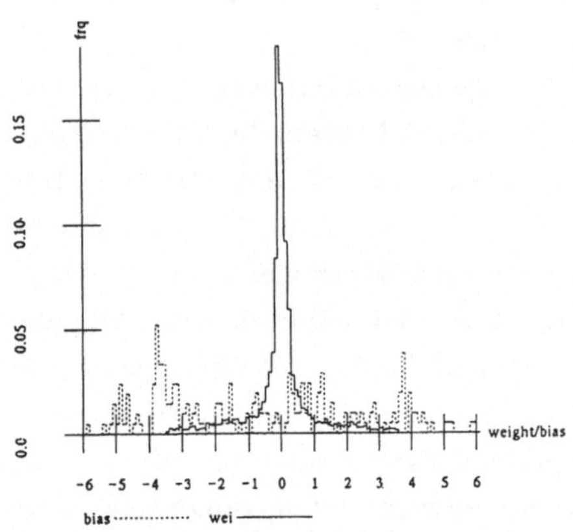

Fig. 4. Distribution of weights and biases for four layers partially connected with weighted updates.
Cutoff [−6,6]: 83% of all biases, 96% of all weights.

biases helped to overcome local minima. (The net tended to "anti-learn" one out of a group of input patterns with same output).

5 Discussion and Outlook

Parallel to this neural net solution, the problem has been solved via *constraint satisfaction search* by an implementation of *backtracking,* selecting the possible assignments by use of *static look-ahead* which incorporates domain-specific *knowledge* (similar to methods studied theoretically by [4]). The efficiency of different versions with different degrees of informedness has been tested (see [12]). The best version actually backtracked only occasionally, i.e. it nearly always found a solution immediately. Therefore we did not implement a *consistency algorithm*. Constraint (C4) could not be implemented guaranteeing an optimal solution without extensive search, similarly to the net solution. It also turned out that the thrashing behaviour is extremely negative, when a (partially) informed version chooses non-optimal nodes, since it prefers to search in wrong areas of search space.

The main difference, however, between the two approaches is of very general character. The connectionist solution makes use of the problem's decomposability and provides a means to *learn* the knowledge for the picking and solving of sub-problems. This method uniquely realizes the ideas of *auto-segmentation* and *knowledge compilation*. The computing effort is concentrated in the learning phase, after which the net performs its task in an effortless manner. If structural parameters change, the scheduler must be adapted according to the problem analysis and the (only possibly in size modified) net can easily be retrained. (Training patterns are only needed up to the size of a maximum sub-problem.)

Opposed to this, the symbolic backtracking solution tries to represent the constraints and heuristics directly in the generate and test routines. Using an informed algorithm, here, a parameter change will be reflected in the static look-ahead and look-back, which implement a case analysis that must preceed this. The backtrack algorithm does not learn the segmentation patterns or the sub-problem solutions. Therefore, the search must be performed again for each problem that is presented, and the computing effort must be made for every search anew. In general, a flexible self-training design can be preferred to the hand-crafted informed algorithm.

There are symbolic algorithms that allow the learning of classification procedures (e.g. ID3 [9]), and this may be extended to cover also a segmentation problem. As outlined in Section 3.3, however, the connectionist approach does not necessarily depend on the presentation of known solutions, as the symbolic method does. Especially, when a problem additionally contains quantitative elements that require an interpolation, the advantages of a neural net become evident. Even if the patterns of the solutions cannot be provided for the learning phase, the existence of a cost function may allow training.

Already in our domain, there exist lower level problems (the module assignment internal to concentrators or connection groups) which can also be viewed as CSP, and – strictly speaking – their optimality criteria interfere with the optimality of the described problem. In contrast with the present bottom-up proceeding (which is also done by the domain experts) we foresee an architecture which allows interaction between different processing levels. This means a design combining several components of the described type, where a connectionist component performs an optimization and a symbolic components serves as scheduler and interface. They must be combined in a hierachical way that allows information flow both bottom-up and top-down in order to solve e.g. an overall optimization problem in which different levels of detail interfere with each other.

6   Conclusion

We have shown that this special constraint satisfaction problem can be iteratively solved due to its decomposability by a two-component architecture with a scheduler and an adequately designed neural net in linear time. The net architecture and its derivation have been related to the actual problem structure. After the learning phase, the internal representation of the net corresponds to a compilation of the possible patterns for the picking and solving of component sub-problems. Due to the absence of a cost function in our case, however, the net must be trained by previously collected patterns. Comparing the described approach to a conventional solution via backtracking, it is noted that the implementation of the static look-ahead and look-back in symbolic programming is case dependent, whereas the desired flexibility of the application may more easily be guaranteed by a self-training neural net. We also foresee an architecture, in which this present realization will constitute one component in a hierachically oriented design that combines the symbolic and connectionist paradigms in a mutually recursive way.

Acknowledgements

This work has been performed with hardware and computer time support by the SIEMENS AG ÖSTERREICH. Wolfgang Ginzel's effort in writing software for plotting the figures is greatly acknowledged.

References

[1]   Abu-Mustafa, Y.S., Neural Networks for Computing?, *AIP Conf. Proc.* **151**, 1986, 1-6.

[2]   Barnden, John A., Neural-Net Implementation of Complex Symbol-Processing in a Mental Model Approach to Syllogistic Reasoning, *Proceedings of IJCAI-89*, Detroit, Mich., 1989, 568-573.

[3]   Ekeberg, Ö., and A. Lansner, Automatic Generation of Internal Representations in a Probabilistic Artificial Neural Network, in: *Neural Networks from Models to Applications* (Personnaz, L., and G. Dreyfus, eds.), Paris: IDSET, 1989, 179-186.

[4]   Haralick, R.M., and G.L. Elliott, Increasing Tree Search Efficiency for Constraint Satisfaction Problems, *Artificial Intelligence* 14 (3), 1980, 61-76.

[5]   Kaindl, H., and H.G. Ziegeler, Some Aspects of Knowledge-Based Configuration, *Proceedings AVIGNON '90: Expert systems & their applications, Specialized Conference: Artificial Intelligence, Telecommunications & Computer Systems*, 1990, 41-54.

[6]   Lapedes, A., and R. Farber, Programming a Massively Parallel, Computation Universal System: Static Behaviour, *AIP Conf. Proc.* 151, 1986, 283-298.

[7]   Mackworth, A.K., Constraint Satisfaction, in *Encyclopedia of Artificial Intelligence* (Shapiro, S.C., ed.), New York, N.Y.: Wiley, 1987, 205-211.

[8]   Nilsson, N.J., *Principles of Artificial Intelligence*, Tioga Publ. Co., 1980.

[9]   Quinlan, J.R., Learning efficient classification procedures and their application to chess end games: in: *Machine Learning* 2 (Michalski, R.S., J.G. Carbonell, and T.M. Mitchell, eds.), Palo Alto, Ca.: Tioga, 1984, 463-482.

[10] Rumelhart, D., J. McClelland *et al.* (ed.), *Parallel Distributed Processing: Explorations in the Microstructure of Cognition*, Cambridge, Ma.: MIT Press, 1986.

[11] Tagliarini, G.A., and E.W. Page, Solving Constraint Satisfaction Problems with Neural Networks, *Proc. IEEE First International Conference on Neural Networks*, San Diego, 1987.

[12] Ziegeler, H.G., and H. Kaindl, A Cyclic Pattern Resulting from a Constraint Satisfaction Search, working paper, to be presented at the *AAAI-90 Workshop on Constraint Directed Reasoning*, July 1990.

Buchstabenerkennung unter Berücksichtigung
von kontextueller Information

Andreas Lebeda
Monika Köhle

Technische Universität Wien
Karlsplatz 13/1804, A-1040 Wien

Abstract

In der vorliegenden Arbeit wird ein neurales Netzwerk zur Buchstabenerkennung vorgestellt. Dabei wird die Wichtigkeit des Einflusses von Kontextinformation auf die Erkennung herausgearbeitet, und bei der Entwicklung des Netzes besonders beachtet. Es werden zwei Systeme entworfen. Einerseits ein Netzwerk, das die verwendete Kontextinformation ermittelt und bereitstellt, indem es aus den bisher erkannten Buchstaben die Wahrscheinlichkeiten für das Auftreten des nächsten bestimmt. Zum anderen wird ein Mustererkennnungssystem entwickelt, das aufgrund des gesehenen Bildes und unter Zuhilfenahme der kontextuellen Information die Buchstaben erkennen soll. Diesem Erkennungsteil liegt das Neocognitron [Fuku 80] zugrunde, das der Aufgabe entsprechend adaptiert und stark abgeändert wurde. Die implementierten und getesteten Entwürfe für dieses Problem werden ausführlich beschrieben und diskutiert.

1. Motivation

Die grundlegende Motivation dieser Arbeit besteht darin, ein visuelles Mustererkennnungssystem durch Einfließen von kontextueller Information (also Information, die durch den Zusammenhang der Buchstaben, der semantischen Bedeutung und aufgrund der Folgehäufigkeiten gegeben ist) in seiner Leistungsfähigkeit zu verbessern. Durch Experimente ([Chan 88]; [Fink 88]; [Ta&Ta 83]; [Tayl 88]; [Town 83]; [To&Be 88]; [We&St 78]) wird klar, daß der Mensch nur dadurch in der Lage ist, den Inhalt einer Textstelle derart schnell zu erfassen, daß er nicht jeden einzelnen Buchstaben seperat erkennen muß, sondern daß er bestimmte Vorstellungen über das Folgezeichen hat, die er dann nur noch anhand der Realität überprüfen muß. Daraus ließ sich die Idee herleiten, daß durch entsprechendes Einbringen von kontextueller Information auch die Erkennungsleistung eines neuralen Netzwerkes verbesserbar sein müßte. Nun war es freilich klar, daß es nicht möglich sein würde, ein System zu schaffen, daß tatsächlich die semantische Bedeutung von Worten erkennen, und somit eine gute Vorhersage für weitere Folgeworte abgeben könnte. Die einzige Möglichkeit, zu einem leichter lösbaren Problem zu kommen, lag darin, eine Ebene tieferzugehen, und die Folgewahrscheinlichkeiten von Buchstaben zu verwenden. Nach der Kenntnis einiger Buchstaben sind eindeutig bestimmte Nachfolger wahrscheinlicher als andere (z.B. wird "qrx" unerwartet kommen, nach "Febr" wird das "uar" allerdings erwartet werden). Der Vorteil, den dies für die Mustererkennung haben kann, ist vor allem der Umstand, daß man plötzlich zwei vollkommen voneinander unabhängige Bestimmungsstücke für den zu erkennenden Buchstaben hat. Ein gutes Beispiel dafür stellen die Buchstaben E und F dar, die sich aussehensmäßig kaum unterscheiden und deshalb von einem rein visuellen System leicht verwechselt werden können. Auf der Ebene der Folgewahrscheinlichkeiten besteht aber dadurch ein großer Unterschied, daß E sicher auf ganz andere Vorkombinationen folgt als F, und somit bei einer eventuellen Ungewißheit aufgrund dieses zweiten Bestimmungsstücks eine eindeutige Entscheidung getroffen werden kann.

Um diese Vorstellung zu verwirklichen wurden zwei Teilsysteme geschaffen, deren Aufgaben vollkommen unabhängig voneinander waren, und die durch Verbindung das gestellte Problem lösen sollten. Das erste Netz ist ein visuelles Mustererkennnungssystem nach der Vorlage des Neocognitron von Fukushima. Der zweite Teil beschäftigt sich mit der Schaffung eines kontextuellen Systems, das aufgrund der Kenntnis der vorangegangenen Buchstaben versucht, den nächsten vorauszusagen. Dieses Netzwerk arbeitet mit der Back Propagation [Ru&Hi 86].

Das dritte hier vorgestellte System stellt schließlich den Zusammenschluß der ersten beiden dar. In ihm wird versucht, die aus dem Kontext kommende Information, die aus dem gleichnamigen System gewonnen wurde, positiv auf die Mustererkennung wirken zu lassen. Hierbei wird das System des Associative Recall (siehe Abschnitt 2), in dem das Wissen um die Wahrscheinlichkeit der Existenz eines Buchstaben im Input dazu benutzt wird, um nach seinen Einzelteilen zu suchen, verwendet. Dabei werden die durch das kontextuelle System ermittelten Auftrittswahrscheinlichkeiten des nächsten Buchstaben verwendet, und speziell nach den Wahrscheinlicheren gesucht. Abschließend werden die Probleme mit dem vorhandenen Ansatz beschrieben und Aussichten auf weitere (notwendige) Verbesserungen des Modells gegeben.

2. Das visuelle Mustererkennungssystem

In diesem Abschnitt wird das System zur visuellen Mustererkennung vorgestellt, das in seinen Ursprüngen an die Ideen Fukushimas [Fuku 84a]; [Fuku 84b]; [Fuku 86] angelehnt ist, sich im Endeffekt aber doch sehr weit vom Neocognitron entfernt hat. Die Aufgabe dieses Systems ist es, auf einen Buchstaben, der in einer Matrix von 21x21 Bildpunkten am Input angelegt wird, mit einer einzelnen Unit "Buchstabe X" zu antworten. Damit sollte es möglich sein, Texte, die zum Beispiel mit einer Kamera aufgenommen wurden, nachträglich zu erkennen, und somit in eine für eine Textverarbeitung zur Verfügung zu stehen.

Das Modell besteht aus sechs Layern, die bis auf den ersten in jeweils 30 Planes geteilt sind. Die Planes werden vom Input zum Output hin immer kleiner. Der erste große Unterschied zum Neocognitron ist das Ausmaß des Inputlayers, nämlich 21x21 (im Vergleich zu 8x8 beim Neocognitron). Die Idee dabei war, eine etwas realistischere Ausgangssituation bezüglich der Möglichkeiten, verschiedenartigste Muster zu erkennen, zu erzielen. Was damit klarerweise einhergeht, ist das Faktum, daß es nun viel schwieriger ist, Muster zu klassifizieren und zu erkennen, da es durch die Größe viel mehr Möglichkeiten gibt. Dennoch scheint es für ein sinnvolles Erkennen die einzig mögliche Variante zu sein, um eine halbwegs tragbare Auflösung zu erreichen. Eine übermäßige Stilisierung ist nicht mehr notwendig, und es wird auch vorstellbar, daß handschriftliche Buchstaben ausreichend erfaßt werden können.

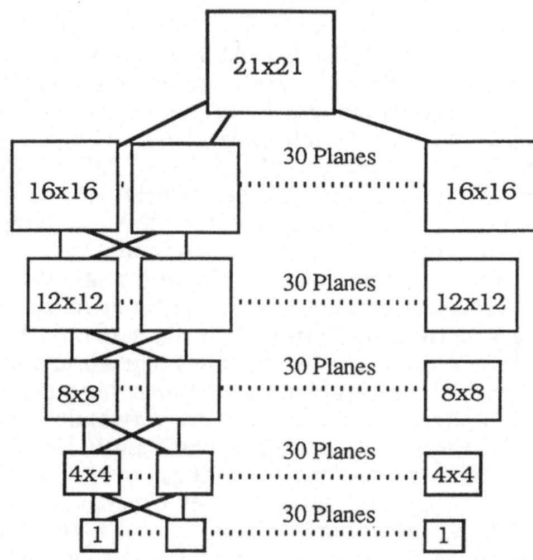

Abb.1: Netzwerksaufbau

Durch die Größe des ersten Layers ergeben sich bei ungefährer Konstanthaltung des Verkleinerungsverhältnisses auch die Größen der folgenden, nämlich:

Layer 2	16x16
Layer 3	12x12
Layer 4	8x8
Layer 5	4x4
Layer 6	1x1

Die Layer sind untereinander voll verbunden, wobei es für jede Unit aus Layer n+1 ein bestimmtes rezeptives Feld (x*x Units) in Layer n gibt, aus dem die Informationen stammen. Das bedeutet, daß jede Unit aus Layer n Verbindungen aus allen 30 Planes des Layers n-1 hat, und zwar jeweils aus demselben rezeptiven Feld. Die rezeptiven Felder überlappen einander, sodaß die Felder zweier benachbarter Units nur um jeweils eine Unit versetzt sind. Zur Illustration seien zwei Units aus Layer 5 mit ihren rezeptiven Feldern in Layer 4 angegeben.

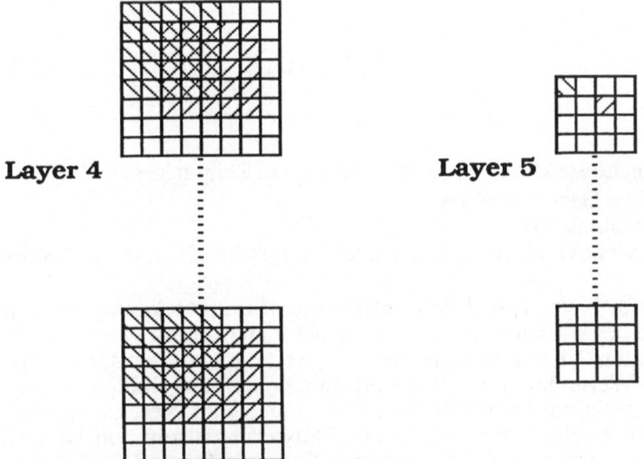

Abb.2: Units mit ihren rezeptiven Feldern. Die Schraffur gibt das rezeptive Feld in Layer 4 der entsprechenden Unit aus Layer 5 an.

Wie man leicht sieht, erreicht man dadurch die oben angeführte Verkleinerung: x*x Units aus Layer n sind mit einer aus Layer n+1 verbunden. Die Nachbarunit aus Layer n+1 hat ein nur um eine Unit verschobenes Feld in Layer n, das Feld von einem Layer zum nächsten genau um x-1 Units in jeder Dimension verkleinert. Um die oben angesprochene Verkleinerung zu erreichen, ergeben sich daher die in der unten angeführten Tabelle enthaltenen Größen der rezeptiven Felder.

Layer 1 nach Layer 2	6x6
Layer 2 nach Layer 3	5x5
Layer 3 nach Layer 4	5x5
Layer 4 nach Layer 5	5x5
Layer 5 nach Layer 6	4x4

Die Verbindungen sind zweiseitig, das heißt, daß es immer Paare von efferenten (absteigenden) und afferenten (aufsteigenden) Bahnen gibt, die jedoch nur ein gemeinsames Gewicht besitzen. Die Bedeutung dieser Tatsache wird später noch ausführlich erklärt. Der Sinn eines derartigen Aufbaus liegt wie schon beim Neocognitron darin, jeden Layer Merkmale einer bestimmten Komplexitätsstufe erkennen zu lassen, wobei die später folgenden Layer das vorher erkannte zu immer größeren Abschnitten zusammenfassen, bis schließlich die Zellen des letzten Layers die ganze "Netzhaut" erfassen können. Sie können also das gesamte Muster betrachten und liefern als Output das Maß an Klassenzugehörigkeit, also praktisch das Erkennungsmaß. In diesem Modell wird es aufgrund der Größe des Inputlayers dazu kommen, daß zum Beispiel im zweiten Layer lediglich primitive Figuren wie Linien erkannt werden, und erst spätere Layer in der Lage sind, Teilfiguren zu erkennen. Wie schon beim Netz Fukushimas ist es die Aufgabe jeder Plane, ein spezielles Muster an allen möglichen Stellen des Inputs erkennen zu können. Daraus folgt gleichzeitig, daß es für jede Plane nur einen Satz von Gewichten gibt. Es ist also für jede Unit in einem Layer die Gewichtsmatrix gleich, es differieren nur die Felder aus denen der Input stammt.

Es ergibt sich für eine Unit in der Netzmitte folgende Aktivierungsfunktion:

$$U_{e, f, d, k, t} = \sum_{a=1}^{w} \sum_{b=1}^{w} \sum_{c=1}^{y} \left(U_{a+e, b+f, c, k-1, t-1} \, G_{k-1, a, b, c, d} \right) + \text{eff}\left(U_{e, f, d, k, t} \right) + h \, U_{e, f, d, k, t-1}$$

$U_{e,f,d,k,t}$ Unit aus Layer k Plane d an Position e,f zum Zeitpunkt t

w   Größe des Gewichtsfeldes
y   Planeanzahl (=30)
h   Konservierungsfaktor (hier: 0.1)
$G_{k,a,b,c,d}$ das Gewicht von Layer k Plane c nach Layer k+1 Plane d an Position a,b

$$\mathrm{eff}\left(U_{p,\,q,\,c,\,k-1,\,t}\right) = \sum_{a=1}^{w}\ \sum_{b=1}^{w}\ \sum_{d=1}^{y}\left(U_{e,\,f,\,d,\,k,\,t-1}\,G_{k-1,\,a,\,b,\,c,\,d}\right)$$
$$\text{mit } a+e=p \text{ mit } b+f=q$$

$U_{p,q,c,k,t}$ Unit aus Layer k Plane c an Position p,q um Zeitpunkt t
w   Größe des Gewichtsfeldes
y   Planeanzahl (=30)
$G_{k,a,b,c,d}$ das Gewicht von Layer k Plane c nach Layer k+1 Plane d an Position a,b

Sonderfälle gelten für Layer 1, in dem kein afferenter Strom vorkommt, da er ja der Inputlayer ist, für Layer 2, in dem der afferente Input aus nur einer Plane kommt (vom Input) und für Layer 6, in dem keine efferenten Verbindungen mehr vorkommen, da er der Outputlayer ist. Das Durchpropagieren der Werte durch das Netzwerk funktioniert auf ähnliche Weise wie beim Netz Fukushimas. Am Inputlayer wird ein beliebiges Muster angelegt. Dieses wird im ersten Schritt auf Layer 2 übertragen. Im zweiten Schritt läuft ein Aktivierungsstrom von Layer 2 nach Layer 3, gleichzeitig einer zurück nach Layer 1. Ein weiterer Strom fließt von Layer 1 nach Layer 2. Diese wechselseitigen Aktivierungen der Layer dauern an, bis die Aktivierung einer der Zellen im letzten Layer einen bestimmten Schwellwert überschreitet. In diesem Moment gilt der Buchstabe als erkannt, und das Netz bricht die Erkennung ab.

Ein weiterer, sehr wichtiger Mechanismus besteht im Konservieren der alten Aktivierungen der Units. Das heißt, daß es bleibt ein Teil von Restaktivierung übrig und wird zum gewonnenen Änderungsbetrag addiert. In diesem Fall wurde die Restaktivierung mit 10% festgesetzt. Dies hat den Sinn, dem Netz eine gewisse Stabilität zu verleihen, indem zumindest ein Teil der Aktivierung im Zeitpunkt n auf den Zustand im Zeitpunkt n-1 zurückgeht.

Ein weiterer, noch wichtigerer Teil betrifft das sogenannte Normieren. Fukushima hat in seinem Modell sehr viele Mechanismen auf die externe Kontrolle von einzelnen Units gerichtet. Dies betrifft zum Beispiel Habituation (also das langsame allgemeine Absinken der Aktivierungen), die dringend für den Vorgang des Associative Recall benötigt wird. Weiters beruht auch der Mechanismus, daß bei allgemein geringer Aktivierung die Selektivität erhöht, bei hoher aber vermindert wird, um eine gleichmäßige Informationsbearbeitung zu gewährleisten, auf derartigen externen Einflußnahmen. Diesem Umstand wird durch Normieren der Werte eines Layers Rechnung getragen. Bei der Normierung wird der Durchschnittswert der Aktivierung im Layer berechnet, daraufhin wird jedes Element durch diesen dividiert und mit dem gewünschten Normwert multipliziert:

$$X_{neu} = \frac{X_{alt}\,\text{Norm}}{\overline{X}_{alt}}$$

Diese Normierung wird nach jeder Berechnung der Aktivierungen durchgeführt.

Der Lernalgorithmus des Systems ist eine Art von Competitive Learning [Ru&Zi 85], wobei der Lernvorgang (Hypercolumns, representative Cells und das Ändern der Gewichte nach der representative cell) genauso aufgebaut ist wie beim Neocognitron. Der Unterschied besteht in der Verwendung einer neuen Lernregel:

$$\Delta G_{k,\,a,\,b,\,c,\,d} = \frac{\left(U_{d+f,\,e+g,\,b,\,a} - \dfrac{\sum\limits_i x_i}{n}\right)L}{\dfrac{\sum\limits_i x_i^2 - \dfrac{\left(\sum\limits_i x_i\right)^2}{n}}{n}}$$

$G_{k,a,b,c,d}$ das Gewicht von Layer k Plane c nach Layer k+1 Plane d an Position a,b

$U_{d+f,e+g,b,a}$ die Unit aus Layer a Plane b an Position d+f,e+g wobei f,g die Koordinaten der Siegerunit aus dem Layer a+1 sind

L   Lernrate

Diese Transformation der Werte der Units auf Gewichtsveränderungswerte entspricht der Transformation einer normalverteilten Zufallsvariable auf eine Standardnormalverteilung. Allgemein bedeutet das, daß alle Gewichte, deren zugehörige Unit mit einem geringerem als dem Mittelwert, also eher schwach, aktiviert war, negativ verstärkt werden, während alle die Gewichte, deren Units stärker als das Mittel aktiviert waren, positiv verändert werden. Die Division durch die Standardabweichung bewirkt die Reduktion der für Gewichtsveränderungen zu hohen Werte der Aktivierungen auf ein akzeptables Maß. Da die Standardabweichung ein Maß für die Ausdehnung der Werte ist, erfolgt bei großen Extremen in den Werten automatisch auch eine stärkere Verringerung, sodaß immer annähernd die selben geringen Werte erzielt werden. Ein weiterer positiver Effekt, den die Teilung am Mittelwert mit sich bringt, ist die Tatsache, daß die Summe der positiven Gewichtsveränderungen genauso groß wie die Summe der negativen ist. Es ergibt sich also nur eine Verschiebung der Gewichtswerte hin zu den Stellen, die zum Muster gehören.

Wie schon weiter oben angesprochen, gehen die Verbindungen zwischen den Units in beide Richtungen. Der Grund für diese Konstruktion ist das Modell des Associative Recall [Fuku 84b]. Es geht davon aus, daß gestörte Muster empfangen werden. Das Netz wird auf eine derartige Eingabe mit einer hohen Aktivierung auf die ungestörten Teile reagieren, auf die gestörten aber kaum. Associative Recall bedeutet, daß Aktivierungen auch von oben nach unten fließen. Ist also zum Beispiel im letzten Layer ein E sehr wahrscheinlich geworden (einige Teile sind erkannt), so fließt von der Unit für E Aktivierung zurück auf alle ein E bildende Teile, und damit auch auf die, die vorher schwach aktiviert waren. Da gleichzeitig durch die Normierung die restlichen Aktivierungen zurückgehen, wird es wahrscheinlicher, daß auch die anderen zu einem E gehörenden Teile ansprechen, falls es irgendwelche passende Aktivierungen aus dem Input gibt. Es wird also "nachgesehen", ob das erwartete Muster (E) nicht doch anliegt.

Ein weiterer verwendeter Mechanismus war der Selektivitätskoeffizient, da zu bemerken war (ein schon von Rumelhart und Zipser beschriebenes Problem [Ru&Zi 86]), daß einige Units nie die Competition gewannen, daher auch nie lernten, und daraufhin zu wenige Planes für die vielen zu erkennenden Muster vorhanden waren. Jede Plane bekam einen Selektivitätskoeffizienten. Gewann eine Unit dieser Plane eine der Competitions, so wurde der Koeffizient vermindert, konnte sie in einem Durchgang nicht gewinnen, so wurde er erhöht. Der Koeffizient wurde multiplikativ mit dem Aktivierungswert verknüpft, wenn es um die Ermittlung des Competitionssiegers ging. Dadurch wurde erreicht, daß auch Units, die sonst kaum je gewonnen hätten, irgendwann einen so hohen Selektivitätskoeffizienten hatten, daß sie auf irgendein Muster ansprachen, und dann auch auf dieses selektiv wurden.

Ursprünglich wurden für das System positive Aktivierungswerte verwendet. Das entsprechende Modell setzte also beim Normieren alle Aktivierungen, die negativ waren, auf Null. Ein neuer ebefalls getesteter Ansatz bestand in einer Veränderung der Regel zur Verhinderung von negativen Aktivierungen. Die Überlegung bestand dabei in der Tatsache, daß einerseits das Nullsetzen aller negativen Aktivierungen zwar notwendig für die Eindeutigkeit der Interpretation ist, andererseits darunter aber die Gleichmäßigkeit der Verteilung der Gewichtsänderungen, die ja von den Aktivierungswerten abhängen (gewaltige Spitze bei Wert 0, Verschiebung des Mittelwertes ins Positive), leidet, und zusätzlich fraglich ist, ob dann das Beibehalten von Restaktivierungen in den einzelnen Units noch sinnvoll ist. Als Lösung dieser Problematik wurde ein weiteres System erstellt, bei dem die negativen Aktivierungswerte gespeichert, und dann nur für die Berechnung der Gewichtsänderungen und in den Restaktivierungen wieder verwendet wurden, während nur die positiven Aktivierungen sich im Netz weiter auswirkten. Man könnte in diesem Modell eine Ähnlichkeit zur Hyperpolarisation bei der menschlichen Nervenzelle sehen, die sich auch nicht durch eine Weitergabe der negativen Aktivierung, wohl aber durch ein Erschweren der positiven Aktivierbarkeit der Unit auswirkt. Dieses Modell zeigte geringfügig bessere Ergebnisse als das erstere. Es erwies sich aber als zweckmäßig, beide für den Zusammenschluß mit dem semantischen System zu verwenden. Im folgenden werden die Ergebnisse dieser beiden Systeme und die daraus ersichtliche Problematik betreffend der Erkennung von Mustern mit einem derartigen System gebracht.

<table>
<tr><td></td><td align="center">**Netz mit Nullsetzen
der negativen Aktivierungen**</td><td align="center">**Netz mit Aufheben
der negativen Aktivierungen**</td></tr>
<tr><td>Klasse1:</td><td>I,X,Leerzeichen</td><td>I,X,Y,Leerzeichen</td></tr>
<tr><td>Klasse2:</td><td>T,Z</td><td>T</td></tr>
<tr><td>Klasse3:</td><td>Punkt</td><td>Punkt</td></tr>
<tr><td>Klasse4:</td><td>N</td><td>N</td></tr>
<tr><td>Klasse5:</td><td>B,E,F,H,K,L,M,P,R,S,Beistrich</td><td>B,E,F,H,K,L,P,R,S,V</td></tr>
<tr><td>Klasse6:</td><td>A,J,V</td><td>A,J,W</td></tr>
<tr><td>Klasse7:</td><td>C,D,G,U</td><td>C,G</td></tr>
<tr><td>Klasse8:</td><td>Y</td><td>M</td></tr>
<tr><td>Klasse9:</td><td>Apostroph</td><td>Apostroph</td></tr>
<tr><td>Klasse10:</td><td>O,Q</td><td>D,O,Q,U</td></tr>
<tr><td>Klasse11:</td><td>W</td><td>Z</td></tr>
<tr><td>Klasse12:</td><td></td><td>Beistrich</td></tr>
</table>

Nun kann man an obigen Ergebnissen zwar sehen, daß das System sehr wohl in der Lage ist, die Buchstabenmenge nach durchaus sinnvollen Kriterien (Form) in Klassen zu ordnen, wobei es mit Klasse 5 auch eine für nicht näher unterschiedene gibt. Auf der anderen Seite ist es aber weder durch längeres Lernen noch durch Veränderung der Parameter möglich, noch viel bessere Leistungen zu erzielen (das Netz mit 40 Planes pro Layer ordnete zum Beispiel den Buchstaben S der Klasse mit den runden Formen [O,Q,U,...] zu). Dadurch stoßen wir auf das eigentliche Problem dieses Ansatzes. Es wird deutlich, daß wir von einem Netz, das ohne teaching input, also ohne Regelung von außen versucht, eine Klassifizierung in eine Mustermenge zu bringen, nicht erwarten können, daß es die gewünschte Klassifizierung trifft. In diesem Beispiel trifft das Netz die Einteilung nach auch für uns sinnvollen Kriterien. Es werden Buchstaben in Kreisform zusammengefasst [O,Q]. Weiters gibt es zum Beispiel eine Klasse mit halbkreisförmigen [C,G]. Für uns als Betrachter ist es aber nicht möglich, dem Netz unsere Unzufriedenheit mit dieser Klassifizierung (bzw. die Unbrauchbarkeit für die gestellte Aufgabe) mitzuteilen – genauso unmöglich wie für das Netz, unsere Wünsche bezüglich der Klassen zu erraten. Die Klassifizierung, die das Netz trifft, kann nur nach den Gesichtspunkten erfolgt sein, die das Netz zur Verfügung hatte, und das ist das Aussehen (E,F,H,L unterscheiden sich nur durch wenige Merkmale). Daß diese Klassenbildung daran liegt, daß die Buchstaben einer Klasse verglichen mit der Gesamtheit der Buchstaben für das Netz wirklich so ähnlich erscheinen, sieht man an vorher mit demselben Netz durchgeführten Versuchen mit nur fünf Buchstaben (E, H, I, L, T). Diese konnten nämlich ohne Probleme auseinandergehaltenwerden. Bei vielen ähnlichen Buchstaben war feiner zu klassifizieren als bei wenigen, die dazu noch erhebliche Unterschiede aufwiesen. Was man daraus folgern kann, ist die Gewißheit, daß man einem Netz, das eine schon vorher festgelegte Klasseneinteilung nach nicht rein aus den Mustern folgenden Kriterien finden soll, doch eine Art von Lehrinput vorgeben muß, wenn man eine Einteilung in derartige spezielle, nicht direkt aus der Mustermenge folgende Klassen erreichen will. Durch die vorangegangenen Versuche scheint aber doch die grundsätzliche Richtigkeit und Berechtigung des vorgestellten Ansatzes gezeigt worden zu sein.

3. Das kontextuelle System

Das Ziel dieses Systems war es, aus einem vorgegebenen Inputmuster, nämlich den dem System schon bekannten Vorgängerbuchstaben, als Output die Wahrscheinlichkeiten des Auftretens aller Buchstaben zu liefern. Es handelt sich also um eine Zuordnungsaufgabe, in der auf ein bestimmtes Inputmuster (Kombination der Vorgängerbuchstaben) ein eindeutiges Ausgabemuster (die Wahrscheinlichkeiten der einzelnen Buchstaben) folgen soll. Back Propagation stellt für solche Aufgaben ein sehr gutes Verfahren dar, da es bei richtiger Wahl der Parameter mit großer Wahrscheinlichkeit zu einer "richtigen" Beeinflussung der Gewichte führt. Dieses Lernparadigma verwendend, wurde daraufhin ein Netzwerk entworfen, das oben genannte Aufgaben erfüllt. Ausgangspunkt bei diesem System ist die Voraussage des achten Buchstaben aus seinen sieben Vorgängern. Diese Grenze deshalb, da es von der Rechenzeit her noch vertretbar ist, auf der anderen Seite aber aus dem achten Vorgänger kaum mehr brauchbare Informationen gewonnen werden konnten. Mit den hier versuchten Lernzeiten lieferte aber selbst der sechste und siebente Vorgänger nur selten einen Beitrag. Das Netzwerk für diese Aufgabe ist in der folgenden Abbildung dargestellt.

Input

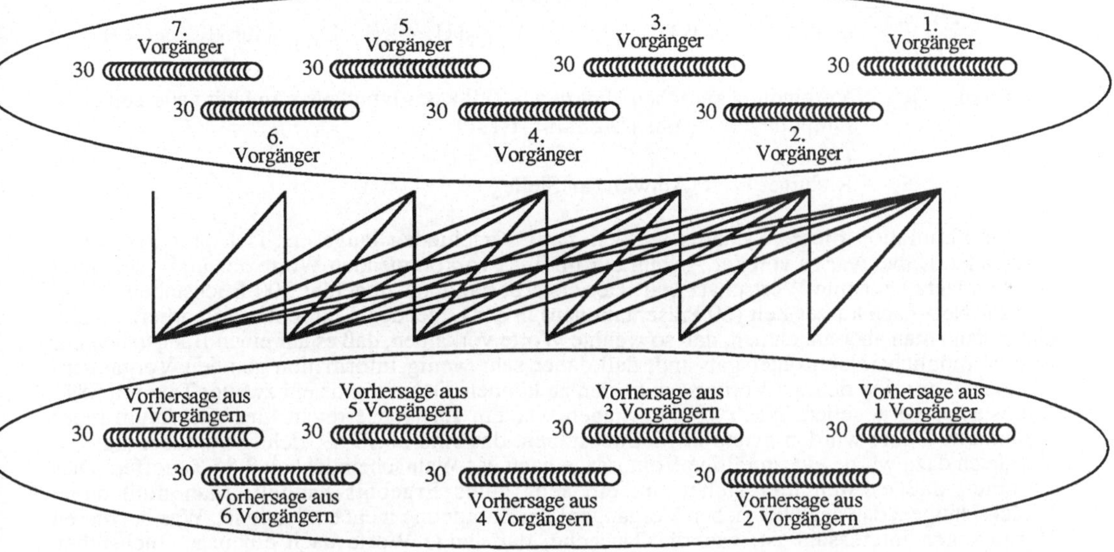

Output

Abb.3: Kontextuelles Netzwerk

Die Verschaltungen wurden so gewählt, weil angenommen werden konnte, daß je nach Abstand vom vorauszusagenden Buchstaben der Vorgänger eine andere Bedeutung haben würde. Somit ist der Inputlayer in sieben Teile mit je 30 Units unterteilt, wobei jeder Teil einen Vorgänger repräsentiert. Ist also Unit $U_{i,j,1}$ aktiv, so bedeutet das, daß der j-te Buchstabe im Alphabet der i-te Vorgänger ist (Index 1 bedeutet, daß es sich um den Inputlayer handelt). Unit $U_{i,j,1}$ liegt also in Teil i des Inputlayers und ist dort die j-te Unit. Ist also der Wortteil "NETZWER" schon bekannt, so sind im Inputlayer die Units $U_{7,14,1}$ (N, der 14te Buchstabe ist siebenter Vorgänger), $U_{6,5,1}$; $U_{5,20,1}$; $U_{4,26,1}$; $U_{3,23,1}$; $U_{2,5,1}$ und $U_{1,18,1}$ aktiviert. Der Outputlayer enthält wieder sieben Teile, von denen erneut jeder aus 30 Units besteht. Dabei bekommt der erste Teil Verbindungen von allen sieben Inputteilen, der siebente nur noch vom direkten Vorgänger. Man erhält also sieben Ergebnisse, die jeweils eine andere Voraussichtsspanne haben. Das Endergebnis erhält man durch Summation der sieben Einzelergebnisse. Dadurch wird erreicht, daß sich die weniger entfernten Buchstaben stärker auf das Ergebnis auswirken, da sie in mehrere der summierten Werte einfließen. Die Spezifikation des Systems ergibt sich wie folgt:

<u>Propagieren:</u>

$$U_{i,j,2} = \frac{1}{1 + e^{\sum_{k=1}^{i}\sum_{m=1}^{30} U_{k,m,1}\,\mathrm{conn}_{k,i,m,j}\,\alpha}}$$

$U_{i,j,2}$ j-te Unit in Teil i des Outputlayers
$U_{k,m,1}$ m-te Unit in Teil k des Inputlayers
α Lernrate
$\mathrm{conn}_{k,i,m,j}$ Verbindung zwischen Unit m Teil k des Inputlayers zu Unit j Teil i des Outputlayers

<u>Gesamtergebnis:</u>

$$E_j = \sum_{k=1}^{7} U_{k,j,2}$$

Gewichtsänderung:

$$conn_{k,i,m,j} = \begin{cases} conn_{k,i,m,j} & \text{für } U_{k,m,1} = 0 \\ conn_{k,i,m,j} + \beta\, U_{k,m,1}\left(V_j - U_{i,j,2}\right) U_{i,j,2}\left(1 - U_{i,j,2}\right) & \text{für } U_{k,m,1} \neq 0 \end{cases}$$

$conn_{k,i,m,j}$	Verbindung zwischen Unit m aus Teil k des Inputlayers zu Unit j aus Teil i des Outputlayers ($1 \leq m,j \leq 30$; $1 \leq i \leq 7$; $1 \leq k \leq i$)
β	Lernrate
V_j	Richtiger Wert (Antwort) an Stelle j

Zur Simulation dieses Systems wurden zwei verschieden lange englischsprachige Texte verwendet. Dabei war es von der Anzahl der im Text vorkommenden Worte abhängig, wie groß der dem Netz bekannte Wortschatz war. Der erste bestand aus ungefähr 300 Buchstaben. Dabei war das Netz nach kurzer Zeit (60 Präsentationen) in der Lage, den Text fehlerfrei vorherzusagen. Dabei kann man aber annehmen, daß so wenige Worte vorkamen, daß es auf einen Buchstaben nur wenige mögliche Nachfolger gab und, daß daher sehr wenig Information aus den Vorgängern ausreichte, um eine richtige Vorhersage treffen zu können. Daher wurde ein zweiter Text mit 3871 Buchstaben vorgegeben. Nach 180 Vorgaben war ein Zustand erreicht, der sich kaum mehr veränderte. Dabei wurden genau 2275 Buchstaben, das sind 58.77 %, richtig vorausgesagt. Im Vergleich dazu würde eine zufällige Voraussage nach der Wahrscheinlichkeit 3.85 % treffen. Dies bedeutet, daß es sich hier sicher um ein sehr gutes Ergebnis handelt. Man muß dabei berücksichtigen, daß auch bei sieben Vorgängern die Zuordnung nicht eindeutig ist. Was bei diesen Voraussagen interessant ist, war die Tatsache, daß lange Worte nach ein paar Buchstaben (Wortanfänge waren meistens falsch -- da es verschiedene mögliche Satzfortsetzungen gibt, ist es nicht verwunderlich, daß hier die Zuordnung uneindeutig ist) richtig erkannt wurden. Dies läßt darauf schließen, daß das Netz das Wort kennt, und aus der Kombination der Anfangsbuchstaben dann auch erkennen kann, daß es sich um dieses Wort handelt. Ein weiterer, leicht zu erkennender Zug des Netzes lag darin, häufig vorkommende Worte besser als seltene zu erkennen.

Als Beispiel möge die Phrase THEMSELVES TO dienen. Dabei ist für jeden Buchstaben der tatsächlich an dieser Stelle stehende, der vorhergesagte, und die zweite Wahl angegeben. Bei den Vorhersagen ist zusätzlich der Wert im Bereich [0,1] angegeben, mit dem der Buchstabe erwartet wird.

tatsächlicher	Buchstabe	Voraussage	2. Wahl
T		T mit 0.1621	W mit 0.0183
H		H mit 0.8708	_ mit 0.0232
E		E mit 0.8812	A mit 0.0336
M		_ mit 0.2578	D mit 0.0273
S		_ mit 0.5780	E mit 0.0353
E		_ mit 0.6332	T mit 0.0366
L		_ mit 0.0507	D mit 0.0137
V		V mit 0.4397	L mit 0.0417
E		E mit 0.9841	I mit 0.0059
S		S mit 0.2912	_ mit 0.0519
_		_ mit 0.7507	E mit 0.0225
T		T mit 0.4425	W mit 0.1777
O		H mit 0.4712	O mit 0.2945

"_" = Space

Man sieht am obigen Beispiel gut, daß das Netz sowohl nach THE als auch nach THEM an ein Wortende "denkt". Nach THEMSE folgt offenbar ziemliche "Ratlosigkeit", denn auch der Sieger-buchstabe hat nur eine sehr kleine Ladung. Nach THEMSEL ist das Wort erkannt, die weiteren Buchstaben folgen mit hohen Ergebniswerten. Lediglich nach THEMSELVE ist für das Netz das Anhängen des S fraglich (_ mit hohem Wert als zweite Wahl), ein Phänomen, das oft auftritt. Bei TO sieht man die Bedeutung des Kontextes zwischen den Worten. Es folgt nämlich im Gegensatz zum ersten Wort, als auf das T klar ein H vorausgesagt wurde hier als eine doch hoch geladene zweite Wahl das richtige O. Als zweites Beispiel sei hier das weniger verwechslungsträchtige Wort SOMETHING angegeben.

tatsächlicher Buchstabe	Voraussage	2. Wahl
S	T mit 0.0199	W mit 0.0185
O	O mit 0.1468	_ mit 0.0366
M	M mit 0.5188	_ mit 0.0395
E	E mit 0.7374	P mit 0.0175
T	_ mit 0.1943	D mit 0.0205
H	H mit 0.8465	_ mit 0.0389
I	I mit 0.7135	E mit 0.2000
N	N mit 0.7422	_ mit 0.0234
G	G mit 0.7330	_ mit 0.0447

Am Wortanfang (1. Buchstabe) wird immer versucht, die häufigsten Wortanfänge T, W zu verwenden. Beim dritten Buchstaben scheint als Alternative das Leerzeichen auf. Dies würde das Wort SO bedeuten. Beim fünften Buchstaben erkennt das Netz das Wort SOME. Die restlichen Buchstaben bereiten nach Erkennen von SOMET kein Problem mehr. Bemerkenswert ist lediglich noch die leichte Tendenz zum THE bei Buchstabe 7.

Was hier gezeigt wurde, ist nur der Nachweis, daß das Netz grundsätzlich in der Lage ist, die gestellte Aufgabe zu lösen. Es wird klar, daß das Beherrschen aller gängigen Wörter und somit ein hohes Wissen über alle möglichen Kontextzusammenhänge einen sehr hohen Lernaufwand bedeuten würde. Trotzdem ist anzunehmen, daß das vogestellte System dazu in der Lage ist, da in der derzeitigen Auslastung die Vorhersage aus dem sechsten und siebenten Buchstaben noch kaum eine Rolle spielt, dort also noch Raum für Informationen zur Verfügung steht. Weiters ist es genauso vorstellbar, die Vorausschauspanne noch zu vergrößern (auch 8. oder 9. Vorgänger als Information heranziehen), eine Maßnahme, die aber erst bei einem Netz mit einem wirklich gewaltigen Wortschatz notwendig sein dürfte.

4. Das vollständige System

Nach der Fertigstellung der beiden Teilsysteme war es das Ziel, die beiden zu einem einheitlichen System zu verbinden, bei dem sich die Information aus dem semantischen Teil positiv auf die Erkennung der Buchstaben auswirkt. Im visuellen System findet sich der Mechanismus des Autoassociative Recall, das ist jene doppelte Flußrichtung der Information durch die Gewichte, die es möglich macht, nur teilweise existente Muster ganz zu erkennen, indem wahrscheinlich gewordene Muster Aktivierungen zurück zu allen Teilen schicken, aus denen sie bestehen. Üblicherweise starten diese Feedback-Verbindungen bei 0 (Aktivierungen im letzten Layer=0), um dann, wenn sie vom Input her Aktivierungen erhalten, diese wieder zurückzustrahlen. Die Erwartung eines bestimmten Buchstaben aufgrund der kontextuellen Information über den Fortgang des Textes stellt aber sehr wohl bereits eine Erwartungshaltung gegenüber dem zu erkennenden Muster dar. Genau gesagt kann man sogar die Werte der einzelnen Folgebuchstaben so übernehmen, wie sie vom semantischen System kommen (gleicher Wertebereich). Es findet daraufhin ein Associative Recall statt. Die Buchstabenteile der eher erwarteten Buchstaben (Ergebnis des kontextuellen Systems) werden also verstärkt, während die der anderen durch die Normierung sogar absinken.

Das System sieht also derart aus, daß zuerst aus den bekannten Vorgängerbuchstaben mit Hilfe des kontextuellen Netzes die Erwartungen bezüglich der Folgebuchstaben bestimmt werden. Diese Werte werden dann in den Outputlayer eingespeist, während gleichzeitig das Muster an den Inputlayer angelegt wird. Es folgt der normale Ablauf des visuellen Systems bis hin zu einer Schwellwertüberschreitung im Outputlayer. Dieses Ergebnis wird ausgegeben und den Vorgängern zugeordnet. Daraufhin erfolgt eine neue Erkennung.

Ein gewaltiges Problem bei der Erstellung eines derartigen Netzes ergab sich aus der Zuordnung der Outputunits der beiden Netzteile, da beim kontextuellen System durch die Back Propagation die Musterzuteilung zwar eindeutig, beim visuellen System aber rein willkürlich durch das System selbst gegeben war. So stellte sich aufgrund der Uneindeutigkeit der Klassen beim visuellen System (mehrere Buchstaben pro Klasse) die Unmöglichkeit dieses Unterfangens heraus. Bei manchen Buchstaben (nur einer in einer Klasse) war die Zuordnung eindeutig: Der Outputwert für den entsprechenden Buchstaben im semantischen System wurde einfach in diese Outputunit übernommen. Das eigentliche Problem stellte sich also nur für die Buchstaben, die keine eindeutige Entsprechung hatten. Man hätte also für O und Q nur dieselbe Outputunit verwenden können - ein für die Mustererkennung unbrauchbarer Vorschlag.

5. Diskussion

Die neuen Aspekte des vorgestellten Systems betreffen vor allem die Verbesserung der von Fukushima vorgeschlagenen Variante. Es wird ein stark vergrößerter Inputlayer verwendet, um genauere Buchstaben erfassen zu können. Weiters wird die Netzarchitektur sowie die Lernregel bedeutend vereinfacht. Dieses System ist in der Lage, das gleiche zu leisten wie das Mustererkennungssystem Fukushimas, nämlich die fehlerfreie Erkennung von fünf verschiedenen Buchstaben. Zusätzlich wurde in dieser Arbeit eine Erweiterung dieses Ansatzes um ein den Kontext einbringendes Back-Propagation Netzwerk behandelt. Dieses Zusatzsystem ist dazu in der Lage, aus sieben Vorgängerbuchstaben einen achten vorauszusagen. Diese Voraussage wirkt sich nachgewiesenermaßen positiv auf den Erkennungsvorgang aus. Ein noch besseres Ergebnis wird lediglich durch Probleme der gegenseitigen Anpassung der Teilsysteme verhindert. Bisherige Versuche dieses Problem zu beheben hatten insoweit Erfolg, als sich eine Verbesserung der Klassenaufteilung erzielen ließ. Dies wurde dadurch erreicht, daß man mit einer Art von Hilfsinput bewußt versuchte, die größeren Klassen aufzuteilen. Allerdings muß hier gesagt werden, daß eine vollständige Verteilung der Klassen, und somit eine eindeutige Zuordnung bis jetzt noch nicht erreicht werden konnte. Diese ist aber notwendig, um eine endgültige Aussage über die Steigerung an Erkennungsrate beziehungsweise eine Zeitersparnis zu machen. Daher ist der derzeitige Stand unserer Arbeiten der Versuch, das visuelle Teilnetz derart zu beeinflussen, daß eine eindeutige Zuordnung der Buchstaben auf die Units des Outputlayers möglich wird.

6. Literatur

[Chan 88]   CHANGEUX,J.P.: Learning and Selection in the Nervous System. - in: deKerkhove,D.(ed.), The Alphabet and the Brain, pp 43-50 Springer-Verlag Berlin, Heidelberg (1988)

[Dorf 89]   DORFFNER G.: Konnektionismus und Subsymbolische AI. - Vorlesungsunterlage (1989)

[Fink 88]   FINKEL,L.H.: Neuronal Group Selection: A Basis for Categorisation by the Nervous System. -in: deKerkhove,D.(ed.), The Alphabet and the Brain, pp 51-67 Springer-Verlag Berlin, Heidelberg (1988)

[Fuku 80]   FUKUSHIMA,K.: Neocognitron: A Self-organizing Neural Network Model for a Mechanism of Pattern Recognition Unaffected by Shift in Position - in: Biological Cybernetics 36 (1980) pp193-202

[Fuku 84a] FUKUSHIMA,K.: A Hierarchical Neural Network Model for Associative Memory - in: Biological Cybernetics 50 (1984) pp105-113

[Fuku 84b] FUKUSHIMA,K.: A Neural Network Model for the Mechanism of Feature Extraction - in: Biological Cybernetics 50 (1984) pp377-384

[Fuku 86]   FUKUSHIMA,K.: A Neural Network Model for Selective Attention Visual Pattern Recognition - in: Biological Cybernetics 55 (1986) pp5-15

[Gr&Th 82] deGROOT,A.M.B., THOMASSEN,A.J.W.M. & HUDSON,P.T.W.: Associative facilitation of word recognition as measured from a neutral prime - in: Memory and Cognition 10 (1982) pp 358-370

[Gutt 82]   GUTTMANN,G.: Lehrbuch der Neuropsychologie 3.,überarb. u. erg. Auflage Huber, Bern,Stuttgart,Wien (1982)

[Hi&Sp 70] HIRSCH,H.V.B & SPINELLI,D.N.: Visual Experience Modifies Distribution of Horizontally and Vertically Oriented Receptive Fields in Cats - in: Science 168 (1970) pp 869-871

[Hube 89]   HUBEL,D.H.: Auge und Gehirn, Neurobiologie des Sehens Heidelberg, Spektrum d. Wiss. Verlagsgesellschaft (1989)

[Hu&Wi 77] HUBEL,D.H. & WIESEL,T.N.: Functional Architecture of Macaque Monkey Visual Cortex - in: Proc. Roy. Soc. Lond. B 198 (1977) pp1-59

[Köhl 90]   KÖHLE,M.: Neurale Netze Springer Verlag, Wien,New York (in Vorbereitung)

[Ru&Hi 86] RUMELHART,D.E., HINTON,G.E. & WILLIAMS,R.J.: Learning Internal Representation by Error Propagation - in: Rumelhart,D.E.&McClelland,J.L.(eds.) Parallel Distributed Processing Vol I, MIT Press Cambridge, MA. (1986)

[Ru&Zi 85] RUMELHART,D.E. & ZISPER,D.: Feature Discovery by Competitive Learning - in: Cognitive Science 9 (1985) pp75-112

[Ta&Ta 83] TAYLOR,I. & TAYLOR,M.M.: The psychology of reading New York, Academic Press (1983)

[Tayl 88]   TAYLOR,M.M.: The Bilateral Cooperative Model of Reading - in: deKerkhove,D.(ed.), The Alphabet and the Brain, pp 322-361 Springer-Verlag Berlin, Heidelberg (1988)

[Town 83]   TOWNSEND,D.J.: Thematic Processing in Sentences and Texts - in: Cognition 13, (1983) pp 223-261

[To&Be 88] TOWNSEND,D.J. & BEVER,T.G.: Knowledge Representation During Reading Depend on Reading Skill and Reading Strategy - in: Gruneberg,M.M., Morris,P.E. & Sykes,R.N. (eds.) Practical Aspects of Memory: Current Research and Issues Volume 2, pp 309-314, John Wiley & Sons Ltd. (1988)

[We&St 78] WEST,R.F. & STANOVICH,K.E.: Automatic contextual facilitation in readers of three ages - in: Child Development 49, (1978) pp 211-219

THEORIE UND ANWENDUNG
STRUKTURIERTER KONNEKTIONISTISCHER SYSTEME

Thomas Waschulzik Hans Geiger
Kratzer Automatisierung GmbH
Maxfeldhof 5–6, D–8044 Unterschleißheim

1. Einleitung

Im Bereich der technischen Informationsverarbeitung gibt es viele Probleme, die mit konventionellen Methoden nicht zufriedenstellend gelöst werden können. Die Gründe dafür sind oft ein Mangel an Flexibilität, Lernfähigkeit und Fehlertoleranz der konventionellen Systeme. Aus diesem Grund befaßt sich die Firma KRATZER AUTOMATISIERUNG seit ca. 5 Jahren mit der Technologie der konnektionistischen Systeme und setzt diese inzwischen auch in Projekten mit Kunden ein.

2. Überblick

Das bisher von uns verwendete konnektionistische Modell wird mit seinen Hauptanwendungsgebieten vorgestellt. Den Abschluß bildet ein Ausblick auf die weitere Entwicklung; schwerpunktmäßig wird dabei auf die Weiterentwicklung des verwendeten konnektionistischen Modells eingegangen.

3. Theorie

Das bisher von uns verwendete konnektionistische Modell soll mit der in [Rumelhart 1986] eingeführten Notation dargestellt werden. Die Verarbeitungseinheiten sind dabei eine Erweiterung des McCulloch-Pitts-Neurons [McCulloch 1943].

Folgende Punkte wurden modifiziert:

- Frequenzcodierung der Knoten (auch als Elemente oder Neurone bezeichnet).
  Die Knoten haben einen Output zwischen 0 und 255 im Gegensatz zu binären Knoten.

- Anpassung der Knoten (modelliert über die Sensibilisierung und Adaptation).
  Bei konstantem Input kann sich die Aktivität eines Knotens in der Zeit verändern. Die Anpassung wird für die Anpassung des Systems an veränderte Umweltbedingungen verwendet, z.B. Veränderung der Helligkeit.
  Eine andere Anwendungsmöglichkeit ist die zeitliche Steuerung von Erkennungsvorgängen, z.B. können verschiedene Objekte auf einem Bild sequentiell nacheinander bearbeitet werden.

- Berücksichtigung der letzten Aktivität des Knotens für die Bestimmung der neuen Aktivität.
  Dies wird vor allem zur Dämpfung von Schwingungen eingesetzt.

- Lineare Approximation der Sigma-Funktion als Schwellenfunktion für die Bestimmung des Outputs eines Knotens auf Grund seiner Aktivität.

Das Modell läßt sich wie folgt mathematisch beschreiben:

Variable	Zahlenbereich	**Interpretation** (jeweils zum Zeitpunkt t)
a_i (t)	[-32768..32767]	Aktivität des Knotens i
o_i (t)	[0..255]	Output des Knotens i
$w_{i,j}$ (t)	[-32768..32767]	Kopplungsstärke von Knoten i zu Knoten j
net_i (t)	$\mathbb{R}$	Nettoinput zum Knoten i
$\Delta sens_i$ (t)	[-32768..32767]	Veränderung der Sensibilisierung
$\Delta adapt_i$ (t)	[-32768..32767]	Veränderung der Adaptation
$adapt_i$ (t)	[-32768..32767]	Adaptation des Knotens i
$sens_i$ (t)	[-32768..32767]	Sensibilisierung des Knotens i

Für die Definition des Modells werden folgende Konstanten verwendet:

Konstante	**Interpretation**
K_UG_i	Untergrenze der Schwelle des Knotens i
K_OG_i	Obergrenze der Schwelle des Knotens i
$NORM\_A_i$	Normaktivität des Neurons i
W1	Gewichtung der Werte von net_i (t), $sens_i$ (t-1) und $adapt_i$ (t-1)
W2	Gewichtung alten Aktivität a_i (t-1)

Erläuterung der verwendeten Funktionen:

Funktion	**Interpretation**
SIGN	Vorzeichenfunktion
A	Funktion zur Berechnung der Veränderung der Adaptation
S	Funktion zur Berechnung der Veränderung der Sensibilisierung

Berechnung der Variablen-Belegung zum Zeitpunkt t, ausgehend vom Zeitpunkt t-1:

$$net_i\ (t) \quad = \sum_j w_{j,i}\ (t-1) \bullet o_j\ (t-1)$$

$$\Delta\ adapt_i\ (t) \quad = A\ (SIGN\ ((a_i\ (t) - NORM\_A_i)),\ adapt_i\ (t))$$

$$\Delta\ sens_i\ (t) \quad = S\ (SIGN\ ((a_i\ (t) - NORM\_A_i\ )),\ sens_i\ (t\ ))$$

$$adapt_i\ (t) \quad = adapt_i\ (t-1)\ +\ ((a_i\ (t) - NORM\_A_i)) \bullet \Delta adapt_{i\ (t)})$$

$$sens_i\ (t) \quad = sens_i\ (t-1)\ +\ ((a_i\ (t) - NORM\_A i)) \bullet \Delta sens_i\ (t))$$

$$a_{i\ (t)} \quad = \frac{W1 \bullet (net_i\ (t)\ +\ sens_i\ (t-1)\ +\ adapt_i\ (t-1))\ +\ W2 \bullet a_i\ (t-1)}{(W1 + W2)}$$

$$o_i\ (t) \quad = \begin{cases} 0 & ,\ wenn\ a_{i\ (t)} <\ =\ K\_UG_i \\[2mm] \dfrac{a_i\ (t) - K\_UG_i}{K\_OG_i - K\_UG_i} \bullet 255 & ,\ wenn\ K\_UG_i < a_i\ (t) < K\_OG_i \\[2mm] 255 & ,\ wenn\ a_i\ (t) >\ =\ K\_OG_i \end{cases}$$

Die Funktionen A und S bestimmen, welche von 8 vorgegebenen Konstanten für die Veränderung der Adaptation und Sensibilisierung verwendet wird.

Für das Lernen verwenden wir folgende Modifikation der Verbindungsstärken $\Delta w_{j,i}$:

$$\Delta w_{j,i}(t) = o_i(t) \bullet \eta_{j,i}(t)$$

Der Lernfaktor $\eta_{j,i}$ bestimmt sich auf Grund von zwei unterschiedlichen Lernregeln:

1. Modifikation der Hebb' schen Regel [Hebb 1949] (für Auto–Assoziation)

   Der Lernfaktor $\eta_{j,i}$ wird aus der nachstehenden Tabelle entnommen: Der Lernfaktor ist abhängig vom Output des der Verbindung vor- und nachgeschalteten Knotens und der aktuellen Kopplungsstärke. Die unten dargestellten 4 Geradenzüge für die Modifikation der Verbindungen und die Lernschwelle werden bei der Knotendefinition festgelegt.

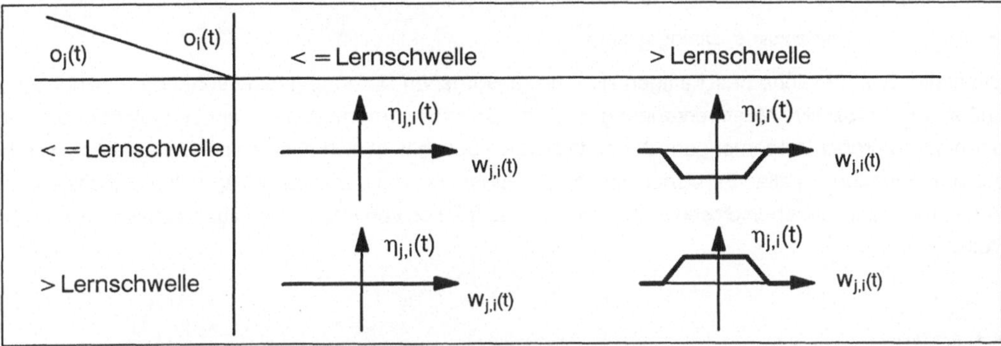

Abb. 1: Schematische Darstellung der modifizierten Hebb'schen Regel für w_{ji}
   $o_j(t)$ = postsynaptische Aktivität zum Zeitpunkt t
   $o_i(t)$ = praesynaptische Aktivität zum Zeitpunkt t
   $\eta_{i,j}(t)$ = Lernfaktor für die Verbindung $w_{j,i}$ zum Zeitpunkt t

2. Modifikation der Delta–Regel (für Hetero–Assoziation)

   Auch hier kann der Lernfaktor von der aktuellen Kopplungsstärke abhängig gemacht werden. Dies hat z.B. den Vorteil, daß der Einfluß einer Synapse eingeschränkt werden kann:

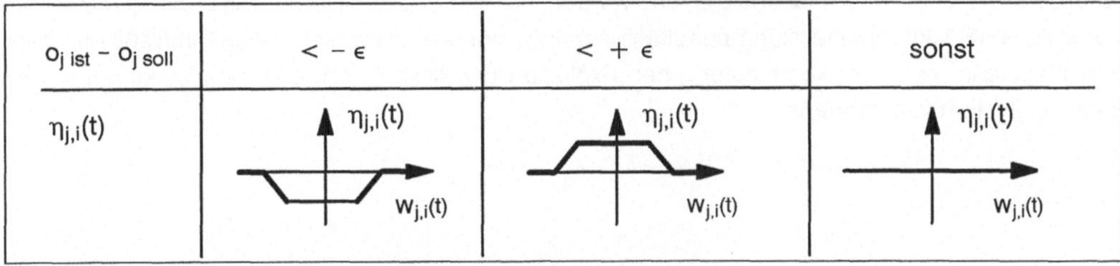

Abb. 2: Schematische Darstellung der modifizierten Delta–Regel
   $o_{j\,ist}(t)$ = Istzustand des Knotens j nach einem Verarbeitungsschritt mit dem Eingabemuster zum Zeitpunkt t
   $o_{j\,soll}(t)$ = Sollzustand des Knotens j zum Zeitpunkt t
   ϵ = Abstand, bis zu dem zwei Aktivitäten als identisch angesehen werden

Semantische Information repräsentieren wir auf zwei alternativen Wegen:

- An einen einzelnen Knoten gebunden (Großmutterneurone)
  Der Output eines Knotens gibt an, ob ein bestimmter Sachverhalt vorliegt oder nicht (z.B. der aktuell bearbeitete Datensatz gehört zu einer bestimmten Klasse.).

- An eine Gruppe von Knoten gebunden (verteilte Darstellung)
  Eine Gruppe von Knoten repräsentiert durch das Muster ihres Outputs einen bestimmten Sachverhalt

(z.B. ein Objekt). Der einzelne Knoten hat dann keine genau definierbare Semantik, sondern erhält sie erst im Kontext mit den anderen Knoten.

4. Anwendungen dieses Modells

Unsere Aktivitäten decken im wesentlichen folgende Themengebiete ab:

- ASMUS   Assoziative Mustererkennung auf Grund visueller Information
- ASFEX   Assoziative Analyse großer Datenmengen
- ASDIS   Assoziatives Dialogsystem

Die ersten zwei Bereiche beschäftigen sich mit sensornahen Daten und sind sehr eng miteinander verknüpft. Die assoziative Mustererkennung auf Grund visueller Information ist ein bedeutender Spezialfall der Analyse großer Datenmengen. Der dritte Bereich beschäftigt sich eher mit der Verarbeitung symbolischer Information. In allen Bereichen spielen das Erkennen von bedeutungstragenden Einheiten und der Zusammenhang zwischen diesen Einheiten für die Extraktion von Information aus Nachrichten eine große Rolle.

4.1 ASMUS

Die assoziative Mustererkennung ist ein klassisches Anwendungsgebiet der konnektionistischen Systeme. Als Beispiel soll hier ein Netzwerk aus diesem Forschungsbereich gezeigt werden, in dem Merkmalsdetektoren visueller Muster in Abhängigkeit von den zu bearbeitenden Bildern herausgebildet werden. Aufbauend auf dieses Modell wird dann eine realistische Anwendung skizziert.

In dem Netzwerk für die adaptive Merkmalsextraktion (Abb. 3),werden nach einer ersten Trainingsphase, in der allgemein interessante Merkmale gelernt werden, nur dann weitere Detektoren herausgebildet, wenn dies durch ein Rückkopplungssignal aus einer wesentlich höheren Hierarchieebene veranlaßt wird. Auf diesem Weg kann man der kombinatorischen Explosion der Anzahl von Merkmalsdetektoren in hierarchischen Systemen entkommen.

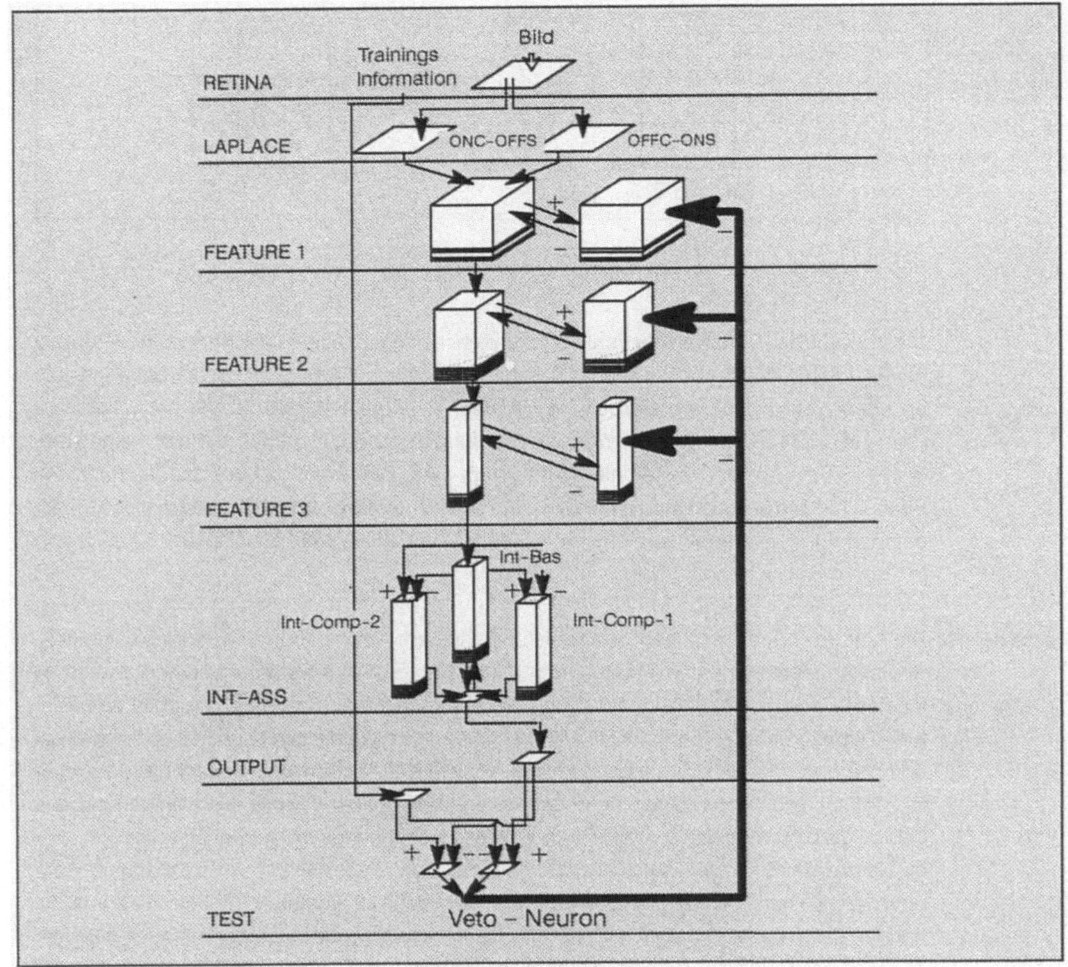

Abb. 3: Netzwerk für die adaptive Merkmalsextraktion aus Bildern

Die einzelnen Hierarchiestufen des Netzwerks für Merkmalsextraktion haben folgende Funktionen:

Retina   In der Ebene Retina wird dem Netzwerk das zu bearbeitende Bild angeboten. Innerhalb dieser Ebene findet keine Informationsverarbeitung statt.

Laplace   Die nächste Stufe besteht aus zwei Ebenen. Jeder Knoten in diesen Ebenen hat ein rezeptives Feld mit 3•3 Knoten in der Ebene Retina. In der On-Center-Off-Surround-Ebene (ONC-OFFS) (s.a. [Grossberg 1975]) haben die Knoten zu dem mittleren Knoten ihres rezeptiven Feldes eine stark positive Verbindung, zu den anderen Knoten eine schwach positive Verbindung. In der Ebene Off-Center-On-Surround (OFFC-ONS) ist die Verschaltungsstruktur analog gewählt, jedoch das Vorzeichen umgekehrt.

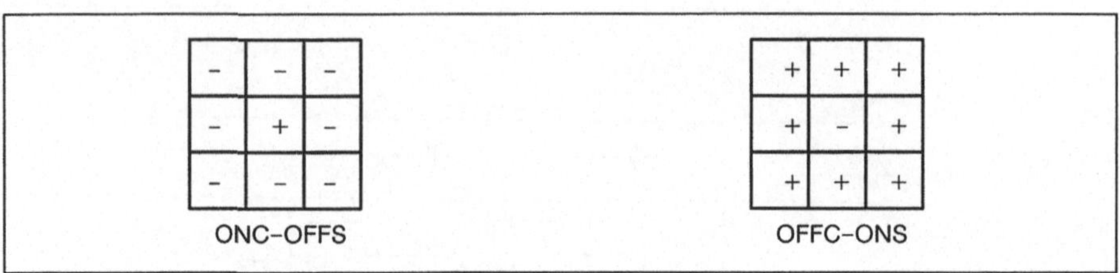

Abb. 4: Rezeptive Felder der Knoten in den Laplace-Ebenen

Diese zwei Ebenen haben die Funktion, zunächst eine Laplace-Filterung zweiter Ordnung der Bildinformation durchzuführen. Diesen Schritt kann man als eine Vorverarbeitungsstufe ansehen. Durch diese Vorverarbeitung wird auch sichergestellt, daß die Aktivität in Teilbereichen der Laplace-Ebenen bestimmten Bedingungen genügt. So erhält man z.B. keine Areale mehr, in denen alle Knoten gleichzeitig aktiv sind. Dies ermöglicht es, zu den nächsten Ebenen mit den üblichen streng lokalen Lernregeln zu lernen, ohne daß die rezeptiven Felder entarten. Eine Lernregel, vergleichbar mit dem Competitive Learning [Zipser 1986], ist also in diesem Fall nicht notwendig.

Feature-1 Die Feature-1 Schicht besteht aus zwei Kuben. In dem linken Kubus sind Feature-Detektor-Knoten angeordnet, in dem rechten hemmende Knoten. Diese hemmenden Knoten werden für eine Winner-Takes-All-Verschaltung (WTA) (s.a. [Grossberg 1988]) zwischen den Feature-Detektor-Knoten benötigt. Die Knoten in den Ebenen der zwei Kuben sind jeweils retinotop angeordnet (d.h. benachbarte Knoten einer Ebene haben auch benachbarte "rezeptive Felder"). Die Knoten einer Säule des linken Kubus haben jeweils das gleiche rezeptive Feld. Sie sind untereinander mit Hilfe der WTA-Verschaltung verbunden, so daß immer nur ein Neuron der Säule aktiv sein kann. Durch Lernen der Verbindungen von der Laplace-Ebene zu den Knoten des Feature-Detektor-Kubus bilden sich Feature-Detektoren heraus. Es hat sich dabei gezeigt, daß eine ONC-OFFS-Verschaltung als Initialisierung auch hier sehr gut geeignet ist und die Lernzeiten erheblich verkürzt. Um die Konvergenz des WTA-Mechanismus zwischen den Feature-Neuronen zu beschleunigen, verwenden wir das folgende Lernverfahren für die hemmenden Verbindungen von den Interneuronen zu den Neuronen des Feature-Detektor-Kubus. Es wird eine hemmende Verbindung dann verstärkt, d.h. ein positives $\Delta w_{i,j}(t)$ abgezogen, wenn der aktuelle Output des der Verbindung nachgeschalteten Knotens niedriger als der Output des vorgeschalteten Knotens ist. Sonst wird die Stärke der Verbindung beibehalten. Auf diese Art und Weise erhält man eine sehr schnelle Konvergenz unabhängig von den Aktivitäten der Neurone [Arnoldi 1989].

Feature-2 Die Verschaltung dieser Hierarchiestufe ist analog zu der Verschaltung von Feature-1, jedoch sammeln die Knoten dieses Feature-Detektor-Kubus bahnenden Input von den Knoten aus Feature-1 und nicht aus der Retina. Es werden in dieser Schicht Kombinationen von einfacheren Features gelernt ([Fukushima 1975] und [Hartmann 1982]). Durch eine Verschaltung, die eine Konvergenz der Information bewirkt, wird die Anzahl der Knoten pro Ebene verringert. Die Anzahl der Ebenen und damit die Anzahl der unterschiedlichen Feature-Detektoren wird vergrößert. Dies ist notwendig, damit sich eine genügend große Vielfalt von Feature-Detektoren bilden kann.

Feature-3 Das in der Hierarchieebene Feature-2 beschriebene Vorgehen wird noch einmal in der Stufe Feature-3 durchgeführt mit einer Verringerung der Knotenanzahl pro Ebene und einer Erhöhung der Ebenenanzahl pro Kubus.

INT-ASS Die nächste Hierarchiestufe sorgt für die Erzeugung einer internen Repräsentation zur assoziativen Abspeicherung. Die interne Repräsentation wird so gewählt, daß der zur Verfügung stehende Zustandsraum optimal ausgenutzt wird. Dies bringt Vorteile durch eine deutlich verbesserte Selektivität bei der Klassifikation von Objekten und eine bessere Speicherkapazität. Die Selektivität ist verbessert, da die interne Repräsentation von unterschiedlichen Objekten so gewählt wird, daß sie einen möglichst großen Abstand im Zustandsraum haben. Auf diese Art und Weise kann man auch sehr gut unterschiedliche Modalitäten zueinander assoziiert abspeichern. Ausführliche Darstellungen dieser Hierarchiestufe finden sich in [Böller 1988] und [Arnoldi 1989]. Die Verschaltung ist durch drei Kuben INT-BAS, INT-COMP1 und INT-COMP2 realisiert. Der Kubus INT-BAS, der auch als Basiskubus für die interne Repräsentation bezeichnet wird, bekommt aktivierenden Input von dem Feature-Detektor-Kubus aus der Hierarchieebene Feature-3. Der Kubus INT-BAS und die Ebene INT-REP sind durch Verbindungen in beide Richtungen sehr eng gekoppelt. INT-REP bekommt zusätzlich noch Input aus den zwei Kuben INT-COMP1 und INT-COMP2. Diese zwei Kuben haben die Aufgabe, ein Fehlersignal zu generieren, wenn in der Trainingsphase ein neues Muster zu einer bereits besetzten internen Repräsentation assoziiert werden soll. Durch das Fehlersignal wird die interne Repräsentation so modifiziert, daß ein neuer Zustand in INT-REP eingenommen wird. Dieser Zustand hat im Zustandsraum eine möglichst große Entfernung von dem zunächst eingenommenen Zustand.

Output Die Output-Ebene liefert das Ergebnis des Erkennungsvorgangs. Hier wird in der Trainingsphase das Muster angeboten, das zu dem auf der Retina angebotenen Aktivitätsmuster assoziiert werden soll. Dies kann z.B. ein Datenbankschlüssel oder wiederum ein optisches Muster sein.

Test An die Outputebene schließt sich eine weitere Hierarchiestufe an. In dieser Ebene wird nach einem Trainingslauf getestet, ob die Trainingsmuster richtig assoziiert werden konnten. Dies geschieht dadurch, daß das gewünschte Testergebnis in der Testebene angeboten wird. Die Output und Testebene werden durch eine spezielle Verschaltung verglichen und erzeugen, wenn eine Abweichung festgestellt wird, ein Rückkopplungssignal auf die niedrigeren Hierarchiestufen Feature-1, Feature-2 und Feature-3. Dieses Rückkopplungssignal der Veto-Knoten modifiziert den WTA-Mechanismus in den hemmenden Kuben derart, daß genau diejenigen Knoten lernen, die am meisten zur Unterscheidung des aktuellen Musters von bereits gelernten Mustern beitragen können.

Mit diesem Schema können in Abhängigkeit vom bisherigen Lernergebnis rückgekoppelt neue Feature-Detektoren gelernt werden.

Aufbauend auf dieses System kann man konnektionistische Systeme für praktische Anwendungen entwickeln. Eine Applikationsmöglichkeit ist die Qualitätskontrolle von Weingläsern vor dem Verpacken.

In der Praxis erwartet man sich von derartigen Systemen im Vergleich zu konventionellen Systemen niedrigere Wartungskosten und eine leichtere Anpassung auf modifizierte Aufgabenstellungen (z.B.: Weißweingläser ☞ Rotweingläser, glatte Gläser ☞ Gläser mit Gravur, ...) .

4.2 ASFEX – Assoziative Analyse großer Datenmengen

In den Anwendungsbereich der Analyse großer Datenmengen ordnen wir z.B. die Klassifikation von Objekten oder den Entwurf von adaptiven Reglern ein. Hier soll nur die Klassifikation von Objekten genauer ausgeführt werden.

Bei vielen technischen Aufgabenstellungen müssen Objekte oder Ereignisse, die durch bestimmte Datensätze repräsentiert sind, in verschiedene Klassen z.B. gut oder schlecht, eingeteilt werden.

Die verwendeten konnektionistischen Systeme bestimmen auf Grund von Trainingsdaten Merkmale, die für die Klassifikation verwendet werden. Dies erfolgt zum Teil mit Netzwerken, die mit dem unter 4.1 dargestellten Netzwerk eng verwandt sind.

Man kann aber auch mit wesentlich einfacheren Netzwerken bereits sehr zufriedenstellende Ergebnisse erzielen, wenn man geeignete Darstellungen für die Repräsentation von Zahlenwerten wählt. So haben wir ein einfaches zweischichtiges Netzwerk mit einem Datensatz aus dem Bereich der Botanik getestet (IRIS-Daten). Dieser Datensatz wird auch als Test für Klassifikatoren verwendet. Es handelt sich dabei um 150 Datensätze mit jeweils 4 Zahlenwerten, die in drei Klassen eingeteilt werden sollen. Wir haben die ersten 25 Datensätze jeder Klasse zum Trainieren des Systems verwendet.

Nach ca. 30 Minuten CPU-Zeit auf einem DESKPRO/386 mit 33MHz von COMPAQ unter dem Betriebssystem SCO/XENIX hatte das Netzwerk diese 75 Datensätze gelernt, d.h. es konnte alle 75 Datensätze korrekt den 3 Klassen zuordnen. Von den restlichen 75 Datensätzen, die man dem System noch nicht angeboten hatte, wurden 69 Datensätze in die richtige Klasse eingeordnet.

4.3 ASDIS – Assoziatives Dialogsystem

Das Ziel von ASDIS ist es, ein assoziatives Dialogsystem zu entwickeln. Dieses System soll dem Benutzer erlauben, ohne die Kenntnis einer formalen Abfragesprache Datenbankabfragen durchzuführen. Die Eingabe in das System soll über Tastatur erfolgen. Im Rahmen dieses Projektes haben wir einen sehr schnellen, fehlertoleranten assoziativen Zugriff auf Wörter realisiert (vgl. [Deffner 1990]).

5. Ausblick

Zu den beiden Punkten Theorie und Anwendung soll aus unserer Sicht ein Ausblick auf die weitere Entwicklung gegeben werden.

5.1 Theorie

Auf Grund von praktischen Erfahrungen und theoretischen Überlegungen sind wir der Meinung, daß man die verwendeten konnektionistischen Modelle grundlegend in folgenden Punkten modifizieren muß:

- Verwendung von unterschiedlichen Verbindungstypen
  Durch die Verwendung von unterschiedlichen Synapsentypen (vgl. Sigma-Pi-Units in [Rumelhart 1986]) kann man wesentlich mehr Informationsverarbeitung in einem einzelnen Knoten durchführen.

- Berücksichtigung der Dendritenbaumstruktur von Knoten
  Durch die Kombination unterschiedlicher Synapsentypen (additiv, multiplikativ, ...) mit einer Strukturierung der Synapsen, kann man Netzwerke erzeugen, die abhängig von dem aktuellen Problem ihre Verbindungsstruktur dynamisch verändern [Waschulzik 1990]. Dies kann z.B. durch Shunting-Inhibition–Synapsen   (Verbindungen) erfolgen, die den Informationsfluß auf dem Dendriten modifizieren. Es können so Teilbäume von bestimmten Aspekten der Informationsverarbeitung (Bestimmung der Aktivität, Lernen, ...) des Knotens abgeschnitten werden. Bei den ersten Simulationen mit derartigen Systemen ergaben sich sehr ermutigende Ergebnisse. Es handelt sich hier um eine Verallgemeinerung der Sigma–Pi–Units aus [Rumelhart 1988]. Siehe auch [Feldman 1982a] und [Feldman 1982b].

- Umstellung auf Single–Spike–Knoten
  Durch die Aufgabe der Frequenzkodierung und die Simulation von einzelnen Spikes erhält man die Möglichkeit, über einen Kanal sehr viele unterschiedliche Arten von Information zu transportieren. Bei der Kodierung von Zahlenwerten kann man diese neuen Möglichkeiten wie folgt ausnutzen:

  o Kodierung des Zahlenwertes durch den mittleren Abstand zwischen zwei Spikes.

  o Zuverlässigkeit des Zahlenwertes durch die Standardabweichung der einzelnen Spikes von der mittleren Feuerungsrate.

  o Zusammenhang von Daten durch synchrone oder asynchrone Bursts.
    Die Knoten feuern nicht permanent, sondern immer nur über eine bestimmte Zeitspanne. Danach sind sie eine gewisse Zeit inaktiv. In der Neurophysiologie entspricht dies den Bursts der Neurone.

Während der aktiven Zeitspanne feuern die Knoten in Abhängigkeit von ihrer Aktivität.
In der folgenden Darstellung seien die Spikes eines Knotens durch senkrechte Striche rechts neben der Knotenbezeichnung dargestellt:

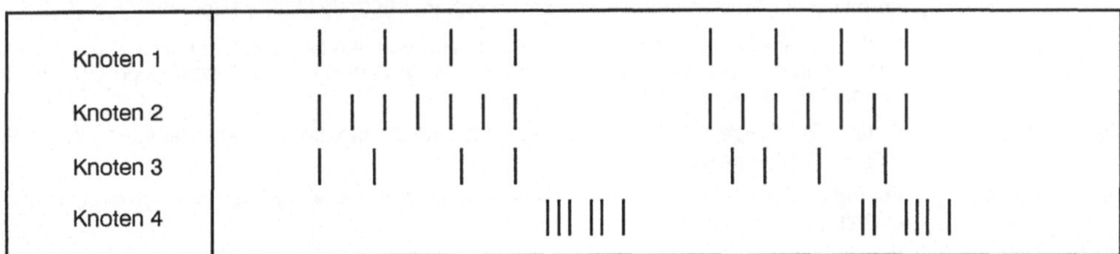

Abb. 5: Korrelation von Spikes und Bursts

Die Knoten 1, 2 und 3 feuern korreliert miteinander, d.h. die Werte hängen semantisch zusammen. Die Information von Knoten 4 hängt mit der Information der anderen Knoten nicht zusammen. Der Zahlenwert, der durch den Knoten 2 repräsentiert wird, ist größer als der Zahlenwert, der von den Knoten 1 und 3 repräsentiert wird. Die Knoten 1 und 3 kodieren den gleichen Zahlenwert, jedoch ist die Zuverlässigkeit des Wertes am Knoten 3 niedriger.

5.2 Anwendung

Bei unseren Kundenkontakten vor allem im Bereich der Großindustrie hat sich in den letzen zwei Jahren ein wachsendes Interesse bemerkbar gemacht. Während sich im Jahr 1989 die Kunden nur über die neue Technik informieren wollten, sind sie ungefähr seit Beginn des Jahres 1990 auch bereit, konnektionistische

Systeme in Projekten einzusetzen. Wir sind überzeugt, daß die konnektionistischen Systeme in nächster Zeit genauso selbstverständlich als Hilfsmittel eingesetzt werden wie heute Datenbanksysteme. Dazu müssen jedoch geeignete Schnittstellen geschaffen werden, die den Anwender von den konnektionistischen Internas abschirmen.

Für die Entwicklung strukturierter konnektionistischer Systeme haben wir eine Methodik erarbeitet und entsprechende Hilfsmittel implementiert. Dies wird in dem Beitrag *Eine Entwicklungsmethodik für strukturierte konnektionistische Systeme* für den Workshop "Strukturierte Netzwerkmodelle" genauer ausgeführt.

Konnektionistische Systeme sind keine Konkurrenz zur "konventionellen" KI: Beide Techniken haben unterschiedliche Aufgabenbereiche, in denen sie optimal eingesetzt werden können. Sofern die Lösung für ein Problem gefunden und formalisierbar ist, sollte man die Aufgabenstellung entweder konventionell oder mit Hilfe der klassischen KI lösen. Kann man den Lösungsweg nicht formal beschreiben, weiß aber, welche Informationen für diese Lösung notwendig sind und hat diese Informationen zur Verfügung, so hat man gute Chancen, eine Lösung mit Hilfe eines konnektionistischen Systems zu finden.

6. Zusammenfassung

Konnektionistische Modelle haben die Forschungsphase verlassen; man ist in verschiedenen Bereichen in der Entwicklung von Anwendungen. Auf dem Gebiet der Neuronenmodelle wird man sich dem biologischen Vorbild noch weiter annähern.

Literatur

[Arnoldi 1989] Arnoldi, M., Mustererkennung mit Hilfe selbstorganisierender, adaptiver Mechanismen. Diplomarbeit an der Technischen Universität München, 1989, Institut für Informatik

[Böller 1988] Böller, D., Realisierung eines hierarchischen neuronalen Netzwerks zur assoziativen Erkennung von Objekten in natürlicher Umgebung. Diplomarbeit an der Technischen Universität München, 1988, Institut für Informatik

[Deffner 1990] Deffner, R., Geiger, H., Recognizing Words with Connectionistic Architectures . INNC–Proceedings 1990, (in press)

[Feldman 1982a] Feldman, J.A.: Dynamic Connections in Neural Networks. Biological Cybernetics, 46, 28–39 (1982)

[Feldman 1982b] Feldman, J.A., Ballard, D.H., Connectionist models and their properties. Cognitive Science, 6, 205–254 (1982)

[Fukushima 1975] Fukushima, K., Cognitron: A Self–Organized Multilayered Neural Network. Biological Cybernetics, 20, 121–136, (1975)

[Grossberg 1975] Grossberg, S., Ellias, S.A., Pattern Formation, Contrast Control and Oscillation in the Short Term Memory of Shunting ON–Center Off–Surround Networks

[Grossberg 1988] Grossberg, S., The Adaptive Brain I, The Adaptive Brain II, North Holland, Amsterdam, New York, Oxford, Tokyo

[Hebb 1949] Hebb, D.O., Organization of Behaviour, John Wiley, New York, 1949

[McCulloch 1943] McCulloch W.S., Pitts, W., A Logical Calculus of Ideas Immanent in Nervous Activity, Bull. Math. Biophys. 54 (1943)

[Rumelhart 1986] Rumelhart, D.E., McClelland, J.L., Parallel Distributed Processing, Volume I, The MIT–Press, Cambridge, Mass. 1986

[Waschulzik 1990] Waschulzik, T., Geiger, H., Arnoldi, M., Böller, D., Nischwitz, A., Brauer, W., New Concepts for Information Processing in Connectionistic Systems. In: Eckmiller, R., Hartmann, G., Hauske, G. (eds.), Parallel Processing in Neural Systems and Computers, North–Holland, Amsterdam, New York, Oxford, Tokyo, 1990

Encoding and Decoding of Patterns
which are Correlated in Space and Time

J.L. van Hemmen and W. Gerstner[1]

Physik-Department der TU München,

D-8046 Garching (bei München)

A. Herz, R. Kühn, B. Sulzer, and M.Vaas

Sonderforschungsbereich 123 an der Universität Heidelberg

D-6900 Heidelberg

Abstract

In the late forties, Hebb postulated his mechanism for learning: Information presented to a neural network during a learning session is stored in the synaptic efficacies in such a way that at a synapse only concurrent events are correlated and encoded. In this paper, three things are done. We study the performance of Hebbian learning in networks with a broad distribution of transmission delays and show that it can handle both stationary and dynamic objects such as single patterns and cycles by the very *same* principle, the delays taking care of temporal changes, if any. Second, we discuss *unlearning*, an unsupervised anti-Hebbian procedure that can deal with unbiased and correlated patterns alike and greatly improves the efficiency of a neural network. Finally, we indicate how to code and retrieve correlated (slow) motion. Here the key idea is to code the *changes* (per unit of time) and use an asymmetric learning rule.

1 Introduction

Coding and faithfully retrieving information is one of the main tasks of a neural network. In thia paper, we want to concentrate on information which is presented in the form of patterns which change in space *and* time and, in addition, may be highly correlated. This type of information presents a challenge to any *local* coding procedure. Local coding is fast, efficient, and easy to program since locality implies that a connection W_{ij} (from j to i) is only determined by the data available to i and j. However, the local coding cannot 'see' the global relations which are present in data correlated over long distances in space and time.

For unbiased random patterns which change on a time scale that is less than the maximal delay time of a network (see below), Hebbian coding is extremely efficient [1 − 3]. Hebb himself formulated the learning mechanism as follows: "When an axon of cell A is near enough to excite a cell B and *repeatedly* or *persistently* takes part in firing it, some growth process or metabolic change takes place in one or both cells such that A's efficiency, as one of the cells firing B, is increased." The axon transports the signals from B to the synapse on A and, as Hebb already observed, the synapse seems to be the most plausible site to store the information.

To implement the Hebb rule mathematically, we specify the dynamics and indicate the important role of the *delays* which are omnipresent in any realistic signal transmission. (After all, it takes the signal some time to travel from B to A.) It is to be stressed that a *broad* distribution of delays (as encountered in the brain) is essential to the capability of a network to learn temporal sequences with different durations. We then formulate the Hebb rule for sequential and parallel dynamics and show its robust performance with respect to space warp and time warp.

---

[1] present address: Dept. of Physics, University of California, Berkeley, CA 94720, USA

Unlearning is an unsupervised anti-Hebbian procedure which 'disentangles' correlated patterns that have been learned by using the Hebb rule but, because of the correlation, could not be discerned yet. Here we concentrate on stationary patterns. Finally, we extend the original Hebbian procedure [1, 2] and describe an efficient (optimal) way of coding slow correlated motion, a notorious problem for any local procedure.

2 Dynamics and Hebbian Learning: Essentials

In order to avoid cluttering the argument by technicalities, we start by considering the simplest possible case, formal neurons and unbiased random patterns. The state of neuron i is specified by the variable a_i that can take only two values: $+1$ (active) and -1 (quiescent). The data presented to the network are patterns $\{\xi_i^\mu; 1 \leq i \leq N\}$ where μ is a label and the ξ_i^μ are independent, identically distributed random variables which assume the values $+1$ and -1 with probability p and $1 - p$, respectively. For the moment, $p = 0.5$ but this condition as well as the independence of the stored patterns will be relaxed later on.

Given the local field h_i, typically of the form $\sum_j W_{ij} a_j$ (see Sect.3), the simplest possible dynamics is deterministic ,

$$a_i(t + \Delta t) = \text{sgn}[h_i(t)]. \tag{1}$$

Noise can be included through a so-called finite-temperature, stochastic dynamics with transition probability

$$\text{Prob}\{a_i(t + \Delta t) = a_i \mid h_i(t)\} = \frac{1}{2}\{1 + \tanh[\beta h_i(t)a_i]\}. \tag{2}$$

Here β is the inverse temperature. As $\beta \to \infty$, we recover (1). The usual updatings are (i) *parallel*, all neurons are updated according to (2) at the same time and independently of each other, and (ii) *sequential*, a single neuron is picked randomly, updated according to (2), all local fields are modified if necessary, the next neuron is singled out, and so on. In the bulk limit $N \to \infty$, sequential dynamics requires a scaling $\Delta t \propto N^{-1}$ so as to guarantee that the number of updates *per neuron* per unit of time remains finite. The global retrieval quality of a pattern, say μ, is measured by the overlap

$$m_\mu = N^{-1} \sum_{i=1}^{N} \xi_i^\mu a_i. \tag{3}$$

We have $m_\mu = 1$ if and only if $a_i = \xi_i^\mu$ for all i; otherwise, $m_\mu < 1$.

In a neuronal network, the information transmission from j to the synapse at i is through the axon, taking τ ms, and it is in the synapses where the data presented to the network are stored. The corresponding synaptic efficacy is denoted by $W_{ij}(\tau)$. It is known that the distribution of the τ's is *broad*, ranging up to $100 - 200$ ms. Following Hebb, we correlate i's activity $a_i(t)$ with what i receives from j, viz. $a_j(t - \tau)$. Adding up all contributions during a learning session $(0 \leq t \leq T)$ and realizing that, as $N \to \infty$, Δt must scale as N^{-1}, we find for *sequential* dynamics [1, 2]

$$\Delta W_{ij}(\tau) = N^{-1} \varepsilon_{ij}(\tau) \cdot \frac{1}{T} \int_0^T dt \, a_i(t) \, a_j(t - \tau) \tag{4}$$

where $\varepsilon(\tau_{ij})$ is a weight to take morphological characteristics into account, and the T^{-1} in front of the integral takes care of saturation effects. Three remarks are in order. First, as it stands, Eq. (4) presupposes unbiased random patterns with $p = 0.5$; the case $p \neq 0.5$ will be handled in Sect. 5. Second, learning proceeds as the patterns come in. The coding is local (only i and j matter for W_{ij}) and there is no programming based on a preceding analysis of the data. Third, Eq. (4) is a *temporal* correlation function, correlating what happens at i at time t with the state of j at time $(t - \tau)$. A broad distribution of delays, which is the key to the robust performance of (4), provides the system with detailed information about changes in space (j as compared to i) and time ($t - \tau$ as compared to t).

For *parallel* dynamics, we have updating at $t = n \cdot \Delta t$ and there is no harm in rescaling time so that $\Delta t = 1$. Then we obtain

$$\Delta W_{ij}(\tau) = N^{-1} \varepsilon_{ij}(\tau) \cdot \frac{1}{T} \sum_{0 \leq t \leq T} a_i(t+1) a_j(t-\tau) \tag{5}$$

since $h_i(t)$ determines what $S_i(t)$ does at time $t + 1$; in other words, one has to correlate the incoming signal at time t with i's state at time $t+1$, and *not* with its state at time t. What is new in (4) and (5) as compared to previous work, is the inclusion of (a distribution of) delays, which, of course, also occur in the retrieval dynamics; see, for instance, Eq.(6) below.

3 Space Warp and Time Warp

The Hebb rules (4) and (5) have been tested extensively on several models $[1-3]$. Here we discuss the performance of one of them. We assume that for each pair (i,j) there is a large number of connections whose delays τ have weights $\varepsilon(\tau)$ independent of i and j. We use a normalization with $\sum_\tau \varepsilon(\tau) = 1$. Summing over the incoming signals we have

$$h_i(t) = \sum_{j(\neq i)} \sum_\tau W_{ij}(\tau)\, a_j(t-\tau) \,. \tag{6}$$

Note that the very same delays which occur in (4) and (5) also appear in (6) — as they should, since the hardware during retrieval is the same as during a learning session. Of course, one also has models $[1-3]$ with only a *single* connection between i and j. The performance hardly depends, though, on the specific model. Neither does it fail in space warp nor in time warp, rather notorious problems in temporal association.

Space warp refers to a fault in phase space. For example, the network has learned the theme $BACH$ and it is now offered a faulty $BHCH$. The timing is correct but the first H in $BHCH$ (in phase space) is wrong. Time warp means that the temporal order is correct but the timing is not. For instance, the network perceives $BAAACH$ with lots of A and little B, C, and H. Figures 1 and 2 show that Hebbian learning overcomes both problems.

4 Unlearning

Suppose now that our patterns are stationary $(T \gg \tau_{max})$, but correlated $(p \neq 0.5)$, as is evident from their correlation coefficients $c_{\mu\nu} = N^{-1} \sum_i \xi_i^\mu \xi_i^\nu \simeq <\xi>^2$ for $\mu \neq \nu$ where the mean $<\xi>$ equals $2p-1$, which is nonvanishing if $p \neq 0,5$. The Hebb rules (4) and (5), which are local, do not 'see' this correlation and give for all delays τ

$$W_{ij}(\tau) = N^{-1} \varepsilon(\tau) \sum_\mu \xi_i^\mu \xi_j^\mu \,. \tag{7}$$

Focussing on a network with instantaneous interactions only $(\tau = 0)$, we immediately observe that no extensive storage capacity is possible. Just put $a_j = \xi_j^\mu$ for all j. Then the local field is

$$h_i^\mu = \sum_{j(\neq i)} W_{ij} \xi_j^\mu = \xi_i^\mu + N^{-1} \sum_{j(\neq i)} \sum_{\nu(\neq\mu)} \xi_i^\nu \xi_j^\nu \xi_j^\mu \simeq \xi_i^\mu + (q-1) <\xi>^3 \tag{8}$$

where q denotes the total number of stored patterns and $<\xi> = 2p - 1 \neq 0$. The signal term ξ_i^μ can dominate the noise $(q-1) <\xi>^3$ only if $(q-1) \cdot \left| <\xi>^3 \right| < 1$, whence q must remain finite.

A way-out is provided by unlearning, originally proposed by Crick and Mitchison [5] to explain dreaming (REM sleep) and implemented by Hopfield *et al.* [6] for $p = 0.5$ and $q \leq 0.15N$.

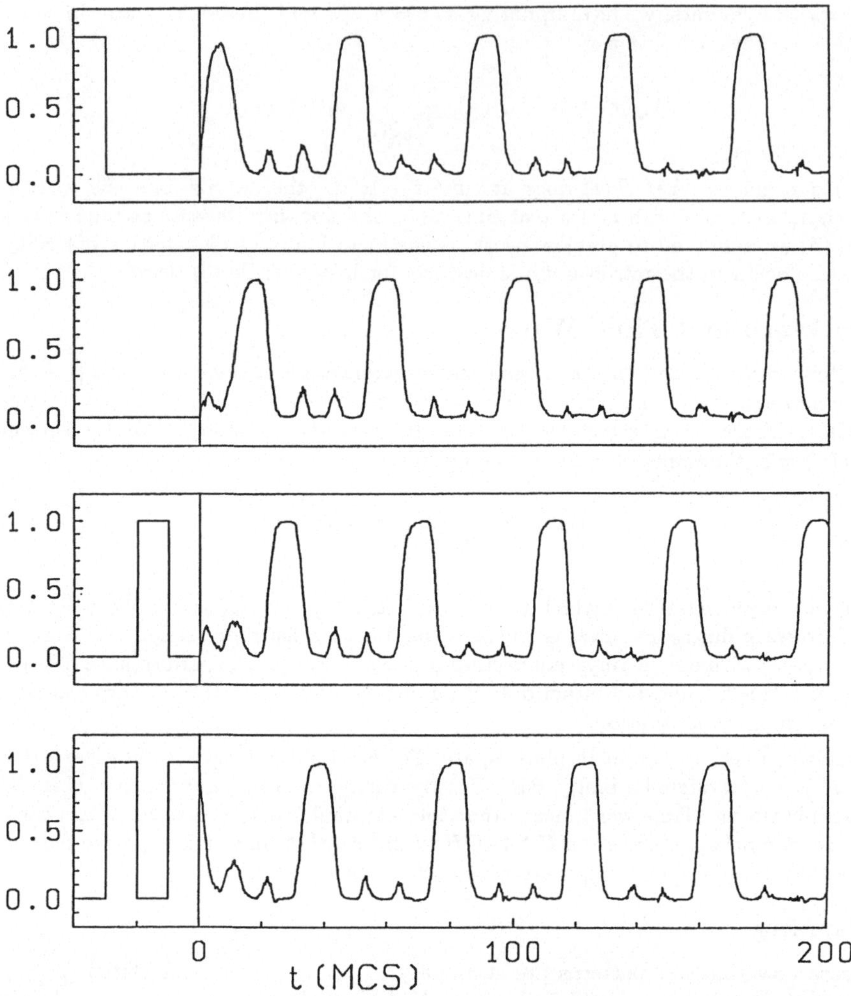

Fig. 1. Space warp. The overlaps with the patterns 1,2,3 and 4 (from top to bottom) have been plotted as a function of time. The network has learned the cycle 1,2,3,4 (or $BACH$). After it has been given the faulty pattern sequence 1,4,3,4 (or $BHCH$) as initial condition for $-\tau_{max} \leq t \leq 0$, the correct order $BACH$ is spontaneously retrieved. Thus $BHCH$ is in the *entrance domain* of $BACH$. The simulation result is shown for $N = 512$ formal neurons and a uniform discrete distribution of axonal delays ($\tau = 0, 1, \ldots, 40$). Here we have sequential dynamics with $\beta = 10$, and the duration of each pattern is $\Delta = 10$. The initial conditions appear in the boxes on the left of $t = 0$.

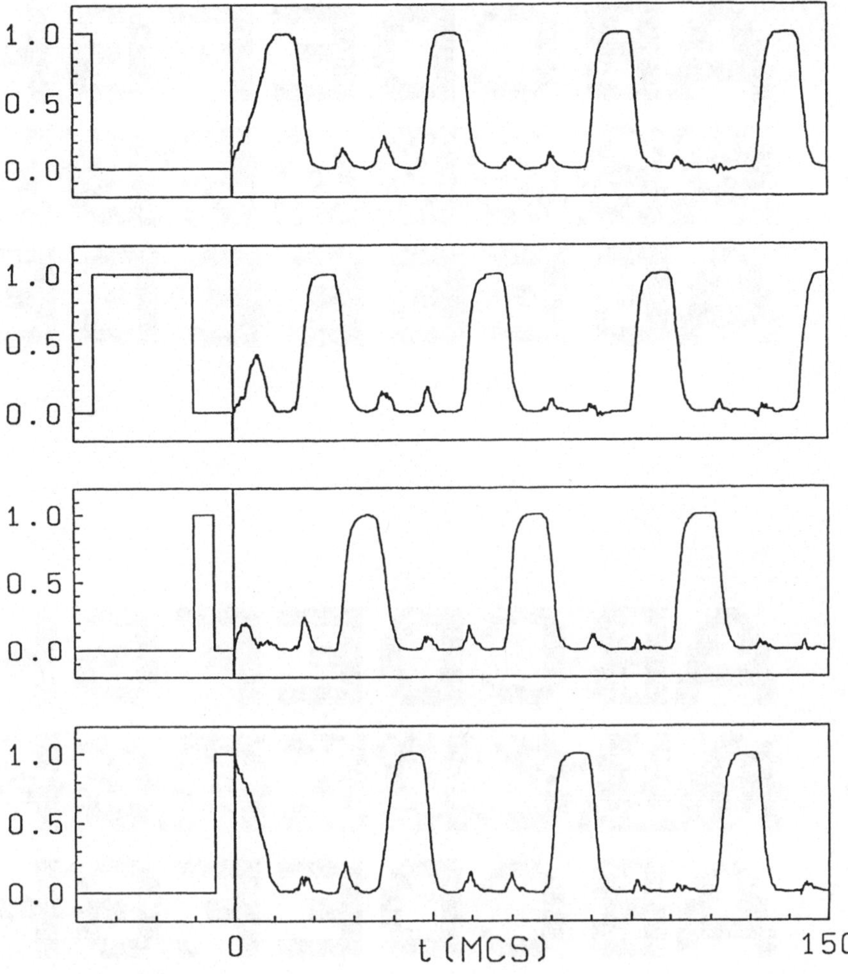

Fig. 2. Time warp. Imagine the system has been taught (again) the theme $BACH$, all notes having the same duration $\Delta = 10$. The overlaps with B,A,C, and H (from top to bottom) have been plotted as a function of time. After the network has been given a pattern sequence with a wrong timing as initial condition for $-\tau_{max} \leq t \leq 0$ (A lasting much longer than B,C, and H), the correct cycle (with its correct timing) is spontaneously retrieved. The simulation result is shown for $N = 512$ formal neurons and a uniform discrete distribution of axonal delays ($\tau = 0, 1, \ldots, 40$). Here we have sequential dynamics with $\beta = 10$. The initial conditions appear in the boxes on the left of $t = 0$.

Fig. 3. Benefits of unlearning. The first eight letters of the alphabet, A – H (top), have been stored in a network of $N = 100$ formal neurons. Corrupted versions (middle) with about 12% noise are presented to the network, which then retrieves the original patterns (bottom). Before unlearning (**a**), the network is unable to discern the letters except for the A. After unlearning (**b**), associative memory has been restored. The retrieved patterns closely resemble but need not coincide with their prototypes.

We start with (7), and use sequential dynamics. The procedure consists of three steps. (i) *Random shooting.* One generates a random initial configuration. (ii) *Relaxation.* The system relaxes under the dynamics (1) to a stationary configuration $\{\eta_i^d; 1 \leq i \leq N\}$. (iii) *Unlearning.* After 'dream' d, all the W_{ij} $(i \neq j)$ are updated according to

$$W_{ij} \rightarrow W_{ij} - \frac{\varepsilon}{N} \eta_i^d \eta_j^d \; . \tag{9}$$

Because of the minus sign, the final state associated with dream d is weakened, it is 'unlearned'. Typically, $\varepsilon = 0.01$. The index d varies between 1 and D, the total number of 'dreams'. A *post facto* justification of anti-Hebbian learning such as (9) can be found in, e.g., ref. [8].

Unlearning greatly improves the efficiency of the network; for example, for $p = 0.5$ the storage capacity is increased by a factor 5. Furthermore, the optimal number of dreams D_{opt} does *not* depend on p,

$$D_{opt}(q,N,p;\varepsilon) = \varepsilon^{-1} \cdot (c_0 + c_1 \cdot N^{-1}) \cdot q \; , \tag{10}$$

where $c_0 = 0.56 \pm 0.08$, $c_1 = 22 \pm 10$, and $\varepsilon \leq 0.05$. Note that, due to (9), nothing is left for $D \gg D_{opt}$. Another new and fascinating aspect, consistent with (10), is that (4) or (5) in conjunction with (10) can store patterns with *varying* activity. Moreover, randomness is not required either, as is demonstrated by Fig. 3. There p is the fraction of black pixels, varying from letter to letter. For all the results mentioned here we refer to [3, 7].

5 Correlated Movements

How, then, should we encode correlated *movements*, for instance, in throwing a ball [9]? If we want to get an impression of how the brain codes, we can also take the visual system where, as is well-known [10], *only changes* in the surrounding are perceived. To solve the coding problem — conventional means such as the pseudoinverse do not work — our key idea is therefore not to code the pictures of the moving object itself but rather the differences between any subsequent pictures [11]. Explicitly, we assume a two layer structure with a receptor layer and a storage layer, and use parallel dynamics. The local fields in the storage layer are taken to be

$$h_i(t) = \sum_{j(\neq i)} \sum_{\tau} W_{ij}(\tau) \left[a_j(t-\tau) - a \right] \; , \tag{11}$$

where $a =< \xi > \simeq -1$ as $p \rightarrow 0$. Instead of (5), the learning rule is asymmetric [11],

$$\Delta W_{ij}(\tau) = N^{-1} \varepsilon_{ij}(\tau) \cdot \frac{1}{T} \sum_{0 \leq t \leq T} a_i(t+1) \left[a_j(t-\tau) - a \right] \; , \tag{12}$$

in agreement with recent neurophysiological data [8]. For stationary patterns, it can be shown that this rule leads to optimal coding [11]. Let the input be $\alpha_i(t), 1 \leq i \leq N$. Then coding and decoding between input and storage layer are given by an 'exclusive or' function (XOR),

$$a_i(t+1) = \text{XOR}\left[\alpha_i(t), \alpha_i(t-1)\right] \tag{13}$$

for the coding process — see Figure 4 — and

$$\alpha_i(t+1) = \text{XOR}\left[\alpha_i(t), a_i(t-1)\right] \tag{14}$$

for decoding. The function $\text{XOR}(x,y)$ equals 1 if $x \neq y$ and -1 if $x = y$. Note that the $a_i(t)$, the 'changes', are to be inserted into (12). The rules (12) - (14) give rise to a rather robust performance, as is illustrated by Fig. 5. What we have depicted there is a storage layer, a 20×20 grating where a pixel is black if $a_i = +1$ and white if $a_i = -1$. The pattern sequence starts in the upper left-hand corner with a single black pixel and broadens into a string perpendicular to the moving direction. During the motion, the number of black pixels increases from 1 to 20 and then decreases to 1 again. Figure 5 confirms once more that Hebbian coding in conjunction with a broad distribution of delays is robust and faithful.

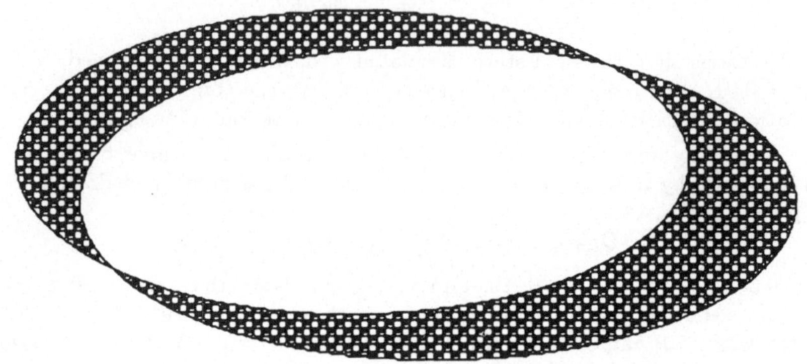

Fig. 4. Coding the motion of an oval. The input layer perceives the two ovals, one of them a single time step later than the other. The symmetric difference (13) is transmitted to the storage layer and encoded via (12).

6 Discussion

In summary, we have studied Hebbian coding itself, viz. (4) and (5), both for cycles and for stationary patterns. A fascinating aspect of a broad distribution of transmission delays is that the network can store temporal sequences with each pattern μ lasting Δ_μ units of time. The Δ_μ need not be equal and can vary from cycle to cycle or pattern to pattern. The only proviso is that (i) $\Delta_\mu < \tau_{max}$ since otherwise the network perceives a pattern as stationary and treats it accordingly, and (ii) the Δ_μ inside a cycle should not differ too much, typically $\Delta_{min}/\Delta_{max} > 0.5$.

Unlearning greatly enhances the efficiency of a network and enables it to store *correlated* stationary patterns. (Cycles are still under study.) Consistent with that, the optimal number of 'dreams' does not depend on the fraction p of active neurons as long as $0.25 \leq p \leq 0.75$. Outside this range we simply have to use another coding, viz., 0/1 instead of $-1/1$.

Correlated *motion* can be handled in rather robust a way by (11) and (12). The moral to be distilled out of these coding procedures is that once a suitable preprocessing and an accordingly adapted representation of neural activity have been chosen, Hebbian learning is a powerful *local* procedure to store spatio-temporal objects, easy to implement in practical work.

Acknowledgments

JLvH and WG gratefully acknowledge the hospitality of professor H. Wagner, Sektion Physik der Ludwig-Maximilians-Universität München, where part of this work has been done. AH thanks the Studienstiftung des Deutschen Volkes (Bonn). We also would like to mention support from the Deutsche Forschungsgemeinschaft via the SFB 123.

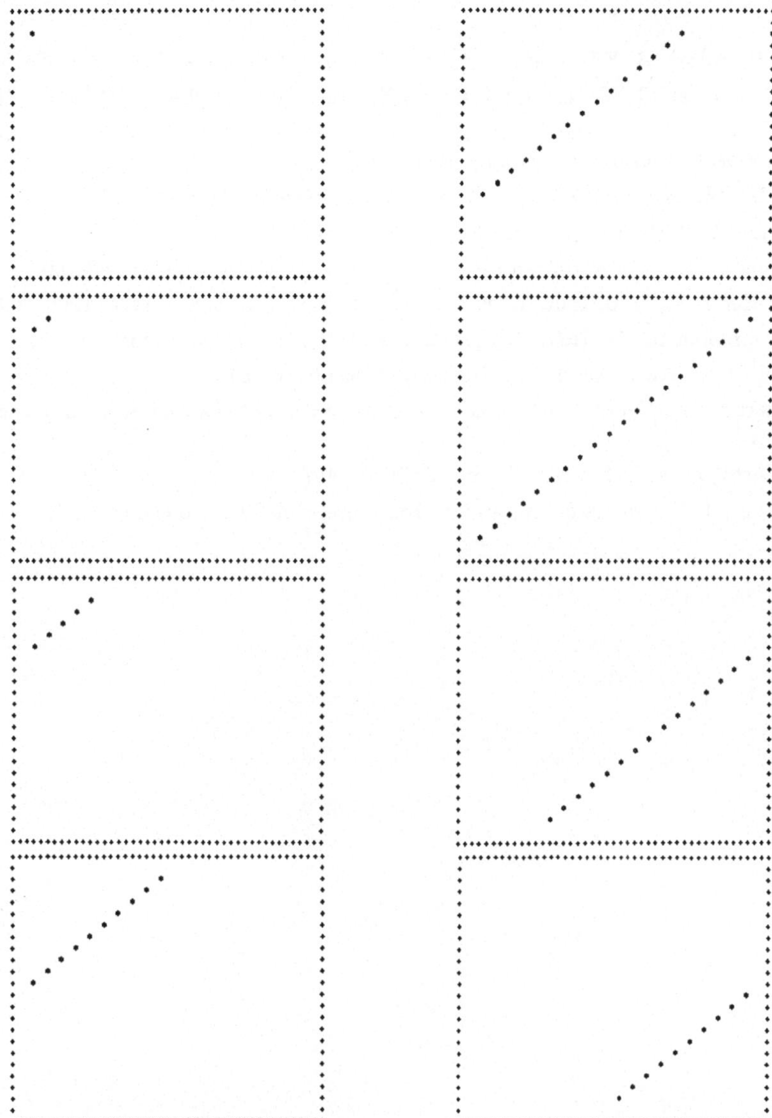

Fig. 5. Motion of a 'phase boundary', a string of black pixels, through a 20×20 storage layer. The system starts with a single point in the upper left-hand corner and the string develops as time proceeds (top to bottom; first left, then right column). During the motion, the fraction of black pixels varies between 1 and 20 but a in (12) does not; it is -1.

References

1. A. Herz, B. Sulzer, R. Kühn, and J. L. van Hemmen, Europhys. Lett. **7** (1988) 663-9
2. A. Herz, B. Sulzer, R. Kühn, and J. L. van Hemmen, Biol. Cybern. **60** (1989) 457-467
3. J.L. van Hemmen, in *Neural Networks and Spin Glasses*, edited by W. K. Theumann and R. Köberle (World Scientific, Singapore, 1990) 91-114
4. D.O. Hebb, *The Organization of Behavior* (Wiley, New York, 1949) p.62
5. F. Crick and G. Mitchison, Nature **304** (1983) 111-114
6. J. J. Hopfield, D. I. Feinstein, and R. G. Palmer, Nature **304** (1983) 158-159
7. J. L. van Hemmen, L. B. Ioffe, R. Kühn, and M. Vaas, Physica A **163** (1990) 386-392
   M. Vaas, diploma thesis (Heidelberg, October 1989), and to be published
8. J. Lisman, Proc. Natl. Acad. Sci. USA **86** (1989) 9574-9578
9. M. Jeannerod, *The Neural and Behavioural Organization of Goal-Directed Movements* (Clarendon, Oxford, 1988)
10. W. Reichardt, Z. Naturforschg. **12 b** (1957) 448-457
11. W. Gerstner, J. L. van Hemmen, and A. Herz, preprint TU München (1990)

ConSTrainer: A GENERIC TOOLKIT for CONNECTIONIST DATASET SELECTION‡

Apostolos N. REFENES
Department of Computer Science
University College London
Gower Street, WC1, 6BT
London, UK.

ABSTRACT

ConSTrainer is a window-based toolkit dedicated to the task of collecting and validating datasets for training connectionist networks. Unlike other connectionist development tools, **ConSTrainer** is an application- and network-independent tool which can be configured to suit the requirements of a variety of applications through a simple-to-use configuration facility. The facility allows the user to create and modify both domain/ranges and domain/range parameters alike. For each parameter in the training exemplar **ConSTrainer** supports the definition of mutually supportive and mutually exclusive parameter sets. A powerful set of consistency and validation checks is also supported, including vector orthogonality, weightsum checking, and re-ordering of the training dataset. This paper introduces the **ConSTrainer** toolkit and discusses its utilization in a non-trivial application for diagnostic decision support in Histopathology.

1. INTRODUCTION

One of the main advantages of connectionist networks over classical expert systems for decision support, is their ability to learn from discrete examples and to generalize over the task domain. This is in sharp contrast to classical rule-based expert systems in which a "knowledge engineer" is required to extract the knowledge from the expert and to formulate rules suitable for reasoning about the task domain. The formulation of such rules is a complex and often ineffective method of developing decision support systems, particularly when the task domain involves incomplete or uncertain information, corrupted data, or dis-oriented features.

On the connectionist front, several interesting gradient-descent procedures have already been discovered for performing learning and generalization tasks. During training, the input and output nodes are clamped into the desired states, and the network is permitted to construct complex internal representations of its environment according to an automatic learning procedure. The learning procedures are capable of modifying connection strengths in such a way that internal units which are not part of the input or output come to represent important features of the task domain. Each connection computes the derivative, with respect to the connection strength, of a global measure of the error in the performance of the network. The connection strength is then adjusted in the direction that decreases the error.

These relatively simple, gradient-descent learning procedures work well for small tasks [Hinton87, AcHiSe85, Hopfie82, McCPit43] and the challenge in the connectionist research community is to find ways of applying them to larger non-trivial tasks. In most non-trivial applications, the training datasets required to clamp the input and output nodes are not always easy to select. It is not always possible to use all the combinations of input-output pairs, nor is it desirable to present the network with random training exemplars. The selection of the most suitable dataset for training connectionist networks is a hard problem, often equal in complexity to that of "knowledge engineering". This is made even harder by the lack of generic methods and tools for application-, and network-independent dataset selection. Connectionist development tools are still in their infancy and concentrate on *network-specific* aspects such as network construction and simulation, network monitoring and visualization, etc.

---

‡ This research is 50% funded by the European Communities Research Programme AIM under contract number A1027 entitled "BIOLAB: The development of an Integrated BIOmedical LABoratory".

‡ The **ConSTrainer** software is implemented in C and X-windows version 11 release 3 and is available for public distribution through the BIOLAB consortium. Some of the optimizations mentioned in this paper as well as others are under continuous development; these are yet to be released.

Unlike other connectionist tools, **ConSTrainer** is dedicated to the task of collecting and validating datasets for training connectionist networks. It is complementary to other connectionist development tools and it is designed to be integrated with some of the more advanced examples such as SFINX [PaGuSk87], CONE [Hanson87], ANSPEC [KraFroRi], and particularly RCS [Goddar89], GENESYS [Gutsch88], and PYGMALION [AngTre89]. **ConSTrainer** is based on a simple system model and formalism which is quite close to the reasoning of the expert. **ConSTrainer** is generic in that it can be configured to suit the requirements of a wide range of applications through a simple-to-use configuration facility. The facility allows the user to create and modify both input/output domains and domain parameters alike. For each domain parameter (i.e. input node cluster) **ConSTrainer** supports the definition of mutually supportive and mutually exclusive parameter sets. A powerful set of consistency and validation checks is also supported, including vector orthogonality, weightsum checking, and re-ordering of the training dataset for certain optimizing network-specific cognitive and performance characteristics. The availability of this type of generic toolkit for connectionist dataset collection offers two major advantages:

[1] simplification and speed-up of the application development cycle. The selection and validation of training datasets is carried out directly by the task domain expert in an environment and reasoning formalism with which he is familiar. This alleviates the need for a "knowledge engineer" and frees the "network engineer" from application specific considerations. Datasets collected in this way are always reliable and can be ported across many connectionist networks.

[2] benchmark datasets. The use of such a toolkit offers the opportunity to make benchmark datasets available to a wider community and to enable researchers to perform meaningful comparisons regarding the cognitive and performance characteristics of different learning procedures.

This paper describes the **ConSTrainer** toolkit and demonstrates its utilization to a non-trivial application for diagnostic decision support. In section 2 of the paper we describe the model underlying **ConSTrainer**. The main problem here is to devise a formalism for selecting training datasets which is close to the way in which the expert reasons about his task domain. In section 3 we describe the architecture of **ConSTrainer** and particularly, the user interface, the tools for re-configuring **ConSTrainer**, and the tools for validating datasets. In section 4 we compare **ConSTrainer** with related work. Finally, in section 5 we conclude that **ConSTrainer**, simplifies connectionist application development, supports portability of datasets, and benchmarking of connectionist algorithms in ways which are not yet generally available in other tools.

2. BUILDING CONNECTIONIST APPLICATIONS WITH ConSTrainer

2.1 Methodology

An attractive methodology for building non-trivial connectionist applications is to decompose the task domain into smaller tasks each of which is easy to model in terms of simpler networks. There are several advantages in using this methodology of de-composing large network systems into their constituent parts:

[1] simplification of training pattern selection. By de-composing the system into smaller subsystems it is easier, and safer, to select training datasets for each subsystem. It is also easier to verify the quality of reasoning and to optimize the cognitive and performance parameters of each sub-system.

[2] explanation facilities. For any decision support system to be acceptable at large, it must have a capability to explain its reasoning. Connectionist systems which are based on large single networks find it hard to support such facilities. By de-composing the system into smaller networks it is possible to fun-out the outputs of the smaller networks and route them into into a general explanation facility.

[3] network performance. One of the major obstacles in using neural network technologies in large scale applications has been the slow speed at which they operate during training. By de-composing the system into smaller sub-subnetworks it is possible to train them independently (fully or partially).

[4] network re-usability. The de-composition of the network allows components which perform routine tasks common to many parts of the application (or shared across applications) to be trained only once and to be re-used.

[5] physiological plausibility: Connectionist networks perform cognition tasks by mimicking the operation of the human brain. The closer a model of the brain as a computational system is to the structure of the biological system, the more effective it is likely to be. It is plausible that the human brain is itself partitioned into specialized heterogeneous neural networks.

The formalism underlying the design of **ConSTrainer** is strongly influenced by these considerations. The principal assumption is that non-trivial applications of connectionist networks would consist of one or more domains of (possibly weighted) inputs which the network classifies into one or more ranges of (possibly weighted) outputs.

2.2 System Model

The system provides the user with a rudimentary model of connectionist computation: the network is "shown" the mapping that is required to learn by clamping an input vector on the input units and clamping the required output vector on the output units. If there are several possible output vectors for a given input vector, each of the possibilities is clamped on the output units with the appropriate probability. The network is then annealed (usually off-line) until it learns to recognize the pattern. The procedure is repeated for all the various input-output pairs. It is not always possible nor desirable to use all the possible input-output pairs. The selection of input-output pairs is carefully selected over the input-output range to represent important features of the task domain. The optimization of the dataset for network-specific cognitive and performance purposes is left to the system. For example, during training, it is often necessary to omit certain training exemplars, and when large datasets are involved it may be useful to re-organize them in order that better performance is achieved. The user view of the system is shown diagramaticaly in figure 2.1.

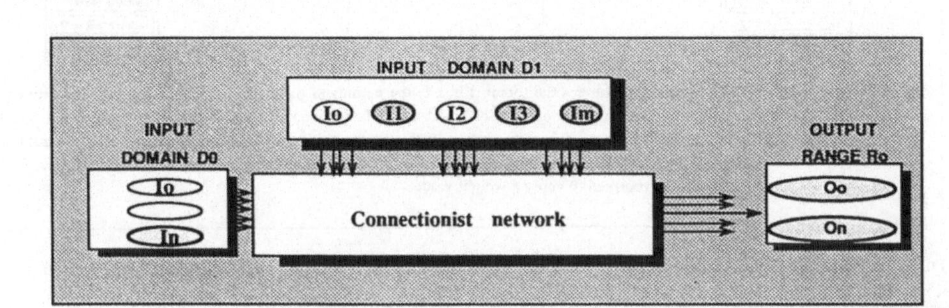

Figure 2.1   *ConsTrainer* System Model - the network is shown the mapping that it is required to learn by clamping the input and output vectors $D_0I_0,...,D_0I_n$, $D_1I_0,...,D_1I_m$, and $R_0O_0,...,R_0O_n$. Typically (e.g. in histopathology), the first input domain, D_0, might represent names of image features such as say CellCounts, InflamatoryPatterns, etc, whilst the second input domain, D_1, might represent symbolic features such as PatientAge, LocationOfTissue, etc. The output range R_0 might represent possible diagnoses such as MalignantTumours. Each input vector has a symbolic representation as an ordered set of weighted domain parameters, themselves possibly the output of another network.

A dataset is composed of several discrete training exemplars carefully selected over the the task domain to represent a complete set of important features in the application. A *training exemplar* consists of an input/output parameter pair. The input and output parameters would span over one or more domains or ranges and they are selected on the basis of causality. Within a training exemplar the parameters can be associated with a relative weight. The semantics of this is described in the sequel.

Informally, the reasoning of the trainer in defining an input/output parameter pair (i.e. training exemplar) proceeds along the following lines:

> *The presense of the parameter set $\{I_0, ..., I_m\}$ in the input domain D_0 taken together with the presence of all the other domain parameter sets, causes $\{O_0,..., O_n\}$ as the output parameter set. Each input and output parameter can be assigned a weight to denote its relative strength.*

This can be formulated more precisely as follows:

$$D_0\{W_iI_i\}\cup...,D_m\{W_jI_j\}...\cup D_n\{W_kI_k\}\rightarrow R_n\{W_rO_r\}$$

where:

D_m denotes the m-th input domain. The presence of more than one input domains (or ranges) is allowed exclusively for brevity as regards the user reasoning and to assist in the decomposition of the application into smaller tasks. The network itself makes no distinction between the parameters.

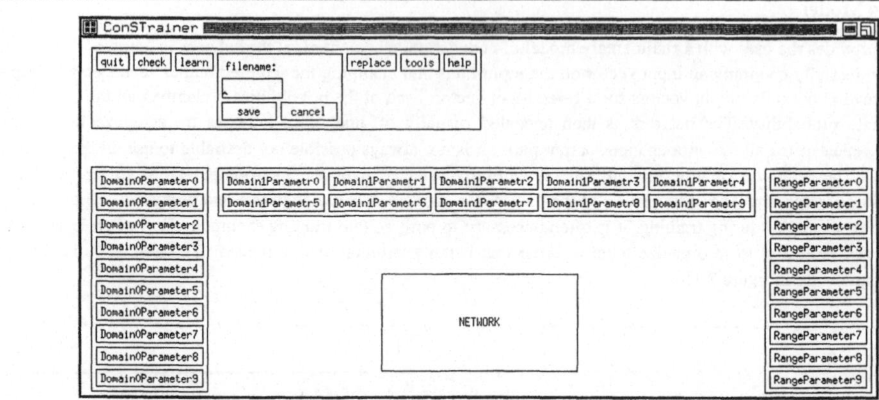

Figure 3.1. **ConSTrainer** User Interface - the topmost box is the command panel. The boxes to the left and immediately above centre represent two input domains. Subsidiary buttonboxes represent the sibling input parameters. Similarly, the rightmost box is the range. The network box in the centre connects **ConSTrainer** to a network simulator. A training exemplar is entered by marking the set of input and output parameters across the domains/ranges. For each parameter the user is prompted to suply a weight value.

$L(D_i)$ denotes the number of elements in the ith input domain D_i. Hence m, i, j, k, and r are bounded as follows: $0 \leq m \leq n$, $0 \leq i \leq L(D_0)$, $0 \leq j \leq L(D_m)$, $0 \leq k \leq L(D_n)$, $0 \leq r \leq L(R_r)$.

$D_m\{W_jI_j\}$ denotes the set of domain specific parameters in D_m $(0 \leq m \leq n)$, $(0 \leq j \leq L(D_m))$. Taken together all these constitute the input vector and support the output parameter set. Each $\{W_jI_j\}$ is likely to have been produced by another network in the system.

w_i denotes the relative weight of the presence of the corresponding domain parameter I_i in the training exemplar. $W_i \in \{0.00,...,0.10\}$.

$\cup$ denotes the union of two parameter sets; and $D_0\{W_iI_i\}$, $\cup ...$, $D_m\{W_jI_j\}$, ..., $\cup D_n\{W_kI_k\}$ can be treated as $D_0\{W_iI_i\}$, $\wedge ...$, $D_m\{W_jI_j\}$, ..., $\wedge D_n\{W_kI_k\}$. Of course this not precisely true since the pattern is supplemented with other patterns before it is input to the diagnostic network.

Several conditions must be satisfied. For example, in each training exemplar T, containing K elements, the weightsum S_T, computed over all input domains would be less than or equal to 1. The same applies to the output range (1).

$$S_T = \sum_{i=0}^{K} W_i \leq 1 \tag{1}$$

Under normal circumstances S_T is exactly equal to 1. Training exemplars with weightsums equal to 1 are said to be the *exact exemplars* in the dataset. If $S_T < 1$ then ε_T (2) means that there is an element of uncertainty associated with the exemplar T:

$$\varepsilon_T = 1 - S_T \tag{2}$$

ε_T is interpreted as a measure of the relative weight of the exemplar T over the entire dataset. It is also possible that $S_T > 1$. Although this is not supported in the present implementation of **ConSTrainer**, in such cases c_T, can be taken as an element of confidence associated withe the domain or range of the exemplar T (with N being the number of exemplars in the dataset).

$$c_T = \frac{\sum_{i=0}^{N} S_i}{N} \tag{3}$$

Such occurrences are noted for later use by the optimizer or by the underlying network-specific learning procedure.

Having described the methodology and model for building applications with **ConSTrainer** we shall next describe the architecture of the **ConSTrainer** toolkit.

3. ConSTrainer: SYSTEM ARCHITECTURE

3.1 Overview

The architecture of the **ConSTrainer** toolkit comprises four principal components: the *user-interface* - implements an interactive graphical interface of the system model; the *tool configuration* software - which is responsible for tailoring the system to user requirements; the *dataset validation* module - which is responsible for performing various validation and optimization operations on the dataset; and the *network-interface* back-end - for translating the training exemplars into network-specific training vectors, pipelining these inputs to various neural network development environments or saving them for off-line training. Figure 3.1 shows the user interface of **ConSTrainer**.

The topmost box in the **ConSTrainer** user interface is the main command panel.Each button supports a distinct function. [help] pops-up the menu of functions and can be used to display manual pages for each command button. Briefly,

[quit] exits the **ConSTrainer** system.

[learn] on-line training. Invokes a connectionist simulator to train the network with each training exemplar. Networks and simulators are part of other toolkits.

[save] off-line training. Saves the entire data set for latter use. The user is prompted for a filename.

[replace] edit last entry. Prompts for weight corrections in the most recent entry.

[check] performs weightsum consistency and other validation checks both globally to the entire dataset, and locally to each exemplar.

[replay] re-displays the exemplar ranges from the dataset to permit corrections.

[tools] the interactive **ConSTrainer** configurations facility.

Having presented an overview of **ConSTrainer** we shall next examine in more detail its facilities for configuration, dataset selection, consistency checking, and replaying.

3.2 Configuring the Toolkit

The user begins by defining their input domains and ranges. Associated with each domain D_i and range R_i there are a finite number of symbolic parameters $D_i \{ W_0 I_0, .., W_n I_n \}$. When the system is first loaded it attempts to retrieve these parameters from the resource database. The resource database is a generic template for setting up an initial configuration of **ConSTrainer**. There are two ways in which the user can configure (tailor-make) **ConSTrainer**: manually by specifying his own resource database from the command line (i.e. `%ConSTrainer -db dbfilename`) or interactively through the [tools] command in the **ConSTrainer** command panel.

The user defined db_file must have a standard format as shown below. Basically, it consists of one or more domain definitions followed by one or more range definitions. A domain or range definition begins with the keyword DMN or RNG followed by its name. Within each domain or range definition there are several domain-specific parameter definitions. Each of these has an associated list of mutually exclusive and mutually supportive parameter names (in the grammar that follows, italics denote non-terminal symbols, and { }* denotes zero or more).

```
FILE          ::=    {domain_def}* {range_def}*
domain_def    ::=    DMN:dom_name {param_def}*
range_def     ::=    RNG:dom_name{param_def}*
param_def     ::=    <param_name [exc_list] [sup_list]>
```

where:

dom_name: is an alphanumeric string of up to 32 characters specifying the name of the input domain or range. This string will appear as a label on the domain widget.

param_name: an alphanumeric string of up to 32 characters specifying the name of the domain parameter. This string will appear as a label inside the command button.

exc_list: is a list of paths i.e. *dom_name.param_name* or simply *dom_name* separated by blank spaces specifying the set of parameters in the present or in any other domain which are mutually exclusive to the parameter presently defined. The selection of the presently defined parameter excludes (deactivates) all the mutually exclusive parameters from the training pattern. The converse is also true. A member of this list cannot re-appear in the list of mutually supportive parameters and vice versa. Likewise, *sup_list:* is a list of names similar to the list of mutually exclusive parameters but with the converse semantics.

The alternative way of configuring the **ConSTrainer** toolkit is interactively through the [tools] facility in the command panel. This action releases a pop-up menu of commands (see figure 3.2) for interactively adding and removing domains, parameters names, and mutually exclusive/supportive lists alike.

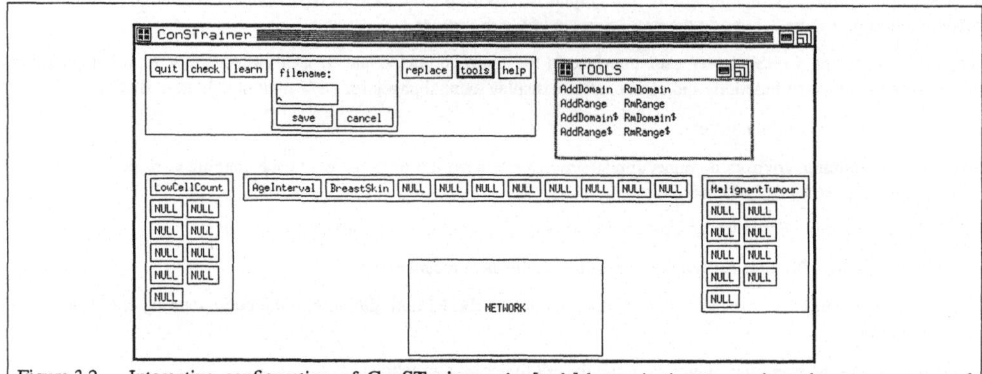

Figure 3.2   Interactive configuration of **ConSTrainer** - the [tools] button in the command panel pops-up a menu of commands for interactively adding and editing tool configuration. Most are self explanatory. The new configuration must be saved before the toolkit can be used for training the network.

There are two main reasons for supporting mutually exclusive/inclusive parameter lists. Firstly, to safeguard against omissions and errors in the training pattern specification and to validate the data at each step. Secondly, to reinforce the network-specific optimizations which are carried out by the system.

3.3 Interactive Dataset Selection

The interactive selection of datasets proceeds along standard lines. Each training exemplar is entered in turn by clicking the mouse over every parameter in the exemplar; domain and range parameters are treated alike. With each parameter the user is prompted to supply a weight value. The process is repeated for all exemplars in the training dataset.

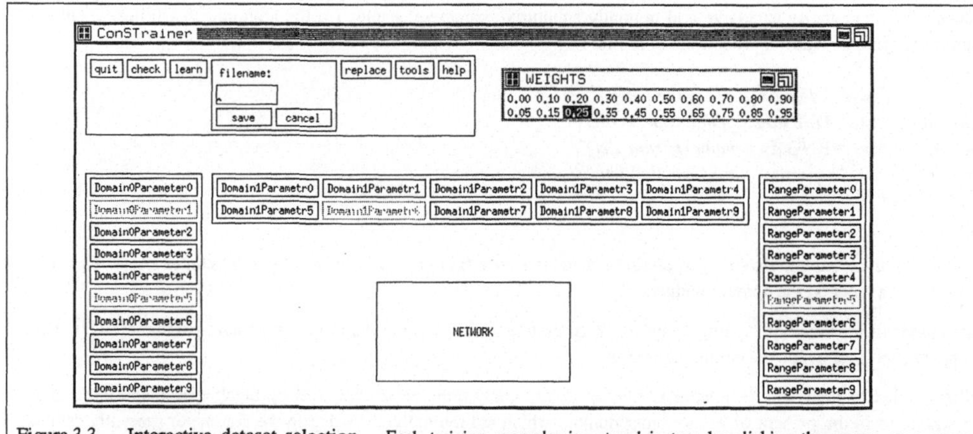

Figure 3.3   Interactive dataset selection - Each training exemplar is entered in turn by clicking the mouse over every parameter in the exemplar; domain and range parameters are treated alike;

On selecting a parameter its iconic entry on the parent domain/range is de-activated and the system releases a pop-up menu prompting for the selection of a weight value (see figure 3.3). All other actions are blocked. On selecting the weight value, the menu is popped down, the selected parameter remains de-activated together with all its mutually exclusive parameters. The list of mutually supportive parameters is placed on a queue and the [learn] and [save] actions are blocked until each member of the list has been selected.

The [cancel] button permits the user to correct the weight of the most recently selected parameter. The [save] button generates a network-specific training vector and like the [learn] button resets the sensitivity on all the parameter buttons and prepares *ConSTrainer* for the next training exemplar.

3.4 Consistency Checking and Optimization

ConSTrainer supports various consistency checks, validations, and optimization operations both locally on each individual training exemplar, and also globally for the entire dataset. It is in many respects an open system and many of the checks and optimization techniques are under continuous development and many are network- and learning procedure-specific. On pressing the [check] button in the command panel, a pop-up menu shows the most common of these (see figure 3.4).

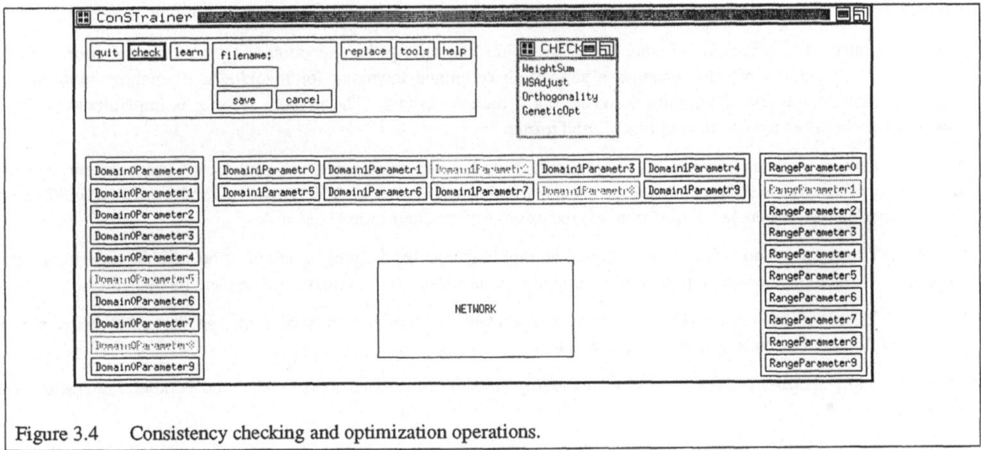

Figure 3.4   Consistency checking and optimization operations.

weightsum checks the domain and range weightsums for equality to unity. Operates on a single exemplar.

wsadjust operates on the entire dataset re-enforcing the relative strength of training exemplars T with $S_T > 1$ and conversely. Under certain conditions this might have implications on the learning procedure. For example in the Boltzmann learning procedure it forces the system to retain the output units clamped if $S_r > 1$ [AcHiSe85].

orthogonality checks for vector orthogonality in the exemplars. This is useful in predicting and explaining the cognitive behaviour of certain gradient descent learning procedures. For example, in Hebbian networks it can be used to determine network recall capabilities (e.g. perfect recall for orthogonal input vectors with length 1 [Hinton87]).

geneticopt generates condition codes for optimization of network behaviour using genetic algorithm techniques [RefKam90].

3.5 Replaying and Editing Datasets

There are several reasons for wishing to retrieve and edit a dataset. First, omissions and errors might have been detected by *ConSTrainer* or by other modules in the integrated network environment. Second, the user might wish to add or modify the dataset or individual exemplars following the *ConSTrainer* [check] facility. Third, the user might wish to safeguard against undue optimizations, etc.

ConSTrainer supports this functionality through the [replay] button in the command panel. On selecting the button, a pop-up dialog widget is released through which the user can specify individual training exemplars by index, ranges of exemplars, or the entire dataset .

The dialog widget contains a small area in which the user types in the range expression. The following are all valid range expressions:

[1]   ; reload and edit exemplar number 1.
[5-16]   ; reload and edit exemplars 5 through to 16.
[0-]   ; reload and edit the entire dataset.

In the last two cases, **Con*STrainer*** would pop-up a [step] through button.

4. RELATED WORK

Programming systems for neural networks, although in their infancy, are developing rapidly. These programming systems range from single simulators; through to research environments such as SFINX [PaGuSk87], CONE [Hanson87], RCS [Goddar89], GENESYS [PaGuSk87], and the ESPRIT-II PYGMALION [AngTre89]; to integrated commercial products such as SAICs SIGMA/ANSpec [KraFroRi] and Hecht-Nielsens AXON [Gutsch88] which are mostly "closed" systems. Below we examine some of the more advanced connectionist development systems which are in the "open" domain and which offer the possibility of adopting **Con*STrainer*** as an additional facility.

4.1 PYGMALION Environment

The ESPRIT-II PYGMALION project is developing a neural programming environment which provides a rudimentary "platform" for neural network applications and which can be easily extended by the application builder [AngTre89]. It also allows trained networks to be moved easily between different machines. The environment consists of five major parts:

[1] Graphic monitor - the graphical software environment for controlling the execution and monitoring of neural network simulation. The graphic monitor includes a simulation command language for invoking a simulation, monitoring its execution, interactively changing values, and saving a trained network. The graphic monitor is implemented using X-windows which makes it easy for adopting **Con*STrainer***.

[2] Algorithm Library - a parameterized library of common neural networks, written in a high level language and providing the user with several validated modules for constructing applications. This fits-in naturally with **Con*STrainer***'s methodology of application de-composition and the use of off-the-shelf trained networks.

[3] High-level Language N - an object oriented programming language for defining, in conjunction with the algorithm library, a neural network algorithm and application. N supports the description of network topology and its dynamics.

[4] Low-level Language nC - a low-level machine independent network specification language for representing partially trained or fully trained sub-networks for specific tasks.

[5] Compilers - to a number of target machines including several Unix-based workstations and parallel Transputer arrays [Barron83].

The PYGMALION toolkit like most such tools is designed to support network development. Currently it does not provide facilities for selection and validation of training datasets. However, it is easy to see how the **Con*STrainer*** toolkit can be incorporated as an integral part of this environment.

4.2 Rochester Connectionist Simulator

The Rochester Connectionist Simulator is the oldest and perhaps the best known system for connectionist network development and simulation [Goddar89]. The original implementation was in LISP but it is now reimplemented in C and X-windows and is publicly available. RCS consists of several modules and options for interfacing to the user and for describing connectionist networks. The main facilities include a graphics interface, a module for network construction, and the simulator itself.

[1] Graphics Interface - the graphics interface is a package that runs as a front-end to the simulator and it supports all the simulation commands. It prime function however, is to allow network monitoring and debugging through iconic representations of particular network aspects such as potential, output, state, links, etc. The graphical interface is a strictly "read-only" interface, but this does not present any difficulties in incorporating **Con*STrainer*** despite its dynamic re-configurability, because **Con*STrainer*** uses its own user-interface.

[2] Network Construction - RCS provides a powerful set of commands for constructing connectionist networks of arbitrary complexity. RCS is based on a generic paradigm according to which each network *node* has several *sites* at which the incoming *links* arrive. Network construction is built-in the simulator by a user program written in C. RCS provides primitive functions for making units, adding sites, making links, naming of units, and other functions for accessing the data structure of the network.

[3] *Network Simulation* - supports an on-line simulation of the network aided by several options for debugging, synchronization, network modification, memory management, etc.

Like the PYGMALION development environment, RCS is designed to support network development at a low-level. The **ConSTrainer** facilities are complementary, and at a higher level in the pyramid of connectionist application construction. This is also true for most of the other "open" neural network development environments such as GENESYS, SFINX, CONE, etc.

5. CONCLUSIONS

We have introduced a reasoning model for dataset collection in connectionist systems, have described the architecture of a generic toolkit based on this formalism. We have used **ConSTrainer** to define and select a training dataset for a non-trivial application in diagnostic decision support for Histopathology. The application involves some 20 parameters in the image domain, 10 parameters in the symbolic domain, and 10 parameters in the diagnostic range (including various types of no diagnoses). Dataset selection was a straight forward process. When the number of parameters is small the recommended methodology is to work out the possible parameter combinations. It is often very useful to start from the range if the number of parameters is smaller (cf backward chaining). If the number of parameters is very large and non divisible into small networks it is important to try and identify mutually exclusive ranges or domain, and mutually exclusive/supportive parameters within ranges and domains. With regard to this application, the system performs well. The strengths were particularly noticeble in three areas:

[1]   providing a simple, efficient, and reliable route for dataset selection, validation, and benchmarking.

[2]   supporting the de-composition of the task domain into its two natural components: a network for low-level feature extraction from images tightly integrated with the second component; a network for high-level diagnostic decision support.

[3]   supporting the capability of an explanation facility.

We believe that the model and it realization in **ConSTrainer** also meet the requirements for a larger class of tasks both in biomedical and in other decision support applications of connectionist models. Some of the most likely candidates are image understanding, command and control systems, and generally most task domains involving low-level sub-symbolic computation integrated with high-level decision support. We are not at present aware of any existing general-purpose toolkit with similar capabilities. By offering an application and network independent toolkit for selecting and validating training datasets for connectionist networks **ConSTrainer**, aims to support connectionist application development, portability and benchmarking which are not yet generally available. It remains to be seen whether this type of system suits the needs of applications like natural language and speech understanding, forecasting, etc.

The future plans include adapting the **ConSTrainer** software to the PYGMALION neural network environment, and extension of **ConSTrainer**'s facilities to include intelligent optimization techniques for specific classes of networks.

ACKNOWLEDGEMENTS

I would like to thank Magali Azema-Barac, Mike Hewetson, John Taylor, and Philip Treleaven of the ESPRIT PYGMALION Project for their support, and useful comments during the implementation of the **ConSTrainer** software. Also Philip Coleridge-Smith of the Department of Surgical Science at Midlesex Hospital, and Alan Rubin of the Department of Histopathology at University College Hospital gave invaluable advice in the field of skin feature and disease state identification. I would also like to thank the CEC research programme AIM for their financial support.

REFERENCES

[AcHiSe85] Ackley D. H., Hinton G. E., and Sejnowski T. J. A learning algorithm for Boltzmann machines, Cognitive Science 9 (1985), 147-169.

[AngTre89] Angeniol B., and Treleaven P. C., "PYGMALION: Neural Network Programming & Applications", proc. ESPRIT conf. 1989.

[Barron83] I. Barron, et al, Transputer does 5 or more MIPS even when not used in parallel, Electronics, 56, 23, November 1983, 109-115.

[Goddar89] Goddard N. H., et all, "Rochester Connectionist Simulator" Technical report TR-233, University of Rochester, Department of Computer Science, (july 1989).

[Gutsch88] Gutschow T., "AXON: The researchers Neural Network Language", Proc., Int. Neural Network Symp. INNS'88, (1988).

[Hebb61] D. Hebb, Organisation of Behavior, Science Editions, New York, 1961.

[Hanson87] Hanson W. A., et al "CONE Computational Network Environment", proc., IEEE First Int. Conf. on neural Networks, pp III-531-538., June 1987.

[Hinton87] G.E. Hinton, "Connectionist Learning Procedures", Tecnical Report, Computer Science Department, Carnegie-Mellon University, 1-46, June 1987.

[Hopfie82] J.J. Hopfield, Neural networks and physical systems with emergent collective computational abilities, Proc. Nat. Acad. Sci, 2554-2558, 1982, 79.

[McCPit43] McCulloch W. S., Pitts W, "A Logical Calculus of the Ideas Immanent in Nervous Activity", Bulletin of Mathematical Biophysics, 5, 115-133, 1943, also in Anderson, Rosenfeld (eds.): Neurocomputing.

[KraFroRi] Kraft T. T., Frostron S. A., MacRtchie B., and Rodgers A., "The Specification of a Concurrent Backpropagation Network Architecture Using Actors", Technical Report SAIC, San Diego, California 92121.

[PaGuSk87] Paik E., Gungner D., and Skrzypek J., "UCLA SFINX a neural network simulation environment", proc., IEEE Int. Conf on Neural Networks, vol 3., pp. 367-376, (1986).

[RefKam90] Refenes A. N. & Kamalati A. H., "Dataset Optimisation for Training Connectionist Systems", Research Note /BIOLAB/RN-19/90, Department of Computer Science, University College London, Submitted IEEE 2nd Int. Symposium on Parallel Systems".

Beschleunigtes Lernen durch adaptive Regelung der Lernrate bei back-propagation in feed-forward Netzen

R. Salomon
Technische Universität Berlin*

Zusammenfassung

Dieser Artikel beschäftigt sich mit back-propagation, einem Lernverfahren für Neuronale Netze. Es wird gezeigt, wie sich durch das Einführen von Testzyklen erstens eine starke Beschleunigung der Konvergenzgeschwindigkeit ergibt, und zweitens aufwendige Experimente, die zum Einstellen lernrelevanter Parameter dienen, entfallen können.

1   Einleitung

In letzter Zeit ist in der Literatur (siehe z.B. [Jac88], [KSV87]) mehrfach gezeigt worden, daß das unter dem Namen back-propagation bekannte Lernverfahren für Neuronale Netze ein Gradientenverfahren ist. Entsprechend läßt sich ein back-propagation Zyklus in der Notation von Rumelhart et.al. mathematisch wie folgt darstellen:

$$W_k = W_{k-1} - \eta \cdot \nabla E \quad , \tag{1}$$

$$E = E(W_k) = \frac{1}{2} \sum_p \sum_i (t_{ip} - o_{ip})^2 \quad . \tag{2}$$

Dabei sind W_k die Matrix der Gewichtungen, E die Fehlerfunktion, η die Lernrate, o_{ip} die Aktivation der unit i bei angelegtem Muster p und t_{ip} die erwartete Aktivation der unit i bei angelegtem Muster p.

Nach dieser Gleichung hängt die Konvergenzgeschwindigkeit entscheidend von einer optimalen Wahl der Lernrate η ab. Dabei bedeutet optimal, daß die gestellte Aufgabe bei festgelegten Fehlerwerten in möglichst geringer Zyklenzahl gelernt wird. Hierbei sind bei jeder neuen Aufgabenstellung folgende Schwierigkeiten zu bewältigen:

1. Das Festlegen der Lernrate: geeignete Werte sind sowohl von der Aufgabenstellung als auch von der durch Zufallszahlen gewählten Initialisierung abhängig. In Extremfällen unterscheiden sich die optimalen Werte um mehrere Größenordnungen. Beispielsweise liegt ein geeigneter Wert bei dem bekannten XOR-Problem bei etwa 0,8 und im Gegensatz dazu bei dem Doppel-Spiral Problem (siehe auch [LW89]) bei etwa 0,002.

2. Die Beträge des Gradienten ändern sich im Laufe des Lernvorgangs sehr stark. Um eine Lösung zu finden, muß die Lernrate in diesen Fällen auf einen verhältnismäßig kleinen Wert gesetzt werden, wodurch sich auch nur eine sehr kleine Konvergenzgeschwindigkeit erzielen läßt.

Um eine möglichst große Konvergenzgeschwindigkeit zu erhalten, muß die Lernrate auf einen optimalen Wert eingestellt werden. Eine Möglichkeit diesen Wert für ein gegebenes Problem (und eine gewählte Initialisierung) zu finden, besteht in der Durchführung zahlreicher Experimente. In jedem Experiment werden jeweils die Lernrate und gegebenenfalls andere relevante Parameter, wie z.B. Momentum, graduell modifiziert. Dieser Vorgehensweise haftet als großer Nachteil an, daß zum Ermitteln der optimalen Lernrate die Aufgabe viele Male gelöst werden muß. Das Ergebnis dieser aufwendigen Versuche ist ein Satz von

*Institut für Angewandte Informatik, FG Informatik in Natur- und Ingenieurwissenschaften, TU Berlin, Sekretariat FR 5–9, Franklinstraße 28/29, 1000 Berlin 12

Parametern, die das erneute Lernen in kürzerer Zeit gestatten. Im Gegensatz dazu ist es wünschenswert, ein Verfahren zu finden, mit dessen Hilfe sich die Parameter sowohl beim ersten Lösungsversuch als auch während des Lernvorgangs selbständig anpassen.

Eine Möglichkeit der dynamischen Anpassung der Lernrate wird von Rush und Salas ([RS88]) im *Gradient Reuse Algorithm* vorgestellt. Dabei wird ein einmal ermittelter Gradient solange verwendet, bis sich keine Verbesserung der Fehlersumme mehr erzielen läßt. Je nach dem, wie oft die alte Gradientenrichtung beibehalten wird, wird bei Unter– bzw. Überschreiten von festgelegten Grenzen die Lernrate modifiziert. Dabei läßt sich nach Rush und Salas beim XOR-Problem eine Reduzierung der benötigten Zyklenzahl um den Faktor vier erreichen. Berücksichtigt man aber, daß in einem feed-forward Netz die Berechnung der Aktivationen (Vorwärtsrichtung) wesentlich aufwendiger als die Bestimmung des Gradienten ist (Berechnen der *e*–Funktion anstelle einfacher Realarithmetik), dann verringert sich die Verbesserung auf den Faktor zwei.

2 Adaptive Regelung der Lernrate

Im weiteren wird gezeigt, wie die oben beschriebenen Probleme durch zwei Änderungen im back-propagation Algorithmus behoben werden können. Diese Änderungen haben folgende Vorteile:

1. Durch die dynamische Anpassung der Lernrate an einen optimalen Wert wird die Konvergenzgeschwindigkeit deutlich verbessert. Des weiteren entfällt dadurch die Notwendigkeit, vieler zeitaufwendiger Experimente.

2. Die Methode ist ohne Schwierigkeiten auf andere Parameter wie z.B. Momentum übertragbar, und eine mathematische Analyse läßt erwarten, daß eine Kombination mit anderen Methoden wie z.B. der in [KSV87] vorgestellten *Partial Conjugate Gradient Method* nach Polak-Ribiere ebenso möglich ist, wie im Falle von standard back-propagation.

Die Änderungen sehen wie folgt aus:

Der Gradient wird in jedem Zyklus normiert. Dadurch werden die oben beschriebenen Probleme der stark unterschiedlichen Gradientenlängen vermieden.

Die konstante Lernrate η in (1) wird durch eine Folge η_k ersetzt, deren Glieder in jedem Zyklus einen anderen Wert haben können.

In jedem Zyklus wird durch das Einführen von zwei **Testzyklen** untersucht, durch welche Variation eine Beschleunigung der Konvergenz erreicht wird. Dabei setzt sich dann die Variation durch, die zu einen möglichst kleinen Wert der Fehlersumme führte. Um dieses zu erreichen, wird im Zyklus k zuerst der Gradient ausgerechnet. Dann werden nach (1) zwei Versuche mit unterschiedlichen Lernraten, die durch Variation der Lernrate des Zyklus $k-1$ entstehen, gemacht. Endgültig wird diejenige Lernrate verwendet, die zu dem kleineren Fehlerwert führt. Der Gradient für den Zyklus k kann mit sehr geringem Aufwand bei der Berechnung der Fehlerfunktion im Zyklus $k-1$ ermittelt werden.

Das führt zu folgendem Gleichungssystem:

$$W_k = W_{k-1} - \eta_k \cdot \frac{\nabla E}{|\nabla E|} \quad . \tag{3}$$

$$E = E(W_k) = E\left(W_{k-1}, \eta_k\right) = E\left(W_{k-1} - \eta_k \cdot \frac{\nabla E(W_{k-1})}{|\nabla E(W_{k-1})|}\right) \quad , \tag{4}$$

$$\eta_k = \begin{cases} \eta_{k-1} \cdot \zeta & \text{wenn } E(W_{k-1}, \eta_{k-1} \cdot \zeta) \leq E(W_{k-1}, \eta_{k-1} \cdot \frac{1}{\zeta}) \\ \eta_{k-1} \cdot \frac{1}{\zeta} & \text{sonst} \end{cases} \tag{5}$$

In den Gleichungen (3) - (5) wird der Paramter ζ zur oben beschriebenen Variaton der Lernrate benötigt: Es wird dadurch keine neue Lernrate eingeführt. Um die geforderte Variation zu erhalten, ist darauf zu achten, daß ζ von eins verschieden ist. Damit eine gleichmäßige Regelung der Lernrate erzielt werden kann, sollte der Wert von ζ auch nicht zu groß gewählt werden. Die durchgeführten Versuche haben einen Wert von etwa $1,3$ als sehr günstig erwiesen; die Einstellung dieses Wertes ist aber nicht kritsch, Werte bis $2,0$ waren akzeptabel. Diese größeren Werte führten sogar zu einer nochmaligen Beschleunigung des Lernvorgangs, es konnte dabei ein schnelleres Einregeln der Lernparameter erreicht werden. Zu große Werte führten allerdings zu Instabilitäten, im Extremfall zu einem Steckenbleiben des Lernvorgangs.

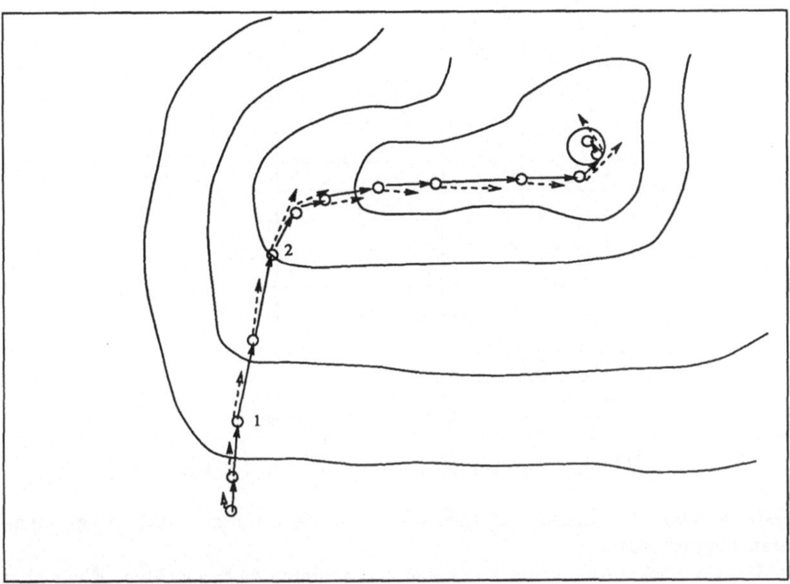

Abbildung 1: Iterationsweg mit geregelten Intervallschritten

In Abbildung 1 ist dargestellt, wie sich beim Lernvorgang die Länge der Iterationsschritte an das "Fehlergebirge" anpaßt. In der Abbildung ist zu erkennen, daß in jedem Punkt zwei Iteratiosschritte mit unterschiedlichen Längen betrachtet werden. Dabei ist der jeweils bessere mit einer durchgezogenen Linie und der verworfenen in unterbrochener Linie dargestellt. Beispielsweise ist in Punkt 1 zu sehen, daß ein größerer Iterationsschritt günstiger als ein kleiner ist, in Punkt 2 verhält es sich umgekehrt.

3 Beschleunigung des Lernvorgangs

Das modifizierte Gleichungssytem (3) bis (5) wurde in einen Algorithmus umgesetzt, und an einer Vielzahl von Problemstellungen getestet. Dabei kamen die Aufgaben u.a. aus den Bereichen Mustererkennung, Klassifizierung und den weit verbreiteten Paritäts–, z.B. Exklusiv–Oder–Gatter und Encoderproblemen. Dabei variierte die Netzgröße von fünf bis über 200 units. Zum besseren Vergleich werden im vorliegenden Artikel nur die beiden letzten Problemstellungen besprochen, da diese sehr weit verbreitet sind und auch von anderen Autoren zur Darstellung ihrer eigenen Ergebnisse herangezogen werden. Einige Ergebnisse sind in den Abbildungen 2 und 3 zu finden.

Bei allen Versuchen wurde ein feed-forward Netz mit je einer input, hidden und output Schicht verwendet. Es existieren nur links von der input zur hidden und von der hidden zur output Schicht.

Bei einem Vergleich der erreichten Zyklenzahl ist folgender Sachverhalt zu berücksichtigen: Durch das Einführen der Testzyklen verdoppelt sich der Rechenaufwand. Entsprechend mußte die erreichten Zyklenzahlen um den Faktor zwei korrigiert werden, was auch in den abgebildeten Diagrammen geschehen ist. Bei Einsatz einer parallelen Rechnerarchitektur können die Testzyklen parallel abgearbeitet werden kann, so daß dann obige Korrektur rückgängig gemacht werden kann.

Im folgenden werden kurz die Ergebnisse beim **4–2–4 Encoder** (Abbildung 2) und dem **Exklusiv–Oder Gatter** (Abbildung 3) besprochen. In beiden Abbildungen ist zu erkennen, daß die adaptiv geregelte Lernrate in den ersten zehn bzw. 60 Zyklen keinen nennenswerten Vorteil gegenüber einer konstanten Lernrate besitzt. In dieser ersten Phase werden in der hidden Schicht die geeigneten Kodierungen der

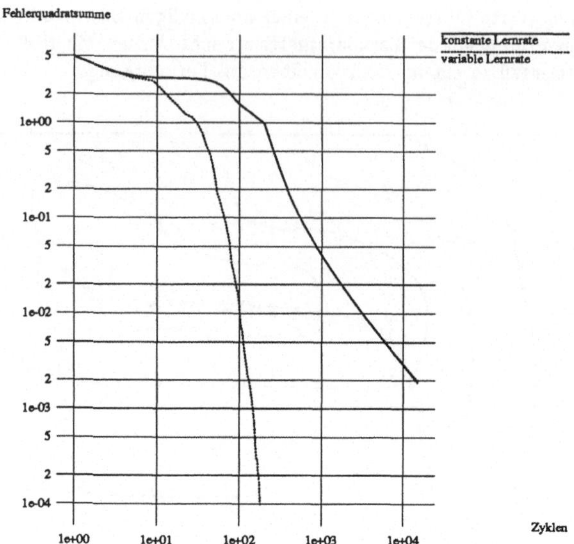

Abbildung 2: Verlauf der Fehlerwerte beim 4-2-4 Encoder

angelegten Muster ausgebildet. Hierfür hat sich, wie in der Literatur mehrfach belegt, eine Lernrate von etwa $0,8$ als brauchbar erwiesen.

Anschließend ist ein starkes Abnehmen der Fehlerquadratsumme zu beobachten. Diese Abnahme beginnt bei einer konstanten Lernrate etwa eine Zehnerpotenz später und wird im weiteren Verlauf immer schwächer. Im Gegensatz dazu wird die Abnahme (bei doppelt logarithmischer Auftragung) bei der adaptiv geregelten Lernrate mit kleiner werdenden Fehlerquadratsummen immer steiler. Für eine Fehlerquadratsumme von $5 \cdot 10^{-3}$ bzw. $5 \cdot 10^{-4}$ beträgt der Vorteil bereits zwei Zehnerpotenzen in der Zahl der Zyklen.

In der Literatur wird häufig auch diejenige Zyklenzahl ermittelt, die benötigt wird, damit ein Netz die gestellte Aufgabe (gerade eben) lernt. Dabei wird häufig der Maximalfehler auf den Wert $0,4$ gesetzt. Beim 4–2–4 Encoder benötigt back-propagation mit konstanter Lernrate dafür etwa 230 Zyklen. Die zugehörige Fehlerquadratsumme hat dann einen Wert von etwa $0,73$. Unter Verwendung der adaptiv geregelten Lernrate ist dieser Maximalfehler bereits etwa nach 25 Zyklen unterschritten, und die Fehlerquadratsumme ist nach gleichem Rechenaufwand bereits um etwa vier Zehnerpotenzen kleiner geworden. Beim Exklusiv–Oder Gatter beträgt der Leistungsunterschied nach etwa 900 Zyklen, die back-propagation mit konstanter Lernrate zum "Lernen" benötigt, sogar 27 Zehnerpotenzen.

4 Diskussion

In Kapitel 2 wurde eine adaptiv geregelte Lernrate und eine Normierung des Gradienten eingeführt. Im Vergleich zur originalen back-propagation zeigt sich eine Reduzierung der benötigten Zyklenzahl um etwa eine Größenordnung. Je kleiner die Fehlerquadratsumme werden soll, um so größer wird der Unterschied in der benötigten Zyklenzahl. Meiner Ansicht nach liegt der größte Vorteil darin, daß sich die Parameter schon beim ersten Experiment auf einen nahezu optimalen Wert einstellen; d.h. es müssen keine aufwendigen Versuche zur Optimierung der Parameter durchgeführt werden.

Bei anderen Verfahren werden spezifische Annahmen über das Verhalten der Fehlerfunktion (Gleichung 2) getroffen, in der Hoffnung daß sie sie in möglichst vielen Fällen zutreffen. Im Gegensatz dazu werden bei der hier vorgestellten Variante keine solche Annahmen gemacht. Das hier vorgestellte Verfahren läßt sich auch auf Gradientenverfahren anderer Fachgebiete übertragen.

Jacobs ([Jac88]) hat in seinen Untersuchungen mit seinem *Delta Bar Delta* bzw. *Hybrid* Algorithmus vergleichbare Verbesserungen erziehlt. Dabei wird nicht mehr eine globale Lernrate benutzt, sondern jedem

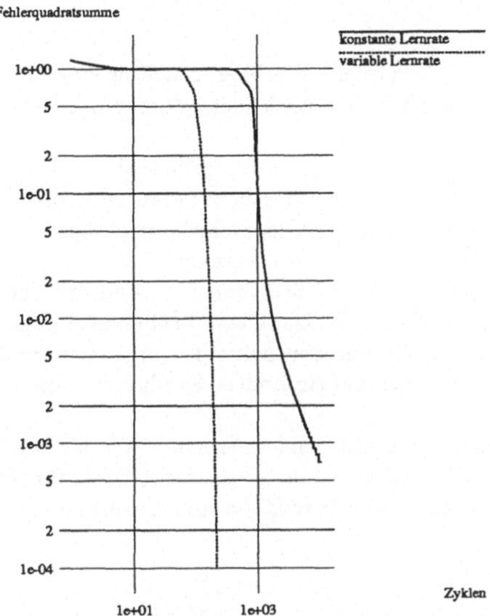

Abbildung 3: Verlauf der Fehlerwerte beim Exklusiv-Oder Gatter

einzelnen link eine individuelle Lernrate zugeordnet. Diese individuellen Lernraten werden mittels dreier neu eingeführter Parameter angepaßt, von denen sich zwei je nach Aufgabenstellung in ihren Werten sehr stark unterscheiden. Diese Parameter müssen wiederum durch zahlreiche Versuche optimiert werden.

Fahlman ([Fah89]) hat mit seinem quick-prop Algorithmus eine Variante vorgestellt, mit der bei einfachen Problemen bessere Ergebnisse erzielt werden. Der quick-prop Algorithmus stützt sich auf zwei (riskante) Annahmen über den Einfluß eines einzelnen link auf die Fehlerfunktion. Die Untersuchungen von Lang und Witbrock ([LW89]) zeigen, daß sich die Verbesserung gegenüber back-propagation beim Doppel–Spiral–Problem auf den Faktor zwei bzw. vier reduziert. Es sind keine Untersuchungen bekannt, wie sich quick-prop bei kleinen geforderten Fehlerquadratsummen, also größerer Genauigkeit, verhält.

Meine eigene Implementierung gestattet auch die adaptive Regelung des Momentum. Dabei werden in jedem Zyklus alternierend Lernrate und Momentum geregelt. Die Leistungsverbesserung gegenüber der Verwendung konstanter Parameter ist teilweise noch wesentlich erhöht.

Eine adaptive Regelung des Momentum macht sich dann besonders vorteilhaft bemerkbar, wenn das Netz eine Lösung relativ schnell finden kann, aber eine hohe Genauigkeit verlangt ist. Ein solches Problem ist z.B. der 4–4–4 Encoder mit 16 Mustern. Bei dieser Aufgabe ist die Lösung nach 24 Zyklen gefunden. Die Fehlerdifferenz liegt pro unit bei etwa 45 %. Bei Verwendung der Regelung des Momentum wird bereits nach 20 Zyklen ein Fehlerwert von einem Prozent erreicht, während Standard-back-propagation zur Erzielung der gleichen Genauigkeit und günstiger Parameterwahl weitere 2000 Zyklen benötigt.

Eine wichtige Eigenschaft von feed-forward Netzen mit back-propagation als Lernverfahren ist die lokale Berechenbarkeit der Aktivationen und Gewichtungsänderungen. Diese Eigenschaft kann durch die Einführung der Gradientennormierung verloren gehen, da der Gradientenbetrag eine globale Größe ist. Die adaptive Regelung ist aber auch ohne Normierung möglich, doch zeigte sich gelegentlich die Notwendigkeit, infolge der sich stark ändernden Gradientenlängen eine Ausnahmebehandlung durch zu führen (siehe [Sal89]). Sowohl bei einer parallelen als auch bei einer sequentiellen Rechnerarchitektur bereitet der Zugriff auf die globale Gradientenlänge keine Schwierigkeiten. Bei einer sequentiellen Architektur muß nur die Reihenfolge der Operationen dahingehend geändert werden, daß zuerst der Gradient vollständig ermittelt wird und dann die links geändert werden. Bei einer parallelen Architektur kann die Länge des Gradienten in einer Art "Carry look ahead"-Addierer ermittelt werden. Die Änderung der links in den oberen Schichten (näher an der output Schicht liegend) muß dann solange verzögert werden, bis die Länge des Gradienten feststeht. Das hat aber keinen Geschwindigkeitsverlust zur Folge, da das nächste Muster erst dann an der input Schicht angelegt werden kann, wenn die links in der untersten Schicht aktualisiert worden sind.

5 Ausblicke

Zur Zeit ist noch eine Reihe von Fragen offen. Die Möglichkeiten von Testzyklen sind von mir in einfachst möglicher Form erprobt worden; es ist bisher noch nicht überprüft, inwieweit ein Ausbau dieser Technik weitere Vorteile bringt.

Die praktische Erprobung hat gezeigt, daß die durch gründliche Analyse entwickelte Technik der Testzyklen tatsächlich zu einer drastischen Reduktion der benötigten Zyklenzahl führt. Diese Ergebnisse sollten durch einen theoretischen Vergleich der Konvergenzgeschwindigkeiten unter Berücksichtigung verschiedener Fehlerkurven und Aufgabenstellungen untermauert werden.

Die Ergebnisse wurden an üblichen Modellproblemen gewonnen. Ich habe mich bemüht, die adaptive Regelung der Lernparameter auf eine Vielzahl von Problemstellungen anzuwenden; es ist aber zum Teil schwierig und manchmal unmöglich, veröffentlichte Testergebnisse anderer nachzuvollziehen. Es wäre wünschenswert, die gewonnenen Aussagen auf ein breites Fundament von verschiedenen Aufgabenstellungen zu stützen.

Ich danke Arnfried Ossen, der mich mit seinen Arbeiten auf back-propagation aufmerksam gemacht hat und mit mir viele hilfreiche Diskussionen führte, Albrecht Biedl für ausführliche Diskussionen bei der Abfassung der Arbeit und Bernd Mahr führ Diskussion und Ermutigung.

Literatur

[Fah89] Scott E. Fahlmann. Faster–learning variations on back–propagation: An empirical study. In David Touretzky, Geoffrey Hinton, and Terrence Sejnowski, editors, *Proceedings of the 1988 Connectionist Models Summer School*, pages 38–51, San Mateo, CA, 1989. Morgan Kaufmann Publishers.

[Jac88] Robert A. Jacobs. Increased rates of convergence through learning rate adaption. *Neural Networks*, I:295–307, 1988.

[KSV87] Alan H. Kramer and A. Sangiovanni-Vincentelli. Efficient parallel learning algorithms for neural networks. *IEEE Computer*, 1987.

[LW89] Kevin J. Lang and Michael J. Witbrock. Learning to tell two spirals apart. In David Touretzky, Geoffrey Hinton, and Terrence Sejnowski, editors, *Proceedings of the 1988 Connectionist Models Summer School*, pages 56–59, San Mateo, CA, 1989. Morgan Kaufmann Publishers.

[RS88] D. R. Rush and J. M. Salas. Improving the learning rate of backpropagation with the gradient reuse algorithm. In *IEEE International Conference on Neural Networks*, pages I–441, San Diego, CA, 1988. The Institute of Electrical and Electronic Engineers, Inc., IEEE San Diego Section and IEEE TAB Neural Network Committee.

[Sal89] Ralf Salomon. Adaptiv geregelte Lernrate bei Back-propagation. Technical Report 89-24, Technische Universität Berlin, 1989. Forschungsberichte des Fachbereichs Informatik.

WORKSHOP:
Strukturierte Netzwerkmodelle
Localist Network Models

Organisator und Leiter: J. Diederich

On High-Level Inferencing and the Variable Binding Problem in Connectionist Networks

Steffen Hölldobler*

International Computer Science Institute

1947 Center Street, Suite 600

Berkeley, CA 94704, USA

ABSTRACT

We present a connectionist inference system for Horn logic. The system is based on a unification algorithm for first-order terms and uses Bibel's connection method. It is restricted in that only one instance of each clause may be used in a proof. But there are no restrictions concerning function symbols or the occurrence of variables. In particular, the inference system handles n-ary function and predicate symbols and multiple occurrences of variables even if these variables are not introduced in the conclusion of a rule. The deductive system has more expressive power than the connectionist high-level inference systems we are aware of. This is elaborated by showing how certain additional restrictions imposed on our system lead to the known inference systems. These additional restrictions are ultimately linked to the way how the variable binding problem is solved.

INTRODUCTION

To formalize and mechanize human thought is one of the main objectives of mathematical logic and automated reasoning. Indeed, many researchers agree that inference is the main process of cognition (e.g. (Fodor & Pylyshyn, 1988)). Unfortunately, most of the approaches taken so far to model inference have neglected the physical constraints given by todays knowledge of the structure and operation of a human brain. Slow neural elements interact by spreading of activation without a central controller. Yet, humans react incredibly fast and this seems to be conclusive evidence that massive parallelism must take place. Connectionist networks aim to model the human brain on an abstract computational level such that the strength as well as the weakness of the brain is preserved (e.g. (Feldman & Ballard, 1982)). Though research in this area has produced exciting new results, there are still considerable problems concerning the modelling of inference. Inference seems to be inevitably linked to structured objects and it is far from being clear how such structured objects can be represented and dynamically created in a connectionist system. Existing proposals for high-level inferencing in connectionist systems are severly limited in their expressive power and it has been argued by J. McCarthy in his response to (Smolensky, 1988), that connectionism suffers from a *propositional fixation*.

It is the goal of this paper to show how structured objects can be represented and how high-level inference can be performed in a connectionist network. We present a connectionist inference system for Horn logic. Besides the author's background there is no particular reason for choosing Horn logic and the same ideas can be applied to build a rule- or frame-based reasoning system. The logic is only restricted in that at most one instance of a clause may participate in a proof. But there are no restrictions concerning function symbols or the occurrence of variables. In particular,

---

*on leave from FG Intellektik, FB Informatik, TH Darmstadt

the inference system handles n-ary function and predicate symbols and multiple occurrences of variables even if these variables are not introduced in the conclusion of a rule.

The inference system is based on a unification algorithm for first-order terms (Hölldobler, 1990b). Therein, terms as well as substitutions are represented as sets of occurrence-label or role-filler (Smolensky, 1987) pairs. This representation can easily be extended to atoms and (sets of) clauses. We know from (Stickel, 1987) or (Bibel, 1987) that finding a proof for a formula requires the identification of an appropriate subset among the connections of the formula. A connection is a link between an atom in the conclusion of a clause and an atom in the hypotheses of a clause where both atoms have the same predicate symbol. The inference system operates by selecting an appropriate subset of connections and, then, simultaneously unifying all connected atoms.

After outlining the system in the following section we try to shed some light into the question how existing connectionist inference systems like the one by Shastri & Ajjanagadde (1990) and Lange & Dyer (1989) are related to more conventional ones. In particular, we demonstrate how their systems can be derived from our inference system by imposing additional constraints. These constraints are linked to the variable binding problem and limit the expressive power of the logic but at the same time they allow a representation of terms and substitutions which is more compact and which can be accessed and computed faster.

A CONNECTIONIST INFERENCE SYSTEM FOR HORN LOGIC

Before we outline the connectionist inference systems let us briefly describe the properties which such a system should have. The system has to handle n-ary function and predicate symbols. The variable binding problem has to be solved and it has to be solved consistently (Barnden, 1984). Variables may occur more than once in the conclusion and/or the hypotheses of a clause. Queries may have more than one answer. Finally, since Horn logic is undecidable we cannot determine in advance how many instances of a clause we may need to answer a query. On the other hand, the ultimate goal is to model human reasoning. Therefore, we would like to have a highly parallel inference system. It should detect tractable fragments of the logic and *execute* this fragments in time linear to the depth of the derivation while using only space linear to the size of the formula.

As mentioned in the introduction our connectionist inference system is based on a unification algorithm for first-order terms and uses Bibel's connection method. We will now exemplify these techniques.

A Connectionist Unification Algorithm

Suppose we want to find a substitution for the variables X, Y and Z such that the terms $f(Y, g(a), g(Z))$ and $f(X, X, X)$ become equal. Obviously, by replacing the variables by $g(a)$, $g(a)$ and a, respectively, we obtain such a substitution. But how can we represent terms and substitutions in a connectionist network?. In (Hölldobler, 1990b) an occurrence-label or role-filler (Smolensky, 1987) representation is used, where occurrences denote positions in a term and labels denote the symbols that occur at this positions. Occurrence-label pairs can be arranged as a matrix M of threshold units such that a unit $M(\pi, s)$ is active if the symbol s occurs in one of the terms at occurrence π. In the example, the symbol f occurs at Λ, Y occurs at 1, g occurs at 2 and 3, a occurs at 21 and Z occurs at 31 in $f(Y, g(A), g(Z))$. Altogether we obtain figures 1(a) and (b) for $f(Y, g(a), g(Z))$ and $f(X, X, X)$. The first step of the unification algorithm is to merge the matrices of the two terms (indicated by the filled circles of figure 1(c)). Then, a finest valid equivalence relation on the occurrence-label representation is computed, which corresponds to the most general unifier for the unification problem. The relation is obtained by computing the closure of the operations

(S)   if $M(\pi, X)$, $M(\pi', X)$, and $M(\pi, s)$ are active, then activate $M(\pi', s)$

and

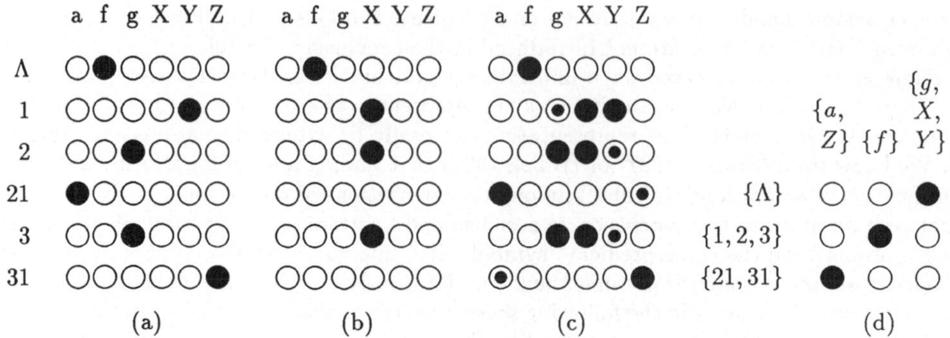

Figure 1: The unification problem $f(Y, g(a), g(Z)) = f(X, X, X)$: (a) the representation of $f(Y, g(a), g(Z))$; (b) the representation of $f(X, X, X)$; (c) the computation of the most general unifier – half-filled circles represent most recent activated units; (d) the compressed final matrix.

(D)   if $M(\pi, X)$, $M(\pi', X)$, and $M(\pi \cdot \pi^*, s)$ are active, then activate $M(\pi' \cdot \pi^*, s)$,

where π, π', π^* denote occurrences, X denotes a variable, and s denotes a symbol. In figure 1(c) the units activated by these operations are depicted half-filled. For example, since $M(1, X)$, $M(2, X)$ and $M(2, g)$ are initially active, $M(1, g)$ is activated by (S). After computing this closure the algorithm checks that there is at most one function symbol at each occurrence, i.e. there is no row π and function symbols f and g such that $M(\pi, f)$ and $M(\pi, g)$ are active. Finally, the algorithm performs an occur check to guarantee that each substitution is acyclic. For our example, both tests are positive and, hence, figure 1(c) represents the output of the unification algorithm. To *read off* the most general unifier we merge columns which have the same activation pattern as well as rows which represent identical variable bindings and obtain figure 1(d). From this compressed matrix the most general unifier can be determined as $\{X \leftarrow g(a),\ Y \leftarrow g(a),\ Z \leftarrow a\}$. For more details see (Hölldobler, 1990b).

The Connection Method

We know from (Stickel, 1987) or (Bibel, 1987) that the problem of finding a proof for a formula consists of finding an appropriate subset among the connections of the formula. A connection is a link between an atom in the conclusion of a clause and an atom in the hypotheses of a clause where both atoms have the same predicate symbol. A set of connections is appropriate iff it is a *spanning* set and all connected atoms can be simultaneously unified. Informally, a spanning set for a formula corresponds to a proof of the formula iff all connected atoms are simultaneously unifiable.

A Connectionist Inference System

We outline the inference system with the help of a small example. Consider a formula, where the atom $P(f(Y, g(a), g(Z)))$ is the conclusion of a clause and the atom $P(f(X, X, X))$ is a conjunct of the hypotheses of a clause. Notice that there is a connection between the two atoms. Since the inference system uses the same representation of terms as the unification algorithm, the arguments of the atoms are represented as in figure 1(a) and (b). Now suppose that each connection in the formula as well as each spanning set for the formula is represented by a unit. Furthermore, assume that these units are connected, such that the activation of a spanning set unit activates all units representing the connections of the spanning set and that the activation of a connection unit triggers the unification of the corresponding terms. Then, as soon as a spanning set is selected all connected atoms are simultaneously unified. If, for example, the connection between $P(f(Y, g(a), g(Z)))$ and $P(f(X, X, X))$ is in the selected spanning set, then the unification depicted in figure 1 is performed as part of the unification of all connected atoms. For more details of the inference system as well as the implementation of reduction techniques see (Hölldobler, 1990a).

DISCUSSION

One of the key problems to be solved in the design of a connectionist inference system is the variable binding problem. We have used a role-filler representation, where the occurrences in a formula are the roles and the variables and function symbols are the fillers. A variable X is bound to a constant c if there is a row π in the matrix M such that $M(\pi, X)$ and $M(\pi, c)$ are active. Since each role π can in principle be filled with any symbol and we have spent a unit for each possibility, one can argue that this a very generous representation or, more bluntly, that it is a waste of units. However, we show in the sequel that a more compact representation which solves the variable binding problem restricts at the same time the expressive power of the logic. This is done by comparing our inference system with existing proposals, notably Shastri's & Ajjanagadde's system[1] (1990) and Lange's & Dyer's Robin[2] (1989). In particular we show how these systems can be derived by imposing step-by-step addional restrictions on our inference system.

Eliminating Function Symbols

Function symbols are difficult to deal with in connectionist systems since they are used to dynamically build up structured objects. Such a structured object can only be represented by a a ensemble of units and it is difficult and expenxive to maintain and update such an ensemble. The absence of n-ary function symbols makes operation (D) in our connectionist unification algorithm unnecessary and as a consequence unification is no longer logspace-complete (see (Dwork et al., 1984)). But, equally important, since the underlying alphabet is finite, the set of terms as well as the set of substitutions becomes finite. This allows Ballard (Ballard, 1986) to prewire all substitutions and then select a substitution by a parallel relaxation algorithm which conforms with a resolution proof. Shastri & Ajjanagadde as well as Lange & Dyer use the fact that the set of terms is finite to assign unique *phases* or *signatures* to constants in the alphabet. These phases or signatures are then propagated along the links in their connectionist network and a variable is bound to a constant if it receives the same phase or signature as the constant.

Eliminating Bindings between Variables

The fact that each variable can in principle be bound to any other variable in a unification problem is responsible for the explicit representation of a binding in our system. For example, if we want to know whether there exist substitutions for Y and Z such that $P(Y, Z)$ follows logically from $P(X, X)$, then the answer should be *yes* with Y bound to Z. This binding is represented by a certain row in the matrix M, where the units for Y and Z are both active. Since neither Shastri & Ajjanagadde nor Lange & Dyer assign phases or signatures to variables they cannot represent such a binding. If we do not allow bindings between variables, then we essentially solve a restricted form of the unification problem – often called *matching problem* – where a term without variables is matched against a term with variables. As laid down in (Hölldobler, 1990b) our unification algorithm solves such a matching problem in two steps.

---

[1] Here we consider the backward reasoning system. For the forward reasoning system we obtain dual results.

[2] We consider only the *deductive* part of Robin. Robin contains also an *evidential* component which allows to automatically select the most likely solution whenever there are more than one.

Eliminating Multiple Occurrences of Variables

If a variable occurs more than once in a clause then the inference system has to guarantee that this variable is consistently bound to the same term at each of its occurrences. This leads to the quadratic[3] number of units in our unification algorithm. Multiple occurrences of a variable are generally not allowed in the inference systems of Ajjanagadde & Shastri and Lange & Dyer. However, the former allow multiple occurrences if the user takes care of the consistent variable binding problem by guaranteeing that a variable which occurs more than once is bound by a query. As a consequence such a variable has to occur in the conclusion of a rule. For example, Shastri & Ajjanagadde can test whether $P(a, a)$ follows logically from $P(X, X)$. If we eliminate multiple occurrences if a variable, then we do not need to unify terms anymore. Unification can be replaced by the weaker concept of parameter passing enriched with a simple test of whether a passed parameter is equal to a certain constant. The parameters are passed from a query to a rule or fact. As a consequence, the number of units can be bound by the size of the formula.

Eliminating Constants in the Conditions of Rules

The elimination of all constants in the conditions of a rule has the effect that only those constants are passed from a goal to the head of a rule which occur in the initial query. This allows Shastri & Ajjanagadde as well as Lange & Dyer to assign phases and signatures only to the constants in the initial query.

Constraining the Search Space

So far the search space was only constrained in that each proof contains at most one instance of each clause. However, Shastri & Ajjanagadde as well as Lange & Dyer require that the whole search space contains only one (or a fixed number) of instances of each clause. Hence, their systems may not find a proof if one of the clauses needed for the proof is already *consumed* by another proof. However, by fixing the number of clauses which can be consumed in the whole search space all possible derivations can be persued in parallel and the time needed to answer a query is bound by the length of the derivation.

Other Approaches

We conclude this section by briefly mentioning two other approaches for modelling high-level inference in connectionist systems. Touretzky's & Hinton's (1988) DCPS is capable of matching a hypothesis of the form $(X\ a\ b)(X\ c\ d)$ against the content of the working memory by searching for a minimum energy state, where X is a variable and a, b, c and d are constants. In Frameville (Mjolsness et al., 1989) a directed acyclic graph with variables is matched against a directed acyclic graph without variables by minimizing an objective function, which specifies the mismatch (or distance) between the dags. However, as Pinkas (1990) has shown all systems based on energgy minimization solve problems equivalent to the satisfiability problem in propositional logic, whereas we want to solve the satisfiability problem of predicate logic.

OPEN PROBLEMS

The connectionist inference system outlined in this paper solves the variable binding problem and shows how structured objects can be represented and dynamically created in a connectionist network. However, many problems remain. We can only use one instance of a clause in the proof of a formula. To deal with multiple instances of a clause we have to recruit units to represent the terms in such clauses. But how can we do this? Another problem is the construction and selection of spanning sets. We could of course implement a certain syntactic or semantic strategy.

---

[3]with respect to the number of occurrences in the unification problem

But we would like to make an informed choice based on previous experience and knowledge about the domain of the application. How can we gather such experience and knowledge?

References

Ballard, D. H. (1986). Parallel Logic Inference and Energy Minimization. In *Proceedings of the AAAI National Conference on Artificial Intelligence*, pp. 203 – 208.

Barnden, J. A. (1984). On Short Term Information Processing in Connectionist Theories. *Cognition and Brain Theory*, 7:25–59.

Bibel, W. (1987). *Automated Theorem Proving*. Vieweg Verlag, Braunschweig, second edition.

Dwork, C., Kannelakis, P. C., & Mitchell, J. C. (1984). On the Sequential Nature of Unification. *Journal of Logic Programming*, 1:35–50.

Feldman, J. A. & Ballard, D. H. (1982). Connectionist Models and Their Properties. *Cognitive Science*, 6(3):205–254.

Fodor, J. A. & Pylyshyn, Z. W. (1988). Connectionism and Cognitive Architecture: A Critical Analysis. In Pinker & Mehler, eds., *Connections and Symbols*, pp. 3–71. MIT Press.

Hölldobler, S. (1990a). A Connectionist Inference System. International Computer Science Institute. *submitted*.

Hölldobler, S. (1990b). A Structured Connectionist Unification Algorithm. In *Proceedings of the AAAI National Conference on Artificial Intelligence. (to appear)* A long version appeared as Technical Report TR-90-012, International Computer Science Institute, Berkeley, California.

Lange, T. E. & Dyer, M. G. (1989). High-Level Inferencing in a Connectionist Network. *Connection Science*, 1:181 – 217.

Mjolsness, E., Gindi, G., & Anandan, P. (1989). Optimization in Model Matching and Perceptual Organization. *Neural Computation*, 1:218–229.

Pinkas, G. (1990). The Equivalence of Energy Minimization and Propositional Calculus Satisfiability. Technical Report WUCS-90-03, Washington University.

Shastri, L. & Ajjanagadde, V. (1990). From Associations to Systematic Reasoning: A Connectionist Representation of Rules, Variables and Dynamic Bindings. Technical Report MS-CIS-90-05, Department of Computer and Information Science, University of Pennsylvania, Philadelphia.

Smolensky, P. (1987). On Variable Binding and the Representation of Symbolic Structures in Connectionist Systems. Technical Report CU-CS-355-87, Department of Computer Science & Institute of Cognitive Science, University of Colorado.

Smolensky, P. (1988). On the Proper Treatment of Connectionism. *Behavioral and Brain Sciences*, 11:1–74.

Stickel, M. E. (1987). An Introduction to Automated Deduction. In Bibel, W. & Jorrand, P., eds., *Fundamentals of Artificial Intelligence*, pp. 75 – 132. Springer.

Touretzky, D. S. & Hinton, G. E. (1988). A Distributed Connectionist Production System. *Cognitive Science*, 12:423 – 466.

Recruitment vs. Backpropagation Learning:
An empirical study on re-learning in connectionist networks

Joachim Diederich

German National Research Center for Computer Science (GMD)
St. Augustin, F.R.G.
and
University of California, Davis
Davis, CA 95616, U.S.A.

Abstract

This paper describes a first comparison between two connectionist learning techniques: backpropagation and recruitment learning. The task is to <u>re-learn</u> a conceptual representation, i.e. to significantly change a representation in an additional training period by the use of new data. Backpropagation denotes to a widely known, supervised learning technique which requires the repeated presentation of a set of training instances. Recruitment learning denotes to a technique which converts network units from a pool of free units into units which carry meaningful information, and can be used for both, instruction-based and similarity-based learning. It will be shown that a learning technique which makes use of structured knowledge (i.e. recruitment learning), re-learns and modifies a connectionist representation faster than backpropagation.

1. Introduction

The objective of this paper is to demonstrate that structure-intensive learning techniques such as "recruitment learning" have advantages in those cases where a connectionist representation must be changed in order to integrate new data.

Similarity-based learning, or "learning by examples," is the original domain for learning in connectionist networks. Backpropagation, competitive, reinforcement and Boltzmann machine learning are all "learning by examples" techniques, i.e. they require the repeated presentation of an ensemble of input vectors. One of the disadvantages of these procedures is, that they make rather strong assumptions about the kind of environment, e.g. the availability of a teaching or reinforcement input, structured data sets etc. One-shot learning, in contrast, is sometimes necessary and has advantages, for instance when a single new fact is available only and has to be integrated in a connectionist representation.

This paper is organized as follows. First, the re-learning task for both connectionist learning approaches is outlined. Next, recruitment and backpropagation learning are briefly introduced and finally a simple empirical comparison of both techniques is described.

2. The task: the modification of a connectionist conceptual hierarchy

The task is to integrate a new concept in a connectionist conceptual hierarchy which has been generated either by backpropagation or recruitment learning. The new integrated concept is a specialization of an existing concept, and is the immediate super-concept of former sub-concepts of the to-be-specialized concept.

The following real-world example describes the type of learning which is realized by both techniques. In the context of this paper, however, we consider the integration of a node in a conceptual taxonomy only, and ignore concept - attribute associations.

For instance, an agent knows car(C_i) where "car" and C_i are concepts and $C_i \in$ (BMW, Porsche). The agent sees one or more instances B_n of "car" with price(B_n, expensive) and forms a new concept "luxury car" which is a "car" with the attribute price(luxury car, expensive). Furthermore, the agent deletes for all C_i: car(C_i), i.e. associations between all C_i and "car" are removed, and asserts for all C_i: luxury car(C_i).

This modification of network structures is a non-trivial process in a highly-connected connectionist system. Some part of the representation must remain unchanged while other parts undergo modifications.

3. Recruitment learning

Recruitment learning is based on layered networks with random connectivity, such as in Feldman (1982), or full connectivity (Diederich 1989). In recruitment learning, a network consists of two classes of units:

<u>Committed Units</u>, these are units which already represent some sort of information or function, e.g. conceptual information. Committed units are connected to other committed units and their simultaneous activation must represent a meaningful state of the network. Committed units are also connected to

<u>Free Units</u>, which represent no meaning yet and which are connected to other free units as well as to committed units.

Recruitment learning is the strengthening of the connections between a group of committed units and one or more free units. This results in the transformation of free units into committed units, constrained by the fact that each stable pattern of activation over a set of committed units must be semantically meaningful.

4. Backpropagation learning

Backpropagation is a supervised, error-correction learning procedure for feedforward perceptrons and simple recurrent networks. Precise teaching data must be available, for instance, when the training data consists of input-output pairs and the task is to predict the output given the input. Backpropagation learning has been described in many publications, the most popular reference is Rumelhart, Hinton & Williams (1986).

5. Architecture and performance of the recruitment learning network

The network used in this study has four modules; each module is a n-layer network with mutual excitatory connections between neighboring layers (in both directions) and inhibitory connections within layers (see Diederich 1989 for a formal description plus complete results). Each layer is a "winner take all" (WTA) network. Competition among units in a layer results in the strong activation of a winner unit, but several units might be active simultaneously if they receive strong excitation. Initially, there are small random weights in this network: weights within a layer are inhibitory [-1, -10] (weights are integers [-1000, 1000], in general), weights to the layer above are initially excitatory [1, 10], as well as weights to the layer below [1, 100]. Recruitment learning can change random initial connections between layers to strong positive weights.

The total network has four "spaces," i.e. three network modules with the architecture described above, and an additional single space containing a set of units without internal organization (the instance space). In detail, there is a space for the representation of structured *objects*, a space for the representation of *attributes*, a space for the representation of *values of attributes*, and the *instance* space. All representations are localist; there is a single unit for the representation of each object, attribute, value or instance.

Units are not only connected with units in the same space, but also with units in other spaces. Object, attribute and value units are connected by *binder units*. A binder unit has three "sites" where symmetric input-lines come in, and it has an activation function which requires input from at least two sites for a positive output. There is one single binder unit for each connection between an object, attribute and value. *Relay units* connect those concept units which have no direct connections, i.e. which are separated by at least one layer. The output of relay units is weaker than the output of concept units (< 250 compared to < 1000).

Units are in one of two states, committed or free. Committed units build a hierarchy, i.e. committed object, attribute and value units are **embedded in a multi-layer network** and form a straight-forward spreading activation network. Initially, there is at least one layer with relay and free units between each layer with committed concept units, i.e. committed concept units in different layers are connected by relay units.

<u>The re-learning procedure.</u>

The input consists of a *goal-concept*, which is part of the object space, and a *single training example* which is an instance of the goal-concept. The goal-concept unit and attribute/value units describing the training example are clamped on. Learning is triggered by clamping on the goal-concept unit with an extremely high activation value, which is out of the range for activation values without external modification. The goal-concept unit sends activations in two directions: in the direction of the top-level layer of the network which results in the (limited) activation of super-concepts of the goal-concept, and in direction of the layer below which causes competition among the free units in this layer.

Attribute and value units representing the training example activate their binder units, and the connected concept units in the object space receive activation. Sub-concepts of the goal-concept which own some of the attributes/values of the training example, and which might own attributes and values not shared by the goal-concept, will receive activation from attribute and value units. During the next time steps there will be a winner unit in the layer below the goal-concept unit as a result of the competition among the free units. The winner unit among the free units establishes excitatory weights to the goal-concept unit in the layer above and to activated units in the layer below by use of a strictly local weight change rule. At this point during learning, the sub-classes of the goal-concept have positive connections to the winner unit in the layer above **and** to the goal-concept unit via the relay units (see Figure 2).

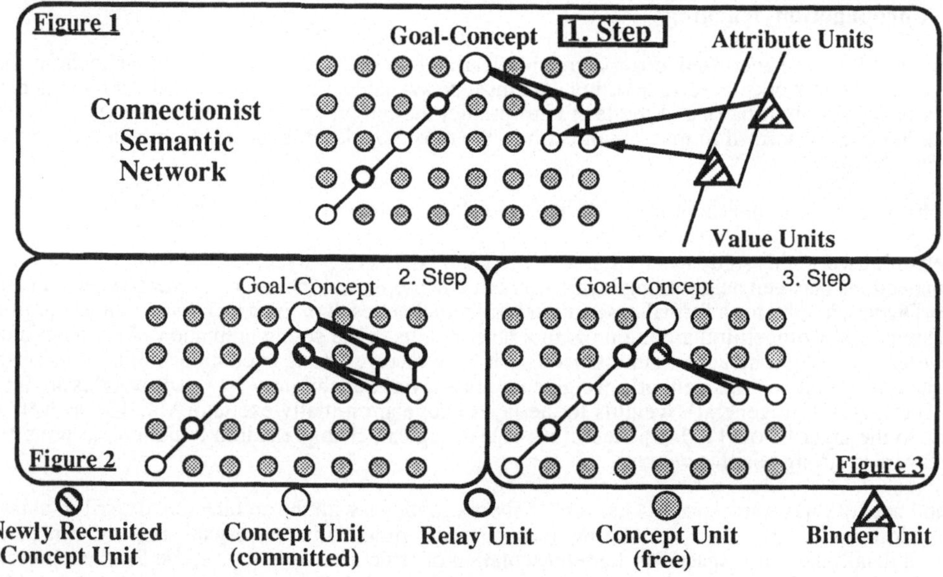

Figure 1-3: (1) The initial network before recruitment learning. Thick lines in the object space show connections which are affected by weight change. (2) Weight change between the winner unit and the goal-concept, and sub-concepts of the goal-concept. (3) The state of the network after cleanup: Sub-concepts of the goal-concept have links to the newly recruited unit.

During the third and final step, the "cleanup" phase, the goal-concept has to decrease incoming weights from its former sub-classes in order to get a full integration of the new concept unit (the winner among the free units). The special characteristics of the weight change rule and the transmission characteristics of the relay units are important at this point. The goal-concept will increase the incoming weight from the new concept unit because both units have a high output. Relay units connecting the goal-concept unit with its sub-classes shut off because there is a winner unit in the same layer. As the relay units decay (or become inactive), the former sub-classes of the goal-concept have no path to the goal-concept anymore, but they do have connections to the new concept unit. The final state of the network is shown in Figure 3.

<u>Simulation results: the integration of an unit in a connectionist semantic network.</u>

Simulations are done with a 400 unit object space, a 100 unit attribute and value space, a 10 unit instance space and 10 binder units. In total, the network has 620 units and 45600 links as part of the multi-layer networks, i.e. links from and to binders are excluded. Fair asynchronuous update is chosen to prevent oscillations due to interactions between spaces. During each update, 50% of all units are randomly selected for firing.

Figure 4 shows the competition among free units in the layer immediately below the goal-concept during the first 15 updates. The goal-concept is clamped on with an output of 15000. Figure 4 shows a clear "winner take all" behavior, due to lateral inhibition. The winning free unit (7) is fully activated after 15 updates, all other free units in this layer have a zero potential and output. This pattern is stable.

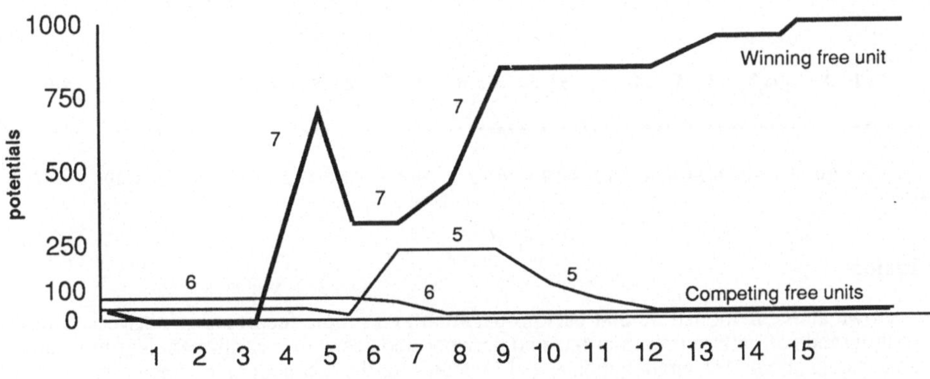

Figure 4: Potentials of free object units in the layer below the goal-concept unit during the first 15 time steps.

6. Architecture and performance of the backpropagation network

The system is a feedforward, single-layer network, i.e. each input unit has a direct link to each output unit. The network is trained with on-line backpropagation. The input and output layer use a binary, localist representation: one unit "on" in each pattern (output = 1.0) while all other units are off (zero output).

The network has 8 input-, and 5 output units. The initial training was done with 8 input-output patterns. A 0.1 learning rate and 0.1 momentum was chosen, and all patterns were learned after 10,000 random pattern presentations.

Next, in order to allow re-learning, a single, **new unit is integrated in the input layer as well as in the output layer.** The new input unit gets random links to all output units [-1.25, 1.25], including the new one. Furthermore, all input units get random links to the new output unit [-1.25, 1.25]. Re-learning is then done with 9 patterns; three of these patterns are different from the original training set (i.e., one new pattern plus two changed patterns).

The following example explains the re-learning process: The 8 input units denote to cars (BMW, Porsche, GM, Ford, Domestic Car, Foreign Car, Car, Motor Vehicle) as well as the 5 output units (Domestic Car, Foreign Car, Car, Motor Vehicle, Vehicle). Each pattern association in learning as well as in re-learning realizes a "concept - super concept" relation. For instance, the input pattern where

"BMW" is "on" is associated with the output pattern where "Domestic Car" is active (Note: this example is based on an European perspective). All 8 pattern associations realize a "concept - super concept" relation (the other 7 relations are: Porsche -> Domestic Car, GM -> Foreign Car, Ford -> Foreign Car, Domestic Car -> Car, Foreign Car -> Car, Car -> Motor Vehicle, Motor Vehicle -> Vehicle).

Several associations are changed during re-learning: Domestic Car -> New Output Unit, Foreign Car -> New Output Unit, New Input Unit -> Car. So conceptually, a new class is integrated in the concept hierarchy which is realized by pattern association.

The parameter which represents speed of learning is "number of random pattern presentations" and not "network updates" as in recruitment learning (although it is easy to translate "random pattern presentations" in "network updates"). Between re-learning trials, learning rate and momentum are manipulated systematically. An initial 0.1 learning rate and 0.1 momentum is increased by an increment of .1 during the following trials (Note: This scheme for the modification of learning rate and momentum between trials is completely arbitrary; see the conclusion section for a discussion).

The following number of random presentations were necessary to correctly learn all 9 pattern association during re-learning, including the three changed pattern (relaxation precision: .001; the correct output unit must have a potential > .9, all other output unit must have a potential < .2).

Learning Rate/ Momentum	.1/.1	.2/.2	.3/.3	.4/.4	.5/.5	.6/.6	.7/.7	.8/.8	.9/.9		.5/0	.9/0
Random Pattern Presentations	4,000	3,000	1,500	1,250	900	850	700	550	575		1,200	700

7. Conclusion

The results shown above demonstrate that backpropagation in a simple feedforward network requires hundreds or thousands of pattern presentations and network updates while recruitment learning can realize the same task in about 100 parallel updates (~15 updates for the competition of free units + ~85 for small weight change). However, a number of comments are necessary:

The systematic modification of learning rate and momentum used here is arbitrary. It is likely that more efficient schemes exist and there is no reason to keep learning rate and momentum fixed during training (see J. Beer in a forthcoming paper). Learning rate and momentum are important parts of backpropagation, however, and techniques for the variation of these parameters should be an integral part of the method and should not be treated as "black magic."

Clearly, the backpropagation network is primitive. We are working on a more extended and realistic comparison based on Rumelhart's PDP realization of semantic networks (Rumelhart 1990).

References

Diederich, J. (1989): *Instruction and High-Level Learning in Connectionist Networks*. Connection Science. Vol.1, No.2, 161-180.

Feldman, J.A. (1982): *Dynamic Connections in Neural Networks*. Biol. Cybernetics, 46, 27-39.

Rumelhart, D.E., Hinton, G.E. & Williams, R.J. (1986): *Learning Internal Representations by Error Propagation*. In: Rumelhart, D.E. & McClelland, J.L. (Eds.): Parallel Distributed Processing. Vol 1.: Foundations. The MIT Press, Cambridge, Mass.

Rumelhart, D.E. (1990): *Brain Style Computation: Learning and Generalization*. In: Zornetzer (Ed.): An Introduction to Neural and Electronic Networks, 405-420. Academic Press, N.Y.

Some Remarks on
Emotion, Cognition, and Connectionist Systems

William M. Rayburn   **Joachim Diederich**[*]
Division of Computer Science   Department of Psychology
University of California, Davis
Davis, CA 95616
U.S.A.

Abstract

Connectionist theories are currently being considered as models of human cognitive processes. If they prove successful in describing cognitive processes, then they may also prove valuable in explaining other processes that display learning, memory, and cognition. Emotions and motivational states can be said to exhibit such processes, and so connectionist theories may someday model emotion and motivational factors. Before this happens, though, the exact roles of learning, memory, and cognition with respect to emotion must first be ascertained.

1. Introduction

Cognitive Psychology, as well as Cognitive Science, is the study of "higher mental processes," which includes attending, remembering, reasoning, imagining, anticipating, planning, deciding, problem solving, and communicating ideas (Zimbardo, 1985). If the eventual goal of Cognitive Psychology is to be able to completely explain away these processes, then a natural extension of that goal would be to completely explain all human mind phenomena. A description of the human mind would be incomplete if higher order processes were someday completely understood, but other facets of the human experience, such as emotion, were not.

Emotion, then, must someday be included in the study of cognitive processes. Emotion is a very real occurrence, *and there must exist a scientific, non-magical explanation for it*. Many of our cognitive processes are used to solve goals. Many of our goals are derived from our emotions (Sloman & Croucher, 1981). Whether or not emotion and cognition are directly related, there must exist some communication process between the two. There must exist a method by which cognitive processes derive information from emotions, and vice versa. If and when the architecture of the human mind becomes fully explainable, this connection between emotion and cognition will necessarily be understood.

The purpose of this paper is to address the question, "Should emotion be represented in connectionist systems, and if so how?" Connectionist systems will be defined, and their importance considered. Then emotion will be addressed; what is emotion, and why are cognitive processes involved in emotion. Finally, the possible connection between neural networks and emotion is discussed.

2. Connectionist Systems

Connectionist models are important for many reasons, among them anatomy, computational complexity, technology, the role of formal languages in science, and the ability to account for learning and memory (Feldman & Ballard, 1982). Anatomically, it is important because animal brains are composed of neural computing elements with complex, parallel connections. If our goal is to determine the exact mechanics of the brain, then being true to anatomical concerns should be paramount.

Humans carry out complex behaviors in only a few hundred milliseconds (Feldman & Ballard, 1982). Because a neuron takes a few milliseconds to carry out a computation, cognitive processing must be completed by only a few hundred parallel processing steps. Current work in symbolic artificial intelligence often requires millions of computations. But results in computational complexity theory (Ja'Ja' & Simon, 1980) suggest that networks of active computing elements can carry out at least simple computations in the required time range.

---

[*] also affiliated with the German National Research Center for Computer Science (GMD), Schloss Birlinghoven, P.O. Box 1240, D-5205 St. Augustin 1, West Germany.

Connectionist theory is important, then, in its ability to account for learning, memory, the speed of human thought, and in its anatomical similarity to the brain.

3. Emotion and Cognitive Processes

Zimbardo (1985) describes emotion as a complex pattern of changes including physiological arousal, feelings, cognitive processes, and behavioral reactions made in response to a situation perceived as personally significant. From this simple description one can gather that emotion covers a wide range of psychological phenomena.

There is a common belief in the theories that will be described below, and that belief is that some form of cognitive processing is necessary for a human to experience an emotion. Given a particular environmental stimulus, a human mind must somehow interpret that stimulus in a particular, and personal, way before that stimulus can elicit any emotion. Though there is disagreement even in this belief (Zajonc, 1984), there is enough evidence to warrant consideration of cognitive processes with respect to emotion.

Lazarus & Smith (1988) stress the need to address two types of cognition that are relevant to emotion: knowledge and appraisal. "...knowledge...consists of cognitions about the way things are and how they work. In contrast, appraisal is a form of personal meaning consisting of evaluations of the significance of this knowledge for well-being" (p. 282). Emotion is dependant on whether we consider a situation important or meaningful. Appraisal is the process of determining a situation's importance. Knowledge provides the foundation upon which we appraise the significance of our encounters with the environment.

Lazarus & Smith (1988) state that they are not implying that there are necessarily predefined sequences or stages that these cognitive processes follow. They allow that "the personal experience of an encounter is often appraised automatically, *and nearly instantaneously*, on the basis of past experiences with similar encounters." But even if knowledge and appraisal seem to constitute an instantaneous event, Lazarus & Smith (1988) stress that knowledge and appraisal are different kinds of cognition. Two people given the same memory, but different appraisal histories, might appraise a given situation very differently, and thus experience very different emotions.

Frijda (1988), in an attempt to make the study of emotion less empirical, has proposed various "laws of emotion." The first three laws he postulates provide a framework for how humans appraise environmental stimuli. The first is the "law of situational meaning:" Emotions arise in response to the meaning structures of given situations; different emotions arise in response to different meaning structures." Frijda (1988) goes on to say:

On a global plane, this law refers to fairly obvious and almost trivial regularities. Emotions tend to be elicited by particular types of event. Grief is elicited by personal loss, anger by insults or frustrations, and so forth. This obviousness should not obscure the fact that regularity and mechanism are involved. Emotions, quite generally, arise in response to events that are important to the individual and which importance he or she appraises in some way. (p. 349)

His next two laws refine the first. One is "the law of concern: Emotions arise in response to events that are important to the individual's goals, motives, or concerns" (p. 351). This law implies the existence of some kind of appraisal process. The other law is "the law of apparent reality: Emotions are elicited by events appraised as real, and their intensity corresponds to the degree to which this is the case" (p. 352). Again, we see that emotion is dependent upon an appraisal process.

Examples of this third law abound. Symbolic information usually does not have the impact that pictures or events actually seen can convey. "A photograph of one distressed child in Vietnam had more effect than reports about thousands killed" (Frijda, 1988, p. 352). Bridger & Mandel (1964) showed that a conditioned fear response, established by the warning that shock would follow a signal light, extinguished at once when shock electrodes were removed. But when a single strong shock reinforcement had actually been delivered, the fear remained, and persisted indefinitely after the shock. The subjects in the latter instance judged that there existed real justification in their fear, whereas the former subjects did not.

These and the rest of Frijda's laws of emotion imply the existence of cognitive processes that determine appropriate emotional response. He makes a distinction between automatic and controlled processing, though. People can control processing, as is evidenced by anyone who puts their emotional responses in check so that they can comply with particular social norms; people tend not to break down and cry among strangers as much as they do around friends.

LeDoux (1989) makes a distinction between cognitive processing and affective processing. He says that cognitive processing is concerned with the relation of a stimulus to other stimuli; saying, for example, that a snake is a vertebrate. Affective processing deals with the relation of a stimulus to the individual; saying that the snake is dangerous. Affective processing corresponds to Lazarus & Smith's (1988) appraisal process. Furthermore, LeDoux (1989) says that by studying brain mechanisms, emotion and cognitive processes are distinct but sometimes interacting functions of the brain, and he claims that the core of the emotional system is a mechanism for computing the affective results of stimuli. Specifically, LeDoux (1989) asserts that affective processing takes place in the amygdala, and that cognitive processing takes place in the hippocampus and neocortex. He stresses that mental information processing takes place largely outside of conscious awareness, with only end-products reaching consciousness (LeDoux, 1989). These products reach consciousness by way of entry into working memory. Emotional experience results when event, affective, and self-representations coincide in working memory.

4. Emotion and Connectionist Systems

There are several facets of the relation between cognition and emotion that can be addressed by connectionist models. The first is simply representing emotions as just a few more nodes in a neural network (Bower, 1987). The second is to provide a cognitive description of how environmental stimuli are appraised, and thus, how they elicit emotion. Most research, however, has emphasized a third possibility: the relation between motivational states and cognitive processes in a connectionist network.

Bower (1987) proposes that emotions be treated as "unique, special-purpose units (or nodes) embedded in each person's associative network which encodes concepts, actions, and events." The emotion nodes would be characterized by what they are connected to, their inputs and outputs. Inputs to the emotion node would be outputs from sets of pattern-recognition rules which identify situations where that emotion is appropriate. Outputs from the emotion node would be connected to "facial expressions, to bodily posture, to our autonomic nervous system and viscera, to word labels for emotion, to concepts which describe the emotion and its pattern, to themes that caused us to feel this way, and finally memories of events when that emotion was strongly aroused and hence associated to the emotion."

The implications of this network theory of emotion fall into three categories. The first is mood-dependent retrieval, which means that recalling learned material is easier to do when you are in the same emotional state as when you learned the material. The second is mood-congruence, which means that people will notice stimuli more if the stimuli in question produce an emotional state that is consistent with people's emotional states. Third is a collection of top-down influences of emotional priming; arousal of an emotion primes concepts and categories that are congruent with how one is feeling.

Bower (1987) admits to not much success in verifying these categories. For example, he tried to find influences of induced moods on word perception. In unpublished research, Bower (1987) recounts finding no consistent mood-congruent interference in a "Stroop task" when subjects induced to feel "happy" or "sad" named the ink color of happy or sad phrases. In more unpublished work, he found no mood-congruent allure of happy vs. sad messages to distract happy vs. sad subjects, respectively, from a dichotic shadowing task.

Bower (1987) then contrasts his failures with the success found when testing patients with clinical mood disorders. Burgess et al. (1981) had agoraphobic and social phobic patients shadow one of two prose passages presented to each ear, and to behaviorally detect occasional presentations of a target word in the attended (shadowed) or unattended (non-shadowed) ear. The target word was either a neutral or threat word relevant to the patient's phobia. Fear words were better detected on the unattended channel (where performance was poor) than on the attended ear (where performance was near-ceiling in detecting the types of targets). Similar results were reported by Foa & McNally (1986) with obsessive-compulsive patients. Target words relevant to the patient's contamination phobias were detected more readily than control words in the unattended but not in the attended channel.

From these and other experiments, Bower (1987) conjectures that laboratory-induced temporary emotions in normal subjects have no impact on perceptual processes, whereas long-standing conditions of trait anxiety or depression, enhance processing of congruent words.

With respect to mood-state retrieval, Bower (1987) has even less luck. The common experiment to test mood-state retrieval is to have hypnotic subjects learn two lists, one after "being made happy," another after "being made sad." A successful result would entail happy or sad subjects better recalling the list when they were in a matching mood. Unfortunately, this result cannot be counted on. Though confirmatory results have appeared (e.g. Bartlett et al. 1982; Schare et al. 1984), they have been offset by failures (Bower & Mayer, 1985; Wetzler, 1985). Bower (1987) regretfully concludes that mood-state-dependent retrieval is probably a small, unreliable effect.

The second possible role in the relation between cognition and emotion is the appraisal process that occurs when humans derive emotional content from their environment; Lazarus & Smith's (1988) appraisal process, LeDoux's (1989) affective processing. All the rules that apply to learning and memory in connectionist systems could conceivably be applied to how we learn and remember emotions. But if connectionist theory proves to be highly explanatory of cognitive processes, then it would be natural to extend its coverage to less traditional cognitive processes.

4.1 Motivational States, Arousal, and Cognitive Learning

In one of the most interesting psychological contributions to the development of connectionist systems, Wickelgren (1979) distinguishes between a lower-level type of S-R associative learning and a higher form of configural pattern learning that he calls "chunking" or "cognitive learning." He notes that patients with damage to the hippocampus show a dichotomy in learning abilities: they can learn simple S-R habits, but cannot do higher forms of learning. Wickelgren (1979) assumes that in order to do higher forms of learning, i.e. form complex memories, *diffuse activation from a hippocampal arousal system* must be active at the same time as the involved neurons process information.

Wickelgren (1979) assumed a set of neurons in the association cortex which encode stimulus features, events, concepts, propositions etc. and these neurons are activated when the corresponding stimulus is presented, or features, concepts etc. are part of thought. Furthermore, he postulated a pool of "free" higher-level units which have no strong connection initially but many weak connections to lower level units.

When a stimulus is presented, lower-level "feature" units are activated and excitation from these units intersect at some higher-level free unit in the association cortex. Wickelgren (1979) assumed that the hippocampus serves as an arousal (motivational) system, projecting diffusely to almost every higher-level free neuron. If the stimulus features a-b-c activate neuron X at the same time as X receives arousal from the hippocampus, then a permanent associative cluster starts to grow slowly. That is, the pathways connecting neurons a-b-c to neuron X are getting stronger. Neuron X then becomes bound to the neurons a-b-c. Neuron X serves the a "chunk node," encoding the association of lower-level features or events in the learned pattern.

"Recruitment learning" approaches such as Diederich (1989) use unspecific arousal for the generation of new network structures, similar to Wickelgren´s (1979) chunking process. If a new instance with unknown features is presented to system, the high activity in the corresponding network module will lead to an unspecific activation of the free space, the set of units which represent no meaning. The free unit with the highest potential and/or random links with the strongest weights will receive this activation (among others) and becomes a clear winner, in part through self-reinforcement. This winner unit is committed during recruitment learning, i.e. will represent information.

5. Conclusion

The purpose of this paper was to address some aspects of emotion and connectionist systems. But the role of emotion in connectionist systems is uncertain. Connectionist systems today do not need the added complexity of emotion.

On the other hand, the study of emotion might entail studying cognitive processes. There is a possibility that the appraisal of environmental stimuli might require some form of cognitive, or affective, processing. If these affective processes are to be explained in further detail, connectionist theories might enter the study of emotion.

References

Bartlett, J. C., Burleson, G., & Santrock, J. W. (1982). Emotional mood and memory in children. Journal of Experimental Child Psychology, 34, 59-76.

Bower, G. H. (1987). Commentary on mood and memory. Behavior Research and Therapy, 25, 443-455.

Bower, G. H. (1985). Failure to replicate mood-dependent retrieval. Bull. psychon. Soc., 39-42.

Bridger, W. H., & Mandel, J. J. (1964). A comparison of GSR fear responses produced by threat and electrical shock. Journal of Psychiatric Research, 2, 31-40.

Burgess, I. S., Jones, R. J., Robertson, S. A., Radcliffe, W.N., & Emerson, E. (1981). The degree of control exerted by phobic and non-phobic verbal stimuli over the recognition behavior of phobic and non-phobic subjects. Behavioral Research Therapy, 19, 233-243.

Diederich, J. (1989). Steps toward knowledge-intensive connectionist learning. In Pollack, J. & Barnden, J. (Eds.) Advances in Connectionist and Neural Computation Theory. Ablex Publ.

Feldman, J. A., & Ballard, D. H. (1982). Connectionist Models and Their Properties. Cognitive Science, 6, 205-254.

Foa, E. B., & McNally, R. J. (1986). Sensitivity to feared stimuli in obsessive-compulsives: a dichotic listening analysis. Cognitive Therapy Research, 10, 477-485.

Frijda, N. H. (1988). The laws of emotion. American Psychologist, 43, 349-358.

Ja'Ja', J., & Simon, J. (1980). Parallel algorithms in graph theory: Planarity Testing. CS 80-14, Computer Science Department, Pennslyvania State University.

Lazarus, R. S., & Smith, C. A. (1988). Knowledge and Appraisal in the Cognition-Emotion Relationship. Cognition and Emotion, 2, 281-300.

LeDoux, J. E. (1989). Cognitive-Emotional Interactions in the Brain. Cognition and Emotion, 3(4), 267-289.

Schare, M. L., Lisman, S. A., & Spear, N. E. (1984). The effects of mood variation on state-dependent retention. Cognition Therapy Research, 8, 387-408.

Sloman, A. & Croucher, M. (1981): Why Robots will have Emotions. Proceedings of the International Joint Conference on Artificial Intelligence, 197-202.

Wetzler, S. (1985). Mode-state-dependent-retrieval: a failure to replicate. Psychol Rep., 56, 759-765.

Wickelgren, W.A. (1979): Chunking and consolidation: A theoretical synthesis of semantic networks, configuring in conditioning, S-R vs. cognitive learning, normal forgetting, the amnesic syndrome and the hippocampal arousal system. Psychological Review, 86(1), 44-60.

Zajonc, R. B. (1984). On the primacy effect. American Psychologist, 35, 151-175.

Zimbardo, P. H. (1985). Psychology and Life. London: Scott, Foresman, and Company.

A Stochastic EM Learning Algorithm for Structured Probabilistic Neural Networks

Gerhard Paaß*, GMD

D-5205 Sankt Augustin, FRG

email: paass@gmdzi.gmd.de

Abstract

The EM-algorithm is a general procedure to get maximum likelihood estimates if part of the observations on the variables of a network are missing. In this paper a stochastic version of the algorithm is adapted to probabilistic neural networks describing the associative dependency of variables. These networks have a probability distribution, which is a special case of the distribution generated by probabilistic inference networks. Hence both types of networks can be combined allowing to integrate probabilistic rules as well as unspecified associations in a sound way. The resulting network may have a number of interesting features including cycles of probabilistic rules, and hidden 'unobservable' variables.

1 Introduction

Probabilistic inference networks [11] have been used to model uncertain causal relations between variables, for instance in a diagnostic system. They consist of a number of rules each of which describes the probabilistic relation of few, typically two to five, variables. Each rule is assumed to model some sort of 'weak' causal dependency. Taken together these rules define the joint probability distribution of a large set of variables. Here we tacitly assume that according to the maximum entropy principle higher order interactions not affected by the rules are set to zero.

The rules should reflect theoretical or empirical knowledge about the corresponding domain. If, however, this knowledge is not available we may capture the probabilistic information in the data by an associative *neural network* [1] consisting of a set of variables which are connected by weighted 'links' modelling the correlation. Its representational power is based upon artificial 'hidden' variables used to approximate higher order interactions. The unkown parameters (weights) of a network are automatically adapted to the data by estimation algorithms. Even complex dependencies can be approximated arbitrarily well if the number of hidden variables is sufficiently large [12].

The *Boltzmann machine* [7] is a neural network which modifies its variables according to a joint probability distribution. Together with the probabilistic inference network it forms a structure which is able to represent the probabilistic rules as well as the associative data. The associative data as well as the probabilistic rules induce different probability measures, which in general will not be compatible. To arrive a single joint distribution we have to find some sort of compromize which is formed according to the relative reliability of the input information. The approach developed in this paper is able to combine conflicting information on probabilities and even may process networks with cycles.

---

*This work was supported by the German Federal Department of Research and Technology, grant ITW8900A7

2 Probabilistic Networks

Consider a problem whose relevant features may completely be described in terms of k atomic propositions $A_1, \ldots, A_k$. Corresponding to each A_i, a random variable x_i is defined taking the values 1 if A_i holds and 0 otherwise. The variables are collected in a vector $x := (x_1, \ldots, x_k)$ whose values $\xi := (\xi_1, \ldots, \xi_k)$ are called 'possible worlds' and form a set Ξ. If $\mathcal{B}$ is the Boolean algebra generated from the A_i, each proposition $B \in \mathcal{B}$ corresponds to a subset of $\Xi_B \subset \Xi$. To arrive at a simpler notation we write $\xi \in B$ instead of $\xi \in \Xi_B$. The available information on the probability of the propositions is compiled into a joint probability distribution $p : \Xi \to [0, 1]$. The probability of some proposition $B \in \mathcal{B}$ is defined as $p(B) := p(\Xi_B) = \sum_{\xi \in B} p(\xi)$.

This setup is used for probabilistic inference networks as well as for associative neural networks. Therefore we can integrate both approaches using the common probability measure $p(x)$. The structure of $p(x)$ is assumed to be known in advance.

Let us first consider a *probabilistic inference network* where the expert's knowledge may be stated in terms of marginal probabilities, e.g. $p(C^r) = q^r$, as well as 'probabilistic rules' which may be interpreted as restrictions on conditional probabilities, e.g. $p(C^r \mid B^r) = q^r$ for propositions $C^r, B^r \in \mathcal{B}$. These restrictions can be reformulated in terms of linear constraints of the form

$$\sum_{\xi \in \Xi} b^r(\xi) p(\xi) = q^r \qquad r = 1, \ldots, d \tag{1}$$

For marginal probabilities $p(C^r) = q^r$ we define

$$b^r(\xi) := [C^r](\xi) := \begin{cases} 1 & \text{if } \xi \in C^r \\ 0 & \text{otherwise} \end{cases} \tag{2}$$

For conditional probabilities $p(C^r \mid B^r) = q^r$ we set

$$b^r(\xi) := (1 - q^r)[C^r \wedge B^r](\xi) - q^r[\neg C^r \wedge B^r](\xi) \tag{3}$$

If the constraints are not contradictory there exists a probability distribution $p(x)$, where all of them hold simultaneously.

As in general the number d of constraints is much lower than the number of all 2^k elementary probabilities $p(\xi)$, there is a large set $\mathcal{P}_d$ of different probability distributions, which simultaneously satisfy all constraints. Similar to [11] we select the distribution from $\mathcal{P}_d$ which *maximizes the entropy* $H(p) = -\sum_{\xi \in \Xi} p(\xi) \log p(\xi)$ subject to the equality constraints (1), as for this distribution lowest 'interactions' between the variables result. It is unique and has the functional form [5]

$$p(\xi) = \mu \exp \left(\sum_{r=1}^{d} \lambda^r b^r(\xi) \right) \tag{4}$$

with a multiplicative constant μ. The parameters λ^r have to be determined in such a way that the constraints (1) hold. It is a *nearest neighbor Gibbs potential* and therefore corresponds to a Markov random field [8]. If the parameters λ^r are known, the equation (4) may be used to simulate the distribution $p(x)$ by successively generating new values for the variables by

$$p(x_i{=}1 \mid \bar{x}_i) = \frac{1}{1 + p(x_i{=}0, \bar{x}_i)/p(x_i{=}1, \bar{x}_i)} \tag{5}$$

where $\bar{x}_i := (x_1, \ldots, x_{i-1}, x_{i+1}, \ldots, x_k)$.

The *Boltzmann machine* [7] is a probabilistic *neural network* where some pairs of variables x_{i_r}, x_{j_r}, $r = 1, \ldots, d$, are connected by links with weights $\lambda_r \in \Re$ indicating the mutual dependency or 'correlation' of x_{i_r} and x_{j_r}. Note that $\lambda_r = 0$ if there is no direct dependency. Using $b^r(\xi) := [A_{i_r} \wedge A_{j_r}](\xi)$ the probability of a possible world ξ is defined [2, p.207] as (4). Hence the Boltzmann machine generates a distribution that has the same form as the maximum entropy distribution subject to the restriction of $p(A_{i_r} \wedge A_{j_r})$, $r = 1, \ldots, d$, to some value. Therefore uncertain reasoning in probabilistic inference networks as well as 'associative reasoning' in neural networks may be combined within one framework. In a neural network some of the variables function as hidden units, for whom there are no observations available. Consequently the corresponding the atomic propositions A_i have no simple symbolic interpretation as they communicate the stochastic relation between the visible variables.

3   Maximum Likelihood Estimation

The structure of the network has to be fixed in advance. Hence we know the functional form (4) of the probabilities except for the numerical parameters. For each probabilistic inference rule there is a $b^r(\xi)$-term according to (1), while each bivariate link in an associative 'neural network' substructure corresponds to an appropriate $b^r(\xi)$-term according to (4).

The probability values assigned to rules and the associative data in general are contradictory. These data items, denoted by $\tilde{q}^r$, are assumed to originate from independent random samples S^r generated according to the true distribution. If $\tilde{q}^r$ corresponds to the probability of some proposition $p(C^r)$, this sample comprizes a number of n^r elements. For each element we do not know the values for all variables x_i but we only know whether C^r holds or not. The fraction of records where C^r holds is just our observed probability $\tilde{q}^r$. Hence we have a missing data situation. We get the binomial distribution $p(\tilde{q}^r \mid q_\lambda^r)$ as the 'sampling distribution' describing the deviation of the observed probability $\tilde{q}^r$ from the theoretical value $p(C^r)$. This deviation gets smaller with increasing sample size n^r. Consequently we can select n^r in such a way that, for instance, the true probability $p(C^r)$ is contained in a given interval $[a, b]$ with a probability of, say, 0.9.

If $\tilde{q}^r$ corresponds to a probabilistic rule $p(C^r \mid B^r)$, the sample S^r is generated in a twostep procedure. First a sample $\check{S}^r$ of size N^r is selected from the complete distribution. Then all sample elements where B^r does not hold are removed. For each element of the remaining sample S^r of size n^r it is only reported whether C^r holds or not. As part of the population is ignored S^r is called a *truncated sample*. The deviation between $\tilde{q}^r$ and $p(C^r \mid B^r)$ again is described by a binomial distribution where n^r can be selected to reflect the reliability of the value.

Data on the associative relation between variables also can be understood as an independent sample $S_{l,ass}$ of size $n_{l,ass}$ covering a subvector y of visible variables. There is no special constraint related to $S_{l,ass}$ as the stochastic relation between the y-variables are communicated by hidden variables not contained in y. To illustrate the situation consider the following example. Assume we have $k = 4$ variables and three pieces of information:

S^1: a sample with $n^1 = 20$ elements on the marginal probability $p(C^1)$ with $C^1 = \{x \mid x^1=1\}$ and an observed relative frequency $\tilde{q}^1 = 0.8$.

S^2: a sample with $n^2 = 10$ elements on the conditional probability $p(C^2 \mid B^2)$ with $C^2 = \{x \mid x^4 = 1\}$ and $B^2 = \{x \mid x^1 = 1 \wedge x^2 = 1\}$ and an observed relative frequency $\tilde{q}^2 = 0.3$.

$S_{1,ass}$: a sample with $n_{1,ass} = 10$ elements on the stochastic relation between the variables $y = (x_2, x_3, x_4)$. To communicate this relation we have symmetric bivariate links between the hidden variable x_5 and the visible variables x_2, x_3, x_4.

Indicating missing data items by '?' we get the following records in the samples:

Sample	Sample Size	No. of Records	x_1	x_2	x_3	x_4	x_5
S^1	$n^1 = 20$						
		4	0	?	?	?	?
		16	1	?	?	?	?
$\check{S}^2$	$N^2 = 10 + ?$						
		?	0	0	?	?	?
		?	0	1	?	?	?
		?	1	0	?	?	?
		7	1	1	?	0	?
		3	1	1	?	1	?
$S_{1,ass}$	$n_{1,ass} = 10$						
		1	?	0	0	0	?
		2	?	1	0	0	?
		2	?	1	0	1	?
		4	?	1	1	0	?
		1	?	1	1	1	?

In the sample $\check{S}^2$ we even do not know the sample size N^r, as part of the records are missing. We may poole together all these samples to a comprehensive sample S. In our example it is defined as $S := (S^1, \check{S}^2, S_{1,ass})$.

Assuming that all information about the parameters of the distribution is contained in S we may use the maximum likelihood approach to determine the optimal parameter $\hat{\lambda}$ as the solution of [9]

$$\prod p(\tilde{q}^r \mid q_\lambda^r) = \max_\lambda \prod p(\tilde{q}^r \mid q_\lambda^r) \tag{6}$$

In [10] the derivatives of this likelihood function with respect to the parameters λ^r are calculated. Starting with some parameter values we subsequently may use gradient techniques to determine the maximum. The resulting 'generalized Boltzmann machine learning algorithm' has the characteristic that for the current λ-values specific probabilities have to be estimated by stochastic simulation using (5).

4 The Stochastic EM-Algorithm

As an alternative we consider a sample-based procedure to determine the parameters of $p(x)$. In essence we reconstructs the missing items of the hypothetical sample $S = (S^1, \ldots, S^d, S_{1,ass}, \ldots) = (x(1), \ldots, x(n))$ which was the basis of the available data. This is just the approach of the stochastic EM-algorithm[4], which is a random version of a general procedure for handling missing data in maximum likelihood problems [6]. This algorithm starts with some arbitrary[1] parameter vector $\hat{\lambda}$ and iterates the following steps:

1. E-step:

    Assume $x(j) = (y(j), z(j))$ is an arbitrary record of the comprehensive sample S and let $y(j)$ be the vector of actually observed values. Then for each $y(j)$ the value of $z(j)$ is randomly generated according to the conditional distribution $p(z(j) \mid y(j), \hat{\lambda})$ given the values $y(j)$

---

[1]The starting parameters should be different from saddlepoints, as the procedure stops there. For associative data this means that the hidden variables should be dependend from the visual variables.

and the current parameter $\hat{\lambda}$. In the case of truncated samples the expected sample size of the truncated portion is estimated. Hence all missing data items are replaced by imputed values.

2. M-step:

In this step a maximum likelihood estimation of the parameters λ is performed using the imputed values as if they were actually observed. With the new $\hat{\lambda}$ step 1 is performed again.

The procedure stops if the parameter vector $\hat{\lambda}$ reaches a stationary point. In some sense the sample S can be understood as a parametrization of the complete distribution. By the law of large numbers the approximation of the distribution gets better if the sample size n is increased, for instance by duplicating each record in S. For $n \to \infty$ the distribution can be represented arbitrarily well.

It has been shown [4] that for $n \to \infty$ under rather general conditions the parameter $\hat{\lambda}$ estimated by the stochastic EM algorithm corresponds to a local minimum of the likelihood function. Empirical evidence shows that the stochastic imputation step allows the algorithm to escape from local minima.

To perform the stochastic E-step we may use (5) together with (4) to generate new values stochastically according to the current value of $\hat{\lambda}$. For each $x(j)$ we start with the present values and randomly select a component of $z(j)$. Its value is randomly determined using (5). After a number of such modifications $z(j)$ fluctuates according to the distribution $p(z(j) \mid y(j))$. The adaption to the new distribution will be particulary fast as the existing values are used as starting states and the difference between the conditional distributions usually will be small.

For the M-step we know that for each variable x_i the conditional probabilities $p(x_i \mid \bar{x}_i)$ should follow the relations (5) and (4). From the binomial distribution we get the log-likelihood function

$$L_i = \sum_{j=1}^{n} \tilde{p}(x_i(j){=}0 \mid \bar{x}_i(j))] \log p(x_i(j){=}0 \mid \bar{x}_i(j)) + \tilde{p}(x_i(j){=}1 \mid \bar{x}_i(j)) \log p(x_i(j){=}1 \mid \bar{x}_i(j)) \quad (7)$$

where $\tilde{p}(x_i(j){=}1 \mid \bar{x}_i(j))$ is the observed probability in record $x(j)$, i.e. has the value 0 or 1. The derivative of L_i with respect to λ^r is given according to (5) by

$$\frac{\partial L_i}{\partial \lambda^r} = \sum_{j=1}^{n} \left[\frac{\tilde{p}(x_i(j){=}1 \mid \bar{x}_i(j))}{p(x_i(j){=}1 \mid \bar{x}_i(j))} - \frac{1 - \tilde{p}(x_i(j){=}1 \mid \bar{x}_i(j))}{1 - p(x_i(j){=}1 \mid \bar{x}_i(j))} \right] \frac{\partial p(x_i(j){=}1 \mid \bar{x}_i(j))}{\partial \lambda^r} \quad (8)$$

$$\frac{\partial p(x_i{=}1 \mid \bar{x}_i)}{\partial \lambda^r} = \frac{-\frac{\partial R_i}{\partial \lambda^r}}{(1 + R_i)^2} \quad (9)$$

with $R_i := p(x_i{=}0, \bar{x}_i)/p(x_i{=}1, \bar{x}_i)$. We have omitted the argument (j) for simplicity. From (4) we get

$$\frac{\partial p(\xi)}{\partial \lambda^r} = p(\xi) b^r(\xi) \quad (10)$$

and with $x_{i,1} := (x_i{=}1, \bar{x}_i)$

$$\frac{\partial R_i}{\partial \lambda^r} = \frac{p(x_{i,0}) b^r(x_{i,0}) p(x_{i,1}) - p(x_{i,1}) b^r(x_{i,1}) p(x_{i,0})}{p(x_{i,1}) p(x_{i,1})} = \frac{p(x_{i,0}) b^r(x_{i,0}) - b^r(x_{i,1}) p(x_{i,0})}{p(x_{i,1}))} \quad (11)$$

$$= R_i [b^r(x_{i,0}) - b^r(x_{i,1})] \quad (12)$$

According to the Hammersley-Clifford theorem [3] the distribution $p(x)$ is completely determined if we know the conditional distributions $p(x_i \mid \bar{x}_i)$, $i = 1, \ldots, k$. Hence the estimation of the conditional distributions from our sample completely determines the unkown parameters λ. We evaluate $\frac{\partial L_i}{\partial \lambda^r}$ for each x_i and modify the current values of λ^r according to $\sum_{i=1}^{k} \frac{\partial L_i}{\partial \lambda^r}$.

5   Discussion

Similar to the Boltzmann machine the stochastic EM-algorithm involves a stochastic simulation of the variables. As only missing data items have to be imputed we have a 'clamped' simulation where the values of variables are used if they are known. A free running simulation is not necessary. Currently empirical investigations are carried out to determine the relative computational efficiency of the stochastic EM-approach. As demonstrated we may mix probabilistic rules with associative data. This allows to include structural information into associative networks.

References

[1] Anderson, J.A., Rosenfeld, E. (1988) *Neurocomputing: Foundations of Research*. MIT Press, Cambridge, Ma.

[2] Aarts, E., Korst, J. (1988): *Simulated Annealing and Boltzmann Machines*. Wiley, Chichester

[3] Besag, J. (1974): *Spatial Interaaction and Statistical Analysis of Lattice Systems*. Journal of The Royal Statistical Society, Series B., p.192-236

[4] Celeux, G., Diebolt, J. (1988): *A Random Imputation Principle: The Stochastic EM Algorithm*. Tech. Rep. No.901, INRIA, 78153 Le Chesnay, France

[5] Darroch, J.N., Ratcliff, D. (1972): Generalized Iterative Scaling for Log-Linear Models. *The Annals of Mathematical Statistics*, Vol.43, p.1470-1480

[6] Dempster, A.P., Laird, N.M., Rubin, D.B. (1977): Maximum Likelihood from Incomplete Data via the EM algorithm (with discussion). *Journal of the Royal Statistical Society*, Vol.B-39, p.1-38

[7] Ackley, D., Hinton, G.E., Sejnowski, T.J. (1985): A Learning Algorithm for the Boltzmann machine. *Cognitive Science* Vol.9 pp.147-169

[8] Kindermann, R., Snell, J.L. (1980): *Markov Random Fields and their Applications*. American Math. Society, Providence, R.I.

[9] Paass, G. (1988): Probabilistic Logic. In: Smets, P., A. Mamdani, D.Dubois, H.Prade (eds.) *Non-Standard Logics for Automated Reasoning*, Academic press, London, p.213-252

[10] Paass, G. (1989): Structured Probabilistic Neural Networks. Proc. *Neuro-Nimes '89* p.345-359

[11] Pearl, J. (1988): *Probabilistic Reasoning in Intelligent Systems*, Morgan Kaufmann, San Mateo, Cal.

[12] White, H. (1989): Some Asymptotic Results for learning in Single Layer Feedforward Network Models. *J. American Statistical Assoc.* Vol.84, p.1003-1013.

[13] Wu, C.F. (1983): On the Convergence properties of the EM algorithm. *Annals of Statistics* Vol.11, p.95-103.

Eine Entwicklungsmethodik für strukturierte konnektionistische Systeme

Thomas Waschulzik Hans Geiger

Kratzer Automatisierung GmbH, Maxfeldhof 5–6, D–8044 Unterschleißheim

1. Einleitung

Für die Abwicklung von Projekten, bei denen konnektionistische Komponenten eingesetzt werden, haben wir eine Entwicklungsmethodik sowie das entsprechende Werkzeug – NETUSE – erarbeitet und setzen beide seit ca. drei Jahren ein. Bei NETUSE handelt es sich um ein reines Software–Paket, das keiner spezielle Hardware voraussetzt.

Eine Darstellung der Anwendungsgebiete und des verwendeten Modells finden Sie in dem Tagungsbeitrag *Theorie und Anwendungen strukturierter konnektionistischer Systeme* in diesem Band.

Das Modell zeichnet sich durch die Verwendung streng lokaler Algorithmen für die Verarbeitung und das Lernen aus. Die von uns verwendeten Netzwerke sind modular aufgebaut und applikationsspezifisch vorstrukturiert.

2. Überblick

Die Methodik und das entsprechende Werkzeug werden parallel, entsprechend dem Vorgehen bei der Entwicklung eines konnektionistischen Systems, vorgestellt. Als Abschluß wird ein Ausblick auf die weitere Entwicklung gegeben.

3. Methodik

Bei der Erarbeitung der Methodik hat es sich gezeigt, daß die Erkenntnisse auf dem Gebiet der Entwicklung großer Programmsysteme in vielen Punkten auch auf die Entwicklung strukturierter konnektionistischer Systeme übertragen werden können. Zentrale Punkte in allen Phasen sind Modularisierung und Standardisierung. Durch ihren gezielten Einsatz kann die Effizienz bei der Abwicklung von Projekten mit konnektionistischen Komponenten erheblich gesteigert werden.

Bei der Modularisierung hat sich bisher ein Vorgehen in drei logischen Hierarchiestufen als sinnvoll herausgestellt:

1. Zerlegung eines Gesamtnetzwerks in Teilnetzwerke, die getrennt erstellt, analysiert und trainiert werden können (siehe 3.2)

2. Zergliederung eines Teilnetzwerks in verschiedene Code–Module.. Jedes dieser Code–Module kann getrennt von dem NBS–Preprozessor (siehe 3.1) bearbeitet werden.

3. Aufbau der Netzwerkbeschreibungssprache aus einfachen, modularen Sprachkonstrukten mit standardisierten Schnittstellen (siehe 3.2).

Unser Entwicklungswerkzeug für konnektionistische Systeme – NETUSE – unterstützt diese Art der Modularisierung. Es besteht aus den drei Komponenten NBS, MERGE und NTS [Waschulzik 1988]. Mit der Netzwerkbeschreibungssprache NBS werden die konnektionistischen Systeme beschrieben und dann durch den NBS-Compiler in Form einer Netzwerkdatei erstellt. Mit MERGE können Teilnetzwerke schrittweise zu immer größeren Netzwerken integriert werden. Die Komponente NTS dient zur Analyse, zum Training und zum Test der erstellten Netzwerke.

Die folgende Tabelle soll die einander entsprechenden Hilfsmittel aus dem Bereich der konventionellen Programmierung und der Entwicklung von konnektionistischen Systemen mit NETUSE darstellen:

konventionelle Programmierung mit C	Netzwerkentwicklung mit NETUSE
C-Compiler	NBS-Compiler
Linker	Merge
Debugger	NTS

3.1 Die Festlegung der Netzwerkstruktur – NBS

Bei der Implementierung eines konnektionistischen Systems legt man in Abhängigkeit von der Aufgabenstellung zunächst die Verbindungsstruktur zwischen den Knoten und die Eigenschaften der Knoten und Verbindungen fest. Dadurch wird das Talent eines Netzwerks bestimmt, d.h. die Art der Aufgabenstellungen, die ein konnektionistisches System nach einem entsprechenden Training erfolgreich bearbeiten kann. Diese Festlegung der Verbindungsstruktur und der Knoteneigenschaften erfolgt im System NETUSE mit Hilfe der Netzwerkbeschreibungssprache NBS. Nach dem Übersetzen mit dem NBS-Compiler erhält man die Netzwerkdatei, in der Struktur des Netzwerks und Eigenschaften der Knoten abgespeichert sind.

Die NBS stützt sich bei der Definition der Netzwerke auf eine konventionelle Programmiersprache, die in diesem Zusammenhang auch als *Wirtssprache* bezeichnet wird. An vordefinierten Stellen der Netzwerkbeschreibung können Code-Stücke in der verwendeten Wirtssprache eingefügt werden. Der NBS-Preprozessor generiert aus der Netzwerkbeschreibung dann den Source-Code in der Wirtssprache. Dieser Source-Code wird anschließend durch den entsprechenden Compiler der Wirtssprache übersetzt. Das so erzeugte Objekt wird nun mit speziellen NBS-Laufzeitroutinen einem konventionellen Linker übergeben und das erzeugte Programm gestartet. Dieses Programm erstellt die eigentliche Netzwerkdatei mit den konnektionistischen Datenstrukturen, dem eigentlichen Netzwerk. Die Gesamtheit aus NBS-Preprozessor, dem Compiler der Wirtssprache, dem konventionellen Linker und Lader wird auch als NBS-Compiler bezeichnet, da aus der formalen Netzwerkbeschreibung die Netzwerkdatei erzeugt wird.

In NETUSE wird bisher nur die Programmiersprache C als Wirtssprache verwendet. Andere höhere Programmiersprachen wie C + + , ADA oder Pascal sind vom Konzept her auch als Wirtssprachen verwendbar.

Wie bereits oben beschrieben, ist für die praktische Anwendung der NBS eine starke Modularisierung der einzelnen Sprachkonstrukte wichtig. Dadurch baut man in kurzer Zeit eine Standardbibliothek aus NBS–Sprachbestandteilen auf. Man verwendet anschließend im Wesentlichen nur noch unterschiedliche Kombinationen dieser bereits ausgetesteten Bestandteile und erreicht so eine sehr hohe Sicherheit und Effizienz bei der Definition neuer Netzwerke.

Der Aufwand für die Definition der Netzwerke sinkt dadurch im Vergleich zur Gesamtentwicklung erfahrungsgemäß nach einer kurzen Anlaufphase auf einen geringen Anteil ab.

3.2 Die Integration von Teilnetzwerken – MERGE

Für die Bearbeitung von komplexen Problemen ist es ebenso wie bei der konventionellen Programmierung sinnvoll, die Gesamtaufgabe in verschiedene Teilaufgaben zu zerlegen, um diese auch in Teilnetzwerken zu realisieren.

Im praktischen Einsatz bringt dies folgende Vorteile:

- Die Entwicklung von komplexen Systemen kann in kleinen, überschaubaren Einheiten erfolgen, deren Verhalten evaluiert ist und die bereits für die Teilaufgabe trainiert worden sind.

- Mehrere Entwickler können gleichzeitig an einem konnektionistischen System entwickeln.

- Es können Systeme schrittweise aus ihren Teilkomponenten aufgebaut werden. Man kann aus Teilkomponenten schrittweise immer größere Komponenten aufbauen und testen. Wenn eine Komponente geändert wurde, sind oft nur die Trainingszeiten für diese eine Komponente und die Zeit für den Abgleich zwischen den Komponenten verloren.

- Der Entwickler muß eine Vorstellung von der Art der Information haben, die an den Schnittstellen zwischen den verschiedenen Komponenten ausgetauscht wird. Diese Informationen, die über diese Schnittstellen ausgetauscht werden, kann man zusätzlich speziellen Netzwerkteilen zur Verfügung stellen. Diese Komponenten können dann so trainiert werden, daß sie als Ausgabe den *semantischen Inhalt* der Information kodieren. So erhält man eine Art Erklärungskomponente, die sowohl beim Test als auch beim praktischen Einsatz von großem Nutzen sein kann.

- Bestehende Systeme können leicht um neue Komponenten erweitert oder Teilsysteme ausgewechselt werden.

- Es können Systeme entwickelt und der Komponententest durchgeführt werden, für die das ursprüngliche Entwicklungssystem nicht genügend Speicherplatz besitzt. Die Hardware für das gesamte System muß erst in der Schlußphase des Projekts für die Integration zur Verfügung stehen.

- Die benötigten Rechenzeiten reduzieren sich drastisch in allen Phasen des Projektes.

3.3 Testen und Trainieren von Netzwerken – NTS

Die so erstellten Netzwerke müssen vor dem praktischen Einsatz noch auf ihre Funktionalität überprüft und entsprechend trainiert werden. Wegen der hohen Flexibilität ist hier einem leistungsfähigen Kommandointerpreter der Vorzug vor einer masken– oder mausgestützten Benutzeroberfläche zu geben.

In dem Softwarepaket NETUSE heißt die Komponente für die Unterstützung bei diesem Prozeß NTS.

Im NTS stehen folgende Klassen von Befehlen zur Verfügung:

- Ein/Ausgabe–Befehle

- Speicherverwaltungs–Befehle

- Initialisierungs–Befehle

- Lern– und Verarbeitungsschritte

- Statistik–Befehle

- Hilfs–Befehle

Der Kommandointerpreter kann Kommandoprozeduren abarbeiten, Formeln und Bedingungen auswerten und parametrierbare Protokolle erstellen. So ist es auch möglich, komplexe und zeitaufwendige Trainingsläufe und Tests im Batchbetrieb durchzuführen. Dies ist notwendig, da man nur so die Komponententests automatisiert durchführen kann.

Muß in einer späten Phase der Entwicklung noch eine Teilkomponente modifiziert werden, so können bei geeigneter Erstellung der Testprozeduren sowohl die Komponententests als auch die Integrationstests automatisiert erfolgen.

In der Praxis hat sich eine hohe Portabilität der Entwicklungswerkzeuge und der Netzwerkstrukturen aus folgenden Gründen als notwendig herausgestellt:

- Schnelle Entwicklung auf dem Hardwaresektor macht oft einen Wechsel der verwendeten Systeme sinnvoll.

- Soft– und Hardwareumgebung werden in der Regel bei Projekten vom Kunden mit vorgegeben.

- Konnektionistische Systeme sind keine Insellösungen, sondern müssen in bestehende Umgebungen integriert werden.

Wegen der schlechten Portabilität von graphischen Oberflächen ist es notwendig, daß die Entwicklungswerkzeuge auch ohne graphische Komponenten verwendet werden können.

3.4 Integration konnektionistischer Komponenten

Konnektionistische Systeme sind, wie oben schon angedeutet, keine Insellösungen. Für die Integration in bestehenden Umgebungen kann man bei NETUSE Funktionen in das durch den Anwender erweiterbare NTS integrieren. Eine andere Möglichkeit der Integration bietet die Call-Schnittstelle des NTS. Sie stellt eine geschlossene Datenstruktur zur Verfügung, über die alle Funktionen des NTS auch aus konventionellen Softwareumgebungen heraus angesprochen werden können.

Bei Verwendung von verteilten Systemen kann das konnektionistische System auch auf einem mit Transputer–Karten ausgestatteten PC-System ablaufen. Die Aufträge an das konnektionistische

System und dessen Antworten können dann mit Hilfe einer "Mailbox–Mailbox–Kommunikation"
über ein lokales Netzwerk gesendet werden.

4. Ausblick

In der Praxis hat es sich gezeigt, daß man auch bereits mit einfachen konnektionistischen Systemen gute Erfolge erzielen kann.

Diese Systeme werden auf einer höheren Abstraktionsebene durch die Spezifikation der Ein- und Ausgabeformate der Zahlenwerte festgelegt werden können. Zusammen mit einer Lernstichprobe, einem Testdatensatz und der Spezifikation des geforderten Leistungsumfangs wird man in einfachen Anwendungsfällen automatisch Netzwerke generieren und testen können.

Dabei wird das System aufgrund der Spezifikation *selbständig* verschiedene Netzwerkstrukturen auswählen und testen können. Dieses Verfahren wird dazu beitragen, die Softwarekosten in dem Bereich, in dem diese Systeme praktisch einsetzbar sind, deutlich zu senken. Ein solches System kann aufbauend auf der Entwicklungsumgebung NETUSE entwickelt werden.

Auf einer niedrigeren Abstraktionsebene hat es sich gezeigt, daß es sinnvoll ist, die Beschreibungssprache für die Definition des Netzwerks zu flexibilisieren, daß der Netzwerkentwickler die Sprachelemente für die Parametrisierung der Knoten- und Verbindungseigenschaften selbst festlegen kann. Dies erleichtert vor allem im Forschungsbereich eine Weiterentwicklung der Neuronenmodelle.

Für die Integration von Netzwerken soll das Werkzeug MERGE zu einem symbolischen LINKER ausgebaut werden, wie dies auch bei der konventionellen Programmierung bisher schon üblich ist. Es muß dazu auch in der NBS symbolisch auf Teilnetzwerke zugegriffen werden können.

5. Zusammenfassung

Konnektionistische Modelle haben die Forschungsphase verlassen, man ist in verschiedenen Bereichen bei der Entwicklung von Anwendungen. Die Entwicklungsmethodik ist so weit fortgeschritten, daß auch komplexe Aufgabenstellungen erfolgreich bearbeitet werden können. Für einfache Anwendungen können bei entsprechender Erweiterung der Werkzeuge die Lösungen inklusive der verwendeten Netzwerke automatisch aus der formalen Spezifikation der Aufgabe generiert werden. Dies wird zu einem Kostenvorteil der konnektionistischen System gegenüber anderen Technologien führen und ein Motor für ihren schnellen breiten Einsatz in der Praxis sein.

Literatur

[Waschulzik 1988]   Waschulzik, T., Optische Mustererkennung in neuronalen Architekturen. Diplomarbeit an der Technischen Universität München 1988, Institut für Informatik

WORKSHOP:
Konnektionismus und Sprachverarbeitung
Connectionism and Language Processing

Organisator: G. Dorffner

This workshop was designed to bring together different views and suggestions on the merits of connectionism in the field of linguistics and natural language understanding (NLU). Among the different contributions to connectionist language processing – including those presented at this conference – there appear to be quite different assumptions as to which is the most appropriate approach to be adopted. They range from attempts to reimplement classical rule-based models of language to the undertaking of designing a self-organizing autonomous machine that understands utterances from experience. This range of approaches should form the basis for the discussions in this workshop.

The contributors to the workshop were asked to give a position paper in which they try to answer the following questions from their point of view:

- how relevant is connectionism for the research on and the modeling of human language?

- what is the most appropriate level of language processing (speech, phonology, lexical access, parsing, semantics, etc.) for connectionism to contribute to NLU? Consider theoretical as well as practical (implementational) aspects.

- does connectionism have any impact on linguistics and our understanding of how language works?

- what – if anything – distinguishes a connectionist approach to language processing from the traditional linguistic approach.

Three of the following papers indeed attempt to arrive at an answer, with considerably different assumptions. Two more papers introduce specific approaches to model aspects of language processing which are used as a basis for the author's arguments as to what the aforementioned questions are concerned. The paper by Sharkey should be read in conjunction with the other article by the same author in the first part of these proceedings.

CONNECTIONISM AND LANGUAGE PROCESSING

Tim van Gelder
Department of Philosophy, Indiana University
Bloomington Indiana 47405 USA

A survey of the field of connectionist work on language reveals a somewhat daunting variety of architectures, formalisms and models. Partly this diversity just reflects the breadth of the domain: language processing embraces everything from phoneme recognition to such areas as parsing, sentence disambiguation, story understanding, and speech generation. Human language processing is a vast complex of distinguishable capacities, and connectionism has been busily chipping away at any aspect that seems to lend itself to neural processing. However, the diversity of connectionist efforts also reflects some real theoretical differences over what kinds of mechanisms one needs, in principle, to be able to generate plausible models and hence adequate explanations. It is an increasingly common observation that, at one end of the connectionist spectrum, there are those who feel that no serious account of language processing can hope to avoid relying on explicit rules, some measure of serial processing, complexly structured representations, variable binding and so forth, and regard neural networks as a useful new way to implement such mechanisms; while at the other end there are those who regard connectionist methods as an excellent excuse to avoid all such baroque entanglements, and hope that self-generated, dynamic, distributed, gestalt-style representations will be the only necessary intermediaries between the ear and the vocal chords. People often think of this as a division between the *conservatives* — those still wedded to old-fashioned devices handed down from previous digital, serial, symbolic paradigms — and the *radicals*, those prepared to embrace fundamentally new approaches. (As in politics, of course, the conservatives see things slightly differently: they tend to regard themselves as the responsible realists, while the radicals are crazed utopian idealists.)

A slightly different perspective on this spectrum of approaches might be more useful. The deep ideological difference can be recast as a matter of the degree of commitment a connectionist has to the idea that there are fundamental similarities between language itself and the internal machinery that produces language; or to the related idea that the various conceptual tools necessary in the *analysis* of language (i.e., in linguistics proper) will be directly mirrored in the actual hardware underlying our linguistic capacities. On this view conservatives are not so much those who cannot relinquish old habits as they are those who think, deep down, that psychology recapitulates linguistics.

For example: we are all probably familiar with the heated debate over the role of rules in the explanation of forms of linguistic performance such as - most famously - the ability of an English speaker to generate past tense verb forms. There is no doubt that a degree of regularity is found in the linguistic behavior itself, and no doubt that this regularity is revealingly captured, in linguistic analysis, by writing out a complex rule governing regular and irregular forms together with their various exceptions. The central point of dispute is the role such a rule might play in the actual generation of the linguistic performance itself; or, more exactly, whether the best explanation of a speaker's ability to form (and to *learn* how to form) the past tense must posit mechanisms which include a representation of that rule. The radical connectionist is the one who denies the need for any such rule-representation, thereby rejecting any neat alignment between the rule-based description of the external phenomena and internal mechanisms responsible for generating those phenomena.

Since from this perspective the conservative connectionist is in substantial agreement with the traditional symbolic theorist, and since my gut inclination is to prefer the radical approach, I propose that (for the moment at least) we think of the real heart of connectionism as lying somewhere nearer the radical end of the spectrum. If we make this move, then the broad question "what does connectionism bring to linguistics or natural language understanding?" has a natural, if very broad, answer: connectionism actively calls into question the assumption that the forms of language itself, and the tools of linguistic analysis, will be found mirrored in the actual structures which underlie linguistic performance. Of course, this kind of skepticism about "the psychological reality of linguistic constructs" is not exactly new in psychology, but connectionist approaches to language take it to new depths. In what follows, I will briefly illustrate by describing various ways in which connectionist practice declines to incorporate, in models of linguistic processing, some remarkably fundamental aspects of language or linguistic analysis.

(1) *Representational form*. One of the most fundamental tenets of traditional symbolic accounts of linguistic processing is the idea that mental representations must themselves have a combinatorial internal structure like that of the linguistic entities being represented; that, in other words, the explanation of language use requires a internal Language of Thought. One of the many powerful arguments in favor of this thesis is based on the "productivity" of our linguistic capacities. It is argued that your ability to understand sentences such as this particular one, which you quite probably never heard or read before, can only be explained if your mental representations of encountered sentences are themselves constructed by concatenating basic symbolic parts in a manner very much akin to the way this sentence itself is constructed.

Now, connectionists do not, by and large, challenge the idea that there must be *some* kind of internal representing of linguistic entities. However they often do reject the inference that such representations must have the same kind of concatenative internal structure as those public linguistic entities. Many connectionist representation schemes are based on the idea of superimposition - many items are stored at once over exactly the same units or weights. A good case can be made that this kind of superimposition is what *distribution* is all about (e.g., van Gelder 1990a), and it can be demonstrated that such representations are inherently non-symbolic in the sense that both natural language and the Language of Thought are symbolic (e.g., van Gelder 1990b). If this is right, these kinds of connectionist approaches to language processing are refusing to assume that the form of external language dictates the *form* of internal representations. According to connectionists, in other words, thoughts of language need not form a language of thought.

(2) *Syntax vs Semantics*. It is difficult to imagine a distinction more basic to linguistic analysis than that between syntax and semantics; whole divisions of the discipline are founded on it. The conservative theorist, whether of connectionist or of symbolic persuasion, generally takes this distinction to be basic for cognitive architecture as well: the mechanisms underlying our lin-

guistic capacities are supposed to divide into those responsible for distinctively syntactic tasks (e.g., parsing) and those which carry out semantically oriented tasks (e.g., disambiguation, case role assignment, material inference).

Connectionists however often decline to build any such distinction into the cognitive architecture itself. They construct models that carry out tasks which depend on *both* syntactic and semantic considerations, but without assigning them any separate mechanisms or processes. Consider McClelland & Kawamoto's (1986) model of sentence interpretation, which takes sentences as inputs and gives appropriate case role assignments (e.g., given "the boy saw the girl with the binoculars," the model tells us that the boy is the agent). Correct case role assignment depends on a complex mix of considerations which include syntactic and semantic factors. The model itself, however, does not record or utilize the syntactic and semantic considerations separately; all the knowledge required to make appropriate assignments is contained in the one set of connection weights, and assignments sensitive to both kinds of consideration are made in one step. Here, then, we find that a distinction central to the *analysis* of language simply fails to be reflected in the actual structure of a network that models (one aspect of) understanding of that language.

(3) *Grammatical well-formedness.* Linguistic analysis of natural language is founded on the distinction between those utterances or inscriptions which are grammatical and those which are not; a major research aim is to produce a set of rules which generate all and only members of the former category for a given language. A cognitive architecture based on this distinction provides mechanisms for language understanding which are designed on the presumption that they will be dealing with grammatically well-formed structures. An essential part of such an architecture is a front-end parser, which converts raw utterances into representations of grammatical structures with their syntactic structure.

Connectionists, by contrast, seem happy enough to construct models of language processing in which this distinction is not one that makes any deep structural difference. An example is Elman's recent work with simple recurrent networks, in which the task for the network is to predict the next word in a partially presented sentence (Elman 1989). The training data consists of a large body of simple sentences concatenated to form one long string. Once trained, the network makes a prediction for any series of words that are input. It makes no categorical distinction between well-formed sequences and word salad; the only difference is that its prediction is likely to be stronger for the more "natural" sequences. It is simply not a precondition of the applicability of the operations within the model that the sequences it is processing be well-formed. This is not to say that the model is completely opaque from the point of view of grammatical structure, since careful analysis of processing reveals such structure reflected in trajectories through state space. Rather, it is to say that grammatical well-formedness, a fundamental aspect of linguistic analysis, is not something built into the actual architecture of the connectionist mechanism.

(4) *Competence vs Performance.* One of the received principles of linguistic analysis is that, although your human linguistic behavior is in many respects finite, the knowledge underlying such behavior is most revealingly described as transcending such limitations. Conservative theorists grant this distinction between competence and performance a psychological reality by postulating a combination of perfectly general processing mechanisms and finite resource limitations

such as memory or attention. An important feature of connectionist work, by contrast, is a refusal to make any firm distinction between central processes and auxiliary resources. For example, the memory of a network is part and parcel of the processing units themselves. Processing is spread throughout memory; what is stored in memory is the ability to process. Performance limitations of a connectionist model cannot be overcome simply by making more memory available to general purpose mechanisms, since there is no real distinction between the two. For the connectionist, finite performance arises from the limits on our capacities embodied in the networks themselves, and not merely from arbitrary limits on auxiliary resources. The utility for linguistics of distinguishing between competence and performance is not in question, but connectionists decline to enshrine any such distinction in the computational architecture.

(5) A fifth example is drawn from a slightly different domain, the neuropsychology of language. How do various aspects of our linguistic capabilities, as revealed in the analysis of overt linguistic behavior, map onto structures in the brain? A fertile source of evidence is the behavior of brain-damaged patients exhibiting deficits in language processing. The fact that some abilities can be lost while others are retained seems to indicate that different abilities correspond in a straightforward way to distinct parts of the underlying cognitive architecture, which in turn correspond to distinct brain regions or pathways. This assumption of a fairly "transparent" correspondence between linguistic function and underlying architecture is being directly challenged by connectionist models of neuropsychological deficits. For example, recently Hinton and Shallice (1990) have produced a connectionist model of a form of "deep dyslexia" in which patients often make semantic errors when asked to read words aloud (e.g., reading "peach" as "apricot"). Curiously, these patients also make visual errors (e.g., reading "cat" as "mat") and mixed semantic/visual errors (e.g., reading "cat" as "rat"). Standard accounts assume that the obvious difference between a semantic and a visual error is reflected in the underlying architecture, such that the different kinds of error result from damage in different places. In the connectionist model, however, all three kinds of error result directly from inflicting damage to the one network; moreover, lesions placed anywhere in the network give rise to qualitatively similar error patterns. Of interest here is the radical explanatory strategy: their explanation of the neuropsychological phenomena only works by rejecting from the outset the standard assumption that there is a transparent mapping between the functions and deficits that linguistic analysis finds in overt behavior and the underlying mechanisms generating that behavior.

I am well aware that in these various cases one could probably find a counterexample - i.e., a model that is connectionist (in the broad sense) but which does in fact incorporate the relevant feature of language or linguistics. But if this shows anything, it shows that the only true generalization about connectionism is that there are no true generalizations to be made. My concern has just been to identify one rather radical and widespread trend or tendency within various branches of connectionist work dealing with natural language processing. There are numerous specific computational virtues of connectionist methods (content-based addressing, approximate matching, etc.), but such virtues tend to be useful in all areas of cognitive modeling. One thing that much connectionist work brings to language processing *in particular* is a deep skepticism concerning the conservative assumption that the mechanisms underlying language use will mirror language itself or the linguistic analysis of language.

References

Elman J. L. (1989) Representation and structure in connectionist models. Center for Research in Language Technical Report 8903, Center for Research in Language, University of California San Diego La Jolla CA 92093.

Hinton G.E. & Shallice T. (1989) Lesioning a connectionist network: Investigations of acquired dyslexia. Connectionist Research Group Technical Report CRG-TR-89-3, Department of Computer Science, University of Toronto.

McClelland J.L. & Kawamoto A.H. (1986) Mechanisms of Sentence Processing. in: McClelland J.L., Rumelhart D.E. and the PDP Research Group (1986) *Parallel Distributed Processing: Explorations in the Microstructure of Cognition*. Cambridge MA: Bradford/MIT Press: 272-325.

van Gelder (1990a) What is the 'D' in 'PDP'? An Overview of the Concept of Distribution. forthcoming in Stich S., Rumelhart D. & Ramsey W. (eds) *Philosophy and Connectionist Theory* Hillsdale N.J.: Lawrence Erlbaum Associates 1990.

- (1990b) Why Distributed Representation is Inherently Non-Symbolic. Proceedings of the Sixth Annual Austrian Artificial Intelligence Conference.

Connectionism for cognitive linguistics

H. Schnelle
Sprachwissenschaftliches Institut
Ruhr Universität Bochum
D-4630 Bochum 1

1. Basic perspectives

Connectionism provides a challenge to current theorizing and modeling in theoretical cognitive linguistics. It has been acknowledged that cognitive linguistics must provide an integrated description and explanation of the knowledge (a) of language structure, (b) of language use, (c) of language acquisition and (d) of the physical mechanisms implementing knowledge, use and acquisition. So far cognitive linguistics has mostly concentrated on the definition of the knowledge of language structure in terms of systems of rules or a set of principles (constraints). Language use is currently specified by algorithms for parsers etc. This is usually confined to uses of regular language. Basic ideas have been advanced about how acquisition of language regularity could be specified in terms of a set of parameters for a system of basic principles for natural languages. No ideas have been given about the empirically justifiable or falsifiable structure of embodiment in physical mechanisms, though it has been acknowledge that we would be concerned with the structure of a biological system.

Seen from the point of view of systems dynamics, processes of regular use of language and of the language acquisition of regularities only mark off special kinds of behaviour (regular behaviour) corresponding to "hills and valleys" in the "landscape" determining the space of dynamic behaviour. If we become concerned with empirically correct descriptions of physical (biological) mechanisms showing language behaviour, we will have to specify the complete dynamics of the behavioural space and not only certain qualitative features of that space.

Connectionism can be taken as a branch of the general theory of dynamical systems, as P. Smolensky has shown. It thus provides an appropriate reference frame for analyses of cognitive phenomena, which by necessity involve structural symbolic descriptions as well as descriptions of mechanisms. The main challenge for an appropriate development of connectionism in view of this task is the relation between structural symbolic descriptions and descriptions of mechanical systems. The analytic framework adopted for connectionist modeling should help in particular to bridge the gap between the abstract regularities of language described in terms of symbolic structures of expressions and the physical or biological mechanisms implementing these linguistic structures in human beings. Solving the problems for the highly structured systems of language may provide a paradigm for the tasks of bridging the gap between different scientific methods (formal calculi and numerical methods).

2. Proposals for solutions in the context of the basic perspective

Hardheaded connectionists believe that structural insight emerges from designing self-organizing systems. This position seems to be highly problematic for a system of high complication such as language. After all, it took a very long time in evolution to come up with an organism having the faculty of language.

Learning of language in the organism occurs in the brains of human beings which have a very specific initial structure which contrasts with that of the other primates such that language is learned naturally in human beings, whereas rudiments of natural language must be skillfully taught to monkeys. No doubt we need insights into the initial structures with respect to which language learning is quick and easy. Such an insight can only be obtained through comparative studies of languages and language behaviours made by linguists by means of structural descriptions. It follows that hard-headed connectionism is imposible for language.

What is needed is a two-level approach, such that one level - the high level in Smolenskys terminology - specifies the structural insights of language - and the other level determines the specific properties of the physical embodiment. There are two alternatives for this approach. The first alternative has been provided by our own approach of net-linguistics. According to this approach, structural insights asvailable in terms of symbolic algorithms are translated into high-level connectionist descriptions. The other alternative is the one applied in the context of Smolensky´s harmonic theory: High level connectionist systems are dirctly compiled on the basis of informal linguistic considerations(cp. Legendre et. al. 1990).

3. The empirically solid development of connectionist approaches to language

The fact that the new perspectives opened by connectionism are fruitful and important must not conceal the fact that the practical development of connectionism in linguistics is still in its beginning. The list of achievements relevant for the complicated areas of the cognitive sciences in general and for linguistics in particular is rather meager. It is easy to argue that most of what has been presented so far is structurally rather simple-minded and even inadequate from the point of view of advanced cognitive science. This holds in particular for linguistics.

It seems, however, that the situation is not dissimilar to Chomskyan linguistics in the late fifties. The proposal opened new perspectives, but compared with the wealth of observational data analysed by American Structuralism at the time it was rather meager. Thirty years of linguistic development has lead to a rather rich framework which determines research in linguistics - be it positive continuation or attempts of refutation.

In reflecting on this development, it should not be forgotten that empirical research in linguistics was paralleled by a development of the mathematical and logical tools for theoretical linguistics. The availability of the framework for symbolic formalization has drastically changed the conditions for understanding the implications of the new linguistics within the last thirty years. Correspondingly, a development of the understanding of the analytic methods of dynamical systems will be needed, before a wider understanding of the implications of connectionist perspectives in linguistics can be achieved.

It follows that a wider acceptance of the fruitful perspectives of connectionism could at best be achieved gradually. This gradual development will not be fostered but rather hampered by many of the specific claims presently advanced by connectionists who vastly underestimate the complexities of the languages or other fields in cognitive science. Claims that languages can be learned by the methods presently proposed are simply proposterous - as indicated above. Such claims must appear ridiculous when the limited range of results so far presented is compared with the complete range of phenomena which would have to be treated.

Such claims can at best be understood as "publicity" for the development of a technical field (such as neurocomputing) where potential "buyers" must be impressed. But we should be more concerned with the progress of empirical science and should not take lightly the empirical criteria. Our claims should rather be based on a confidence of justifiability and not merely on hope.

To sum up : Connectionism opens extremely fruitful perspectives of scientific research in the cognitive sciences. Its present achievements are respectable if considered as a start. Their value as a field with definite achievements should not be exaggerated.

4. How should we proceed in developing connectionism in the field of language processing?

Strategically, it is absolutely essential to obtain a cooperation of linguists and experts in connectionism if we want to speed up progress.. In the present situation, this aim should be assigned primary importance. It can be attained in at least three ways:

A. One tries to show how facts for which well-known linguistic descriptions exist can be represented in terms of connectionism. The value of descriptions of this type lies in the fact that the linguist can learn the content and the techniques of the new methods on the basis of the knowledge available to her or him. Our own approach is motivated by this strategy.

B. One tries to show how linguistic facts which the linguist knows and which he usually treats in certain ways in the context of symbolic approaches appears in another light and has a better explanatory value when approached by methods inspired by connectionism. Some approaches of so-called harmonic grammar (Lakoff, Goldsmith, Legendre and Smolensky) are of this type.

C. One tries to show that notoriously difficult problems in linguistics, such as describing the mechanisms of the variability of language relating to defective forms, context, disambiguation can be explained and modeled in a connectionist framework. Many connectionist models of recent years had these aim. But their achievements so far have not been very persuasive. The reason seems to be that the structure of these connectionist models were poor and the learning or adaptation rules were not yet powerful enough. More research will be necessary before a better insight in initial structures and powerful learning rules will be available.

All three of these strategies will have to take the following into account: Current misunderstandings of the content and the possibilities of connectionism must be corrected! Thus the misunderstanding that some critics of connectionism had shown that it cannot represent complicated linguistic structure - such as unlimited combinatory or compositional structure - and that at best certain types of layered pattern matching could be represented. We have shown in our approaches (cp. the contributions at this conference: Wilkens, Kunze) that this is not the case and that any constituent structure grammar could be translated into a connectionist network, which has a finite part mirroring the structure of the grammar and a homogenous unlimited part in which patterns of triggers for grammatical processing in the grammar network represent linguistic structure for a given expression.

5. Connectionist modeling of efficient learning and adaptation of complicated cognitive processes

Connectionist models of language learning have only be successful for very limited phenomena. Even there the number of iterations needed is enourmous and uncomparable with the empirical facts about learning in human beings. Thus the learning processes proposed are not very efficient and far from applicable to complicated phenomena. The reason seems to be that the initial architecture assumed is typically rather poor - usually a three-layer network with unspecified feedforward relation . At best a handful of learning rules has been tried so far. It is absolutely necessary to come to more efficient learning rules and to a much better insight into initial architectures, in which learning becomes efficient.

The connectionist attempts made so far are laudable in principle since the explanation of language acquisition and of use adaptation to a large variety of situations is indeed a central task for the understanding of language. But, given the necessity to come to a better insight into the architectures of processing another more indirect strategy should be tried, which starts from modeling adaptation rather than attack complete processes of learning right away.

I would recommend one of the two following strategies. Both are in line with our present approach. The first starts with stating a number of principles defining the constraints on possible natural language knowledges. We then derive implementation of the system of principles in a certain connectionist network. With respect to this network learning consists in changing the initial connectivities. The connectivities are parameters; thus learning consists in setting these parameters. The second strategy tries to give the variability of the language the primary role. This strategy is to be applied in several stages: The first stage starts from connectionist implementations of complicated cognitive processes for standard or idealized cases, such as parsers (or understanders) of well-formed expressions. It applies adaptation or learning rules to deviant expressions presented to the system and studies how the connectionist network adapts to these situations and relates them to the standard ones. Thus the standard processes initially implemented by the definition of a dynamics for designated trajectories will be enriched by trajectories (with corresponding dynamics) initiated by ill-formed expressions. On the second stage one tries to apply the results of the adaptation studies to developmental studies relating a part of a language to an extended part. The processes of language extension should have similarities to adaptation processes. On the third stage one will study sequences of language extension and relate them to observations of stretches of language acquisition. These studies on various stages will provide a basis for defining empirically based proposals for the initial structure of the learning system and the learning rules to be applied.

6. Summary

If the task of linguistics involves an integration of linguistic structure with physical embodiements I do not see an alternative to the connectionist approach. Since it is a fruitful branch of dynamical systems theory which has provided insight on the mapping of high level symbolic structure and low-level physical structure it should be tried in a systematic and responsible way. Establishment of its methods in linguistics will take time and will require theoretical and didactic developments whose success should not be blocked or hampered by exaggerated claims.

A Radical View on Connectionist Language Modeling

Georg Dorffner
Austrian Research Institute for Artificial Intelligence

The two previous papers have presented quite different opinions on how connectionism can be best used in natural language processing. I would like to follow up on van Gelder's suggestion of a radical view of connectionist language modeling, albeit under some preconditions, and briefly present the approach undertaken at the Austrian Research Institute of Artificial Intelligence (ARAI). I will also discuss some consequences of this approach and comment on Schnelle's suggestions.

What connectionism can do for natural language processing (NLP) and whether it can provide anything new most certainly depends on what one expects from the NLP endeavour. There seem to exist at least two extremes:

- one might expect a system that actually performs in a real world application.
- or one might simply hope to get an understanding of what human language is all about, and how it might work.

Although they need not be, at the present moment these two expectations appear to exclude each other. Conventional AI has come up with quite a few impressing NLP systems which – I dare to say – do not contribute very much to our understanding of the human cognitive process of language, at least not what all those subtle aspects of everyday language are concerned that make this human ability so fascinating. Such systems appear so brittle and inflexible that they are at best a crude approximation of processing a still formal language.

This is where connectionism can come in. If used properly it might be capable of providing the foundation for a model that has the right amount of flexibility and richness to account for subtle phenomena in language processing. To get away from the brittleness of earlier systems, the best way is to free oneself – as van Gelder suggested – from the notion that the interior of the model has to consist of language-like structures. This is identical to the suggestion by Smolensky (1988) and others to introduce a sub-symbolic level of processing where knowledge is not represented by concatenated symbols but by a large number of uninterpreted elements. By doing this, however, one appears to give away the chance of implementing a real-world application, considering the current level of research and computing power.

At the Austrian Research Institute for Artificial Intelligence we have adopted the most radical viewpoint and have therefore started with the assumption that connectionism can be at its best when used for a sub-symbolic and self-organizing model. Such a model should not make specific assumptions about representations – be they explicit or implicit according to the distinction by Sharkey in this volume – of both the syntactic and semantic kind. The short term goal of such an undertaking is to arrive at a thorough understanding of human language, a runnable real-world system is expected only in the distant future (this does not exclude useful hybrid systems on a shorter term). By 'understanding' I do not mean a step-by-step explanation of every process involved but a model we can examine and that itself can stand as an 'explanation'. For when we give up the idea that the model consists of formal representations, we cannot expect to understand every single part on a verbal level. An outline of this radical approach and its consequences follows.

The first assumption of the approach reflects the aforementioned abandoning of internal formal representations. The approach attempts to clear up a great misunderstanding: Although language brings into play the *symbols* which seem to be so important for high-level human cognition, language processing itself is *not symbol manipulation* in the sense of conventional AI. That is, language understanding (and production) is primarily an unconscious associative process which – according to the sub-symbolic hypothesis – is not borne out by symbolic representations. Nevertheless, within this process symbols play a large role, as language in its transmittable form is recognized as a concatenation of symbols. I say 'is recognized as ...' because the symbolness cannot be in the language signal itself, but has to be projected into it by a cognitive individual.

Therefore a connectionist model of language processing has to explain how symbols as the elements of language are embedded into the sub-symbolic process of associating something with those elements and their concatenation. Smolensky has shown that connectionist networks are most appropriate for sub-symbolic models, thus they are appropriate for language models.

Another assumption of the approach is closely related to the previous one. Initially I have said that the internals of the model do not consist of representations. To put it more strictly, that means that no verbalized or otherwise formalized notion is implanted into the system by its designer, neither explicitly nor made implicit (see Sharkey). That is what symbolic representation was all about in conventional AI. The designer of a system expresses his or her knowledge of the world and inserts it by means of symbol concatenations. It is not very likely, that is, it is even impossible that humans at birth are equipped with such detailed descriptions of the world and even about language itself. It is at least arguable that humans have the knowledge about things like a *noun* or a *phrase* pre-wired instead of acquiring it. For a plausible model of language it is therefore necessary to include the process of acquisition by self-organization based on an adaptive interaction with the environment. In other words, structured knowledge is acquired and made implicit (in Sharkey's sense) by the system itself.

This leads to the third assumption of this approach. Adaptive acquisition of (primarily sub-symbolic) knowledge is also necessary to account for a variety of phenomena in language processing. A conservative in van Gelder's sense could still try to get away by saying that explicit representations in connectionist models saves the time for the tedious process of training and learning. By saying this, the conservative forgets that symbolic representations are only approximations to what really happens in our minds and that they neglect individual differences. Such differences, however, are what accounts for many subtle aspects and also limits of language.

This brings us right to the notion of *meaning*. Instead of assuming that the meaning of a word is god-given and one just has to identify it and insert it into a model, it seems much more plausible to think of meaning as an associative response happening inside an adaptive individual. To learn about the meaning of a word (symbol), the individual first has to learn to form a concept according to the current situation, then to identify the symbolic function of the word, and finally to tie the two together. At all three steps the process is susceptible to factors quite unique to the very individual and the very situation. First, no two individuals are exactly alike. Secondly, no two individuals have exactly the same history of experiences. Therefore, concepts and the links between symbols and concepts will differ to one degree or another for each individual. This gives rise to phenomena of 'misinterpretation', individual uses of language, etc. which are not just side aspects but ubiquitous phenomena which make language so interesting.

Meaning thus becomes an individual's response to identifying a language utterance. More precisely, it becomes the conceptual response of the individual, *concepts* being special states of the system that are acquired from experience in the environment. This last comment turns out to be very important: If we succeed in building a model that can learn how to form concepts from experience and how to tie them to the symbols in a language, we will have succeeded in explaining how meanings can be grounded to the system's internal states. That is, we will have come closer to understanding how humans acquire meaning without an external designer pre-wiring it. From a more practical viewpoint, we might no longer have to rely on a designer's ability of identifying meaning and foreseeing appropriate system reactions. Considering the onset of the approach – we want to get some feeling of how humans process language – this is an extremely important aspect, neither conventional AI nor the conservative connectionist approach can handle.

There are several consequences and also drawbacks to this approach of connectionist language modeling. First, for the moment we are restricted to very simple models of very fundamental processes, such as naming tasks or word-induced conceptualization. By abandoning many lingusitic representations on a high level, we have to work ourselves up from rather basic things. This approach, however, does not neglect the complexities of language (as Schnelle suggested) but assumes that these complexities have to be rooted in simpler mechanisms and can only be understood until such simpler ones can be handled. This makes sense considering how language probably has evolved in history and how it is acquired by a child. Of course, the approach would be doomed to fail if we discover that complex language aspects are impossible to be included in a distributed non-representationalist sub-symbolic model. However, there is great evidence that it is possible. For example

- structure can be reflected in distributed patterns in a non-classical sense (see the references in Sharkey's invited paper about representations and Rotter & Dorffner in this volume)
- sequences of 'grammatical' inputs can be dealt with appropriately without ever assuming explicit representations of rules (see Elman 1988, 1989)

Secondly, we do not know if this approach can succeed. Self-organization in more complex models could still turn out to be so difficult that the models are useless. The approach does *not* want to simulate evolution, but the difficulty might still be unsurmountable. However, it has been argued here that the approach is not impossible for theoretical reasons (see Schnelle) but might be on a larger scale for more practical grounds. Then again, even small models can help us in gaining an understanding about language.

Thirdly – as the most severe consequence – a self-organizing non-representationalist approach is limited to what today's artificial systems can experience. In other words, concepts can only be based upon basic sensory experience (e.g. visual) and basic motivational aspects that can be handled by modern machines. We can expect an artifical intelligence to learn and to communicate about a concept like *apple* – what its visual appearance and maybe tactile properties are concerned – but we cannot expect a machine to acquire the meaning of concepts like *freedom* or *currency* anytime soon.

Finally, an approach as outlined here cannot work without any architectural considerations guided by the designer's knowledge. To the contrary, it is assumed that the model has some quite complex internal structure that is pre-wired and not subject to adaptation. So, instead of defining the detailed representations necessary for language, one has to come up with basic principles and build appropriate modules for them. As those knowledge-guided designs are on a higher level than specific concepts we could call them *representations on a meta-linguistic level*. For the first model implementations at the ARAI (Dorffner in press) such meta-linguistic representations are model components for

- the conceptualization capacity of the system
- the ability to identify the symbolic function of a word
- internal realizations of symbols

In this sense it is assumed that there do have to be innate structures in a system processing language – as Schnelle argued – but those are not on any language-specific level. At the same time one has to recognize that the approach cannot totally free itself from the designer's knowledge – which, on the other hand, was not really necessary to begin with.

In summary I would like to argue that connectionism can provide a genuinely novel perspective to language research if we adopt a more radical approach to modeling. Such an approach should not be based on explicit representations but on processes of self-organization in a complex initial architecture. It can help with the design of plausible models of human language that bring us closer to an understanding of how language might work. In particular, it can help in explaining the grounding of meanings in an individual's experience. In this very respect radical connectionist models seem to achieve more than both conventional approaches and conservative connectionism can.

Dorffner G.: A Step Toward Sub–Symbolic Language Models without Linguistic Representations, in Reilly R., Sharkey N.(eds.): Connectionist Approaches to Language Processing (Vol. I), Lawrence Erlbaum (in press).

Elman J.L.: Finding Structure in Time, UCSD, CRL Technical Report 8801, 1988.

Smolensky P.: On the Proper Treatment of Connectionism, Behavioral and Brain Sciences 11(88), p.1–74, 1988.

Word Recognition as a First Step Towards Natural Language Processing with Artificial Neural Networks

Renate Deffner Klaus Eder Hans Geiger
Kratzer Automatisierung GmbH
Maxfeldhof 5–6, D–8044 Unterschleißheim/München

Introduction

Object of this analysis is the association of a natural language statement with one of a finite number of predefined actions such as generation of a database query, display of required information and/or generation of a natural language response. A neural network will be used for collecting, storing and evaluating context information which in turn will modify the retrieval of information from the associative lexicon. Restricting the system to problem–dependent analysis of input statements should allow correct responses to incomplete, corrupt or (syntactically) ambiguous inputs.

As a first step to natural language understanding an associative system for recognizing words has been implemented.

What do we Expect from a Natural Language System?

In order to control the communication process and compare the results of man–machine interaction we can use an imitation test like the Turing test. For us the relevant aspect of the interaction is a pragmatic one, i.e. the question whether the system is able to solve the given task like a cooperative human partner would under the same conditions.

Therefore we define "understanding" as an emipircal system property:

> A statement is understood if and only if the system responds in the
> way the human dialogue partner expects and understands.

We do not require from our system that the rules, procedures and knowledge representations it builds for the problem–solving must be analogous to human thinking but rather accept that an 'alternative intelligence' might turn out < Habel > . Also the machine is not expected to act more intelligently than a human dialogue partner would be able to if he had the same information at his disposal. In addition to the theoretical and practical requirements any intelligent system has to meet < Geiger > , a NL–system must be able to:

- Form associative links between the input words and the words in its database.
  These associations must be able to express similarities in respect to e.g. ASCII–coding, phonetic likeness, syntactic features and semantic properties. Defining a *distance* between two words (or equivalent syntactic entities) cannot be restricted to a single value but must rather take into account the context which defines the set of features to be used for computation of the distance.

- Classify unknown words according to their context and their similaritiy to the words in the database.

- Store and update the history of the ongoing dialogue in order to resolve ambiguities using information gained previously.

- Tolerate typing and spelling errors as well as syntactically incorrect input statements,

According to our definition the system can prove that it 'understood' the natural language input by selecting a corresponding formal output frame and correctly instantiating the dependent variables.

When a parser is used for sentence processing, a complete linguistic analysis takes place. There is no possibility to stop when the sentence has already been understood by using only part of the information. The possibility to stop at certain best guesses is only given when a statistical analysis of NL–statements is included < Waltz > . In a connectionist system the statistical information is derived from the data and included automatically.

By chosing a pragmatic approach (reaction of the system as criterion) for evaluation of the performance of a NL-system we avoid the problem of finding out how deep (or to which extent) a statement will have to be analyzed in order to be understood. This is highly desirable because the discriminating criteria depend on the data. In a connectionist system the criteria are dynamically changing < McClelland >.
As is shown in < Kahler > and < Krempl >, connectionist methods also allow incomplete, ambiguous and even incorrect information to be handled.

Symbolic Information in Neural Networks

Neural networks have widely been used for adaptive pattern recognition. A pattern is defined as a representation of an object that is described by a set of real numbers together with information on the meaning of these numbers. This is adequate to describe an object by its physical attributes, where the real numbers give a numeric value for one particular attribute (e.g. size, coordinates, temperature). We arrive at non-numeric descriptions of objects by replacing physical attributes with symbolic information and the associated numerical value with a logical value describing certain aspects of an object (such as "red", "little", "fruit" ...). This logical value is not necessarily binary. It can be weighted, thus giving more or less importance to it or it can be provided with a probability, thus representing a measure of confidence.

Pattern recognition using numerical attributes can be understood as selecting one of a finite number of predefined ("learned") patterns in response to the presentation of an unknown pattern. The selection is done by "similarity", which in this case is also easily defined as the smallest (vector) distance between the input pattern and the stored patterns. In neural nets this may be accomplished by using autoassociative algorithms, the advantage in comparison to conventional table lookup processes being the implicit definition of "similarity" and also a certain degree of immunity to noise: the most similar pattern is reconstructed, as long as the superimposed noise does not change the relative distances between input and stored patterns.

For many cases computing the Hamming distance is sufficient, provided the symbols are coded in binary patterns. If linguistic information is represented in this form, however, there arise a few difficulties:

Applied to linguistic problems, patterns are representations of single words. Presenting the ASCII-representation, this being a subset of the complete pattern, the recognition process should complete the pattern by adding the missing symbolic values. Using the above definition, this would be done by selecting the complete pattern whose ASCII-part is identical to or similar to the ASCII-representation of the input word. This, however, is not unambiguous, since the other properties necessary for understanding the input statement are not parts of one ASCII-pattern. Thus, the database must either include several patterns with identical ASCII-parts or there must be a set of different algorithms for computing the missing parts of the pattern for one word.

In both cases a simple pattern match is not sufficient to solve the recognition problem. In addition to the ASCII-representation of one word, one must necessarily include some kind of context information to resolve the inevitable ambiguities mentioned above. This can be done by looking at the whole statement (possibly even additional information of a more global nature) as one pattern. Since it cannot be expected, that all possible statements are stored in the database used, this precludes the definition of recognition as a matching process between patterns. Rather, the database stores known ASCII-representations of words together with all the known features for this word < Deffner >.

In our approach the typical properties (relaxation process) of neural networks allow a parallel investigation of several possible solutions. The recognition process thus consists of a selection of those dynamically weighted features, that give a best fit into the context. With this method, besides the factual knowledge obtained by evaluating binary features, rule based knowledge coded in the same network as dependencies (connections) between the features can be used (see fig. 1).

Words and their Internal Representation

The internal representation used in this work is a vector of binary values each signifying the presence or absence of a certain feature of the coded word. As features for achieving tolerance with regard to misspelling we use groups of 2, 3 and 4 successive characters < Kohonen, Wickelgren > . These features give a certain amount of redundancy on one hand and on the other hand make sure that different words have a different coding.

Example:
The word "fruit" consists of the following set of features:

$$\text{"fr", "ru", "ui", "it", "fru", "rui", "uit", "frui", "ruit"}$$

During the construction of the lexicon a table of character groups is built. Along with each group the frequency of the group within the lexicon is stored in order to weight the features during retrieval.

This kind of coding shows several advantages:

- It is easy to compute and shows great tolerance with regard to misspelling. Words are correctly recognized when up to 40 % of the characters are wrong or missing.

- There are no training times because the connections between features and words are explicitly given.

- There are no requirements for the set of input data, especially no restrictions to the statistical correlations between different objects. Therefore, adding a new word does not result in crosstalk between this and other previously stored words.

- When storing a great number of words, the number of character groups increases more slowly and a certain saturation is reached, e.g. for 5000 names each on average 12 characters long, less than 20000 groups were found (as compared to the theoretical limit of approx. $26^4 = 456\,976$).

- Using weighted character groups, relevance can be expressed in relation to the frequency of groups dependent on the criteria used for defining the similarity of words (e.g. in order to recognize street names the information that the searched name is ending with the word "street" has small discriminating effect compared to the rest of the name).

The above coding is not restricted to groups of ASCII–characters. To improve recognition according to phonetic likeness of words a phonetic code instead of the ASCII–code may also be used < Krempl, Wickelgren > .

In order to extend the description of words to syntactic and semantic information the vector of features of each word is expanded, e.g. together with the word "red" the syntactic property *is_adjective* and the semantic property *is_colour* may be set < McClelland >

Computing a Measure of Similiarity between Words

When computing a distance (modified Hamming–distance) as a measure of similarity with this strategy, it is necessary to define the meaning of similarity. The criteria for this definition are strongly dependent on the application where word recognition is used. So the computation is a highly dynamical process:

When using the above coding for simple word recognition (e.g. as an associative dictionary) the weights of features may be given by the user, thus defining one special (intuitive) meaning of similarity.

When using word recognition as a part of a larger system (e.g. sentence recognition) the weights of features are set by a neural network according to the most appropriate kind of similarity (e.g. when a best fit to the input "ret talble" is looked for, first only adjectives representing a colour with a spelling similar to "ret" and then only nouns representing furniture with a spelling similar to "talble" are searched). ,

The process of computing the similarity between an input word and the words stored in the lexicon is as follows:

- Give (or compute) the weights for all the features (see above).

- Compute the similarity according to:

$$\text{dist} (word_i , word_l) = \sum_k w_k \cdot \| F_{ik} - F_{lk} \|$$

where:
dist : measure of similarity
k : summation index running from 1 to the number of features
$word_i$: input word
$word_l$: word from the lexicon
w_k : weight of feature k
F_{ik} : Binary value (0,1) for feature k of input word
F_{lk} : Binary value (0,1) for feature k of lexicon word

The connectivity matrix representing the connections between features and words which leads to the above calculation of $dist(word_i, word_l)$ may be regarded as a neural net, where information about words and features is stored:

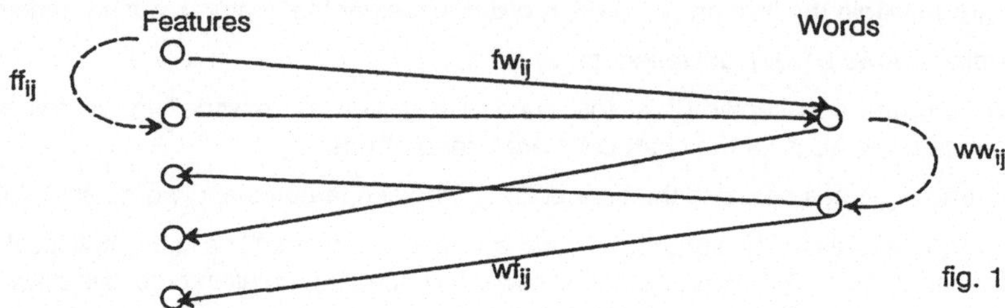

ff_{ij} = 0 Connections between features, not used here.
These connections would constitute a fully associative memory.

ww_{ij} = 0 Connections between words, not used here.

wf_{ij} = 0 Inputs from words to features, not used here.

fw_{ij} = Inputs from features to words.

$$fw_{ij} = \begin{cases} 1 & \text{if feature i is present in word j} \\ -1 & \text{if not} \end{cases}$$

$$fw_{ij} = \sum_{i=F_n}^{F_n-1} -\Sigma \frac{fw_{ij} + 1}{2} \quad \text{and } x_{F_n} = 1 \; \textit{(Dummy–Feature)} \quad \rightarrow \quad -\sum_{i=1}^{F_n} x_i \, fw_{ij} = H(\vec{x}, \vec{w_j})$$

$H(\vec{x}, \vec{w_j})$ = modified Hamming distance: number of features present in $\vec{x}$, but not in $\vec{w_j}$.

For $\vec{w_j}$ is contained in $\vec{x}$, $H(\vec{x}, \vec{w_j}) = 0$

Alternatively:

$$fw_{ij} = \begin{cases} 1 & \text{if feature i is present in word j} \\ 0 & \text{if not} \end{cases}$$

$H(\vec{x}, \vec{w_j})$ yields number of features present in $\vec{w_j}$, but not in $\vec{x}$.

For $\vec{x}$ is contained in $\vec{w_j}$, $H(\vec{x}, \vec{w_j}) = 0$

$\vec{x}$: search pattern
F_n : number of features

Advantages of the Associative Recall Compared to Conventional Strategies

- A continuous measure for similarity can be defined. Therefore the whole database can be sorted automatically according to similarity. In a conventional way one would get only two disjunct sets (search condition is true/false). Thus the user can expand or restrict the retrieval result without modification of the search pattern.

- The use of "wildcards" is unflexible for database retrieval and may lead to undesired results (too much resulting data/ no result at all etc.). With an associative search the use of wildcards is replaced by a continuous modification of the maximum distance. With this the n most similar entries can be displayed and it is guaranteed that those n entries will be found in any case.

- A search run will not be aborted because of typing errors in the search pattern. The n most similar entries will be found anyway, the result being highly identical with the result gained with a correct search pattern.

- Connectionist architectures are massively parallel by nature and thus lend themselves readily to implementation on parallel hardware. Using the simple algorithms of our model it is possible to achieve significant acceleration of access times with little effort.

- Context information (in the form of attributes) can very easily be used to modify relative weights during computation of similarities (see above). This serves to resolve ambiguities and enhances fault tolerance on the semantic level.

The last point shows how this word recognition system can in a natural way be extended to include understanding of complete natural language statements.

Discussion

As stated above, the primary goal under study is understanding a complete natural language statement. We define *understanding* as selecting one out of a finite number of actions that are expected by the human partner. Using this definition, pattern recognition as defined above seems applicable to the task. We could assume that the possible actions are stored as symbolic patterns including variables that are to be instantiated for a particular statement. In this case, *understanding* would consist of transforming the input statement into a form where a pattern matching could thus be performed by selecting the best fitting output statement.

Necessary for recognition of natural language statements is the generation of an internal representation of the words in the input statement. This representation must contain the following information:

- *Static Information*
  This information is gained from the knowledge base (lexicon). The search is based on the ASCII-representation of the input words. Similiarities between the input and the entries in the knowledge base are evaluated using a number of given weights for the features. The information retrieved from the knowledge base is context independent and contains syntactic and semantic information which is at this point not necessarily unambiguous! The result of this lookup is a pattern containing a superset of information (generally a combination of information from several lexicon entries).

- *Dynamic Information*
  Applying pattern matching to the static information obtained in the first step the information is compared to predefined ("learned") statements in a process similar to the pattern recognition shown above. As a result of this pattern recognition weights for certain discriminating features are changed in order to complete the recognition process.
  The use of connectionist methods for the pattern matching process avoids the backtracking component otherwise necessary for this step. Analogous to the process of word recognition it turns out that statement recognition using neural networks is highly tolerant regarding syntactical or semantical uncertainties.

References:

<Deffner>   Deffner, R., Geiger, H., Assoziative Worterkennung mit neuronalen Netzen, in: Rieger, B., Schaeder, B. (eds.),Lexikon und Lexikographie, GLDV–Proceedings 1990 (in press)

<Geiger>   Geiger, H., Storing and Processing Information in Connectionist Systems, NSMS–Proceedings 1990, (in press)

<Habel>   Habel,C., Prinzipien der Referentialität (Berlin, 1986)

<Kahler>   Kahler, R., Untersuchungen zur Anwendung selbstorganisierender, assoziativer Netzwerke für Zugriffe auf Datenbanken (Diplomarbeit an der TU München, 1986).

<Kohonen>   Kohonen,T., Content Addressable Memories (2nd Edition), Springer Berlin, New York 1987

<Krempl>   Krempl, T., Automatische Transkription mit Hilfe selbstorganisierenderNetzwerke (Diplomarbeit an der TU München, 1986)

<McClelland>   McClelland, J.L. and Kawamoto, A.H., Mechanisms of Sentence Processing: Assigning Roles to Constituents, in: McClelland, J.L. and Rumelhart, D.E., (eds.), Parallel Distributed Processing, Vol. 2, (MIT Press, 1986), pp. 272 – 326

<Waltz>   Waltz, D.L. and Pollack, J.B., Massively Parallel Parsing, Cognitive Science 9, (1985), pp. 51 – 74

<Wickelgren>   Wickelgren, W.A., Context-sensitive Coding, Associative Memory and Serial Order in (Speech) Behaviour, Psychological Review 76, (1969), pp. 1 – 15

IMPLEMENTING SOFT PREFERENCES FOR STRUCTURAL DISAMBIGUATION

Noel E. Sharkey[1]
Department of Computer Science
University of Exeter
Devon, U.K.

A simulation is presented here that demonstrates how a standard BP net, taking whole sentences as input, may be trained to perform a structural disambiguation task and to generalise to novel examples. It is argued that, during learning, the net implements *raw* attachment preferences in the relationship between the upper and lower weights. An analysis is provided of how these preferences are implemented, and it is shown how each individual word may be assigned a raw preference value (RPV) which may be used as an indicator of its structural bias. Moreover, it is shown how the activation function makes use of the raw preferences by modulating their strength of their biases in a manner that is contextually sensitive to the structural biases of all the other words in a sentence.

A major stumbling block in the automation of natural language processing is that natural language is pervasively ambiguous i.e. there is a one-to-many mapping between surface strings and their representations. Consider the sentence: "The groundsman chased the girl with a large stick."; the prepositional-phrase (PP), *with a large stick*, is attached directly to the verb-phrase (VP), and the sentence may be bracketed: ((The old man) (chased (the girl) (with a large stick))) i.e. the groundsman had the stick and he chased the girl with it. But this sentence cannot be parsed on the basis of syntactic information alone. This is because syntactically equivalent substitutions within the sentence affect the syntactic structure. For example, if "long hair" is substituted for "large stick", the result is that the PP, *with long hair*, would now be attached to the noun-phrase (NP) *the girl* instead of the VP. The new bracketing would be: ((The groundsman) (chased (the girl (with long hair)))) i.e the girl had the long hair and she was being chased by the groundsman. Thus, it appears that contextual variable can influence the assignment of syntactic structure.

Some linguists have attempted to develop parsing rules for getting round the problem of structural ambiguity. For example, Kimball (1973) used Right Association in which the preferred attachment was to the directly preceding noun; and Frazier and Fodor (1978) used Minimal Attachment in which the parse prefers an attachment in which the minimal number of nodes are created in the parse tree. Other linguists and AI researchers have attempted to solve the structural problem by attributing a more important role to the lexicon during parsing. The best attempted solutions have involved introducing syntactic preference rules (e.g. Ford, Bresnan, and Kaplan, 1982), or semantic preference rules (e.g. Wilks, Huang, and Fass, 1985) into the lexicon. Nonetheless, it has proved difficult to develop rules that do not demand continual updating to handle new examples. And it is difficult to find a *sufficient* set of syntactic and/or semantic features.

---

[1]This project was funded by an award from the British Telecom Research Laboratories at Martlesham Heath (under the CONNEX iniative). I would like to thank Richard Sutcliffe (RA on the project) for running the simulation and Paul Day for conducting the normative study. I would also like to acknowledge Don Mitchell, Ajit Narayanan, and Peter Wyard for their support and suggestions.

The aim of the present paper is to explore how lexical preference rules can be learned from a sample set of sentences. To begin, a simulation is described in which a standard BP net (2-layer) learns to bracket input sentences into NP or VP attachments. This was done to find out if the learned representations could capture contextual regularities underlying the attachment task. Next, the net is analysed to find ways in which to characterise the "soft" preference rules associated with the input vocabulary. First, the *raw* or *static* preferences are discussed in terms of Euclidean distances between the lower and upper weights in the learned net. It is shown how these distances can be used to assign raw preference values (RPVs) for individual words. Second, the *dynamics* of the soft preference rules[2] are discussed by examining how they operate during the processing of entire sentences. It is after all not individual words that determine a particular attachment, but their interactions with the other words in the sentences containing them.

A SIMULATION

The task was to take five-word sentences as input and compute correct structural interpretations (bracketing) as output. Two input sentences and their target bracketings are shown in Example 1. There were two major components in this task: (i) mapping the input words onto the output (the autoassociative task); and (ii) bracketing the output string (the structuring task) for either noun-phrase attachment (NPA) or verb-phrase attachment (VPA).

<u>Example 1. A simplified bracketing for NP and VP attachments</u>

John hit dog in market -> (John (hit (dog in market)))

John hit woman with stick -> (John (hit woman (with stick)))

Materials. The sentence materials were made up from 29 words, shown in Table 1, distributed in the categories NOUN1, VERB, NOUN2, PREPOSITION, NOUN3. This word set was used to generate all possible 1048 strings. These strings were subjected to a human normative study with the result that the corpus was reduced to 173 meaningful sentences for training the net (55 NPA and 118 VPA sentences). A further 16 sentences (8 NPA and 8 VPA) were reserved for testing generalisation.

For input and output, a simple localist representation was chosen for each word and bracket. To preserve the structure of the input and output strings, the vector frame method (e.g. Hinton, 1981) was employed. In this method the input vectors were conceptually divided into five partitions representing slots in a sentence frame: NOUN1, VERB, NOUN2, PREPOSITION, NOUN3. The units in each partition represent the possible slot fillers[3]. Thus the five-word input sentences[4]

---

[2]See McMillan & Smolensky, 1988; and Hanson & Burr, in press, for alternative discussions on the implementation of rules in connectionist nets.

[3]There are serious restrictions with this type of representation (cf Sharkey, 1990 - this volume), however, in the current context, it serves the useful purpose of making the input and output representations easier to analyse.

[4]Extraneous elements such as articles were removed from the sentences. The word order was also held constant to enable the learning algorithm to concentrate on the main task of separating the attachments without having to develop other syntactic constraints. Such cannonical representations could easily be produced by an initial parse.

were encoded in an *n* dimensional binary input vector (the vector frame) such that five elements were set to +1 (one in each partition) and *n* - 5 were set to 0. The output targets consisted of a vector representation of five words from the corresponding input sentence and 5 brackets. Only two different output bracketings were employed; one for noun-phrase attachments and one for verb-phrase attachments.

Noun1	Verb	Noun2	Prep	Noun3
John	played	woman	by	stick
	made	music	with	child
	hit	dog	in	market
	saw	money	on	demand
				telescope
				ear
				mate
				subway
				stage
				anger
				night
				park
				radio
				fraud
				lottery
				room

Table 1. The words used to generate the training samples

Architecture and learning. The back propagation learning algorithm (Rumelhart, Hinton, & Williams, 1986) was employed in a network architecture consisting of two weight layers and three layers of units (29-20-36) as shown in Figure 1. The required number of hidden units was determined[5], after some experimentation, to be twenty.

Results. With a learning rate of 0.1 and a momentum term of 0.5, both the autoassociative and structural components of the task were learned, for all 173 sentences in the training set, in 1730 training cycles.

After the learning was completed, generalisation was tested by presenting 16 novel test sentences to the net for a forward pass with no weight adjustments. The test set consisted of 8 pairs of novel sentences. These were chosen such that each sentence in a pair differed from its partner by only one word which flipped the attachments. Two pairs of sentences differed on VERB, two on NOUN2, two on PREPOSITION, and two on NOUN3.

After each test sentence was presented, the states of the output vector were examined for the preferred attachment. Since novel examples produce weaker output signals, the acceptance criteria for a unit to adopt the +1 state was gradually reduced until a complete bracketed structure appeared in the output. The learned representations proved to be general enough to correctly bracket for the input for 11 out of the 16 test sentences. This was reasonably powerful

---

[5]There is a newly published technique for dynamically reducing the number of hidden units to a minimum (Mozer & Smolensky, 1989).

generalisation, given the difficulty of the novel test set and the small size of the experimental sample.

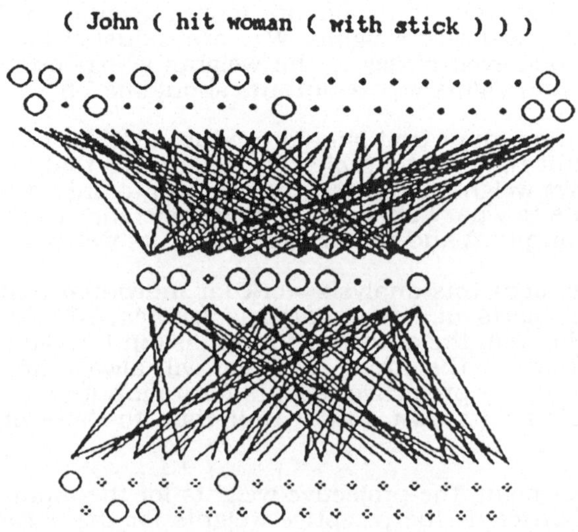

Figure 1 is a diagram of the learned net with circles representing the units - their size indicates their current activity level. The lines between the circles represent weighted connections. The state of the net shows its activation after presentation of the sentence "John hit woman with stick."

ANALYSIS OF PREFERENCES

The first question to be addressed in this section is, what is the causal role of the individual words in the task of disambiguating the structures. Answering this question presents a potentially difficult problem, because the net only ever saw the words in complete sentences, and it was the complete sentences that were the patterns to be classified. So the problem amounts to finding a way to extricate the influence of individual words from the influence of the sentences that contain them.

One approach to this problem begins by examining the relationship between the upper and lower weights in the BP net. My argument is that the development of this relationship during learning implements a set of "soft preferences" that take on the role of lexical preference rules in Simulation 1. In this view, each word has, in a sense, a weighted preference that is used to "vote" for one of the attachments. However, unlike standard preference rules, the strength of a word's vote may change according to the company it keeps i.e. the other words in the sentence.

The importance of weight relationships may be clarified by briefly examining their development during learning. In the forward operation of the net, the input vector $\mathbf{v}$ is mapped onto the hidden unit vector $\mathbf{h}$ by the squash function $S:\mathbf{W}_1\mathbf{v} \rightarrow \mathbf{h}$ (where S is $1/1+e^{-x}$, and $x = \mathbf{W}_1\mathbf{v}$). Then $\mathbf{h}$ is mapped onto the output vector $\mathbf{o}$ using the same squash function on the upper weight matrix: $S:\mathbf{W}_2\mathbf{h} \rightarrow \mathbf{o}$. Next, $\mathbf{o}$ is compared with the target vector $\mathbf{t}$ to determine its correctness. If $0 > \mathbf{t} - \mathbf{o} > 0$ then, in the backward operation, the error correction procedure adjusts the weights matrices $\mathbf{W}_1$ and $\mathbf{W}_2$ such that $\mathbf{o}$ is closer to $\mathbf{t}$.

In order to understand how the preferences are implemented in the weights, it is instructive to view the learning process geometrically. First, the upper weights, W_2, are adjusted so that the weight vectors for output units that want to be 'on' are moved closer to the current vector of hidden unit activations; and weight vectors for outputs that want to be 'off' are moved away from the current hidden unit vector. Second, the lower weights, W_1, are adjusted to push the vector of hidden unit activations even closer to the weights whose outputs should be 'on' and further away from weights whose outputs should be 'off'.

The upshot is that if an input unit should produce a "1" as output on unit A, and a "0" as ouput on unit B, then the projective weights for that input unit should be closer to the receptive weights of output unit A than to output unit B. This weight relationship amounts to what I shall call a "soft preference rule". That is, the input unit weights prefer output A and so moves closer to its weights.

Now the question is, does this analysis work for individual units (words) that are always employed as parts of larger patterns (sentences)? We can find out by examining the results from the autoassociation task in the Simulation. Recall that any word that appears in the input sentence will always appear in the ouput. Thus, for a given word, the projective weights for its input unit should be closer to the receptive weights for its own output unit than to those of any other output units.

To support this latter point, the projective weights for the input units were plotted in the same weight space as the receptive weights for the output units. Then the squared Euclidean distance was computed from each input projective weight vector to each output receptive weight vector. An example of this analysis is given in Appendix 1 for the input word "saw". Input-saw is much closer to output-saw than to any other output word in the vocabulary list. This distance result was replicated across all input words with only one exception (input-made was slightly closer to output-ear (65.22) than to output-made (68.67) for which I presently have no explanation).

What the above analysis of the relationship between the upper and lower weights tells us is that the input words have a raw or static preference for producing themselves as output. This is not really surprising, but it enables us to take the next step in working out the preferences for the structuring task. First it should be noted that the structural interpretation is really carried by the positioning of the third bracket in the output. For verb-phrase attachment, the third bracket appears just before the preposition e.g. (John (hit woman (with stick))); whereas for noun-phrase attachment, the third bracket appears just before the subject noun e.g. (John (hit (dog in market))). We would expect these brackets to develop mutually exclusive receptive weight representations during learning. This is borne out by an examination of the weights developed in Simulation 1 as shown in Table 2. Each weight in the noun-phrase vector is approximately equal in magnitude, but in the opposite direction, to each weight in the verb-phrase vector.

To analyse the attachment preferences for each of the input words, their projective weight vectors were plotted in the same space as the receptive weight vectors of the attachment brackets (shown in Table 2). Then the squared Euclidean distance was computed between each of the projective vectors and the two receptive vectors (the results are shown in Appendix 2).

	1	2	3	4	5	6	7	8	9	10
NPA	+7.5	−3.7	−5.3	−2.2	−2.6	+5.6	−0.3	−2.9	−0.6	+2.9
VPA	−7.4	+3.7	+5.0	+2.1	+2.1	−5.8	+0.2	+2.8	+0.4	−2.9

	11	12	13	14	15	16	17	18	19	20
NPA	−1.0	+3.6	−1.6	−7.9	−1.8	−1.0	−4.3	+2.5	+1.3	+6.1
VPA	+0.7	−3.6	+1.3	+8.0	+1.4	+1.1	+4.3	−2.5	−1.3	−6.3

Table 2. The receptive weights for the brackets responsible for noun-phrase attachments (NPA) and verb-phrase attachments (VPA) - rounded to one decimal place. The integers across the top indicate the hidden unit numbers.

In this way, it is possible to tell whether a given input word preferred (was closer to) the noun-phrase or verb-phrase attachment bracketing. The distribution of preferences across word classes is given in Table 3.

CLASS	NPA	VPA
VERBS	2	2
NOUN1	2	2
PREPS	2	2
NOUN3	9	7

Table 3. Distribution of the attachment preferences across the various word classes used in Simulation 1

Despite a heavy bias in the training set (118 VPA versus 55 NPA sentences), the word preferences were fairly equally divided between the two attachment classes with NPA = 15, and VPA = 13. Thus the net appears to compensate for the unbalanced training set. However it should be noted that the numbers in Table 2 do not represent absolute preferences. The projective weights for some words may be very close to the receptive weights for one of the brackets and far from the other. For example, from Appendix 2, it can be seen that the weights for the word "saw" are much closer to the NPA bracket (15.23) than they are to the VPA bracket (20.71). In contrast, some words, such as "money" may be almost the same distance from the NPA bracket (18.28) and the VPA bracket (18.09) with a slight bias towards VPA. Obviously, some means must be developed for indicating the strength of a word's preference. As a first step, we define the *raw preference value* (RPV) of a word as difference between the Euclidean distances, d, between the two brackets i.e. RPV = d_{NPA} - d_{VPA}. Using this calculation, the RPV for "saw" is 5.48_n and the RPV for "money" is 0.19_v. These values clearly reflect the relative static biases of the two words. The RPV for all the words used here are given in Appendix 2.

The reason why some words exhibit weak preferences is because during learning they may be combined with other words which already have strong preferences in the target direction. Consequently, there may be only a very small change in the weights, and, as a result, weak or uncommited words would have little or no room to acquire strong preferences. For example, the word "money" appears more than twice as often in VPA sentences (39 times) than it does in NPA sentences (18 times) and yet it has only a very small VPA preference (RPV = 0.19_v). This is because out of its 53 appearances it occurs as the subject of the strongly NPA verb "saw" (RPV_{saw} = 5.48_n) twenty-three times, and as subject of the strongly VPA verb "money" (RPV_{made} = 5.05_v) thirty-two times. Thus "made" had no room to develop strong preferences.

In the main, these raw preferences work very well. It is possible to estimate the particular attachment of a sentence simply by summing the values for the noun preferences and subtracting them from the sum of the verb preferences. If the sum is positive, the sentence is VPA, and if it is negative, the sentence is NPA. Surprisingly, this provides the correct answer for a large proportion of the training sample and exhibits as good generalisation properties as the net itself. However, like any static preferences, it fails because it is not sensitive to contextual change. Such a failure is shown in Example 2.

Example 2. Using RPVs for sentences.

```
(.66_v)      (5.48_n)     (0.19_v)     (0.86_v)      (1.76_n)
S1: John      saw          money        on           telescope.
```

Total RVP_{S1} = 5.53_n - correct NPA

```
(.66_v)      (5.48_n)     (0.19_v)     (3.41_v)      (1.76_n)
S2: John      saw          money        with         telescope.
```

Total RVP_{S2} = 2.98_n - incorrect NPA (should be VPA)

The two sentences in the example differ only on the the prepositions "on" and "with". The preposition "with" should change the role of "telescope" to be the instrument of the seeing rather than the surface on which the money sits. Although the RPV_{with} has a relative strong VPA value, it is not strong enough to overpower the RPV_{saw} which keeps the sentence as an NPA. If the sentence had been "John saw money in night", then "night" would overpower "saw" and the sentence would be VPA. However, to be flexible enough, the system needs a dynamic way in which to assign preferences. This facility is already built into the operation of the net as we shall now see.

Dynamic preference values.

In order to see how the attachment preference of a word modulates according to context, it is necessary to examine the function that maps the input states onto the hidden units. The function used in the simulation was the non-linear (but monotonic) sigmoidal function: $1/1+e^{-x}$, where x = sigma $w_{ij}a_i$ + bias, w_{ij} is the weight from the ith input unit to the jth hidden unit, and a_i is the activation state of the ith input unit. Now, if the activation value of a hidden unit was determined by a linear combination of the binary input activation, then we could say that the preference value of an input unit in the +1 state was simply the value of the weight from it to the hidden unit. However, because the combination is non-linear we must use a less direct method to compute the preferred attachment of a word in a sentence.

Let f be the sigmoid function, $\mathbf{x}$ is a vector of the weighted sums of the input activations and biases for a sentence S, and $\mathbf{x}'$ is a vector of the weighted sums of the input activations and biases of S - k, i.e. the input sentence S with the kth word deleted. Then the dynamic preference value, v, of unit k to the hidden unit vector is given by:

$$v^k = f(\mathbf{x}) - f(\mathbf{x}')$$

We are now in a position to understand how sentence contexts affect the magnitude of a word's preference vote. To simplify matters, we shall examine a net with only one hidden unit, and with the weighted value of the kth input unit held constant at 0.5 A graph of the inputs and corresponding outputs of the hidden unit is shown in Figure 2. To find out how the magnitude of x' affects v^k, an arbitrary point on the horizontal axis of the graph in Figure 2 is chosen for x', the horizontal coordinate for x is then $x' + 0.5$. The vertical axis gives us $f(x)$ and $f(x')$.

Note that the steepest increase is from $f(x')$ to $f(x)$, and hence the largest value of v^k is when $x' = 0$. The size of v^k diminishes progressively on both sides of zero.

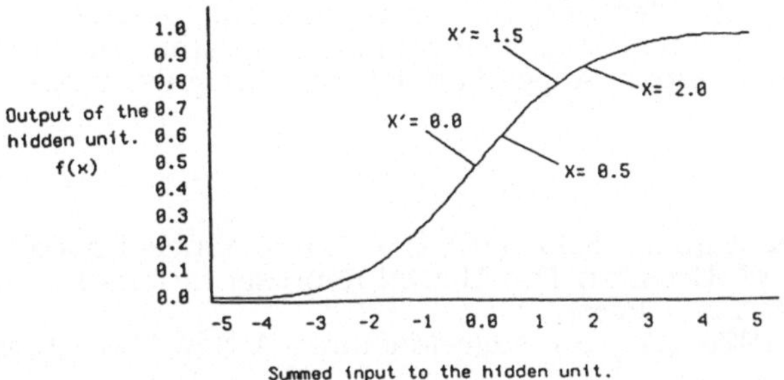

Figure 2. A plot of the inputs and outputs to a hidden unit

Now that we have seen how dynamic preferences operate, we shall return to examine the sentences in Example 2 in the previous section (S1: John saw money *on* telescope. S2: John saw money *with* telescope.) It was noted, in the previous section, that the raw preference values were defeated by their inflexibility for these sentences. The problem was that the word "saw" had a very strong RPV which could not be overpowered by the change in prepositions. We now show how the dynamic preferences for the word "saw" are modulated by the change in prepositions (see Example 2). For illustration, we shall use hidden unit 1. As can be seen in Table 2, hidden unit 1 has the largest positive weight to the NPA bracket and the largest negative weight to the VPA bracket. Thus it has a potentially large say in biasing the attachment towards NPA.

For sentence S1 (Example 2), the preference strength for "saw" on hidden unit 1 is $v^{saw} = f(3.49) - f(1.88) = 0.10$; and for sentence S2, it is $v^{saw} = f(4.61) - f(3.00) = 0.04$. These figures show a 60% reduction in the preference strength of "saw" from S1 to S2. Using such contexual modulation on all of the hidden units, the net computes the correct alternative output bracketing for both of the sentences even though they were not part of the training set. It is the ability to modulate the preference value of the input words that gives the net its ability on the structural disambiguation tasks.

CONCLUSIONS

The simulation presented here demonstrates how a standard BP net may be trained to perform a structural disambiguation task and how it learns to generalise to novel examples. Even though the net was trained on whole sentences it was shown that it implemented raw preferences, foreach word, in the relationship between the upper and lower weights during learning. The analysis of how the raw preferences were implemented was used to assign an RPV to words that indicates the strength of their structural bias. The addition of RPVs for the the words in a sentence, turned out to produce a reasonable estimate for the correct structural assignment of a sentence. However, for many cases, like those in Example 2, the rigidity of the raw preferences prevented correct assignment.

This rigidity is overcome in the normal operation of the net; by the nature of the activation function. We showed how the activation function utilises the raw preference in a way that is sensitive to sentence context; minor word changes in a sentence can lead to dramatic changes in the preference strength of a word. This is just the type of flexibility that is required from lexical preference rules if they are to structurally disambiguate a large variety of sentences. This work is only a preliminary investigation of the idea of a net containing soft preference rules. So far the idea seems like a promising one for making a start on training the preference rules required for a wider range of structural ambiguity tasks.

References.

Ford, M., Bresnan, J.W. & Kaplan, R.M. (1982) A Competence Based Theory of Syntactic Closure. In J.W. Bresnan The Mental Representation of Grammatical Relations. Cambridge, MA:MIT Press.

Frazier, L. & Fodor, J.D. (1978) The Sausage Machine. A New Two-stage Parsing Model. Cognition 6.

Hanson, S.J. & Burr, D.J. (in press) What Connectionist Models Learn: Learning and Representation in Connectionist Networks. Behavioral and Brain Sciences, New York:CUP.

Hinton, G.E. (1981) Implementing Semantic Networks in Parallel Hardware. In G.E. Hinton & J.A. Anderson (Eds) Parallel Models of Associative Memory. Hillsdale, N.J.:Lawrence Erlbaum.

Kimball, J. (1973) Seven Principles of Surface Structure Parsing in Natural Language. Cognition 2.

McMillan, C. & Smolensky, P. (1988) Analyzing a Connectionist Model as a System of Soft Rules. Technical Report CU-CS-393-88, University of Colorado, Boulder.

Mozer, M.C. & Smolensky, P. (1989) Using Relevance to Reduce Network Size Automatically. Connection Science 1.1.

Rumelhart, D.E., Hinton, G.E. & Williams, R.J. (1986) Learning Internal Representations by Error Propagation. In D.E. Rumelhart & J.L. McClelland (Eds) Parallel Distributed Processing Volume 1. Cambridge, MA: MIT.

Wilks, Y. Huang, X. & Fass, D. (1985) Syntax, Preference and Right Attachment. Proceedings of IJCAI.

APPENDIX 1: The squared Euclidean distance between the projective weight vector for the input word "saw" and the receptive weight vectors for all of the output words in Simulation 1.

```
OUTPUT WORDS       Squared Euclidean (rounded)

played              199
made                220
hit                 210
saw                  62  *****
woman               161
music               180
dog                 157
money               166
by                  169
with                171
in                  166
on                  140
stick               132
child               149
market              147
demand              149
telescope           128
ear                 136
mate                136
subway              145
stage               131
anger               206
night               152
park                129
radio               128
fraud               122
lottery             131
room                180
```

APPENDIX 2: The squared Euclidean distance between the projective weight vector for each of the input words and the recptive weight vectors for the NPA and VPA brackets.

```
INPUT WORDS      Euclidean d.
```

INPUT WORDS	NPA	VPA	RPV
John	17.83	17.17	0.66v
played	19.6	16.4	3.10v
made	20.35	15.3	5.05v
hit	17.09	19.31	2.23n
saw	15.23	20.71	5.48n
woman	17.61	18.65	1.05n
music	19.16	17.12	2.04v
dog	17.83	18.71	0.88n
money	18.28	18.09	0.19v
by	17.32	19.34	2.02n
with	19.72	16.31	3.41v
in	17.86	18.49	0.63n
on	18.41	17.55	0.86v
stick	17.26	19.36	2.10n
child	13.89	22.47	8.58n
market	19.18	18.19	0.99v
demand	21.79	14.83	6.96v
telescope	17.35	19.10	1.76n
ear	20.12	16.00	4.12v
mate	16.88	19.42	2.53n
subway	19.08	17.83	1.25v
stage	17.26	19.36	2.10n
anger	20.10	16.22	3.88v
night	22.00	14.76	7.24v
park	19.54	18.38	1.16v
radio	17.61	19.26	1.65n
fraud	17.66	19.16	1.49n
lottery	16.73	19.82	3.09n
room	18.38	18.89	0.51n

WORKSHOP:
Massiver Parallelismus und Kognition
Massive Parallelism and Cognition

Organisator und Leiter: C. Lischka

ADAPTIVE LOOK-AHEAD PLANNING

Sebastian Thrun[†‡] · Knut Möller[‡] · Alexander Linden[†]

[†]German National Research Center for Computer Science
D–5205 St. Augustin, Postfach 1240, F.R.G.
e-mail: st@gmdzi.uucp, al@gmdzi.uucp

[‡]University of Bonn
Department of Computer Science
D–5300 Bonn, Römerstr. 164, F.R.G.

Abstract

We present a new adaptive connectionist planning method. By interaction with an environment
a world model is progressively constructed using the backpropagation learning algorithm. The
planner constructs a look-ahead plan by iteratively using this model to predict future reinforcements. Future reinforcement is maximized to derive suboptimal plans, thus determining good
actions directly from the knowledge of the model network (strategic level). This is done by
gradient descent in action space.

The problem of finding good initial plans is solved by the use of an "experience" network
(intuition level). The appropriateness of this planning method for finding suboptimal actions
in unknown environments is demonstrated with a target tracking problem.

Keywords: planning, reinforcement learning, temporal credit assignment problem, gradient descent, target
tracking

Introduction

Undoubtedly planning is an important and powerful concept in problem solving [12]. Planning concerns
the synthesization of a sequence of actions to achieve a specific goal.

Connectionist approaches so far rely on an associative mapping, which selects good actions given environmental state descriptions. These are based on the interaction of a world model and an action generating
network [1, 2, 6, 10, 11, 14, 15, 20]. We recognize three major problems with these approaches:

1. Since no explicit consideration of the future is made, future effects of actions must be directly encoded
   into this world model mapping, thus model learning becomes complicated.

2. After learning the integration of additional constraints is not possible.

3. While the model network is an essential part of the training of the action network, the learning of
   the latter lags behind that of the former.

In this paper we present a new connectionist planning procedure. Our model network learns one-step predictions by observing the environmental mapping [2, 6, 11]. In this way training information is immediately
available and model learning is easier and faster. With such a model network a look-ahead plan is constructed and subsequently optimized. We demonstrate the performance of this planning procedure through
simulations on a target tracking problem.

Reinforcement Learning

In common supervised learning tasks usually an explicit target pattern is known for each situation. E.g.
if we train a network to find optimal actions in a controlling task, supervised learning can only be used if
these optimal actions are known to the teacher. However, when supervised learning is used for tasks where
only a simple reinforcement signal is received, then the optimal actions (the targets) are not known a priori.
Instead this reinforcement signal evaluates all past actions: the better the actions of the past, the better the

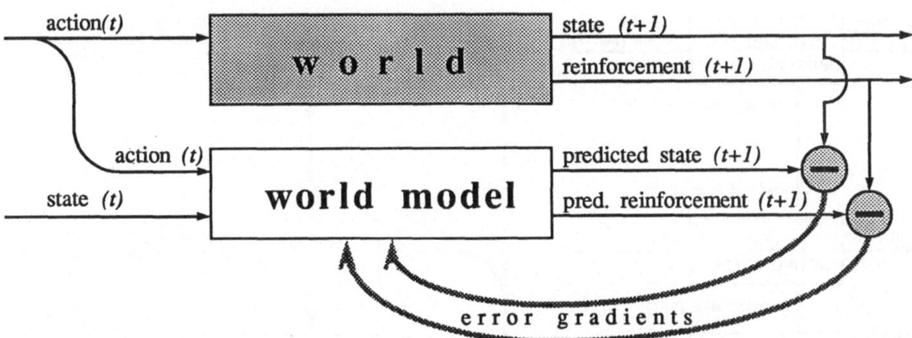

Figure 1: Training of the world model by error comparison and backpropagation. The model is learning to predict subsequent world states and reinforcements.

reinforcement. Since the reinforcement is an unstructured overall signal, the problem with reinforcement learning tasks is the assignment of particular reinforcements to particular actions in the past. This problem is called the *temporal credit assignment problem*.

Many approaches use a network which solves this problem directly [1, 11, 17]. This network, the controller network, learns to generate actions that optimize the whole future reinforcement. Obviously the quality of actions depends strongly on future actions. Thus if the controller generates an action, future actions are implicitly contained in this decision.

The planning procedure presented in this paper does not solve the temporal credit assignment problem directly, although the experience network described below can be considered as a solution for this problem. Instead of assigning a quality value to each possible action, actions are optimized by a look-ahead planning procedure which optimizes actions with respect to the next N reinforcements. This implies the assumption that the effect of a certain action to the reinforcement occurs in the next N time steps – similar assumptions are also made in [1, 17]. N can be an arbitrary number – the computational costs of the optimization steps are linear in N. Moreover, N can be determined at planning time dynamically.

The World and the World Model

Planning is a hypothetical process, in which future states and future actions are involved. If we consider future events for finding optimal actions, it is not sufficient to work with the real world only. Indeed, some kind of a world model is demanded, which learns gradually to mimic the qualities of the real world. The training of this world model is a system identification task.

In this paper, we use a multilayer differentiable, non-recurrent connectionist network for modeling the world (c.f. figure 1). This network is trained by backpropagation to predict the behavior of the world [1, 2, 6, 10, 14, 20].

Formally, the world considered in this paper is defined as a mapping, which maps an action vector $\vec{a}(t)$ with a current state $\vec{s}(t)$ to a subsequent state $\vec{s}(t+1)$ and reinforcement $\vec{r}(t+1)$. Before training, the mapping of the world is unknown. Hence by exploring the world we obtain training information for the world model: if we change the world's state at time $\vec{s}(t)$ by an arbitrary action $\vec{a}(t)$ (e.g. random action), we obtain a subsequent state vector $\vec{s}(t+1)$ and a corresponding reinforcement $\vec{r}(t+1)$. These signals are used as a teacher signal for training the world model. At the same time we use the model network for predicting the state $\vec{s}_{pred}(t+1)$ and reinforcement $\vec{r}_{pred}(t+1)$. If we compare predicted and real state and reinforcement, we can compute an error gradient, which is used for adapting the internal parameters of the model network – namely the weights and the biases – in order to decrease the prediction error (c.f. figure 1). This is done by propagating the error back through the network using the backpropagation algorithm [16, 18].

Adaptive Look-Ahead-Planning

The planning procedure presented in this paper is an approximation procedure, which starts with a initial plan and improves this plan stepwise by gradient descent in order to maximize the next N reinforcements. Let us assume we have such an initial N-step look-ahead plan. This is a sequence of proposed actions for

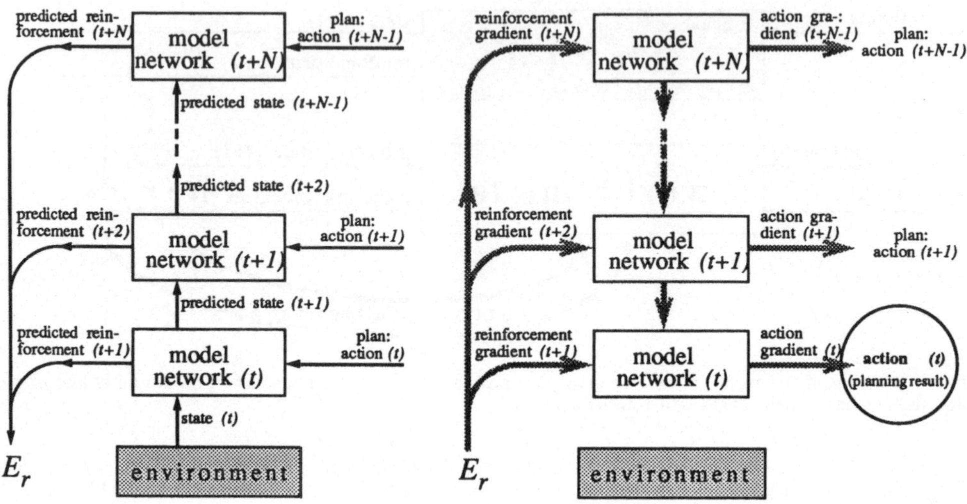

Figure 2: Planning with a chain of adaptive model networks. The black arrows indicate the activation stream, the grey arrows the energy gradient flow. With the actual world state the reinforcement for the next N steps is predicted with respect to a plan. Then the plan is changed in small steps in order to maximize the reinforcement.

the next N time steps starting at the actual time t:

$$\vec{a}_{plan}(t), \vec{a}_{plan}(t+1), ..., \vec{a}_{plan}(t+N-1).$$

(Some heuristics for obtaining initial plans are explained below.)

Now we can use the model network for predicting the subsequent state $\vec{s}_{pred}(t+1)$ and reinforcement $\vec{r}_{pred}(t+1)$. If we assume that this prediction is a good approximation of the real state, we can build up a chain of N copies of the model network for forecasting the next $N-1$ states and reinforcements (c.f. figure 2). Thus we obtain a prediction for all reinforcements

$$\vec{r}_{pred}(t+1), \vec{r}_{pred}(t+2), ..., \vec{r}_{pred}(t+N)$$

in this look-ahead window.

For improving the actions with respect to the predicted reinforcement we use a gradient descent algorithm in action space [7, 8, 19], which will be derived in detail in the next section. It computes the gradients of the reinforcement with respect to the plan, which give us the information, how to change the plan in small steps in order to improve its performance.

The whole procedure described above is to be repeated. After a fixed time or if convergence is observed the algorithm is terminated and the first action of the resulting plan $\vec{a}_{plan}(t)$, the result of the planning procedure, is executed from the environment

$$\vec{a}(t) \;=\; \vec{a}_{plan}(t).$$

This action is a (sub-)optimal action, i.e. which yields (sub-)optimal reinforcement regarding the current model network.

In the next section we derive a feed-forward algorithm for computing the desired gradients and then we discuss how to obtain initial plans.

The Feed-Forward Algorithm for Gradient Search in Action Space

As mentioned above the environment is modeled by a non-recurrent multilayer backpropagation network. This restriction is sufficient for our simulation results – the extension of the algorithm to recurrent networks [3, 4, 5, 9, 13, 14, 15, 21] is straightforward and shown in [18].

The external input of the world model network is a state vector $\vec{s}(t)$ and an action vector $\vec{a}(t)$. Both state and action vector are the external input $\vec{I}(t)$ of the model network; for all non-input units this external input is 0. The output of the network is the predicted state and the predicted reinforcement, thus the number of input units, which receive state values, is equal to the corresponding output units – this is crucial for concatenating the world models.

Let the activation function of each unit be given by

$$x_k(t) = \sigma_k(net_k(t)) + I_k(t) \quad \text{with} \quad net_k(t) = \sum_j w_{kj} x_j(t) + \theta_k. \tag{1}$$

Here $x_k(t)$ denotes the activation value of unit k at time t, w_{kj} the weight from unit j to unit k, θ_k the bias of unit k, $I_k(t)$ the external input of unit k at time t and σ_k denotes an arbitrary differentiable squashing function, usually $\sigma_k(net_k(t)) = (1 + e^{-net_k(t)})^{-1}$.

Let us assume that we have some initial plan. As described in figure 2, the actual state of the world $\vec{s}(t)$ and the actions of the plan are propagated through the chain of models using the activation function (1). Note that the external input $I_i(t+s)$ for each state input unit i of the sth copy of the model network ($1 \le s \le N-1$) is fed with the activation $x_{i'}(t+s-1)$ of the corresponding state output unit i' of the preceding model copy. The external action input $I_j(t+s)$ is fed with the corresponding action $a_{j'}(t+s)$ of the plan.

Unlike the state predictions, which are used directly in the plan evaluation chain, the reinforcement predictions $\vec{r}_{pred}(t+\tau)$ ($1 \le \tau \le N$) are used for optimizing the performance of the plan. In order to improve these future reinforcements we define a *reinforcement energy function* E_r:

$$
\begin{aligned}
E_r \;&=\; \tfrac{1}{2} \sum_{\tau=1}^{N} (\vec{r}_{opt} - \vec{r}_{pred}(t+\tau)) \cdot I\vec{g}(\tau - 1) \cdot (\vec{r}_{opt} - \vec{r}_{pred}(t+\tau))^T \\
&=\; \tfrac{1}{2} \sum_{\tau=0}^{N-1} \sum_{k} g_k(\tau)(r_{opt,k} - x_k(t+\tau))^2
\end{aligned}
\tag{2}
$$

(this holds since the predicted reinforcement $\vec{r}_{pred}(t+\tau)$ is the activation of some output units $x_k(t+\tau-1)$, c.f. figure 2.) Here I is the identity matrix, $\vec{g}$ is a weighting function, in the simplest case $\vec{g} \equiv (1, ..., 1)$, and $\vec{r}_{opt}$ is the *optimal* reinforcement, e.g. $\vec{r}_{opt} = (1, ..., 1)$.

In the sequel we show how to compute the gradients of E_r with respect to the plan. These tell us how to change the actions of the plan in order to improve the predicted reinforcement, thus how to optimize the plan with respect to our world model.

One way of computing the gradients of E_r with respect to the actions is using backpropagation through the spatial unfolded time-structure [16, 19]. Since no dynamical determination of the plan length N is possible by using this backpropagation-in-time technique, we will derive a pure feed-forward algorithm for computing these gradients.

Let us define the gradient of each activation x_k with respect to the external input $I_i(t+s)$ by

$$\xi_{is}^{k}(\tau) \;\equiv\; \frac{\partial x_k}{\partial I_i(t+s)}(t+\tau). \tag{3}$$

If we know these gradients for all input units i, all reinforcement prediction units k and all time steps $s, \tau \in \{0, 1, ..., N-1\}$ we can compute the desired gradients for changing the actions with the stepsize $\eta > 0$:

$$
\begin{aligned}
\Delta I_i(t+s) \;&=\; -\eta \frac{\partial E_r}{\partial I_i(t+s)} \\
&=\; \eta \sum_{\tau=0}^{N-1} \sum_{k} g_k(\tau)(r_{opt,k} - x_k(t+\tau)) \cdot \frac{\partial x_k}{\partial I_i(t+s)}(t+\tau) \\
&=\; \eta \sum_{\tau=0}^{N-1} \sum_{k} g_k(\tau)(r_{opt,k} - x_k(t+\tau)) \cdot \xi_{is}^{k}(\tau)
\end{aligned}
\tag{4}
$$

It remains to show how to compute these $\xi_{is}^{k}(\tau)$.

Obviously $\xi_{is}^k(\tau) = 0$ holds for all $s > \tau$, since no activation depends on a future action. For all τ, for *all* units k and for all $s \leq \tau$ $\xi_{is}^k(\tau)$ can be propagated forward through the network by[1]

$$\xi_{is}^k(\tau) \overset{(1)}{=} \frac{\partial \sigma_k(net_k(t+\tau))}{\partial I_i(t+s)} + \frac{\partial I_k(t+\tau)}{\partial I_i(t+s)}$$

$$= \sigma_k'(net_k(t+\tau)) \sum_j w_{kj} \frac{\partial x_j}{\partial I_i(t+s)}(t+\tau) + \delta_{ik}\delta_{s\tau}$$

$$= \sigma_k'(net_k(t+\tau)) \sum_j w_{kj}\xi_{is}^j(\tau) + \delta_{ik}\delta_{s\tau} \tag{5}$$

Since at non-recurrent multilayer networks input units receive only external input (i.e. $net_k \equiv 0$) and the remaining units, the hidden and output units, receive only internal input ($I_k \equiv 0$), (5) reduces to:

$$k \text{ action input unit:} \quad \xi_{is}^k(\tau) = \delta_{ik}\delta_{s\tau}$$

$$k \text{ no input unit:} \quad \xi_{is}^k(\tau) = \sigma_k'(net_k(t+\tau)) \sum_j w_{kj}\xi_{is}^j(\tau) \tag{6}$$

So far, we have derived a rule for propagating gradients through one copy of the model network, namely to derive the gradients of the output activations from those of the input units. It remains to state a propagation rule for propagating these gradients forward through the whole chain of model networks. Since the state prediction $\vec{s}_{pred}(t+\tau)$ is used as the state input $\vec{s}(t+\tau+1)$ for the next time step, for each state input unit k and the corresponding state output unit k' the gradients are equivalent:

$$k \text{ state input unit:} \quad \xi_{is}^k(\tau) = \xi_{is}^{k'}(\tau-1) \tag{7}$$

With the equations (6) and (7) the gradients of the reinforcement energy function with respect to all actions of the plan are computed. According to (4) these actions are changed in small steps in order to decrease E_τ:

$$\vec{a}_i(t+s) \longleftarrow \vec{a}_i(t+s) - \eta \frac{\partial E_\tau}{\partial I_{i'}(t+s)} \tag{8}$$

for all action vector components i, the corresponding input units i' of the model network and all plan steps $s \leq N-1$.

Variable Plan Lengths

The advantage of our feed-forward algorithm unlike backpropagation-through-time is the possibility to determine plan lengths dynamically at planning time. During construction of the model chain we propagate both activations and gradients ξ forward through the network. Thus after each look ahead into future we know by definition (3), how an infinitesimal small change of the first action of the plan $\vec{a}_{plan}(t)$ effects the actual state predictions $\vec{s}_{pred}(t+\tau)$.

Instead of the real world we use the world model for planning and predicting future effects. Hence this model does not match the world exactly but approximates its behavior, look-ahead planning can be cut as soon as the estimated error of the current model network is larger than (a constant c times) the maximal estimated effect of $\vec{a}_{plan}(t)$ to activations of the actual copy of the world model. Then the model is too inaccurate – further look ahead is not expected to turn out precise new information. One obtains an estimation for the error from the model training procedure: for example, the minimal or average observed error can be taken as a lower bound of this error.

Initial Plans – The Experience Network

There are a lot of different strategies for finding initial plans. They can be derived by heuristics like

- random, last or average action (if exists),
- rest of the last plan (if exists) or

---

[1] δ denotes the Kronecker delta.

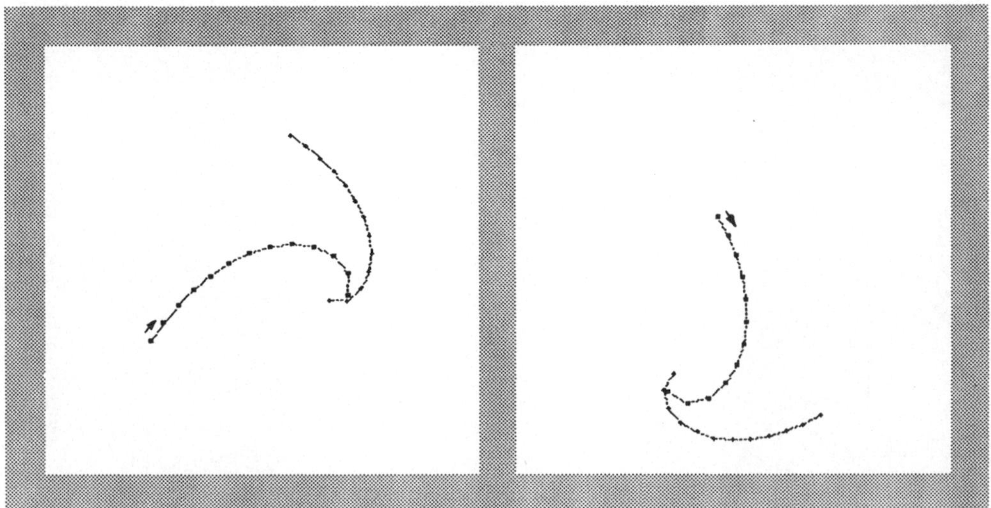

Figure 3: Target tracking – basic strategy: The system (boxes, arrow) moves always into the target's (crosses) direction.

- local optimization: Starting with one of the above initial actions only the one-step reinforcement is optimized by gradient descent. This strategy produces suboptimal actions with respect to the immediate next predicted reinforcement.

If some planning took place before, one should use the rest of the previous plan, N–1 actions, as the first N–1 actions of the new plan. This reduces the problem of finding an initial plan to finding the last action of the initial plan only.

Despite of those fast static strategies it is interesting to investigate adaptive modules for determining initial actions. One adaptive way of finding initial plans is the use of an *experience network* in addition to the world model network. This network is trained in a supervised manner (e.g. with backpropagation) to compute the resulting action of the training procedure from the current state. The experience network is similar to the *control network* described in [1, 17], but it is used in a different way. Its output is optimized by our planning procedure before it is given to the world.

The advantage of using an experience network is that the time-consuming planning procedure is shifted gradually to the *experience* in the experience network. This decreases the whole planning computation time.

Simulation Results: Target Tracking

We tested our planning method on a target tracking task. The system tried to reach a target in a two-dimensional space. The target's policy was not to flee in a fixed direction, but to move always 90° to the current direction of motion of the system. The system had to learn the policy of the target for reaching the target as quick as possible.

It was sufficient to use a one layer world model network for predicting states and reinforcements. The state input and output consisted of the actual coordinates of system and target object. The action was also a two-dimensional vector, which pointed into the movement direction of the system – the length and thus the speed of a movement was fixed. The goal was to minimize the euclidian distance between system and target. Corresponding to the two dimensions of the plane the reinforcement was split into a horizontal and a vertical component, each of which was simply defined as the difference between target and system coordinate. The reinforcement error function E_r described above measured the euclidian distance, such that minimizing E_r was equivalent to minimizing this distance. In addition, we used a two-layered experience network with four hidden units for learning the planning results and proposing good initial plans.

For reaching the target in as few steps as possible, the immediate reinforcement should not be optimized due to later reinforcements. This is illustrated in figure 4: if the system uses the simple strategy to maximize

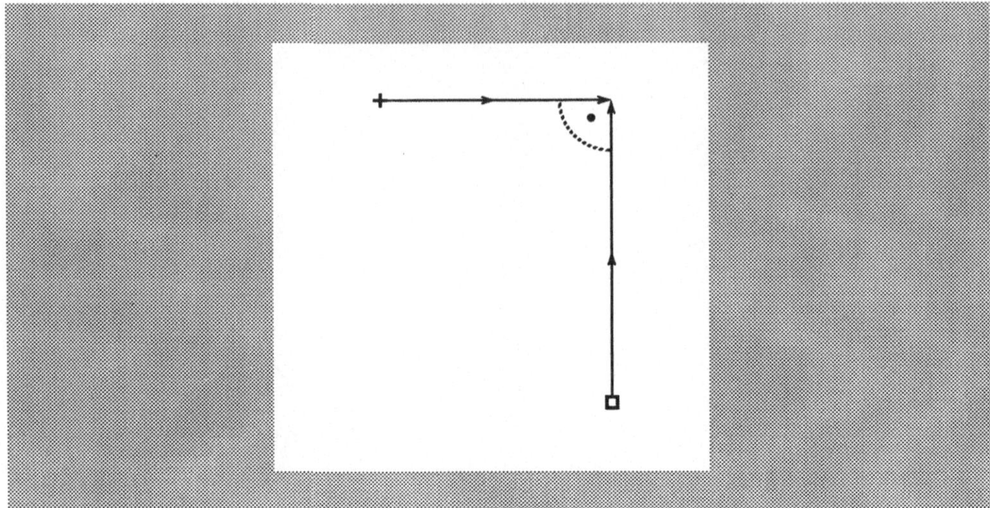

Figure 4: Target tracking – the analytical optimum

the next reinforcement – this would be a non-planning system expected to do – the system will always move in the direction of the target. Obviously this is not the optimal trajectory. The theoretical optimum is shown in figure 5. In this case neither system nor target changes its direction.

The planning process was conducted with a look-ahead $N \leq 7$. The reinforcement weighting function was $g_k(\tau) = 2^\tau$ and the adaptation rate depended also on τ: $\eta = \frac{1}{2} \cdot 2^{-\tau}$. The learning rate of the model and experience network were $\eta_{\text{model}} = 0.1$ and $\eta_{\text{exp}} = 0.05$.

After about 3500 training cycles we observed the trajectories shown in figure 6. The planner always found a close to optimal solution. This demonstrates the appropriateness of the method for finding suboptimal actions at the target tracking task.

Discussion

The optimization technique used in this paper is a gradient search procedure. Since look-ahead planning, as it is presented in this paper, does not depend on a special optimization method, one can use arbitrary numerical optimization like genetic algorithms etc. as well. In using gradient search techniques we have made certain assumptions about the environment. One is continuity, i.e. similar actions imply similar subsequent states and reinforcements. This has also been assumed in the use of continuous connectionist networks for modeling the environment. Another is that the initial plan is in the E_r-valley of the resulting plan. Therefore the choice of the initial plan is essential for the quality of the planning result.

On control problems usually many solutions exist for achieving a certain goal. E.g. inverse kinematics are often characterized by infinitely many solutions with different properties. Many connectionist approaches reduce this one-to-many mapping to a one-to-one mapping [1, 17, 11, 2, 6, 10, 11], since the action generator, the control network, is a mathematical function. Therefore often a marginal constraint like smoothness etc. is also optimized. The planning procedure, as it is presented above, is able to perform one-to-many mappings as well. For example, this can be done if the selection of initial plans is a probabilistic process or if the adaptation of the plan's action might be combined with a probabilistic search procedure, such that the planner is able to find different results at the same configuration. Up to now no simulation results are available – maybe we will present a probabilistic planning procedure in a later paper.

Acknowledgements

The authors wish to thank Frank Śmieja for fruitful discussions. The preparation of this paper was supported in part by grant ITR 8800 L7 from the German Federal Ministry for Scientific Research and Technology (BMFT).

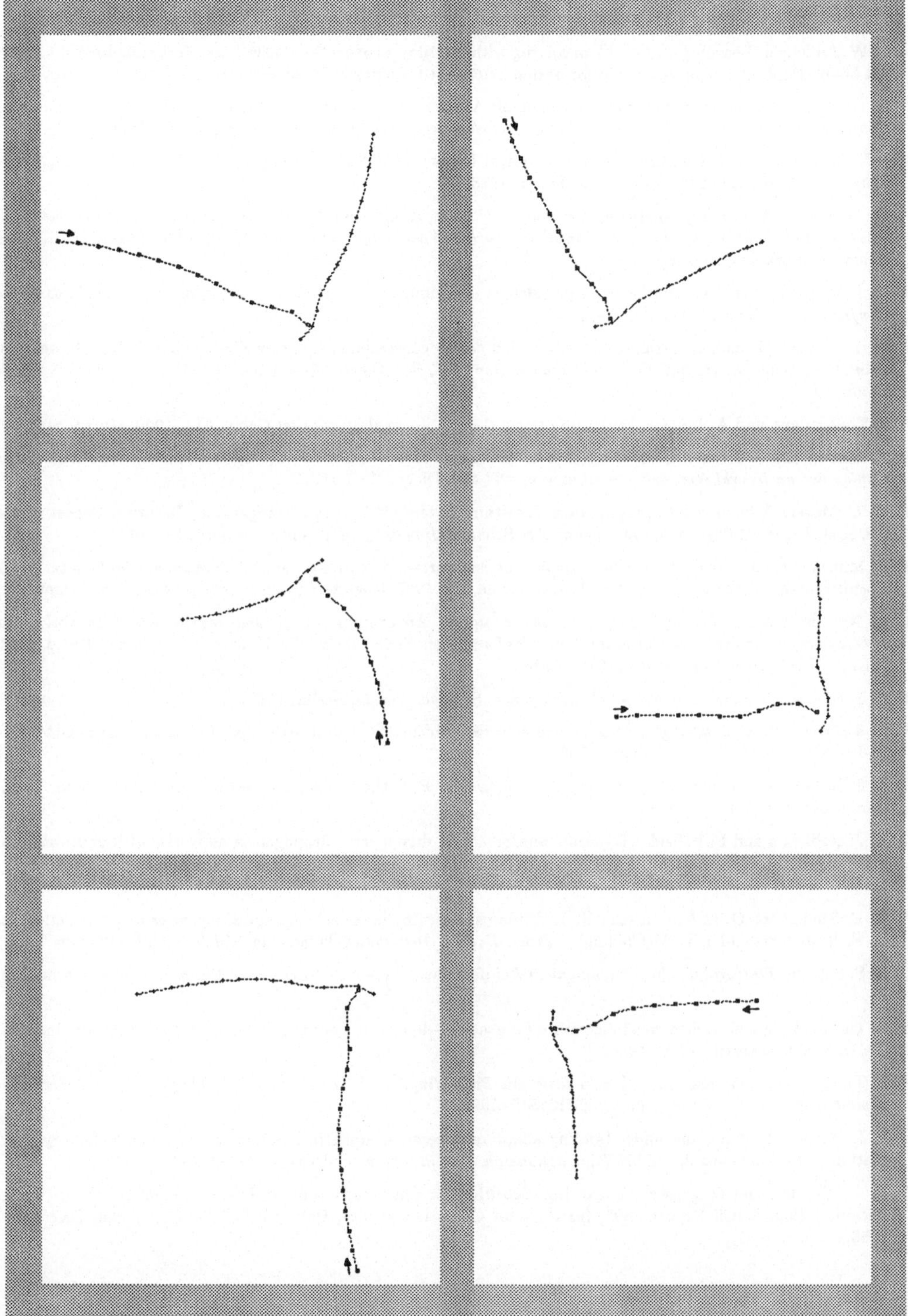

Figure 5: Target tracking by planning with an adaptive world model. The system always moves very close to the optimal direction.

References

[1] C. W. Anderson. Learning and problem solving with multilayer connectionist systems. Technical Report COINS TR 86-50, Dept. of Computer and Information Science, University of Massachusetts, Amherst, MA, 1986.

[2] A. G. Barto. Connectionist learning for control: An overview. Technical Report COINS TR 89-89, Dept. of Computer and Information Science, University of Massachusetts, Amherst, MA, September 1989.

[3] J. L. Elman. Finding structure in time. Technical Report CRL Technical Report 8801, Center for Research in Language, University of California, San Diego, 1988.

[4] M. Gherrity. A learning algorithm for analog, fully recurrent neural networks. In *Proceedings of the First International Joint Conference on Neural Networks, Washington, DC*, San Diego, 1989. IEEE, IEEE TAB Neural Network Committee.

[5] M. I. Jordan. Attractor dynamics and parallelism in a connectionist sequential machine. In *Proceedings of the Conference on Cognitive Science*, 1986.

[6] M. I. Jordan. Generic constraints on unspecified target constraints. In *Proceedings of the First International Joint Conference on Neural Networks, Washington, DC*, San Diego, 1989. IEEE, IEEE TAB Neural Network Committee.

[7] J. Kindermann and A. Linden. Inversion of neural nets. *Journal of Parallel Computing*, 1990. (to appear).

[8] A. Linden and J. Kindermann. Inversion of multilayer nets. In *Proceedings of the First International Joint Conference on Neural Networks, Washington, DC*, San Diego, 1989. IEEE.

[9] M. C. Mozer. A focused backpropagation algorithm for temporal pattern recognition. Technical Report CRG-TR-88-3, Depts. of Psychology and Computer Science, University of Toronto, Toronto, Jun 1988.

[10] P. Munro. A dual backpropagation scheme for scalar-reward learning. In *Ninth Annual Conference of the Cognitive Science Society*, pages 165–176, Hillsdale, NJ, 1987. Cognitive Science Society, Lawrence Erlbaum.

[11] D. Nguyen and B. Widrow. The truck backer-upper: An example of self-learning in neural networks. In *Proceedings of the First International Joint Conference on Neural Networks, Washington, DC*, San Diego, 1989. IEEE, IEEE TAB Neural Network Committee.

[12] N. J. Nilsson. *Principles of Artificial Intelligence*. Springer Verlag, Berlin, 1982.

[13] B. A. Pearlmutter. Learning state space trajectories in recurrent neural networks. Technical Report CMU-CS-88-191, Carnegie Mellon University, 1988.

[14] A. J. Robinson. *Dynamic Error Propagation Networks*. PhD thesis, Cambridge University Engineering Dept., Cambridge, UK, February 1989.

[15] A. J. Robinson and F. Fallside. Dynamic reinforcement driven error propagation networks with application to game playing. to be presented at the Eleventh Annual Conference of the Cognitive Science Society, Ann Arbor, 1989.

[16] D. E. Rumelhart, G. E. Hinton, and R. J. Williams. Learning internal representations by error propagation. In D. E. Rumelhart and J. L. McClelland, editors, *Parallel Distributed Processing. Vol. I + II*. MIT Press, 1986.

[17] R. S. Sutton. *Temporal Credit Assignment in Reinforcement Learning*. PhD thesis, University of Massachusetts, 1984.

[18] S. Thrun. A general feed-forward algorithm for gradient-descent in neural networks. Technical Report In press, GMD, Sankt Augustin, FRG, 1990.

[19] S. Thrun and A. Linden. Inversion in time. In *Proceedings of the EURASIP Workshop on Neural Networks, Sesimbra, Portugal, February 15-17*. EURASIP, 1990.

[20] P. J. Werbos. Building and understanding adaptive systems: A statistical/numerical approach to factory automation and brain research. *IEEE Transactions on Systems, Man, and Cybernetics*, SMC-17:7–19, 1987.

[21] R. J. Williams and D. Zipser. A learning algorithm for continually running fully recurrent neural networks. Technical Report ICS Report 8805, Institute for Cognitive Science, University of California, San Diego, CA, 1988.